Students & Families

One-Stop Internet Resources

drivered.glencoe.com

Online Learning Center

- Chapter Objectives
- eFlashcards
- Practice Tests

Web Site Links

- AAA Foundation
- Department of Motor Vehicles for all 50 states
- Safety-related links
- Auto maintenance–related links
- Tips for dealing with pedestrians and bicyclists
- Information about driving and substance abuse

Glencoe

RESPONSIBLE DRIVING

drivered.glencoe.com

 **Glencoe**

New York, New York   Columbus, Ohio   Chicago, Illinois   Peoria, Illinois   Woodland Hills, California

Consulting Authors

Dr. John W. Palmer, Professor
Department of Health, Education, and Traffic Safety
St. Cloud University

Dr. Maury E. Dennis, Professor
Center For Alcohol and Drug Education Studies
Texas A & M University

Dr. Dale O. Ritzel, Professor
Health Education and Safety Center Director
Southern Illinois University, Carbondale

Dr. Leanna Depue, Director
Missouri Safety Center
Central Missouri State University

Walter Barta, Product Manager
Driver Education
Alberta Motor Association

Charles A. Butler, National Driving Solutions
Traffic Safety Director
AAA National Office (Retired)
Lake Mary, FL

William E. Van Tassel, Ph.D.
Manager, Driver Training Operations
AAA National Office

The McGraw·Hill Companies

Send all inquiries to:
Glencoe/McGraw-Hill
21600 Oxnard Street, Suite 500
Woodland Hills, CA 91367

ISBN 0-07-867812-9 (Hard Cover Student Edition)
ISBN 0-07-867814-5 (Soft Cover Student Edition)
ISBN 0-07-867813-7 (Teacher Wraparound Edition)

Printed in the United States of America

2 3 4 5 6 7 8 9   027   09 08 07 06 05

Reviewers

Well, this is it. You're going to learn to drive, and you're probably in a big hurry to get behind the wheel. However, driving is something that you cannot rush into. There is a great deal of essential driving information that you need to know first. It's important that you understand that risk is always present for the driver but that good drivers learn more effectively to manage risk. Good drivers reduce risk by managing visibility, time, space, and the available traction. We want you to be a good driver.

We've spent many years working on safe driving strategies and attitudes and at the same time working with young people such as you. *Responsible Driving* has been written with you in mind. We want you to know the rules and the facts about driving, but we also want you to know why they are important. This book tells you the What and How about driving, and it always tells you the Why.

The American Automobile Association, which you probably know as the AAA or Triple A, is part of the team that helped put *Responsible Driving* together. The AAA is an organization that has the greatest resources in the world on driving. We have used these resources in *Responsible Driving* to help you understand what driving is all about.

Dr. John W. Palmer
Dr. Maury E. Dennis
Dr. Dale O. Ritzel
Dr. Leanna Depue
Walter Barta
Charles A. Butler
William E. Van Tassel, Ph.D.

Brief Contents

Contents

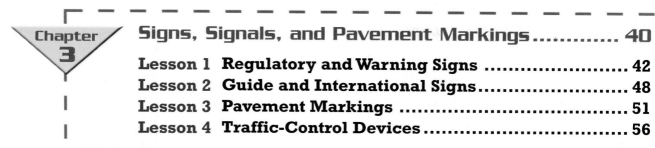

Contents

Contents

Contents

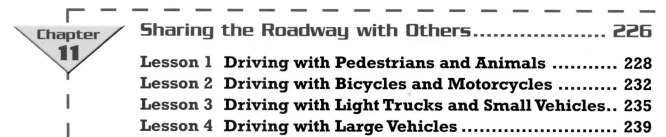

Contents

Contents

BUILDING Skills

Content

Getting the Most Out of Responsible Driving

Becoming a safe and responsible driver is easy with *Responsible Driving*. Follow the guidelines below to make the most out of each lesson.

Preview the Lesson

Get a preview of what's coming by reading the lesson objectives. You can also use this feature to prepare for quizzes and tests.

Review Key Terms

Find each vocabulary term in the text and read its definition. The terms are boldfaced and highlighted in yellow so you can locate them easily!

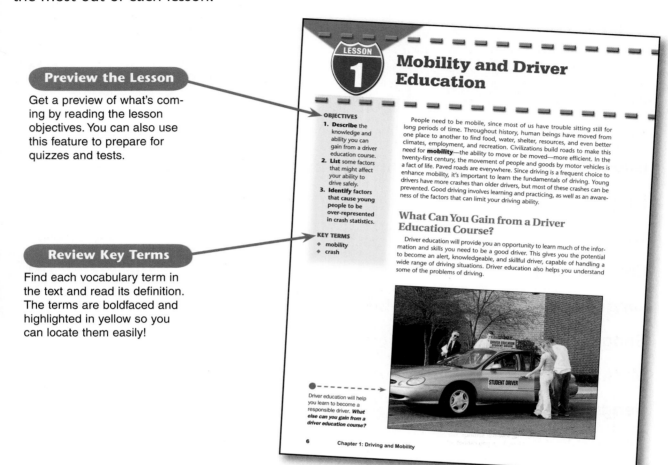

LESSON 1

Mobility and Driver Education

OBJECTIVES

1. **Describe** the knowledge and ability you can gain from a driver education course.
2. **List** some factors that might affect your ability to drive safely.
3. **Identify** factors that cause young people to be over-represented in crash statistics.

KEY TERMS
- mobility
- crash

People need to be mobile, since most of us have trouble sitting still for long periods of time. Throughout history, human beings have moved from one place to another to find food, water, shelter, resources, and even better climates, employment, and recreation. Civilizations build roads to make this need for **mobility**—the ability to move or be moved—more efficient. In the twenty-first century, the movement of people and goods by motor vehicles is a fact of life. Paved roads are everywhere. Since driving is a frequent choice to enhance mobility, it's important to learn the fundamentals of driving. Young drivers have more crashes than older drivers, but most of these crashes can be prevented. Good driving involves learning and practicing, as well as an awareness of the factors that can limit your driving ability.

What Can You Gain from a Driver Education Course?

Driver education will provide you an opportunity to learn much of the information and skills you need to be a good driver. This gives you the potential to become an alert, knowledgeable, and skillful driver, capable of handling a wide range of driving situations. Driver education also helps you understand some of the problems of driving.

Driver education will help you learn to become a responsible driver. **What else can you gain from a driver education course?**

6   Chapter 1: Driving and Mobility

Use Glencoe's *Responsible Driving* Web Site to Boost Your Driving Smarts!

▲ Boost current driving knowledge by checking out the links for each chapter.

▲ Get specific information from your state's Department of Motor Vehicles Web site.

▲ Check out the Web link exercises.

▲ Use the eFlashcards to test your knowledge of critical driving vocabulary.

▲ Take the online quizzes for each chapter to practice for your driving test.

Tips for New Drivers

IDENTIFYING INFORMATION

Identify these objects and conditions as you drive:

► vehicles, pedestrians, or objects that are in your path or could enter your path

► vehicles, pedestrians, or objects close to the back or sides of your vehicle

► vehicles, objects, or roadway features that limit your visibility and may conceal objects or conditions

► signs, signals, and roadway markings

► roadway-surface conditions

Dealing with the UNEXPECTED

HANDLING HYDROPLANING

When you are driving in rainy conditions, it is possible that your car will start to hydroplane. If this happens, follow these guidelines.

▲ Avoid braking or turning suddenly because doing so could cause the car to skid.

▲ Ease off the gas pedal until the car slows down and you regain traction.

▲ If you need to brake, gently pump the brake pedal.

▲ If your car has antilock brakes, you should brake as you normally would. The antilock brakes will prevent the wheels from locking.

Read the Tips for New Drivers and Dealing with the Unexpected

As you go over each chapter, look at the features such as **Tips for New Drivers** and **Dealing with the Unexpected**. These features will provide you with valuable information when you get behind the wheel.

Answer the What Would You Do Feature

The **What Would You Do** feature allows you to make decisions from the driver's point of view. First, look at the picture. Then read the caption. Based on what you have learned in the lesson, determine the best response to the situation.

WHAT WOULD YOU DO? What factors might limit your ability to drive safely here? How should you handle them?

restricted by law to safe, low-risk settings. Unfortunately, even if you restrict your driving to low-risk settings, you cannot totally avoid risk. You will eventually be faced with making decisions in higher-risk settings.

Young drivers drive differently. Do 15- to 20-year-old drivers drive like older drivers? The answer is no. The youngest drivers from 15 to 17 years old do a much better job of avoiding alcohol-impaired driving than 18- to 40-year-old drivers. Unfortunately, that is the only good news when young and older drivers are compared. Young drivers tend to speed and not pay attention to their driving more often than older drivers. In addition, young drivers have weaker visual search and space management skills than older drivers. To make matters worse, young drivers are less likely to use protective devices such as safety belts and motorcycle helmets. There is a staggering cost to the over-representation of 15- to 20-year-old drivers in motor-vehicle crashes—$16 billion per year in economic losses, more than 10,000 people dead, and hundreds of thousands more people injured each year.

There are a few simple steps you can take to begin to avoid this problem. Make sure you always travel at the safest speed limit, make driving the focus of your attention, and always use protective devices when you are in a vehicle. In addition, practicing driving will help you sharpen your visual search and space management skills.

Lesson 1 Review

❶ List three skills or abilities you will gain from a driver education course.

❷ What are some factors that might affect your ability to drive safely?

❸ What factors cause young drivers to be over-represented in crash statistics?

Chapter 1 Lesson 1   9

Complete the Lesson Reviews

Completing the lesson reviews can help you see how well you know the material you have just studied.

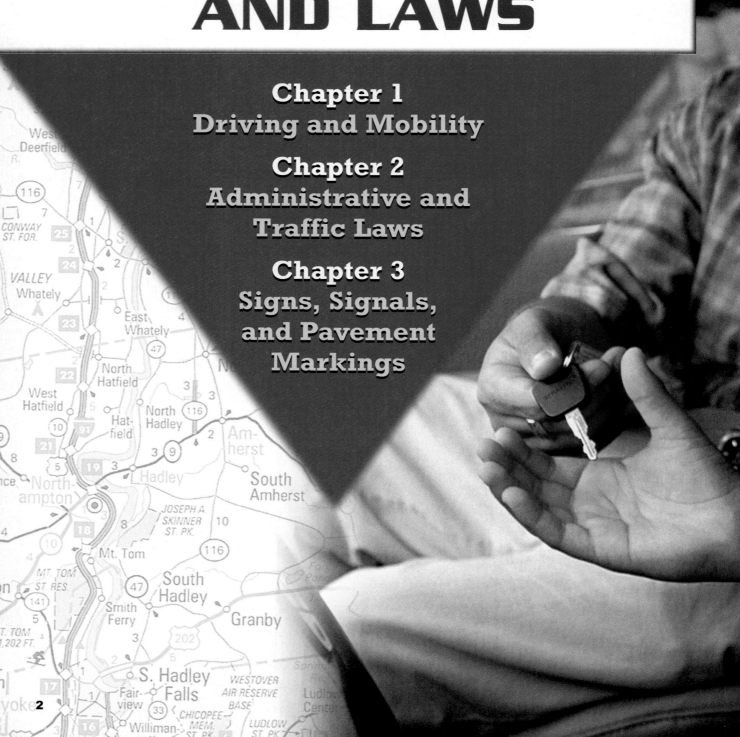

UNIT 1

DRIVING, MOBILITY, AND LAWS

Chapter 1
Driving and Mobility

Chapter 2
Administrative and
Traffic Laws

Chapter 3
Signs, Signals,
and Pavement
Markings

How do you become a good driver?

Becoming a good driver begins with learning the fundamentals of the road. These basics are second nature to good drivers and should become second nature to you as well. This unit will help you learn the first steps toward becoming a good driver.

Chapter 1

Driving and Mobility

What Are the Costs of Driving?

Think about some of the costs associated with driving. You probably recognize that driving involves the cost of gasoline and maintenance. But did you think about the costs associated with crashes or the environment? In this chapter you will learn about the costs of driving, as well as the importance of driver education, the basics of the highway transportation system, and the foundations for managing risk.

Driver Ed *Online*

For additional activities, visit **drivered.glencoe.com**. Here you will find:

◆ **Web Link Exercises**

◆ **eFlashcards**

◆ **Practice Driving Tests**

LESSON 1

Mobility and Driver Education mr. Gabrys 23'S MEN

OBJECTIVES

1. **Describe** the knowledge and ability you can gain from a driver education course.
2. **List** some factors that might affect your ability to drive safely.
3. **Identify** factors that cause young people to be over-represented in crash statistics.

KEY TERMS

◆ mobility
◆ crash

People need to be mobile, since most of us have trouble sitting still for long periods of time. Throughout history, human beings have moved from one place to another to find food, water, shelter, resources, and even better climates, employment, and recreation. Civilizations build roads to make this need for **mobility**—the ability to move or be moved—more efficient. In the twenty-first century, the movement of people and goods by motor vehicles is a fact of life. Paved roads are everywhere. Since driving is a frequent choice to enhance mobility, it's important to learn the fundamentals of driving. Young drivers have more crashes than older drivers, but most of these crashes can be prevented. Good driving involves learning and practicing, as well as an awareness of the factors that can limit your driving ability.

What Can You Gain from a Driver Education Course?

Driver education will provide you an opportunity to learn much of the information and skills you need to be a good driver. This gives you the potential to become an alert, knowledgeable, and skillful driver, capable of handling a wide range of driving situations. Driver education also helps you understand some of the problems of driving.

Driver education will help you learn to become a responsible driver. *What else can you gain from a driver education course?*

When you learn to drive and have access to the use of a motor vehicle, your life changes. The increased mobility can be fun or profitable. You have more freedom to choose when and where you travel. You no longer have to wait for your ride to arrive or to travel on a schedule set by someone else. You can go to the big game, go to that popular movie, make a trip to a beach, and go to your new job. You might even be a professional, and drive to make money. However, the biggest restriction on your mobility will probably be money.

In a driver education course, you will gain useful knowledge; learn to manage visibility, time, and space; and become aware of limiting factors.

USEFUL KNOWLEDGE

Of course, in order to drive, you need to understand the basic facts about how a vehicle works and what to do in an emergency. Driver education can also help you understand several other important concepts:

- how your personality, emotions, and maturity affect your driving
- how to maneuver and control your vehicle to minimize risk in different driving environments
- how alcohol and other drugs impair your ability to drive, and a knowledge of the penalties for their use
- how to interpret traffic laws, rules of the road, signs and signals, and roadway markings
- an awareness of limiting factors for yourself and your vehicle
- how a vehicle works
- a knowledge of what to do in an emergency situation

MANAGING VISIBILITY, TIME, AND SPACE

Driver education increases your awareness of the roadway and its surroundings. You will learn how to better manage visibility, time, and space. This knowledge helps assure your safety and the safety of your passengers, other drivers, and pedestrians.

AWARENESS OF LIMITING FACTORS

To become a safe and responsible driver, you need more than driving skill. Other factors that can seriously interfere with your ability to drive safely include:

- the foolish feeling that there is little or no risk involved in driving and that if a collision occurs, it's "the other person's fault"
- an illness or injury that you have, or the side effects of the medicine you may be taking for it
- your emotional state at the time you are driving
- the effects of alcohol and other drugs

You gain knowledge of the rules of the road through driver education. You gain experience and ability by spending time behind the wheel. Learning and practicing will improve your driving skills. Experience will sharpen your decision-making abilities. How you actually drive, however, is up to you. Only you can decide to be a responsible driver.

Driver Ed Online

Topic: New Drivers

For a link to more information on safety tips for new drivers, go to **drivered.glencoe.com**.

Activity: Use the information provided at this link to create a poster or Web page that illustrates three tips to help teens be safer drivers.

Why Is Driver Education Important for Young Drivers?

When it comes to driving safely, younger drivers have a lot to learn since they are involved in more crashes than other drivers.

When a motor vehicle hits another motor vehicle, a pedestrian, an animal, a bicyclist, or a fixed object, this is called a **crash**. Some people call these crashes "accidents," but traffic safety professionals prefer the term *crash* or *collision* because it is factual and specific. Whether you call what might happen a crash, collision, or an accident, what is really important is taking every possible action to avoid being involved in one yourself. Unfortunately, young drivers are involved in crashes too frequently.

The over-representation of young drivers results in twice as many motor vehicle crashes or accidents involving 15- to 20-year-olds than would normally be expected. Drivers aged 15 to 20 are only 7 percent of the driving population, but they are involved in about 14 percent of the motor-vehicle crashes each year—double what you might expect. Because younger drivers are so over-represented in crash statistics, driver education becomes that much more important.

FACTORS OF OVER-REPRESENTATION

There are several factors that can be attributed to the over-representation of young drivers involved in crashes.

Young drivers lack experience. Since young drivers usually drive fewer miles than older drivers, you might expect that they would have fewer crashes. This is not true. Part of the reason for young drivers' more frequent crashes is their lack of experience and lack of practice in driving, which can result in driving mistakes.

The best way to overcome this obstacle is to practice driving as much as possible with a parent or trusted adult in various driving environments. The more you practice driving with an adult, the more experience you will gain and the better you will be able to handle different situations and environments when you drive alone. Another good method for overcoming your lack of experience is observing how experienced drivers handle various situations when they are driving.

Young drivers drive at dangerous times and transport passengers. Another part of the over-representation comes from the times when young people usually drive and who rides with them. Driving at night is more dangerous than driving during the day for all drivers. The probability of a crash also increases with each passenger riding with the young driver, although this is not true for older drivers. Laughing, talking passengers are one reason why young drivers are over-represented in crashes, where inattentive driving is listed as a cause of the crash. It's sometimes tempting to pay attention to your passenger, and take your attention off the road.

Once you are a licensed driver, you could choose to drive alone and not drive at night. This would reduce the chances that you will be in a crash. Many safety advocates believe that until young drivers have gained experience and have had more practice at solo driving, their driving should be

WHAT WOULD YOU DO? ❓
What factors might limit your ability to drive safely here? How should you handle them?

restricted by law to safe, low-risk settings. Unfortunately, even if you restrict your driving to low-risk settings, you cannot totally avoid risk. You will eventually be faced with making decisions in higher-risk settings.

Young drivers drive differently. Do 15- to 20-year-old drivers drive like older drivers? The answer is no. The youngest drivers from 15 to 17 years old do a much better job of avoiding alcohol-impaired driving than 18- to 40-year-old drivers. Unfortunately, that is the only good news when young and older drivers are compared. Young drivers tend to speed and not pay attention to their driving more often than older drivers. In addition, young drivers have weaker visual search and space management skills than older drivers. To make matters worse, young drivers are less likely to use protective devices such as safety belts and motorcycle helmets. There is a staggering cost to the over-representation of 15- to 20-year-old drivers in motor-vehicle crashes—$16 billion per year in economic losses, more than 10,000 people dead, and hundreds of thousands more people injured each year.

There are a few simple steps you can take to begin to avoid this problem. Make sure you always travel at the safest speed limit, make driving the focus of your attention, and always use protective devices when you are in a vehicle. In addition, practicing driving will help you sharpen your visual search and space management skills.

Lesson 1 Review

❶ List three skills or abilities you will gain from a driver education course.

❷ What are some factors that might affect your ability to drive safely?

❸ What factors cause young drivers to be over-represented in crash statistics?

The Highway Transportation System

LESSON 2

OBJECTIVES

1. **Name** the three parts of the highway transportation system.
2. **Identify** the role of motor vehicles in transporting goods and people.
3. **Explain** how the highway transportation system is regulated.

KEY TERMS

♦ highway transportation system (HTS)
♦ collision

As a licensed driver, you must use the vast network of highways, streets, and roads that crisscross the United States. Each day, millions of drivers share these roadways. As you prepare to join the other drivers on the road, remember that your goal is not just to learn to drive. It is to learn to navigate roads and highways safely and responsibly.

What Is the Highway Transportation System?

Motor vehicles, streets and highways, and people are the components of the **highway transportation system (HTS)**. The main goal of this complex system is to enable people and goods to move from place to place as safely and efficiently as possible whether they are cyclists, pedestrians, or drivers.

Nearly 4 million miles of different kinds of roadways link the towns, cities, counties, and states of the United States. These roadways include twisting country roads, vehicle-choked city streets, and multilane superhighways. Some roadways are smooth and well maintained, while others are riddled with cracks, bumps, and potholes. Driving the very different roads within the HTS can be a challenge, especially at night or in poor weather.

HISTORY OF THE HTS

Human beings have been walking, running, pushing, riding, paddling, and sailing for many centuries. With the invention of the wheel in 3500 B.C., humans began developing carts and wagons that made it possible to move people and goods more easily. Continuing improvements in the movement of goods and people ultimately led to today's highway transportation system.

It's hard to believe, but in the United States, the HTS is only about 100 years old. Originally, horses outnumbered cars. In 1902, only 23,000 motor vehicles and more than 17 million horses used a highway system that had 150 miles of paved roadway. Today, over 230 million registered motor vehicles travel a total of 42 trillion miles a year on 4 million miles of paved roadways. It is rare to see a horse on the roadway. But it certainly is not rare to see another motor vehicle when you are out for a ride.

Motor vehicles are no longer a novelty, they're a basic necessity. Today, motor vehicles move a majority of people and goods. If motor-vehicle traffic stopped tomorrow, 60 percent of freight would not arrive at its destination, and 79 percent of personal trips would not occur. In the last ten years alone, personal trips by motor vehicles increased 11 percent (including 2 percent alone in the year after 9/11). Since the number of motor vehicles actually exceeds the number of licensed drivers, motor vehicles are the first choice for moving goods and people.

Did You Know?

In 1893, Charles and Frank Duryea—two bicycle mechanics—built the first successful gasoline-powered automobile in America. Two years later, in Springfield, Massachusetts, the brothers established the first automobile-manufacturing company in the United States.

DESIGNING GOOD HIGHWAYS

Early American roads were built along the routes of existing trails. Many were constructed with little or no thought to the future. Nowadays, an army of engineers designs more complex highways.

Engineers must determine the best route, taking into consideration all the people who will use the road. They also plan the construction of bridges along the route, exit and entrance ramps, the location of traffic signs, and anything else pertaining to the highway. Curves must be planned carefully to make sure they are banked, or tilted, properly so that vehicles won't run off the roadway.

VEHICLES

More than 230 million registered vehicles travel the HTS. These range from large vehicles, such as tractor-trailers and buses, to small vehicles, such as motorcycles and mopeds. Along the HTS, you see vehicles of every imaginable description, from flashy new luxury cars to battered old pickup trucks.

Vehicles also vary in how difficult they are to handle and drive. A heavy truck, for instance, does not accelerate, turn or brake the same way that a lightweight sports car does. Motor vehicles vary, too, in safety features and in their ability to provide protection to drivers and passengers in case of a **collision**, or crash. For example, drivers of solidly built vehicles equipped with air bags are far less vulnerable to injury than are drivers of subcompact cars or motorcycles. How well an owner cares for his or her vehicle also affects its performance and safety.

DRIVERS

The highway transportation system is often crowded. More than 194 million licensed drivers and 55 million pedestrians and bicyclists use the HTS—in other words, just about everyone! Most of these drivers, riders, and walkers act responsibly when using the roads. Unfortunately, some people behave in an unsafe or irresponsible manner. They drive recklessly, cross streets without looking, or weave their motorcycles or bikes through heavy traffic. Such people pose a serious danger to other roadway users. As a driver, you must anticipate and learn to cope with these unsafe practices.

✔ Tips for New Drivers

IDENTIFYING INFORMATION

Identify these objects and conditions as you drive:

► vehicles, pedestrians, or objects that are in your path or could enter your path

► vehicles, pedestrians, or objects close to the back or sides of your vehicle

► vehicles, objects, or roadway features that limit your visibility and may conceal objects or conditions

► signs, signals, and roadway markings

► roadway-surface conditions

?

WHAT WOULD YOU DO?
What vehicle safety features required by law would help you manage risk in this situation?

How Is the HTS Regulated?

Federal, state, and local governments work together to regulate the highway transportation system. For example, federal law established a maximum speed limit of 55 miles per hour on all U.S. roadways in 1974. This law was changed in 1995 to allow individual states to set their own highway speed limits. State and local police enforce speed limits and all other traffic laws.

FEDERAL AND STATE REQUIREMENTS

To set uniform standards for vehicle and driver safety, the federal government made two important laws.

The National Traffic and Motor Vehicle Safety Act requires automakers to build certain safety features into their vehicles, such as safety belts and shatterproof windows. This law also requires manufacturers to correct vehicle defects discovered after vehicle models are sold.

The National Highway Safety Act establishes specific guidelines for state motor vehicle safety programs. Each state must follow these federal guidelines. Guidelines govern vehicle registration and inspection, driver licensing, traffic laws and traffic courts, and highway construction and maintenance. The National Highway Safety Act also allows each state to make its own laws concerning highway safety. Many of these state laws are of special interest to teenage drivers. In most states, for example, teens under a certain age—usually 17 or 18—are not allowed to drive at night. In some states, teenagers must be enrolled in high school before they can get and keep their driver's licenses.

Cities and towns, too, pass driving regulations that affect drivers within their city limits. In many cities, for instance, drivers may turn right at red lights except where expressly prohibited.

Lesson 2 Review

❶ What are the three parts of the highway transportation system?

❷ Who regulates the highway transportation system? Give examples.

❸ What is the significance of the way highways are numbered?

The Risks of Driving

As a licensed driver, you are faced with some risks when you drive a motor vehicle. These risks are not all well known. Learning what some of the risks are and how to manage them can make you a better driver.

Are Drivers Actually at Risk?

Driving involves **risk**—the possibility of personal injury or damage to vehicles and property. The first thing you must understand as a responsible driver is that these risks are real—and much more likely than you think. Here are some important facts:

- In any given year, the likelihood of your being involved in a crash is about 1 in 9.
- In any given year, your chances of suffering a disabling injury are about 1 in 83.
- Motor-vehicle crashes kill about 38 percent of all people who die between the ages of 15 and 20.
- Approximately 85 percent of these traffic deaths occur in the first collision in which the vehicle's occupants are involved.
- More than 57 percent of all fatal crashes involve only one vehicle.

No matter how confident you may feel that you've mastered the basics of driving, the risk of being involved in a crash is always present. However, there are several ways you can maximize your control while driving and minimize risk.

REDUCING THE RISKS

Many factors contribute to the risks of driving. Some risks are obvious, such as bad weather. Others, such as distractions, may be less obvious but are just as important. Driving responsibly means assessing your risks and doing all you can to reduce or control them. Here are five ways to reduce or control risk.

Keep your vehicle in top condition. Are your brakes working properly? Are your tires properly inflated? Are all your windows clean? When your vehicle is in good condition, you have more control over it.

OBJECTIVES

1. **Describe** five ways that you can reduce risk when using the highway transportation system.
2. **Identify** the foundations of effective driving.

KEY TERMS

- ◆ risk
- ◆ visibility
- ◆ time
- ◆ space

Risk is always present. The chance that you will be in a collision within the year is 1 in 9. *How can you reduce your chances of being in a collision?*

Most drivers overestimate their ability to manage risk and underestimate actual risk. ***What are some steps you can take to manage risk when driving?***

SAFETY TIP

"Better safe than sorry" is a maxim with special relevance for drivers. Never assume that a driver, cyclist, or pedestrian sees you and will not enter your path of travel. When appropriate, tap your horn or flash your lights. Always be prepared to steer or brake to avoid a collision.

FYI

During daylight hours, you can see the low beams of an oncoming vehicle from 4,700 feet away, or a little less than a mile. You can see an oncoming vehicle without headlights only from 2,500 feet away, or about half a mile.

Anticipate the actions of others. Wise drivers drive defensively. Identify cues or behaviors that help you predict how other roadway users might act or react. Because drivers and pedestrians often act without thinking or telling you what they're going to do, you must watch them for clues.

Protect yourself and others. Do what you can to protect yourself and others. Just fastening your safety belts can save you and your passengers from death or serious injury. Turning on your low-beam headlights at all times, even during daylight hours if your vehicle is not equipped with automatic daytime running lights (DRLs), reduces the risk of a crash because other drivers can easily see you.

Drive only when you're in sound physical and mental condition. Are you feeling alert and clearheaded, or not? Are you concentrating on your driving—or daydreaming about tomorrow night's date, drinking an alcoholic beverage, or talking on a cell phone? To drive safely, you need to be in sound physical and mental condition.

Make a conscious effort to develop your driving skills. Driving skills can be developed. Learn good driving habits and try to improve your own driving ability, to help protect you and your passengers.

BUILDING A GOOD DRIVING FOUNDATION

Driving a vehicle is challenging because you need to do many things at once. You have to simultaneously control the vehicle, watch the roadway and off-road areas, read signs, and be alert for the sudden actions of other people.

As a young person, you have good reflexes, but you don't have the driving experience of older drivers. You need to clearly see what you're doing, make good decisions, and handle your vehicle safely to become a good driver.

Because you have so much to keep track of when you're driving, it is helpful to have a system to gather and process information so you make sound decisions and reduce driving risk.

What Are the Foundations of Effective Driving?

The foundations for effective driving include searching and giving meaning, understanding options and choices, and mastering basic driving skills. You must use your senses to see and hear other drivers and to search for information from road signs, markers, and surrounding traffic. As you drive, you constantly encounter choices and options. Applying the knowledge you have learned, and utilizing your experience to make good choices will help you master most driving situations. To be an effective driver, you must use your driving skills to get where you want to go safely with the least amount of risk.

WHAT WOULD YOU DO?
What factors are contributing to risk? What steps can you take to reduce risk?

VISIBILITY, TIME, AND SPACE

The wise management of visibility, time, and space, come into constant play when you are driving.

Visibility refers to what you can see from behind the wheel and how well you see it. Visibility also refers to the ability of others—pedestrians and other drivers—to see you. When you are driving, less visibility means more risk. On the other hand, when you can see clearly, you decrease risk.

Time involves the ability to judge your speed and the speed of other vehicles and highway users. Time can also refer to how long it will take your vehicle or another vehicle to stop or intersect paths.

Space refers to distance. As a wise driver, you must keep a margin of space between your vehicle and other vehicles and highway users when you drive. This margin of space allows you plenty of room to safely maneuver or to stop if necessary.

You will read about visibility, time, and space throughout this book, because all three are crucial elements in safe and responsible driving and in reducing risk as you drive.

Lesson 3 Review

❶ What are the five ways that you can reduce or control risk when driving?

❷ Describe visibility, time, and space as they relate to driving.

❸ What factors may contribute to driving risk?

LESSON 4

The Costs of Driving

OBJECTIVES

1. **List** the various costs of motor vehicle use.
2. **Describe** the nature of the motor-vehicle crash problem.
3. **Identify** noncrash costs of motor-vehicle use.

KEY TERMS

◆ cost
◆ cost-benefit ratio

Driving may look like it's free, but it's not. Great mobility has many benefits, but it also has many risks and many costs. **Costs** are measured in dollars and lives. The basic costs of mobility can be grouped into two categories: crash costs and noncrash costs.

What Are the Costs of Mobility?

Mobility has a price. Crashes can be tragic and very expensive since they cost billions of dollars each year. It also costs money to operate a car, even if you never have a collision. Think about the costs of driving before you choose to become a driver.

CRASH COSTS

In the United States, the total cost of motor-vehicle crashes has been estimated at more than $230 billion every year. If this cost were divided equally between everyone in the United States, motor-vehicle crashes would cost more than $800 per person every year. In addition to fixing the wrecked vehicles, money is spent cleaning up after the crash, repairing property damage, caring for the injured, and burying the dead. More time and money is spent on lost wages, lost production, and traffic delays from motor-vehicle crashes.

The most important costs of motor-vehicle crashes are deaths and injuries. Crashes have forever changed the lives of hundreds of thousands of people, many of whom were young people. In the United States more than 42,000 people die each year as a result of motor-vehicle crashes. Each one of these fatalities was someone's child, friend, or relative.

Motor vehicle crash costs affect everyone. *How do motor vehicle crashes affect everyone?*

Dr. John W. Palmer

St. Cloud State University
St. Cloud, MN

Drivers enjoy the freedom to choose where and when to travel. Freedom comes with a price. By enrolling in driver education, you are spending your time wisely, but even the best instruction does not replace experience. You will continue to learn about driving when you drive solo. Remember, two-thirds of teen drivers killed in motor-vehicle crashes were not wearing safety belts. Please avoid paying a heavy price for mobility freedom.

What other tips do you think are important to remember when you begin driving solo?

MINIMIZING CRASH COSTS

When you see the causes associated with motor-vehicle crashes, you can identify driver actions that could reduce the cost of crashes. The National Highway Traffic Safety Administration, part of the United State's Department of Transportation, has identified three high-priority actions to reduce crash costs. These actions are using protective devices, such as seat belts, not drinking alcohol before driving, and driving at an appropriate speed.

If everyone used protective devices such as safety belts and helmets, about 10,000 people would not die in crashes each year. If drivers would not drive while under the influence of alcohol, some 13,000 fatalities, 360,000 nonfatal injuries, and nearly $40 billion in economic costs would be avoided.

Finally, if drivers operated at appropriate speeds over 12,000 fatalities, 690,000 nonfatal injuries, and 2.3 million damaged vehicles might never happen.

Other driver mistakes linked to high numbers of crashes include inattention, failure to yield the right of way, and driving while drowsy. Most mistakes such as these can be prevented.

NONCRASH COSTS OF DRIVING

Not all the costs of driving come from crashes. The noncrash costs of driving can be grouped into three categories: operating costs, fixed costs, and environmental costs.

Operating costs. Operating costs maintain the motor vehicle you drive and include money you spend for gas, oil, and tires. Operating costs vary based on the number of miles you drive. The more miles you drive, the greater your operating costs.

Fixed costs. Fixed costs include the purchase price of the car and insurance and licensing fees. These costs occur no matter how much you drive. Fixed costs are spread out over all the miles you drive. The more miles you drive a vehicle, the smaller the fixed costs are per mile. The American Automobile Association's annual *Your Driving Costs* study reported recently that motorists driving 15,000 miles in 2003 would have spent an average of $7,754 on all auto-related expenses, or 51.7 cents a mile.

Energy Tip

Save fuel by carpooling, or ridesharing, to school or work, whenever possible. Driving less frequently not only conserves energy but also cuts the cost of gas, oil, vehicle upkeep, tolls, and parking. Having fewer cars on the road makes carpooling an environmentally sound idea, too.

Environmental costs. Some people link air pollution, hazardous waste dumping, and urban sprawl to motor-vehicle use. Efforts have been under way for decades to reduce motor-vehicle-related pollution and to regulate or recycle the hazardous wastes motor vehicles create.

Urban sprawl made possible by society's increased mobility is also a hot political topic. Some people dream of moving to a big city. To other people, moving to a rural area is the fulfillment of their dreams. The constant movement of people from urban settings to suburbs or rural areas increases the strain on the environment because more roads, garages, and gas stations have to be built. However you look at this movement of people, there are environmental costs that need to be considered when determining the full cost of motor-vehicle use.

THE COST-BENEFIT RATIO

The choices you make as a driver can increase or decrease the total **cost-benefit ratio** of driving, that is, the way you weigh the benefits you receive from driving versus what driving a vehicle actually costs. The most direct way you can help minimize the cost of driving is by making choices that reduce the probability of a crash or making choices that protect you if a crash occurs. Understanding and managing your costs is a big part of the driving experience.

?

WHAT WOULD YOU DO?
It's a nice day, and you have a few errands to run in the neighborhood. Will you walk, ride your bike, or take your car?

Lesson 4 Review

❶ List some of the crash costs of driving.

❷ Describe three noncrash costs of driving.

❸ How can you minimize the crash costs of driving?

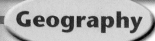
USING THE MAP SCALE

People drive to get from one place to another. But they don't always know how to get there or how far they will have to drive. One way to make sure of your destination and the distance you'll need to travel is to use a road map.

Suppose you want to drive from San Jacinto, California, to Indio, California. You'll travel north on highway 79 to Route 10 and then southeast to Indio. Now you know how you're going to drive there, but how can you determine approximately how many miles you'll be traveling?

Look at the map scale to help you figure out the distance. The numbers along the top show the distance in miles. The scale shows you that 1 inch on the map is equal to about 25 miles. You can use a ruler or a piece of string to estimate your traveling distance. Just find out how many inches long your route on the map is and then multiply by 25.

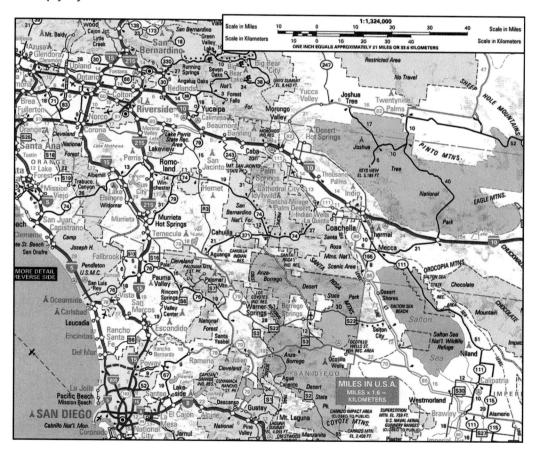

TRY IT YOURSELF

❶ About how far is it from San Jacinto to Indio along highways 79 and 10?

❷ If you travel at an average speed of 50 miles an hour, how long will it take to get from San Jacinto to Indio?

❸ Driving at the same average speed, how long will it take you to get from Perris to La Jolla?

Key Points

Lesson 1

1. Driver education can help you learn how your personality, emotions, and maturity affect your driving; how to maneuver and control your vehicle; how alcohol and drugs impair your ability to drive; and how to interpret traffic laws, rules of the road, signs and signals, and roadway markings. You will also learn how to better manage visibility, time, and space. (Page 7)

2. Factors that affect your ability to drive safely include feeling that there is little or no risk involved in driving, an illness or injury that you have, your emotional state while driving, and the effects of alcohol and other drugs. (Page 7)

3. The following factors can be attributed to the over-representation of young drivers involved in crashes: lack of experience, driving at dangerous times, transporting passengers, and different driving styles of young drivers. (Pages 8–9)

WHAT WOULD YOU DO?
What factors might limit your ability to drive safely here? How should you handle them?

Lesson 2

1. The three parts of the highway transportation system are motor vehicles, streets and highways, and people. (Page 10)

2. Motor vehicles move a majority of people and goods for business and pleasure. (Page 10)

3. The highway transportation system is regulated by federal, state, and local laws and regulations.

Two important laws are the National Traffic and Motor Vehicle Safety Act and the National Highway Safety Act. (Page 12)

Lesson 3

1. Five ways that you can reduce risk when using the HTS include keeping your vehicle in top condition, anticipating the actions of others, protecting yourself and others, driving only when you're in sound physical and mental condition, and making a conscious effort to develop your driving skills. (Pages 13–14)

2. The foundations for effective driving include searching and giving meaning, understanding options and choices, and mastering basic driving skills. (Page 15)

WHAT WOULD YOU DO?
What factors are contributing to risk?
What steps can you take to reduce risk?

Lesson 4

1. The various costs of motor-vehicle use include crashes and the costs associated with operating a vehicle. (Page 16)

2. Crash costs include fixing the wrecked vehicles, cleaning up after the crash, repairing property damage, caring for the injured, and burying the dead. (Page 16)

3. Noncrash costs of driving include operating costs, fixed costs, and environmental costs. (Pages 17–18)

On a separate sheet of paper, write the letter of the answer that best completes each sentence.

1 Driving with your headlights on during daylight hours
   a. increases your chances of being seen.
   b. increases engine efficiency.
   c. allows you to pass in a no-passing zone.

2 Operating costs for your vehicle include
   a. hazardous wastes.
   b. the purchase price of your car.
   c. money you spend on gas, oil, and tires.

3 Under the National Traffic and Motor Vehicle Safety Act, automakers must
   a. provide for vehicle registration.
   b. build certain safety features into their vehicles.
   c. offer a choice of models to customers.

4 The risk of being involved in a crash
   a. does not pertain to good drivers.
   b. depends on the confidence of the driver.
   c. is always present.

5 The yearly total cost of motor-vehicle crashes in the U.S. has been estimated at
   a. $230,000.
   b. $230 million.
   c. $230 billion.

6 Driver education can provide you with
   a. knowledge of the rules of the road.
   b. discounts on vehicle purchases.
   c. automobile insurance.

On a separate sheet of paper, write the word or phrase that best completes each sentence.

fixed	facts
visibility	HTS

7 The goal of the _____ is to enable people and goods to move safely and efficiently.

8 When you drive, reduced _____ means increased risk.

9 The more miles you drive a vehicle, the smaller the _____ costs are per mile.

10 In order to drive, you need to understand the basic _____ about a vehicle.

Writing

Driver's Log

In this chapter, you have learned about ways to manage risk while driving. Write two paragraphs that give your personal view on the following:

- How would you evaluate the possibility of your being involved in a collision? Explain.
- What kinds of situations do you feel hold the greatest risk for you as a driver? How will you manage risk?

Projects

❶ Obtain a copy of your state driver's manual. Read the table of contents, and then take some time to skim through the book. What topics are emphasized? What charts and illustrations are included? Are sample test questions included?

❷ As a passenger, identify objects on or near the road ahead. What actions might you take to minimize driving risk? Try to predict what other drivers will do. Compare your predictions with what actually happens.

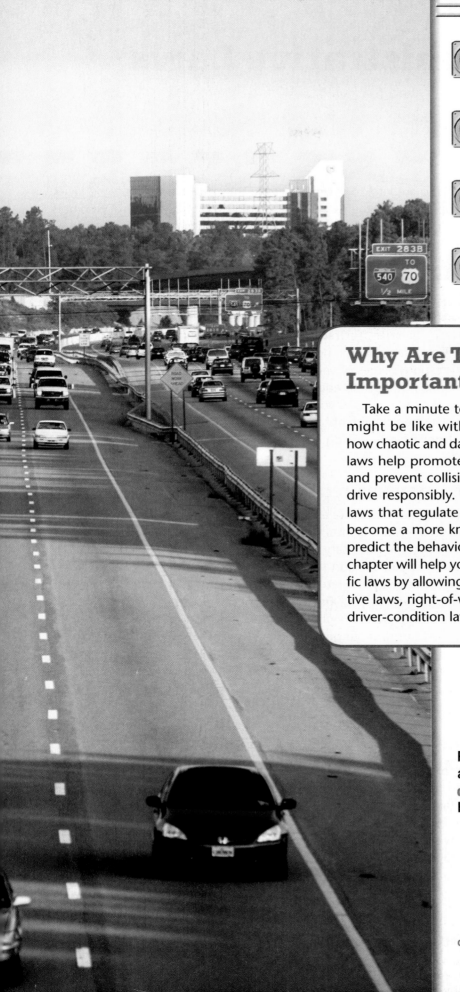

 LESSON 1
Administrative Laws

 LESSON 2
Right-of-Way Rules

 LESSON 3
Speed Limits

 LESSON 4
Driver-Condition Laws

Why Are Traffic Laws Important?

Take a minute to think about what driving might be like with no traffic laws. Imagine how chaotic and dangerous it would be. Traffic laws help promote the orderly flow of traffic and prevent collisions. They also help you to drive responsibly. When you understand the laws that regulate driving, it will help you to become a more knowledgeable driver and to predict the behavior of other drivers, too. This chapter will help you begin to understand traffic laws by allowing you to explore administrative laws, right-of-way rules, speed limits, and driver-condition laws.

Driver Ed
Online

For additional activities, visit drivered.glencoe.com. Here you will find:

◆ **Web Link Exercises**

◆ **eFlashcards**

◆ **Practice Driving Tests**

Administrative Laws

LESSON

1

OBJECTIVES

1. **Identify** the procedures that are regulated by administrative laws.
2. **Discuss** suspending and revoking driver's licenses as well as the point system.

KEY TERMS

◆ administrative laws
◆ suspend
◆ revoke
◆ point system

Rules and laws are vital to society because they establish limits to behavior that help people live together peacefully. Administrative laws control who gets and keeps a driver's license and regulate vehicle ownership and operation.

What Are Administrative Laws?

Each state has laws that control its highway transportation system. **Administrative laws** establish the procedures for issuing and removing people's driver's licenses, for registering a vehicle, and for securing a title, which proves ownership of the motor vehicle. Other administrative laws cover the financial responsibilities of vehicle owners and drivers and establish standards for the minimum safety equipment and care of a vehicle.

To drive and own a vehicle, you are required to follow your state's motor-vehicle laws. This begins with obtaining a license to drive. It includes following the laws that govern safe driving, owning and operating a car, and insurance requirements.

GETTING A DRIVER'S LICENSE

Granting a license to operate a motor vehicle is a function of state government. To obtain a driver's license, you must pass a series of tests. After you pass these tests and pay the necessary fees, you will receive your driver's license.

Each state gives you a vision test, since you need to be able to see what you are doing to drive a car. States also test your knowledge of signs, signals, and markings, as well as your understanding of the state's traffic laws and safe-driving practices. Tests may be verbal, written, and/or on a computer. In most states, the last hurdle to getting a driver's license is the road test, or the in-vehicle driving test. This tests your ability to actually drive.

In some states, younger drivers may need to take more than one driving test. Graduated driver-licensing laws for teen drivers have been enacted in 48 of the 50 states.

SUSPENDING AND REVOKING LICENSES, THE POINT SYSTEM, AND VIOLATIONS

States also have the power to take licenses away. States can **suspend**, or temporarily take away, licenses for a specified period of time. Licenses are typically suspended for 30 to 90 days and always fewer than 365 days. States also have the power to **revoke**, or take licenses away, for a year or more. If your license is revoked, after the time of revocation is finished, you must apply for another driver's license.

States decide when to suspend or revoke your driver's license based on a **point system**, which assigns each driver points for violations. Each traffic violation "costs" a number of points, depending on its seriousness. The points you accumulate are put on your driving record, and they can affect your ability to keep a driver's license.

If a driver whose license has been suspended continues to get points, the license can be revoked. Some violations are so serious that convicted offenders lose their licenses immediately. The most serious violations include driving under the influence of alcohol or other drugs, leaving the scene of a collision in which there has been an injury, or using a motor vehicle in the commission of a crime.

CERTIFICATE OF TITLE

States issue a certificate of title when you buy a motor vehicle, which proves that you legally own the vehicle. The state keeps a copy of the title. Anyone selling a motor vehicle must supply a certificate of title to the buyer. The certificate lists the name of the owner and the make, style, vehicle identification number (VIN), and engine number of the vehicle. This information proves that a particular person owns a particular car, so the certificate should be kept in a safe place outside the vehicle.

VEHICLE REGISTRATION

When purchasing a vehicle, you must also register your vehicle with the state. Registration shows who is responsible for operating the vehicle. When you register a car, you'll receive a registration certificate and one or two license plates. If the state requires liability insurance, you must also provide the name of your insurance company. Registration must be renewed every year or two. Keep your registration in the vehicle, and put the registration sticker on the license plates as legally required.

INSURANCE

Financial responsibility is another aspect of driving. Auto insurance pays some of the bills when you crash, and many states require it. Auto insurance can pay for the damages you may cause that result in death, injury, or property damage to others.

Energy Tip

Excessive speed causes crashes and can "cost" you points in the point system states use to monitor your driving. Excessive speed also wastes fuel. Be responsible!

Did You Know?

The first license plates began to appear on U.S. automobiles in 1901.

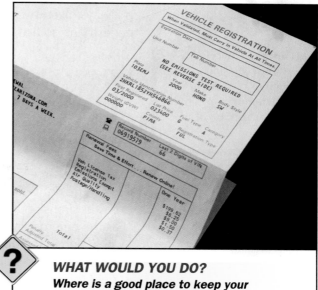

?

WHAT WOULD YOU DO?
Where is a good place to keep your vehicle's registration?

Lesson 1 Review

❶ What do administrative laws require you to do?

❷ What is the difference between a certificate of title and vehicle registration?

❸ Why is it advisable to purchase auto insurance?

Right-of-Way Rules

OBJECTIVES
1. **Define** the meaning of the term *right-of-way*.
2. **Identify** when you should yield the right-of-way.

KEY TERM
◆ right-of-way

FYI

A majority of drivers fail to stop at stop signs. It is important to keep this in mind when you try to anticipate the actions of other drivers.

When you drive, other drivers don't always want to share the road with you. You can avoid a collision by knowing who should go first and who should wait. To do this, you need to know the rules that govern right-of-way. Right-of-way laws in every state are based on the Uniform Vehicle Code, which are vehicle laws recommmended by a national committee and used in part by all states. The laws about when drivers should yield the right-of-way are the same from state to state.

What Is Right-of-Way?

As a good driver, you will often have to yield the **right-of-way**, or the right to proceed first. Never assume that you have the right-of-way. Right-of-way is always given by someone. Often, the correct move is to let other drivers or pedestrians go first.

When Should You Yield the Right-of-Way?

Right-of-way laws are very clear in identifying who should yield to whom in almost every situation. However, human beings make mistakes. The rule that you must yield the right-of-way in order to avoid a collision overrides all other rules.

Here are three situations in which you must always yield the right-of-way:
- Yield the right-of-way to any emergency vehicle, such as an ambulance, that has its sirens on and its lights flashing. If you are going in the same direction as the emergency vehicle, move to the far right of the road and stop. If you are going in the opposite direction on a multiple-lane road, you do not necessarily have to stop, but you should always move to the right.
- Yield the right-of-way to people who are blind and are carrying a white cane or using a guide dog, no matter where they cross the street.
- Yield the right-of-way to all pedestrians, especially those using crosswalks.

In **Figures 2.1, 2.2,** and **2.3,** you will find some of the right-of-way situations that occur most often. In each picture, the red car is required to yield. In all these situations, drivers must yield to pedestrians who are crossing at crosswalks.

MINIMIZING YOUR RISK

One of the most common causes of fatal collisions is one driver's failure to yield the right-of-way to another driver. Never assume that others will yield to you. Other drivers do not always yield the right-of-way, even if you are on a major street or on the right at a four-way stop. Stay alert! It is almost always

SAFETY TIP

When you are on a side street approaching a well-traveled road, stop at the intersection even if a stop sign is not present. Proceed when you are sure you have enough time and space to do so safely.

FIGURE 2.1   RIGHT-OF-WAY SITUATIONS

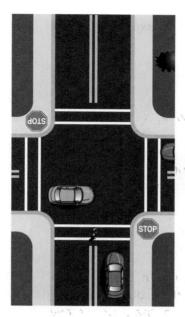

At STOP signs, yield to traffic
on the through street.

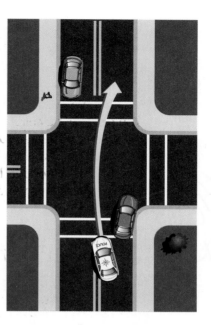

When an authorized emergency vehicle
approaches, move to the right (clear of
an intersection), stop, and remain in such
position until the authorized emergency
vehicle has passed.

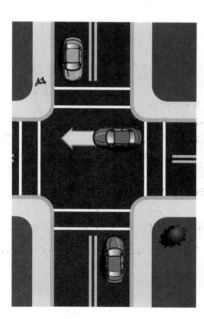

At intersections not controlled by
traffic signs or signals, yield to
vehicles already in the intersection.
Drivers on the left must yield to
those on their right.

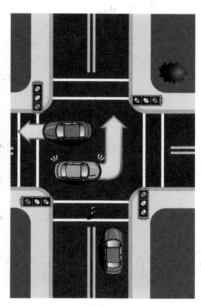

At traffic lights, yield to vehicles still
in the intersection when the light
changes.

FIGURE 2.2 **MORE RIGHT-OF-WAY SITUATIONS**

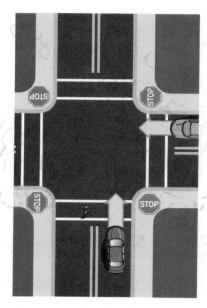

At four-way stops, yield to vehicles that arrive first. If you arrive at the same time, yield to a vehicle from the right.

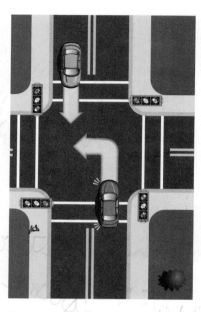

When you are turning left at an intersection, yield to all oncoming vehicles until you have the time and space to make a turn.

Coming out of a driveway or alley, yield to all vehicles in the roadway.

At all YIELD signs, yield to all vehicles on the cross street.

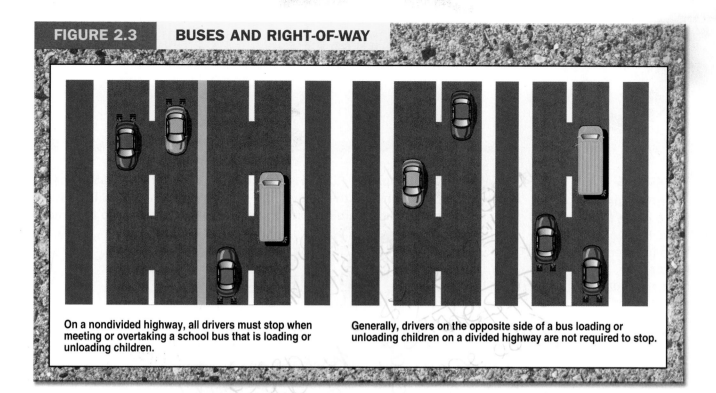

FIGURE 2.3 | **BUSES AND RIGHT-OF-WAY**

On a nondivided highway, all drivers must stop when meeting or overtaking a school bus that is loading or unloading children.

Generally, drivers on the opposite side of a bus loading or unloading children on a divided highway are not required to stop.

safer to yield, even if the other driver is required by law to yield to you. To minimize your own risk, remember that others will not always obey pavement markings, traffic signs, and traffic signals. Make yourself as visible as possible, and identify an escape route in case something goes wrong in a particular driving situation. When signaling a move left or right into a lane being used by other drivers, you must yield to any vehicle that is passing you or to any vehicle that appears to be so close that it presents a danger.

?

WHAT WOULD YOU DO?
To whom would you yield? Why?

Lesson 2 Review

❶ What does right-of-way mean?

❷ In which situations should you yield the right-of-way?

❸ How can you minimize your risk of collision?

Speed Limits

OBJECTIVES

1. **Define** the meaning of the following kinds of speed limits: fixed and advisory.
2. **Explain** under what conditions posted speed limits do not apply.

KEY TERMS

◆ fixed speed limit
◆ advisory speed limit

Did You Know?

In Great Britain, the Locomotive Act (Red Flag Act) of 1865 imposed the first speed limits. They were 2 miles per hour in cities and towns and 4 miles per hour in the country.

What is a safe speed? Posted maximum speed limit signs attempt to answer this question, but they only apply under ideal conditions. The different types of speed limits are important to understand if you are to become a responsible driver.

What Are the Different Kinds of Speed Limits?

When you are behind the wheel, it's important to understand the various types of speed limits. All states post speed limits on their roadways in the form of speed-limit signs. Speed limits are set and posted to protect all drivers. Traffic engineers set speed limits by studying road conditions. They evaluate the road surface, the average amount of traffic, and any hidden dangers. Traffic engineers also know how many collisions have happened at any given location. A speed limit is set only after all these factors have been taken into consideration.

Posted speed limits do not really tell you how fast to drive. They only state that you cannot safely go faster than the posted speed—the *maximum* speed at which you can drive under the best weather and road conditions. While you might drive the maximum allowable speed on a clear day, you would not do so in bad weather. For example, you would never try to drive at the maximum allowable speed in the middle of a snowstorm.

All states also have basic speed limits that mean you cannot drive at speeds faster or slower than conditions safely permit. Visibility, time, and space determine the speed at which you can travel safely.

A few interstate roads have speed limit signs as high as 75 mph. **When may this speed not be reasonable?**

FIXED SPEED LIMIT

A **fixed speed limit** is a maximum or minimum speed that a vehicle may be driven on a particular roadway. Fixed speed limits do not change. Drivers may never legally travel at speeds faster than the maximum posted speed. Drivers who travel at speeds greater than the posted maximum limit can be issued a citation and be made to pay a fine.

In a few special cases, speed limits are set for a minimum allowable speed, where drivers can be ticketed for driving too slowly. A vehicle traveling below the minimum posted speed limit can be dangerous to other drivers who must suddenly slow down when they approach this vehicle. On high-speed highways, slow drivers can make other drivers nervous or angry and cause traffic tie-ups and congestion.

ADVISORY SPEED LIMIT

All roads are not straight and flat. Many roads go up and down hills, over bridges, and around sharp curves. Drivers need to adjust their speed for these changes. An **advisory speed limit** advises drivers to interrupt their normal driving speed for a limited time. Advisory speed limits provide valuable, safe guidelines for adjusting your speed.

For example, a warning sign is usually posted before a sharp curve or before an exit ramp. If the curve is very sharp, a square, yellow advisory speed sign may be posted beneath the warning sign to advise you of the maximum safe speed for that curve. In addition, chevron-shaped markings may be used to emphasize the risk. Like all speed limits, advisory limits are based on ideal road conditions.

Note the advisory speed limit sign. *What is the maximum speed you should travel around this curve?*

DAY AND NIGHT SPEED LIMITS

Some states have lower speed limits at night. Night driving is much more dangerous because it is harder to see the road and any obstacles in the dark.

Driving at a lower speed gives drivers more time to search for visual clues and to identify dangerous objects or road conditions that increase risk. In 2002, two out of every three drivers under 21 years old involved in a fatal, single-vehicle crash were killed at night.

What Are Basic Speed Laws?

No matter what the speed limit sign says, all states have a basic speed law. The basic speed rule is: Always drive at a speed that is reasonable and proper for existing conditions. Your ability to manage visibility, time, and space also determines what is a safe speed at any given time.

A safe speed at any particular time is determined by the type and condition of the road. Also important are factors such as the traffic, weather, and light. Following the basic speed law, drivers must go more slowly than the minimum posted speed if road or traffic conditions make that posted speed unsafe. If you are given a ticket for breaking the basic speed law, the officer issuing the ticket must show that the driver was going too fast for the weather, road, or traffic conditions at that time. Drivers can also be cited for driving too slowly. In these cases, the officer must show that the speed was so slow that it caused danger to other drivers going at a reasonable speed.

More than half of all fatal crashes occur on roads with posted limits of 55 mph or more. Driving faster than the posted speed limit is never safe or reasonable, and it's always against the law.

Take note of these facts about speed. The higher the speed:

- the less time the driver has to spot dangerous situations and take action.
- the greater the time and distance it takes to change direction or stop a vehicle.
- the greater the chance the vehicle will skid or roll over on a turn.
- the greater chances of a collision, personal injuries, and property damage.

Driving within the posted speed limits and slowing down when road or weather conditions are difficult will make you a more responsible driver.

?

WHAT WOULD YOU DO?
Snow is on the ground and you see this sign. At what speed would you drive?

Lesson 3 Review

❶ What are the different kinds of speed limits?

❷ What are the basic speed laws?

❸ In what circumstance would a posted speed limit not be reasonable?

Driver-Condition Laws

When you get behind the wheel, your physical, mental, and emotional conditions affect your ability to drive safely. Driving a motor vehicle while your judgment is impaired by alcohol, drugs, fatigue, lack of sleep, or emotional upset increases your chances of a serious crash. Laws against driving while your judgment is impaired help minimize the number of crashes.

How Do You Recognize High-Risk Behavior?

You have probably seen someone driving a car or truck in a careless, dangerous, or unacceptable manner. These incidents happen frequently. Consequently, states are enacting laws with severe consequences to discourage these high-risk behaviors.

Improper driving can be unintentional, reckless, or criminal. Basically, this depends upon the behavior of the driver and the conditions under which the behavior occurred. When you are driving, you may have an impulse to operate your vehicle in a careless, dangerous, aggressive, or reckless manner. For your own safety, try to not act on these impulses.

DRIVING WHILE IMPAIRED

Impaired driving is an extremely high-risk behavior. In 2002, some 41 percent of 42,815 deaths occurred in alcohol-related crashes. One in every 122 licensed drivers (1.5 million) is arrested for driving while under the influence of alcohol, an offense commonly called a DWI (driving while intoxicated) or DUI (driving under the influence). Between 10 and 22 percent of drivers involved in crashes test positive for drug use.

Most people agree that no one under the influence of alcohol or other drugs should operate a motor vehicle. As a result, states have passed many alcohol and drug driving laws. For instance, every state has enacted an **illegal per se law** that makes it unlawful for a person to operate a motor vehicle with a blood alcohol concentration (BAC) above a certain level. For drivers over 21, that level is .08 percent in 45 states. Drivers who hold a commercial driver license can be arrested for DWI at a lower BAC of .04 percent. For persons under age 21 the BAC limit is often even lower—.02 percent in 37 states, .01 percent in 2 states, and .00 percent in 11 states.

Implied consent laws have been enacted in all states. When receiving their licenses, drivers agree that if stopped for cause and charged with the offense of drinking and driving, they will take a test for the presence of alcohol. This means you must agree to take a blood alcohol concentration test if requested to do so by a police officer.

OBJECTIVES

1. **Define** the meaning of the following terms: *implied consent, aggressive driving,* and *vehicular homicide.*
2. **Identify** the three conditions that must exist to uphold a charge of reckless driving.

KEY TERMS

- ◆ **illegal per se law**
- ◆ **implied consent laws**
- ◆ **aggressive driving**
- ◆ **vehicular homicide**

Dealing with the UNEXPECTED

ROAD RAGE

What should you do if you have inadvertently triggered another driver to become enraged? Here are some tips for dealing with road rage.

▲ Do not make eye contact with an angry driver. Eye contact could make the person even angrier.

▲ Remain calm and courteous. Do not exchange insults or gestures with an enraged driver.

▲ Give an angry driver plenty of room. Allow as much distance as possible between your car and the other vehicle.

▲ If you think that an enraged driver is following you or you feel that you are in danger, get help. If you have a cell phone, call the police. Otherwise, drive to a police station, shopping center, convenience store, or other place where there are plenty of people.

In 32 states, drivers who either test above the BAC limit established by law or who refuse to take the BAC test face immediate penalties. These drivers will have their licenses suspended or revoked immediately for 7 to 180 days for a first offense. In addition, persons who refuse to take a test for blood alcohol concentration still may be charged with DWI based on observed erratic driving and physical behavior.

AGGRESSIVE DRIVING

Aggressive driving is a high-risk behavior that threatens the safety of others, and it's a moving traffic violation. Aggressive driving includes speeding, running red lights or stop signs, tailgating, frequent and unsafe lane changes, and passing on the shoulder. Aggressive drivers have low regard for other people. They use their vehicles to express their personal anger and frustration without regard for others.

Aggressive driving has increased so much that seven states have enacted laws to combat it. Typically, two or more of these dangerous and high-risk behaviors must occur before a driver is charged with aggressive driving and faces increased penalties.

Here are some examples of aggressive driving:

- driving at an inappropriate speed (15 to 20 mph above the posted limit)
- tailgating
- failing to stay in the right lane except to pass
- frequent and unsafe lane changes (weaving in and out of traffic)
- passing on the shoulder during heavy traffic

Because failure to follow basic traffic laws can cause aggression, avoid triggering others to drive aggressively.

Driver Ed
Online

Topic: Driver Distractions

For a link to more information on driver distractions, go to **drivered** .glencoe.com.

Activity: Using the information provided at this link, work with two or three other students to create a chart that identifies the most common driver distractions and presents important tips for staying focused while driving.

RECKLESS DRIVING

Driving recklessly endangers other drivers. Driving is considered "reckless" when three conditions exist. First, a driver must consciously and intentionally drive in a dangerous manner. Second, the driver knows or should know that his or her actions place other people at increased risk. And third, the conditions—including time and place of occurrence, weather, traffic volume, and vehicle and driver condition—make the increased risk obvious and serious.

Reckless driving always involves improper driving acts, such as driving under the influence, going to sleep while driving, speeding, and failure to yield right-of-way. However, conditions at the time of driving might make it "reckless" rather than an ordinary violation of a traffic law. For instance, exceeding the speed limit by 20 to 25 miles per hour in a school zone when children are present is reckless driving, as is drag racing on a city street when other vehicles are present.

Willful and *wanton* are key legal terms in a reckless driving violation charge. These terms imply that a person purposefully and willfully committed an act without regard for the rights and safety of others. The words *willful* and *wanton* indicate that the person knows what he or she is doing. More importantly, they indicate that the person intended to commit the act, even though the person did not intend or desire to do harm.

Whenever reckless driving causes the death of another person, the driver or drivers involved may be charged and convicted of **vehicular homicide**.

INATTENTION AND DISTRACTIONS

Inattention is a leading cause of motor-vehicle crashes and another high-risk behavior. Failure to pay full attention to driving was a contributing factor in nearly 50 percent of the 6.3 million collisions reported to the police in 2002 according to the National Highway Traffic Safety Administration.

Younger drivers are frequently guilty of inattention. Research conducted by the American Automobile Association (AAA) revealed that inattention is the primary cause of 25 percent of all crashes involving 16- to 18-year-old drivers. Eating, drinking, tuning the radio, talking on the cell phone, falling asleep, or talking to other people in the car are a few of the distracting things people do while driving. Trying to do any of these things when you're behind the wheel distracts you from the task of driving. So far, seven states have enacted laws restricting the use of cell phones while driving.

Don't get distracted while driving. *How can you do so?*

Elizabeth Vermette

AAA Public Affairs
Washington, DC

Driving is a risky business. Last year in the United States, more than 42,800 people were killed and almost 3 million were injured in motor-vehicle crashes. Motor-vehicle crashes are the leading cause of death and injury for teens.

Young drivers can reduce teen crashes through compliance with graduated driver's licenses, rights-of-way, speed limits, and driver condition laws.

How can compliance with graduated driver's licenses, rights-of-way, speed limits, and driver condition laws help reduce teen crashes?

? WHAT WOULD YOU DO?
What steps can the driver take to avoid vehicle audio system distractions?

As a young driver, you are more likely to be distracted by other teenage passengers. Statistically, the chance of a crash occurring increases dramatically as the number of teen passengers increase. For this reason, graduated driver license (GDL) laws in 25 states restrict young beginning drivers from transporting other teen passengers during the learner's and/or intermediate licensing stages, usually during the first 6 to 18 months of licensure.

You will learn more about inattention and distractions in Chapter 17.

Lesson 4 Review

❶ What are the meanings of the terms *implied consent, aggressive driving,* and *vehicular homicide*?

❷ What three conditions must exist before a person can be arrested for reckless driving?

❸ List three actions that can cause a driver to be distracted.

BUILDING Skills — Geography

USING COORDINATES

You want to find Port Allen, Louisiana, on the map. How can you do that quickly? First find Port Allen on the map index. It is listed alphabetically. Beside the name, you will see H-12. These are coordinates.

Look at the map. There are letters along the left side and numbers along the bottom. Find the H and put your left finger on it. Now find the 12. Move your left finger straight across the map until it is above the 12. Port Allen is in that area.

Notice the ◉ beside Port Allen. This means it is a county seat. A ○ stands for a town, a ● stands for a city, and ★ stands for the state capital. If you scan the map quickly, you can see that the names of cities and towns are written in different-sized type: the larger the type, the greater the population.

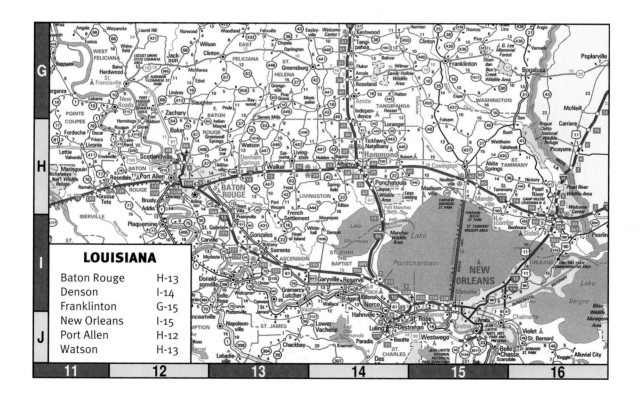

TRY IT YOURSELF

❶ Find Denson on the map. Is its population greater or less than the population of Port Allen?

❷ Find Franklinton and Watson. Which is a county seat?

❸ Find Baton Rouge and New Orleans. Which is the capital of Louisiana? Which has the smaller population?

Key Points

Lesson 1

1. Administrative laws establish procedures for issuing and removing people's driver's licenses, for registering a vehicle, and for securing a title that proves ownership of the motor vehicle. (Page 24)
2. States can suspend or temporarily take driver's licenses away for a specified period of time. They also have the power to revoke or take licenses away for a year or more. States decide to suspend or revoke a license based on a point system. (Pages 24–25)

Lesson 2

? WHAT WOULD YOU DO?
To whom would you yield? Why?

1. Right-of-way is the right of one vehicle to proceed before another vehicle. (Page 26)
2. You must yield the right-of-way to emergency vehicles, people who are blind, and all pedestrians. You must also yield at intersections not controlled by signals or signs, to vehicles already in the intersection, at stop or yield signs, to traffic on the cross street, at traffic lights, to vehicles still in the intersection when the light changes, when moving into a lane used by other drivers, and to passing vehicles. You also must stop when a school bus stops to pick up or discharge students. (Pages 26–29)

Lesson 3

1. Fixed speed limits are the maximum or minimum speeds that a vehicle may be driven. Advisory speed limits provide valuable, safe guidelines for adjusting vehicle speed. (Pages 30–31)
2. A posted speed limit sign does not apply when you are unable to drive at a speed that is reasonable and proper for existing conditions. (Page 32)

Lesson 4

? WHAT WOULD YOU DO?
What steps can the driver take to avoid vehicle audio system distractions?

1. Implied consent is an agreement you make that if stopped for cause and charged with the offense of drinking and driving you will take a BAC test. Aggressive driving is a high-risk behavior that threatens the safety of others. Vehicular homicide occurs when reckless driving causes the death of another person. (Pages 33–35)
2. To be charged with reckless driving, a driver must consciously and intentionally drive in a dangerous manner, know that his or her actions place other people at increase risk, and understand that conditions make the increase in risk obvious and serious. (Page 35)

On a separate sheet of paper, write the letter of the answer that best completes each sentence.

1 If you are driving while impaired, get in a collision, and the other driver dies, you could be charged with
 a. reckless driving.
 b. vehicular homicide.
 c. aggressive driving.

2 Posted speed limits
 a. tell you at what speed you must drive.
 b. are only on interstate highways.
 c. indicate the maximum speed you can drive given weather and road conditions.

3 On a two-lane street, an ambulance is coming from behind with its siren blaring and lights flashing. You should
 a. pull over to the left and stop.
 b. pull over to the right and stop.
 c. increase your speed.

4 Your driver's license can be revoked if you
 a. are convicted of DUI or DWI.
 b. get into a collision.
 c. drive below the minimum speed limit.

5 Right-of-way rules determine
 a. minimum speed limits in each state.
 b. procedures for turning right.
 c. who should yield the right-of-way.

6 You must pass a series of tests in order to
 a. increase your number of driving points.
 b. obtain a driver's license.
 c. obtain a certificate of title.

On a separate sheet of paper, write the word or phrase that best completes each sentence.

A Uniform Vehicle Code
B point system
C aggressive driving
D basic speed law

7 The __D__ states that you should always drive at a speed that is reasonable and proper for existing conditions.

8 Tailgating is an example of __C__.

9 Most states use a(n) __B__ to keep track of traffic violations by individual drivers.

10 All states have right-of-way laws that are based on the __A__.

Writing

Driver's Log

In this chapter, you have learned about the rules and laws that govern the roadways and the motorists who use them. Write about the five rules or laws you think you will have the most trouble obeying.

Projects

1 Find out the location of your area's department of motor vehicles to obtain a copy of your state's driver's manual. Do the same with two neighboring states. Report on laws that are the same in each state and those that are different.

2 Ask at least four drivers if they can name five facts about roadway speed. Prepare a report on your findings. You may want to compare your report with the reports of others in your class and put together a combined report.

Signs, Signals, and Pavement Markings

What Do Signs Really Mean?

Take a minute to think about all the various traffic signs that you see on the road. You probably know the meaning of certain signs. For example, you know that a stop sign requires you to stop your vehicle. But do you recognize and understand the meanings of all traffic signs? In this chapter, you learn about traffic signs as well as traffic signals and pavement markings.

Driver Ed
Online

For additional activities, visit **drivered.glencoe.com**. Here you will find:

◆ **Web Link Exercises**
◆ **eFlashcards**
◆ **Practice Driving Tests**

Regulatory and Warning Signs

OBJECTIVES

1. **Identify** the shapes and colors and describe the purpose of regulatory signs.
2. **Describe** the actions to take at regulatory signs.
3. **Identify** the shapes and colors and describe the purpose of warning signs.
4. **Describe** how to respond to warning signs.

KEY TERMS

◆ regulatory sign
◆ warning sign

Roadway signs provide important information about where you are, where you are going, and what rules or laws to follow. If there were no signs, how would you know you were on the right road? Imagine how difficult it would be to manage risk if there were no speed limits or rules regulating when or where to yield. You can also imagine the numerous collisions that would take place at intersections without stop signals.

Designed for easy understanding, traffic signs have uniform shapes and colors. In addition, signs may display words, symbols, or a combination of both. You read word messages from left to right or from top to bottom. However, you read most symbols from bottom up. Once you know the general meanings, you can quickly identify the intended message.

There are two types of traffic signs: regulatory signs and warning signs. Each possesses the characteristics just mentioned and helps to make your driving experience safer.

What Are Regulatory Signs?

A **regulatory sign** regulates or controls the movement of traffic. These signs inform you of laws that apply at a given time or place. Regulatory signs are red, white, black, green on white, or white on black. Most regulatory signs are vertical rectangles (taller than they are wide). Such signs show speed limits, turning restrictions, lane use, and pedestrian and parking controls. A red circle with a red slash through it, on any of these signs, means NO. **Figure 3.1** shows you examples of regulatory signs. At each of these signs, you must take a specific action.

What Actions Should You Take at Regulatory Signs?

Regulatory signs give commands or set limits. The four most common regulatory signs include:

● stop signs and speed-limit signs
● yield signs and railroad crossbuck signs

Stop signs are eight-sided, red, and tell you where to stop. Yield signs are inverted triangles with a red border. They require you to slow and yield (give way) to traffic on the crossroad or the road onto which you are merging if close enough to cause a conflict or a collision. Speed-limit signs indicate the maximum speed you may drive under ideal conditions. Railroad crossbuck signs indicate that railroad tracks are crossing the roadway.

Energy Tip

Save fuel by letting up on the accelerator well in advance of a red light, stop sign, or yield sign.

FIGURE 3.1

REGULATORY SIGNS

Yield
Triangle
Red

Stop
Octagon
Red

Railroad crossing
Crossbuck
White

Speed limit
Vertical rectangle
White

One way
Horizontal rectangle
Black

Do not enter
Square
Red

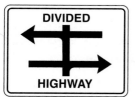

Divided highway
Horizontal rectangle
White

Wrong way
Horizontal rectangle
Red

Keep right
Vertical rectangle
White

Intersection lane
Control
Square
White

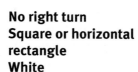

No right turn
Square or horizontal
rectangle
White

Time-limit parking
Vertical rectangle
White

Stop signs are most frequently placed at one or more corners of an intersection. **Where should you stop at a stop sign?**

STOP SIGNS

Most often you will see a stop sign at the intersection of two roadways. There may be stop signs on all four corners or on only one or two corners of an intersection. In some places, stop signs are located in the middle of the block; these indicate crosswalks.

You must come to a full stop at a stop sign. Often a white stop line is painted on the pavement in line with the sign. There may be two white lines indicating a pedestrian crosswalk just beyond the stop line, or there may be walk lines and no stop line. You are required to stop in front of the first white line you come to. If there are no lines, stop just in front of, or in line with, the sign.

After you stop, if there is no cross traffic from the right or left, you may proceed. When there is traffic on the other roadway, you must decide what to do. If there are stop signs for cross traffic and another vehicle has reached its stop sign before you reach yours, you must let it go first. If you and the other vehicle arrive at the same time, the driver on the left must let the driver on the right go first. If you are the driver of the vehicle on the right, make sure the driver of the vehicle on the left is going to wait. Then proceed cautiously.

YIELD SIGNS

At a yield sign, you move from one roadway onto or across another one. As you approach the yield sign, slow down and check oncoming traffic and the traffic behind you. Search left and right for cross and oncoming traffic. If a vehicle is coming toward you, you will have to judge its distance and speed and decide whether you can safely enter or cross the road. You may need to slow down or stop and wait until the roadway is clear of traffic before you proceed.

SPEED-LIMIT SIGNS

Speed-limit signs show the maximum, or fastest, speed allowed on a roadway. Driving faster than the posted speed is illegal. Some speed-limit signs also post minimum speeds. These signs are usually on expressways. You should not travel slower than the minimum speed posted, unless road or weather conditions make it unsafe to travel at that speed.

RAILROAD CROSSBUCK SIGNS

A railroad crossbuck sign is located where railroad tracks cross the roadway. On multilane roadways and in heavy traffic areas, signal bells, flashing red lights, and railroad gates may also warn and protect drivers. Regardless of whether or not lights and gates are present, if a train is coming, you *must* stop.

What Are Warning Signs?

A **warning sign** alerts you to changes in the condition or use of the roadway ahead. Warning signs include those that tell you about road construction and maintenance; school zones and crossings; railroad crossings; curves; intersections; changes in road width; and pedestrian, animal, and vehicle crossings. You may see a warning sign when a road or lane is closed, near a school, or when there is a dangerous road condition. If you do not know what a particular warning sign means, remember that all warning signs are either yellow, fluorescent yellow-green, or orange with black letters; they use numbers or symbols; and most are diamond shaped.

Figure 3.2 on page 46 provides you with examples of warning signs. Knowing the shapes and colors associated with warning signs will give you a better idea of what to do should you come across an unfamiliar sign.

What Actions Should You Take at Warning Signs?

When you see a warning sign, increase your level of alertness to changes in the roadway, in traffic, or in environmental conditions. Always proceed with caution. Be especially careful when you see a pedestrian or school-zone sign, a railroad advance-warning sign, or a slow-moving-vehicle sign.

Yield signs and speed-limit signs are two examples of regulatory signs. *What are other examples of regulatory signs?*

FIGURE 3.2 | **WARNING SIGNS**

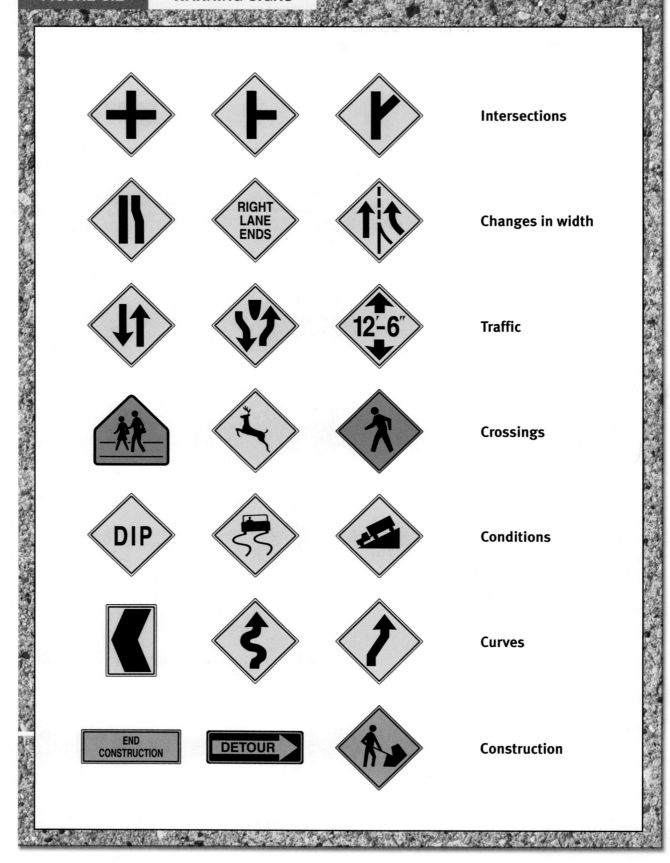

Intersections

Changes in width

Traffic

Crossings

Conditions

Curves

Construction

PEDESTRIAN OR SCHOOL-ZONE SIGNS

When you see a pedestrian or school-zone sign, you must slow down and proceed with caution. Inattentive pedestrians and children playing nearby may dart into the street. When lines representing a sidewalk are added to the yellow-green diamond-shaped sign or the five-sided sign shaped like a house, it warns drivers of a pedestrian or school crossing. If pedestrians and children are present, stop and wait for them to cross the roadway.

RAILROAD ADVANCE-WARNING SIGNS

Be especially careful when you come to a railroad advance-warning sign. Slow down before you reach the tracks, and be prepared to stop. Determine if there is more than one set of tracks, and look in both directions to see if a train is approaching. If there is more than one set of tracks and a train is approaching, make sure a second train is not approaching from the opposite direction on another set of tracks before you proceed.

SLOW-MOVING-VEHICLE SIGNS

Use caution when you see a slow-moving-vehicle sign. This special warning sign appears on the back of horse-drawn, tractor-drawn, and self-propelled farm equipment as well as slow-moving construction and maintenance machinery. It is yellow-orange and bordered in dark red.

Driver Ed Online

Topic: Traffic signs
For a link to more information on traffic signs, go to drivered.glencoe.com.

Activity: Using the information provided at this link, get with several other students to make a bulletin-board display of common traffic signs.

WHAT WOULD YOU DO?
The symbol on these signs is called a chevron. What do the signs mean? What would you do in this situation?

Lesson 1 Review

❶ How can you tell which roadway signs are regulatory signs?

❷ What should you do when you see a stop sign? a yield sign? a railroad crossbuck sign?

❸ How do you know which signs are warning signs?

❹ How should you proceed at pedestrian zones, school zones, railroad advance-warning signs, and slow-moving-vehicle signs?

Guide and International Signs

Highway signs do more than just warn you and inform you of what you can and cannot do. They can provide information about where you are, where you are going, how to get there, how far you have to go, and what services and sites are available to help make your trip more comfortable and enjoyable.

As you drive, you will see highway signs that convey information through colors, shapes, symbols, words, and numbers.

What Are the Functions of Guide Signs?

As you travel along the roadways, you will see four kinds of guide signs. A **guide sign** identifies roadways and routes; provides information about mileage to certain destinations; points out roadside services, such as rest stops and service stations; and directs you to recreational areas, such as nearby sites of interest.

ROUTE MARKERS

Route markers identify which route you are driving on. Routes are the numbered roadways that crisscross the continent. Various symbols and colors are used to identify the route as an interstate highway or a state or county road. **Figure 3.3** provides you with different route markers.

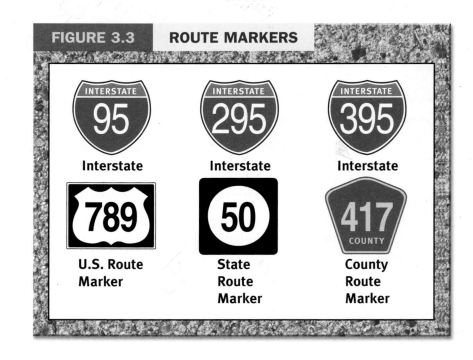

FIGURE 3.3   ROUTE MARKERS

INTERSTATE 95 — Interstate

INTERSTATE 295 — Interstate

INTERSTATE 395 — Interstate

789 — U.S. Route Marker

50 — State Route Marker

417 COUNTY — County Route Marker

Routes that run north and south are odd numbered signs. For example, Interstate 5 on the West Coast connects Seattle, Washington, in the north with San Diego, California, in the south, while I-95 on the East Coast connects Portland, Maine, with Miami, Florida.

East–west routes are even numbered. For example, I-10 in the south connects Jacksonville, Florida, on the East Coast with Santa Monica, California, on the West Coast. And I-90 in the north connects Boston, Massachusetts, with Seattle, Washington.

Interstate routes that lead *into* cities have three digits and begin with an odd digit (195, 395, and so on). If a three-digit route begins with an even digit (295, 684), the route goes *around* a city and connects to interstate highways at both ends.

DESTINATION AND MILEAGE SIGNS

You will often see destination and mileage signs mounted over highway lanes. These signs tell you where you are, which lane to take to get to your destination, what exits are coming up, and how far away the exits are. Smaller signs on the side of the road also inform you how far you are from different places. Destination and mileage signs are green with white lettering. You can find examples of these signs in **Figure 3.4.**

WHAT WOULD YOU DO?
What does this sign mean? What should you be alert to when you see this sign?

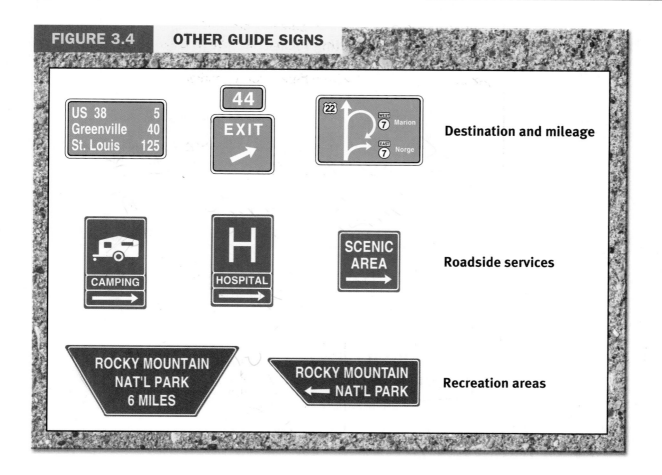

FIGURE 3.4   OTHER GUIDE SIGNS

US 38 5 Greenville 40 St. Louis 125 44 EXIT ➚ 22 ↰ WEST 7 Marion / EAST 7 Norge	**Destination and mileage**
CAMPING ➡ H HOSPITAL ➡ SCENIC AREA ➡	**Roadside services**
ROCKY MOUNTAIN NAT'L PARK 6 MILES ⬅ ROCKY MOUNTAIN NAT'L PARK	**Recreation areas**

ROADSIDE-SERVICE SIGNS

When you want to stop for gas or food or make a phone call, look for blue signs with white lettering. These are roadside-service signs. Refer to Figure 3.4 for examples of roadside-service signs.

RECREATIONAL-AREA SIGNS

Recreational-area signs are brown with white lettering. These signs guide you to state and national parks, historic sites, and other places of interest. Figure 3.4 provides you with examples of recreational-area signs.

Which International Signs Are Used in the United States?

An **international sign** is one you can understand without knowing another language. Because so many U.S. citizens travel abroad and foreign residents travel in the United States, more traffic-control signs are using colors, shapes, and symbols to provide fast, accurate communication. You can see different international signs in **Figure 3.5.**

FIGURE 3.5   INTERNATIONAL ROAD SIGNS

No entry for cycles

Falling rocks

No U-turn

First aid station

Telephone

Gas station

Lesson 2 Review

❶ Which signs are guide signs?

❷ How are route numbers designated?

❸ Why are international signs used in the United States?

Pavement Markings

You have probably noticed lines, arrows, and words painted on streets and highways. These markings give drivers and pedestrians important information, directions, and warnings about roadway travel. You need to understand pavement markings in order to control and reduce risk.

What Do Yellow and White Lines on the Roadway Mean?

Yellow and white roadway lines provide directions or warnings for drivers. Yellow lines divide traffic traveling in opposite directions. White lines parallel to the roadway separate same-direction traffic into lanes. White lines perpendicular to the roadway indicate pedestrian crosswalks and where drivers must stop at intersections and railroad crossings.

YELLOW LINES

Yellow lines are used to separate traffic traveling in opposite directions and the left edge of multiple-lane, divided highways. Yellow lines may be single, double, solid, or broken. A single, broken yellow lane line, or a broken yellow lane line (on your side) to the right of a solid yellow line, means that you can pass *if* it is safe to do so. A solid yellow lane line (on your side) to the right of a broken yellow lane line means that it is dangerous and illegal for you to pass.

OBJECTIVES

1. **Identify** the meaning of yellow and white roadway lane markings.
2. **Describe** the meaning of arrows and other nonlane roadway markings.

KEY TERMS

- **shared left-turn lane**
- **reversible lane**
- **high-occupancy-vehicle (HOV) sign**

Double broken yellow lines mark lanes in which traffic changes direction at different times of the day. *Why would traffic change directions at different times of the day?*

When two solid, double yellow lines divide a roadway, neither you nor drivers traveling in the opposite direction can cross them to pass another vehicle. You may, however, turn left across them to turn into a driveway, if it is safe to do so.

Shared left-turn lanes. On some three- and five-lane roadways, each side of the center lane is marked by parallel solid and broken yellow lines and with white arrows that point alternately left and right. This lane is called a **shared left-turn lane**. Vehicles moving in either direction can use this lane to make left turns off the roadway into an entrance. Drivers who want to make left turns onto the roadway can also move into the shared left-turn lane and wait for a gap in traffic.

You may not pass on a two-way road divided by double yellow lines. *When can you pass on a two-way road?*

Use shared left-turn lanes safely:

1. *Don't get in the lane too soon.* The longer you drive in the center lane, the more likely you are to meet someone traveling in the opposite direction. Give yourself just enough time to check traffic in all directions, signal, enter the lane, straighten out your vehicle and, if necessary stop, and yield before turning.
2. *Watch for vehicles pulling out of driveways and cross streets.* Other drivers may cut across in front of you or turn into the shared lane to wait for a gap in traffic.
3. *Use the shared left-turn lane only to turn left.* If you do not intend to turn, stay out of the lane!

Reversible lanes. Double-dashed (broken) yellow lines are used to mark a **reversible lane**. A number of large cities with heavy rush-hour traffic use reversible lanes to improve traffic flow in one direction in the morning and the opposite direction in the evening. Except during rush hour, there are typically an equal number of lanes open to traffic moving in either direction. During nonrush hours, drivers may pass vehicles moving in the same direction by crossing the double dashed lines on their side of the highway, as long as it is safe to do so.

✓ Tips for New Drivers

SHARED LEFT-TURN LANES

Here are tips for using shared left-turn lanes safely.

▶ Do not move into the lane too soon. The longer you stay in the lane, the more likely it is you will meet someone coming in the opposite direction.

▶ Watch for cars pulling out of entrances and side streets. They may cross in front of you, cutting you off.

▶ Do not use a shared left-turn lane for anything but turning left.

REVERSIBLE LANES

Here are some methods for learning how to use reversible lanes safely.

- ▲ Know the pavement markings that designate the lane as a reversible lane.
- ▲ Know the location, direction of traffic, and lanes to use during specific times of day.
- ▲ The first time you travel in a reversible lane do so as a passenger.
- ▲ The first time you drive in a reversible lane do so at the beginning or end of rush hour when traffic may be lighter.
- ▲ If you are ever confused about how to use reversible lanes drive in the outer lane(s) to the right.

To reduce the chance of a crash between you and other drivers moving in opposite directions, signs, signals, and markings are used to inform drivers which lanes to use during specific hours. When you see doubled-dashed lines on the pavement, check both sides of the highway for signs and overhead signals that tell you which lane(s) you can use.

WHITE LINES

White lines that are parallel to the roadway mark the lanes for traffic moving in the same direction. If the lines are broken, you can move from lane to lane when it is safe to do so. Solid white lines between lanes of traffic moving in the same direction are meant to *discourage* passing at high-risk locations but *may not prohibit* passing.

Solid white lines are used to indicate the right side of the roadway. These lines are especially helpful at night because they mark the outer edges of the road, which are otherwise hard to see. A solid white line may also mark a bicycle or breakdown lane on the right side of the roadway.

The broken white lines indicate that you may change lanes or pass. The solid white edge line marks a breakdown lane. You should not travel in a breakdown lane. ***How do white lines and yellow lines differ?***

FIGURE 3.6

OTHER ROAD
MARKINGS

Ⓐ Shared left-turn lane

Ⓑ High-occupancy-vehicle (HOV) lane for use by vehicles carrying **2** or more occupants

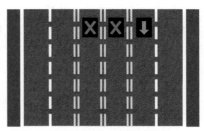

Ⓒ Reversible lane at different times of day may be used by traffic moving in opposite directions

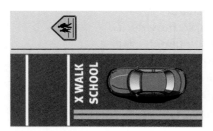

Ⓓ Pedestrian crosswalk

Ⓔ Road exit ramp

Ⓕ Stop line

Ⓖ Disabled-driver parking

What Do Other Markings on the Roadway Mean?

Other roadway markings may include lines, arrows, symbols, and lettering designed to guide drivers and pedestrians. Solid white lines running across traffic lanes are used to identify stopping points and pedestrian crosswalks. White arrows and words on the pavement identify movements that may or must be made from or within a lane. **Figure 3.6** shows you various road markings.

Many road markings contain a combination of solid lines, broken lines, and arrows. For example, shared left-turn lanes consist of all three in order to show drivers where they can make left turns. Reversible lanes are also made up of all three elements. They allow drivers to know in what direction the lane may be driven.

RESTRICTED-LANE MARKINGS

On heavily traveled city streets and expressways, restricted-lane markings appear. During certain hours of the day, traffic in certain lanes may be restricted to buses, turning vehicles, and/or high-occupancy vehicles. A **high-occupany-vehicle (HOV) sign** specifies the minimum number of passengers required (2 to 3 or more) to use the restricted lane. Such lanes are often designed to serve as an incentive for people who carpool because they are able to avoid some traffic by traveling in these lanes.

Be certain that when driving alone you do not drive in the HOV lane. Fines for doing so can be several hundred dollars. In some states, motorcycle drivers may be permitted to occupy this lane. In addition, drivers of hybrid vehicles may be allowed to drive in these lanes regardless of the number of people in the vehicle.

? WHAT WOULD YOU DO?
You are driving alone. Are you allowed to use this lane? Why or why not?

Lesson 3 Review

❶ Which pavement markings indicate that it is legal to pass? That it is illegal to pass?

❷ How is a shared left-turn lane marked? How would you use it?

❸ How is a reversible lane marked? How would you use it?

❹ How is a restricted-use lane marked?

Traffic-Control Devices

A traffic-control device keeps traffic moving in an orderly manner. The most obvious traffic-control device is a traffic signal. Other traffic-control devices include pedestrian signals and traffic officer's signals. Each of these devices allows you to know when to stop or move your vehicle through traffic.

What Does Each Traffic-Control Device Mean?

As a user of the highway-transportation system, your movement, whether you're a driver or pedestrian, is controlled by a series of traffic signals, arrows, flashing lights, pedestrian signals, or the directions of a traffic officer.

TRAFFIC SIGNALS

Traffic signals are usually located at intersections, where the level of risk increases. Today, more fatalities occur at intersections than at any other locations. **Traffic signals** are used to control traffic by indicating who has been granted right-of-way. It is important for you to know what each color and symbol means and respond in the appropriate manner. **Figure 3.7** provides the meanings of and appropriate responses to each traffic signal.

Special-use signals may operate during specific hours or on demand at school zones, fire stations, and some intersections. Traffic signals may be vertical or horizontal and may have one to five separate lenses that give information to roadway users. The most common lenses are circles, but the use of arrow lenses is also becoming more common.

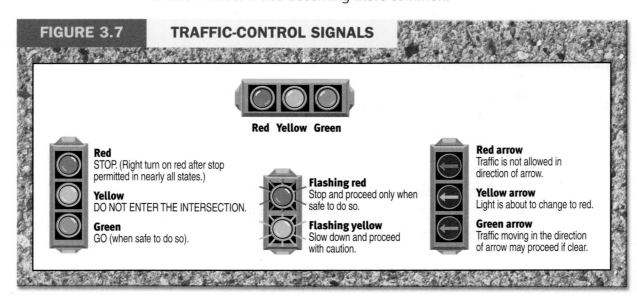

FIGURE 3.7   TRAFFIC-CONTROL SIGNALS

Red Yellow Green

Red
STOP. (Right turn on red after stop permitted in nearly all states.)

Yellow
DO NOT ENTER THE INTERSECTION.

Green
GO (when safe to do so).

Flashing red
Stop and proceed only when safe to do so.

Flashing yellow
Slow down and proceed with caution.

Red arrow
Traffic is not allowed in direction of arrow.

Yellow arrow
Light is about to change to red.

Green arrow
Traffic moving in the direction of arrow may proceed if clear.

Signal sequence. The standard signal sequence is green-yellow-red-green. To assist drivers who may be color-blind or whose view may be partially blocked, signal head colors are always in the same position.

When signals are in the *upright* position, the red light is on top, the yellow light is in the middle, and the green light is at the bottom. When lights are mounted *horizontally*, the red light is on the left, the yellow light is in the center, and the green light is on the right.

Additional signals. At a **flashing traffic signal** you must either stop or slow down, depending on the color of the light. If you see a flashing red signal, you *must* come to a full stop, just as you would at a stop sign. You must slow down and proceed with caution at a flashing yellow signal.

PEDESTRIAN SIGNALS

In cities, you will find **pedestrian signals** at busy intersections. Some are also located in the middle of the block. They may have either words or signals telling pedestrians, or people on foot, how to proceed. **Figure 3.8** shows you the meanings of pedestrian signals.

Flashing pedestrian signals. If you're driving and the pedestrian signals start to flash an orange "Don't Walk," you can expect that pedestrians in the crosswalk will continue to cross the street and your traffic signal is going to turn from green to yellow to red. However, just don't watch the pedestrian signals. Pay attention to the pedestrians and the traffic signals controlling vehicle traffic.

TRAFFIC OFFICER'S SIGNALS

Keep in mind that a police officer can take place of and overrule traffic-control signals. Thus, when an officer is present and directing traffic, you should follow the officer's signals even if they go against those of an automatic traffic signal or stop sign.

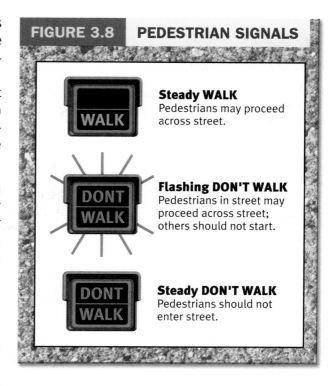

| FIGURE 3.8 | PEDESTRIAN SIGNALS |

Steady WALK
Pedestrians may proceed across street.

Flashing DON'T WALK
Pedestrians in street may proceed across street; others should not start.

Steady DON'T WALK
Pedestrians should not enter street.

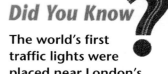

Did You Know?

The world's first traffic lights were placed near London's House of Commons in 1868.

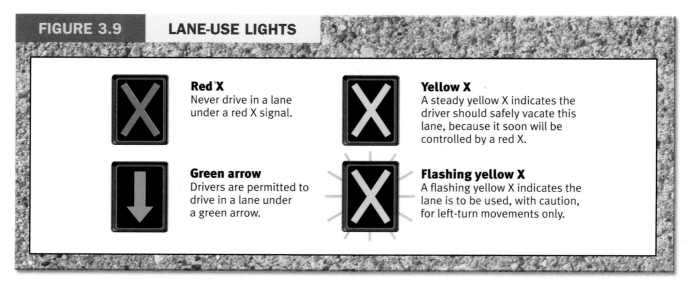

| FIGURE 3.9 | LANE-USE LIGHTS |

Red X
Never drive in a lane under a red X signal.

Green arrow
Drivers are permitted to drive in a lane under a green arrow.

Yellow X
A steady yellow X indicates the driver should safely vacate this lane, because it soon will be controlled by a red X.

Flashing yellow X
A flashing yellow X indicates the lane is to be used, with caution, for left-turn movements only.

Mark Kulewicz

Auto Club of New York
Garden City, NY

Highway and traffic engineers design traffic-control devices to convey a simple, clear, uniform message to all highway users. As a driver, you must recognize and understand the meaning of these devices by their color, shape, legend, and placement. This enables you to respond properly and take the actions needed to maneuver your car safely in different traffic, terrain, and weather conditions.

What might happen if you were unable to recognize and fully understand the meaning of traffic-control devices?

Are There Signals That Let You Know Which Lanes You Can Use?

On heavily traveled multiple-lane roadways, you may see lane-use lights mounted above the roadway. It is important for you to know what to do in response to these signals because they are used when lane traffic is reversed during rush hour to improve flow. **Lane-use lights** indicate which lane(s) you can use at any given time. Sometimes they are used to facilitate traffic flow in tunnels and on bridges. **Figure 3.9** provides you with the lane-use lights.

WHAT WOULD YOU DO?
You are stopped at a red light and want to turn right. Should you make the turn now?

Lesson 4 Review

❶ What are the colors and the meanings of the colors of traffic signals?

❷ What is the sequence of traffic signals?

❸ What are the colors and the meanings of pedestrian signals?

❹ What are lane-use lights?

READING AND INTERPRETING A BAR GRAPH

A bar graph presents information in a way that makes it easy to compare quantities.

The bar graph below shows the number of U.S. licensed vehicle drivers in different years. The numbers along the vertical axis, going up the left side of the graph, stand for tens of millions. So 1 equals 10 million, 5 equals 50 million, and so on.

The years in which the number of drivers are being compared are written along the bottom of the graph, on the horizontal axis.

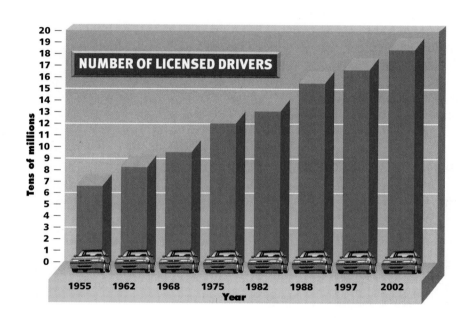

NUMBER OF LICENSED DRIVERS

Tens of millions — Year: 1955 1962 1968 1975 1982 1988 1997 2002

TRY IT YOURSELF

❶ About how many licensed drivers were there in 1968? in 2002?

❷ About how many more licensed drivers were there in 1982 than in 1962? About how many more were there in 2002 than in 1988?

❸ Which year shown on the graph had the smallest increase in the number of new drivers?

❹ Between which two years shown did the number of licensed drivers nearly double?

❺ What is the approximate average number of new licensed drivers each year? (Figure the difference between the last and the first years shown. Then divide by the number of years.)

❻ If the trend in numbers of licensed drivers between 1982 and 2002 continues, about how many licensed drivers would you expect in the year 2010?

Key Points

Lesson 1

1 Regulatory signs control the movement of traffic. They are red, white, black, green on white, or white on black. Most are vertical rectangles. (Page 42)

2 Completely stop at stop signs, yield to cross traffic at yield signs, drive no faster than the limit posted on speed-limit signs, and prepare to stop at railroad crossbuck signs. (Pages 44–45)

3 Warning signs alert you to changes in the condition of the road. They are yellow, fluorescent yellow-green, or orange with black letters. Most are diamond shaped. (Page 45)

4 Respond to warning signs by increasing your level of alertness, slowing down, and proceeding with caution. (Page 47)

WHAT WOULD YOU DO?
The symbol on the sign is called a chevron. What does the sign mean? What would you do in this situation?

Lesson 2

1 Guide signs include route markers, destination and mileage signs, roadside-service signs, and recreational-area signs. They provide information. (Pages 48–50)

2 International signs are ones you can understand without knowing another language. (Page 50)

Lesson 3

1 Yellow lane markings divide traffic moving in opposite directions. White lane markings separate traffic traveling in the same direction. (Pages 51–53)

2 Arrows direct you into lanes from which you can turn. Other road markings include lines, symbols, and letters designed to guide drivers and pedestrians. (Page 55)

WHAT WOULD YOU DO?
You are driving alone. Are you allowed to use this lane? Why or why not?

Lesson 4

1 Stop your vehicle at a red traffic signal. Do not enter the intersection at a yellow traffic signal. Go at a green traffic signal. (Page 56)

2 WALK signals indicate that pedestrians may cross the street. Flashing DON'T WALK signals indicate that pedestrians in the street may proceed across the street but that others should not start. Steady DON'T WALK signals indicate that pedestrians should not enter the street. (Page 57)

3 A red X signal indicates that you should not drive in that lane. A green arrow indicates that you may drive in that lane. A steady yellow X indicates that you should vacate the lane as soon as possible. A flashing yellow X indicates that the lane may be used with caution to make left turns. (Page 57)

On a separate sheet of paper, write the letter of the answer that best completes each sentence below.

1 White lines parallel to the road separate
   a. traffic moving in the same direction.
   b. traffic moving in opposite directions.
   c. vans from trucks.

2 A yield sign indicates that a driver
   a. has the right of way.
   b. may need to stop and wait until the roadway is clear of traffic before proceeding.
   c. must move to a different lane.

3 Two solid yellow lines on a roadway indicate that
   a. passing is permitted in either direction.
   b. the left lane may be used only for left turns.
   c. no passing is permitted in either direction.

4 When approaching a flashing red traffic signal, you should
   a. slow down and proceed with caution.
   b. respond as if it were a stop sign.
   c. immediately turn right.

5 A steady yellow X posted above a highway lane indicates that
   a. vehicles should move slowly.
   b. vehicles should move to a different lane.
   c. the lane will become an exit ramp.

6 Blue signs with white lettering indicate
   a. roadside services.
   b. roadway conditions.
   c. construction areas.

On a separate sheet of paper, write the word or phrase that best completes each sentence below.

A. advance-warning
B. pavement markings
C. high-occupancy-vehicle
D. regulatory

7 You may be permitted to drive in ___C___ lanes if your vehicle has two or more occupants.

8 A(n) ___D___ sign indicates what a driver must or must not do.

9 Traffic signals, signs, and ___B___ provide drivers with information.

10 A railroad ___A___ sign is round and yellow with black markings.

Writing

Driver's Log

Signs, signals, and pavement markings communicate information to drivers. Imagine you are driving and see a traffic sign that you are not familiar with. Write about some of the features of a traffic sign that would help you understand what to do.

Projects

1 Find out how intersections in your state are marked where right turns on red lights are prohibited. Describe what you believe to be the advantages and disadvantages of allowing right turns on red lights.

2 Do you find certain signs, signals, or pavement markings confusing? Create a sketch showing how you would improve each one.

This review tests your knowledge of the material in Chapters 1–3 and will help you review for your state driving test. On a separate sheet of paper, select the answer that best completes each statement.

1. Driving a motor vehicle gives you
   a. freedom to express yourself.
   b. increased mobility.
   c. more money.

2. To insure the safety of your passengers when you are driving, you should manage your
   a. personality and grooming habits.
   b. vehicle inspection stickers.
   c. time, space, and visibility.

3. Being a responsible driver is dependent on
   a. making responsible decisions.
   b. having a good road map.
   c. owning your own car.

4. The highway transportation system consists of
   a. regulations.
   b. cars, drivers, and roads.
   c. superhighways.

5. Most goods and people are transported by
   a. railroads.
   b. motor vehicles.
   c. air transport.

6. A person is less likely to be seriously injured in a collision when driving a
   a. subcompact car.
   b. motorcycle.
   c. vehicle equipped with an air bag.

7. The highway transportation system is regulated by the
   a. drivers' association.
   b. rules of the road.
   c. federal, state, and local governments.

8. The highway transportation system is used by more than
   a. 194 million licensed drivers.
   b. 19.4 million licensed drivers.
   c. 1.94 million licensed drivers.

9. The law that establishes specific guidelines for state motor vehicle safety programs is
   a. the National Highway Safety Act.
   b. the National Safety Enforcement Act.
   c. the National Motor Vehicle Safety Law.

10. Risk when you are driving a car is
    a. not likely if you follow all the rules.
    b. not intensified by distractions.
    c. likely to increase when you drive in bad weather.

11. You can reduce the risks of driving by
    a. ignoring your vehicle's mechanical condition.
    b. turning on your low-beam headlights at all times.
    c. driving aggressively.

12. Your license may be suspended if you
    a. don't have a perfect score on your written test.
    b. acquire a certain number of points for moving violations.
    c. misplace your driver's license.

13. A certificate of title for your car
    a. must be kept inside the vehicle at all times.
    b. gives you permission to drive the car.
    c. provides proof of ownership of your car.

14 You must yield the right-of-way
   a. to avoid a speeding ticket.
   b. when you drive on the right side of the road.
   c. to avoid a collision.

15 If you see an advisory speed limit, you should
   a. resume normal driving speed.
   b. watch out for a potentially dangerous driving situation.
   c. be aware of speed-control devices.

16 When you follow the basic speed laws, you should always
   a. drive at the posted speed limit.
   b. drive at a reasonable speed for road conditions.
   c. drive more slowly and with extreme caution.

17 When you drive at a higher rate of speed, you have
   a. less time to react to a dangerous situation.
   b. a better chance for controlling your vehicle.
   c. more time to change directions.

18 Actions that can prevent or reduce costs of crashes include
   a. removing most protective devices.
   b. driving at excessive speeds.
   c. avoiding the consumption of alcohol.

19 An illegal per se law makes it against the law to
   a. fail to stop for a flashing light.
   b. drive on an expired driver's license.
   c. operate a motor vehicle with a blood alcohol content above a certain level.

20 A regulatory sign may be used to
   a. give limitations for using a particular lane of traffic.
   b. give directions to the hospital.
   c. warn of approaching danger.

21 Warning signs may
   a. be green with white letters.
   b. warn you about road construction.
   c. require you to stop an action immediately.

22 If you need mileage information to a certain destination, you should look for a
   a. sign with flashing lights.
   b. multicolored sign.
   c. guide sign.

23 International signs are used in the United States for
   a. traffic control.
   b. giving information about foreign cities.
   c. welcoming visitors.

24 A shared left-turn lane is used by
   a. drivers traveling in opposite directions who want to make left turns.
   b. emergency vehicles.
   c. drivers in vehicles moving in the same direction.

25 A high-occupancy-vehicle sign indicates that a traffic lane is
   a. temporarily closed.
   b. too crowded.
   c. restricted for multipassenger vehicles.

Challenge Questions

1 When you approach an intersection,
   a. obey directions of the traffic officer rather than the traffic signal.
   b. ignore flashing pedestrian signals at night.
   c. the signal light sequence goes from red to green to yellow to red.

2 To develop safe highways, engineers must plan carefully for
   a. future designs of cars.
   b. anticipated volume of people.
   c. banking of curves on the roads.

UNIT 2

BASIC VEHICLE CONTROL

Chapter 4
Systems and Checks
Prior to Driving

Chapter 5
Basic Control Tasks

Chapter 6
Basic
Maneuvers

How do you control your vehicle?

Controlling your vehicle will become less mysterious to you as you learn what the mechanical systems are and how to use them. Understanding these systems helps you understand how your vehicle operates and how to maneuver it safely. This unit will provide you with the foundations for basic vehicle control.

Systems and Checks Prior to Driving

 LESSON 1
Comfort and
Control Systems

 LESSON 2
Visibility and
Protective Systems

 LESSON 3
Information and
Communication
Systems

 LESSON 4
Checking Your Vehicle
Before Driving

What Should You Do Before You Start Your Vehicle?

You probably know that before you turn on your vehicle you must fasten your seat belt and put the key in the ignition. But do you also know the other steps and safety precautions you should take before entering your vehicle? In this chapter, you will gain a better understanding of the various safety checks you should conduct before operating your vehicle as well as your vehicle's various systems.

Driver Ed *Online*

For additional
activities, visit
drivered.glencoe.com.
Here you will find:

- ◆**Web Link Exercises**
- ◆**eFlashcards**
- ◆**Practice Driving Tests**

Comfort and Control Systems

OBJECTIVES

1. **Describe** four devices that help make you comfortable in a vehicle.
2. **List** eight devices that enable you to control a vehicle, and explain what each one does.

KEY TERMS

- ignition switch
- accelerator pedal
- brake pedal
- power brakes
- steering wheel
- gear selector lever
- clutch pedal
- parking brake
- cruise control

SAFETY TIP

Cruise control should not be used when driving where the traction between the tires and road is poor or where frequent speed adjustments are necessary.

Vehicles are equipped with comfort and control devices to help you drive comfortably and safely. It is important that you learn what these devices are, where they are located, and how they operate.

Suppose you're driving along and suddenly you see a light blink on your control panel. What does that blinking light mean? If you don't know the answer, it could be costly to you. Your ignorance might put you, your passengers, and other drivers at risk. The following section gives you a general idea about the lights on your control panel. To learn about all the lights on your control panel, refer to the owner's manual for your vehicle.

What Devices Help Make Driving Comfortable?

Discomfort behind the wheel can distract you from the driving task. Being comfortable helps you concentrate on driving. Vehicles have several devices that help make you comfortable, and you can use them to your best advantage. Some comfort devices help reduce muscle strain and make driving less tiring. Others control the interior climate of your car. You can usually adjust your seat position, the steering wheel, and the ventilation system.

SEAT-POSITION CONTROLS

The driver's seat should be comfortable and provide you with good visibility and access to the vehicle's controls. Don't sit so close or so far away from the steering wheel that driving is uncomfortable for you or so high or low that you can't easily see where you're going. Adjustments are best made before driving. In a vehicle with a steering-wheel air bag, adjust the seat so you are at least 10 inches from the steering wheel.

Front seats usually move up or down, forward or back, or tilt a little to provide you with a better fit to the vehicle. In vehicles without power seats, the seat-adjustment lever is usually located on the lower left side or lower front of the driver's seat. Pulling back or up on the lever while pushing or pulling the seat allows you to adjust the seat forward or back for better access to vehicle controls and switches.

Many vehicles have power-seat-adjustment controls, which allow you to mechanically adjust the front seat. These controls are often located on the driver and passenger door-trim panels or on the side of the driver's seat. Some luxury vehicle seats have a heating option or contain an inflatable lumbar support pad in the seat's back with the controls located in about the same place as the power-seat-adjustment controls. Never adjust the seat while the vehicle is moving.

STEERING WHEEL

To make sure you can comfortably see, align the steering wheel with your body. The top of the steering wheel should be no higher than the top of your shoulders. If you are a shorter driver, you may need to use a wedge-shaped seat cushion to bring yourself up to a proper driving height in vehicles without an adjustable steering wheel.

Many newer vehicles have an adjustable steering wheel, which tilts up or down. The lever to tilt this type of steering wheel is located on the steering column. You can adjust these steering wheels to a comfortable position that gives you good visibility and control. Never adjust the steering wheel while the vehicle is moving.

AIR CONDITIONER AND HEATER

If you're too hot or too cold, the air conditioner and heater can make you more comfortable. Use the air conditioner to cool the vehicle and lower the humidity. The heater warms the vehicle interior and also clears fogged windows. You can adjust your air conditioner and heater to various levels or temperatures so that you are comfortable while driving.

AIR VENTS

Even cars without air conditioners have air vents, which also help cool the interior of the car. Adjustable air vents allow outside air to flow into the vehicle. They are usually located on the dashboard or on the front lower left and right sides of the vehicle in front of the doors. These vents also allow the air from the air conditioner and heater to enter the car.

How Can You Control the Movement of Your Vehicle?

Each vehicle's control system enables you to start the vehicle, stop the vehicle, and control its speed and direction. The vehicle's control system consists of
- the ignition switch,
- the transmission and clutch,
- the steering wheel,
- the accelerator and brakes.

Each of these components enables you to have movement control when you drive.

IGNITION SWITCH

Start the car's engine by inserting the key in your vehicle's **ignition switch** and turning the key. The ignition switch is usually found on the steering column but sometimes is located on the dashboard to the right of the steering wheel. As shown in **Figure 4.1**, ignition switches normally have five positions: Accessory, Lock, Off, On, and Start. When you are finished driving, turn the ignition switch to Lock, and remove the key.

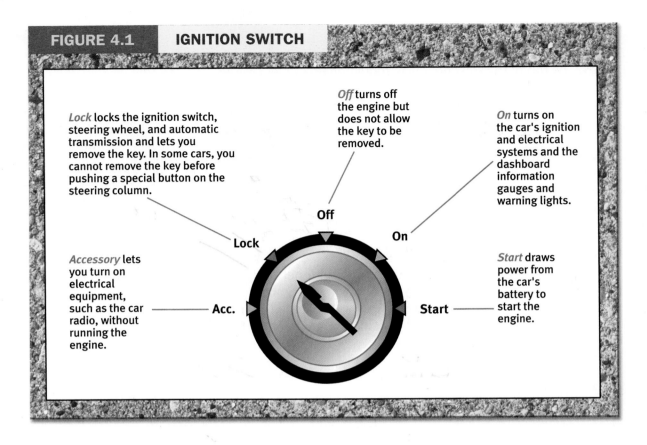

FIGURE 4.1   IGNITION SWITCH

Lock locks the ignition switch, steering wheel, and automatic transmission and lets you remove the key. In some cars, you cannot remove the key before pushing a special button on the steering column.

Off turns off the engine but does not allow the key to be removed.

On turns on the car's ignition and electrical systems and the dashboard information gauges and warning lights.

Accessory lets you turn on electrical equipment, such as the car radio, without running the engine.

Start draws power from the car's battery to start the engine.

Off

Lock

On

Acc.

Start

ACCELERATOR (GAS PEDAL)

To move the vehicle forward and control its speed, press on the **accelerator pedal**, or gas pedal. Use your right foot to press the accelerator pedal, which is always the foot pedal on the far right side at your feet. The harder you push on the accelerator, the faster your vehicle goes. Pushing the accelerator causes more fuel to flow into the engine, the power plant of the vehicle. Taking your foot off the accelerator pedal helps reduce your driving speed.

BRAKE PEDAL

The **brake pedal** enables you to slow or stop your vehicle. To do so, press down on the pedal with your right foot, the same foot you use to press the accelerator. The brake pedal is always located just to the left of the accelerator pedal. **Power brakes** require less foot pressure to operate than nonpower brakes. However, power brakes do not shorten the distance needed to stop the vehicle.

STEERING WHEEL

You control the direction of your car by turning the **steering wheel**, located in front of the driver's seat. When moving forward, the car always goes in the direction of the front wheels. In cars equipped with power steering, it's very easy to turn the steering wheel.

FIGURE 4.2   AUTOMATIC GEAR SELECTOR LEVER

Neutral (N) is the out-of-gear position, which can be used when the car is idling. In Neutral, the wheels are free to roll.

Drive (D) is the forward gear you'll normally use while driving.

Low (L or *2* and *1)* allows the engine to deliver more power to the wheels at slower speeds. Use low gears to drive up and down steep hills.

Reverse (R) is used for backing the car.

Park (P) locks the transmission. Your car should be in Park when you start the engine.

SELECTOR LEVER FOR AUTOMATIC TRANSMISSION

The transmission helps a vehicle move forward efficiently. Transmissions are either automatic or manual. On vehicles that have automatic transmissions, choose the gear you want by moving the **gear selector lever**. This lever is located either on the steering column or on the floor to the right of the driver's seat. To move the gear selector lever on the steering column, pull the handle toward you and then adjust it to the gear that you want to be in. When your gear selector is on the floor, move the handle backward and forward to the gear that you want to be in. Often times you will also have to push a button in to move the gear selector. This button ensures that a simple tap on the handle will not put your car into another gear when you did not intend to do so.

Your gear selector lever allows your car to stay parked and move forward and backward. It is connected to your vehicle's transmission.

A vehicle with an automatic transmission will start only in Park or Neutral. It's safer to start the car in Park, which is also the gear in which you should leave the car. When you start the car in Park, the vehicle will not roll. A car in Neutral *will* roll on an incline when the parking brake is released.

The five standard gear selections for an automatic vehicle are:

- Park
- Reverse
- Neutral
- Drive
- Low

Refer to **Figure 4.2** to obtain a better understanding of the functions of each gear.

FIGURE 4.3   **MANUAL GEARSHIFT**

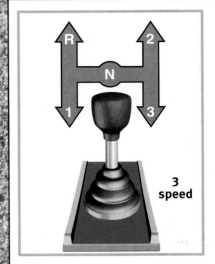

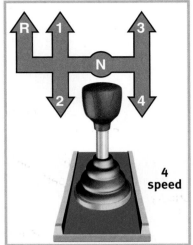

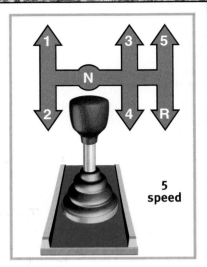

Cars with a manual transmission have a gearshift instead of a selector lever. The gearshift can have 3, 4, or 5 speeds.

GEARSHIFT FOR MANUAL TRANSMISSION

To start and move a vehicle with a manual transmission (or stick shift), you will need to use the clutch. A car with a manual transmission has a **clutch pedal**, a third foot pedal located to the left of the brake pedal. To start this vehicle, step down on the clutch pedal and move the gearshift to the gear you need (usually First or Reverse).

The gearshift is located on the floor to the right of the driver's seat or on the right side of the steering column as seen in **Figure 4.3**. Always press the clutch pedal down when you start the car and when you change gears. The gearshift may have three, four, five, or even six forward speed positions. The fifth or sixth gear serves as an overdrive gear, which allows the engine to run more slowly and fuel efficiently at high speeds. In Chapter 5, you will learn more about how to operate a manual transmission while driving.

PARKING BRAKE

When your drive is over, you need to set the **parking brake**. Frequently called the *emergency* or *hand brake*, the parking brake keeps a vehicle from rolling away after it is parked. The parking-brake control can be a small pedal located to the left side of the floor panel, a hand lever located under the left side of the dashboard, or a floor-mounted hand lever located to the right of the driver's seat.

To set your parking brake, pull the lever up as far as it will go (or press down on the pedal)—it will feel tight and locked into place. When you want to release the parking brake, press in the button on the lever and push it down (or step on the pedal to release it upwards).

When a vehicle with power steering stalls, the power steering is lost. If the vehicle cannot be started and needs to be rolled off the road, the steering wheel will be very difficult to turn.

CRUISE CONTROL

On longer trips, **cruise control** (or speed control) is a feature that lets you maintain a constant speed without keeping your foot on the accelerator. On cars or trucks that have it, the cruise-control button or switch is located on the turn-indicator arm or on the steering wheel. Using cruise control lets you rest your right foot while maintaining a constant speed, which is also more fuel efficient.

To set cruise control, first accelerate to the speed you want, taking into consideration the posted speed limit, road conditions, and traffic. Decelerate slightly, and switch on cruise control. You can turn the cruise-control switch off manually whenever you choose. As a safety measure, cruise control goes off any time you touch the brake pedal.

Cruise control is mostly intended for flat highway driving in situations where you can maintain a particular rate of speed for a fairly long period of time. It should not be used in the city or on wet, snowy, icy, gravel, sandy, and curving roads or difficult driving terrain such as hills and mountains.

Cruise control is a convenience, but be careful when you use it because cruise control may lead you to be less alert than you need to be.

Energy Tip

Consider using cruise control when driving on the highway. Cruise control helps you maintain a constant speed, which improves gas mileage.

WHAT WOULD YOU DO?
You are driving in the right lane at 50 mph. What actions will you take to minimize risk? What vehicle controls will come into play?

Lesson 1 Review

❶ What equipment is designed to make drivers comfortable?

❷ What devices control the vehicle? What does each device do?

❸ When would you apply the parking brake?

LESSON 2

Visibility and Protective Systems

OBJECTIVES

1. **Name** at least five aids to visibility.
2. **Describe** four features that are designed to protect you and your passengers from injury.
3. **Name** three antitheft devices.

KEY TERMS

- ◆ blind spot
- ◆ defroster
- ◆ active safety device
- ◆ passive safety device
- ◆ head restraint
- ◆ air bag
- ◆ antitheft device

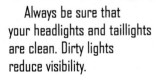

SAFETY TIP

Always be sure that your headlights and taillights are clean. Dirty lights reduce visibility.

Safety features reduce driving risk. Many do so by helping you see what's around you. Others protect the driver and passengers from injury or guard the vehicle against theft.

What Devices Aid Visibility?

Seeing and being seen by other roadway users are critical factors in controlling risk. Several devices make driving easier and safer. A vehicle's visibility system lets you see the roadway better and helps you be seen by others as well.

LIGHTS

Some lights in and on your vehicle that help you see and be seen by other vehicles include headlights, taillights and side-marker lights, daytime running lights, and fog lights.

Headlights. Turning on your headlights helps other roadway users see you both at night *and* during the day. Headlights help you see better at night, in dim light, and in bad weather. The switch to turn on your headlights may be on the dashboard or on the left side of the steering column. Headlights can be switched to low beams or brighter high beams. You either pull the lever toward you or push it away to change to high or low beams. In some older vehicles, the switch that dims and brightens the lights is a button located on the left side of the floor panel. Most of the time you drive, you will use the low beams.

Taillights, side-marker lights, and dashboard lights. Taillights and side-marker lights help other drivers see your vehicle. When you turn on your headlights, your taillights and side-marker lights simultaneously come on. At the same time, the dashboard gauges, dials, and controls also light up. You can dim or brighten the dashboard lights by turning a knob located on the instrument panel or turn-indicator lever. In many vehicles, the same knob used to turn on the headlights also controls the brightness of the dashboard lights and the interior dome light.

Daytime running lights. Many new vehicles have daytime running lights that automatically come on and stay on while the engine is running, which help other drivers see you. Daytime running lights do not turn on taillights or side-marker lights. Some vehicles have an Autolamp On/Off Delay System. This system turns on the lights automatically at night, turns off the lights automatically during daylight, and keeps the lights on for a period of time after you turn the key off.

Fog lights. Special headlights that are designed to project light low to the ground are fog lights. These lights are best used in fog or when it is snowing. Fog lights have their own switch to turn them on and off.

REARVIEW AND SIDEVIEW MIRRORS

Rearview and sideview mirrors help the driver see behind the car and to the side. They are particularly useful when you are starting out or changing lanes. The rearview mirror should be easy to see without moving your head. You must turn your head a little to use the side- view mirrors and also to check over your shoulder, but limit this to a quick glance. Even when correctly adjusted, however, rearview and sideview mirrors cannot eliminate all **blind spots**—areas of the road that you cannot see while driving the vehicle (see **Figure 4.4**).

Before you drive, adjust your mirrors. Adjust the inside rearview mirror so you can see as much as possible out the rear window. You should be able to use this mirror with a shift of the eyes, not a turn of the head. Drivers 6 feet tall or more may find it helpful to turn the mirror upside down so that the day/night switch is on the top of the mirror. This action raises the mirror about 2 inches and eliminates a blind spot to the front.

Adjust the sideview mirrors so you can see past each side of the car as much as possible. To adjust the driver's side mirror, place your head against the driver's side window and set the mirror so you can just see the side of the car. For the passenger's side mirror, position your head in the middle of the car and adjust the mirror in the same way, so you can just see the right side of the car. Someone may need to help you adjust the passenger side mirror because you view the side mirrors from the driver's seat. These mirror settings help minimize blind spots. Remember that even properly adjusted mirrors will not eliminate all blind spots.

Glance often in your rearview and sideview mirrors. How does this help you when driving your car?

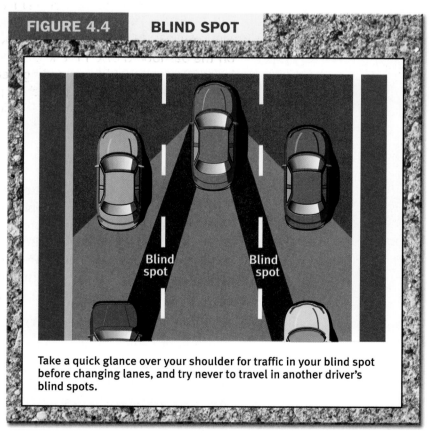

FIGURE 4.4   BLIND SPOT

Take a quick glance over your shoulder for traffic in your blind spot before changing lanes, and try never to travel in another driver's blind spots.

Tips for New Drivers

DEFROSTING THE WINDSHIELD

In cold weather, frost can build on your windshield. To defrost your windshield, leave the blower off and turn the temperature control to the hottest setting for the first couple of minutes. This allows the air to warm up and prevents that initial ice-cold blast from freezing the inside of the windshield.

When you are planning to change lanes, check your blind spots, and make certain they are clear. You will need to use the mirrors and check over your shoulder. You must make a final check to the sides before you make any lateral move (see Figure 4.4). Turning your head to use the sideview mirrors or to check over your shoulder should be limited to a quick glance to detect the presence of objects and not to gather detailed information.

WINDSHIELD WIPERS AND WASHER

Windshield wipers help you see through the front windshield in the rain and allow you to clean a dirty windshield. Windshield wipers may be two speed, three speed, or operate at variable speeds. Some vehicles also have a wiper for the rear window.

Variable-speed wipers can be set to move at a very slow or very rapid rate. This feature is useful when only an occasional wipe is needed to keep the window clear, as during a light drizzle. Variable speeds are also helpful when driving in the rain where a faster rate of wiping is needed.

When you just need to clean the windshield, the windshield washer squirts water or a cleaning solution stored in a container under the hood onto the windshield. After you squirt the windshield, windshield wipers will clean it off.

SUN VISORS

Often when you are driving at certain hours of the day, the sun can reduce your visibility. If the sun makes visibility difficult, sun visors can be moved up and down and turned to the side to prevent the sun from shining in your eyes. You sometimes need to use the sun visor in the early morning or just before sunset. However, be careful not to let the visors interfere with your view of the roadway or traffic to the side. Sun visors are meant to aid visibility, not diminish it.

DEFROSTER (DEFOGGER)

In cold or rainy weather, use the **defroster** to help you see. This device—sometimes called the *defogger*—clears moisture or frost from the front, rear, and side windows. A few minutes of heat from the defroster can also make it easier to scrape ice from the windows before you drive. In most vehicles, front and rear defrosters have separate controls.

What Features Protect You from Injury?

Protective features help reduce risk by guarding you and your passengers against injury in case of a collision or sudden emergency maneuver.

Some safety features, such as manual safety belts, are **active safety devices** that require drivers and passengers to take action to protect themselves. Other safety features, such as air bags, are called **passive safety devices**. Passive safety devices operate without the user having to do anything.

SAFETY BELTS

Safety belts (seat belts) save lives and prevent injuries. They lessen the chance that you or your passengers will be thrown against the dashboard, through the windshield, or out a door that has sprung open in a crash. In addition, safety belts help keep you behind the wheel and in control of the vehicle if you have to swerve or brake abruptly or are struck by another vehicle.

You and your passengers should always wear safety belts whenever the vehicle is moving. Shoulder-lap safety belts are the safest. If you wear a shoulder-lap belt in a crash, your risk of being killed is reduced by 45 percent and your risk of moderate to critical injury is reduced by 50 percent. For occupants of light trucks, seat belts reduce the risk of being killed by 60 percent and reduce the risk of moderate to critical injury by 65 percent.

Forty-nine states have passed laws that require the driver and front-seat passengers to wear safety belts.

HEAD RESTRAINTS

Head restraints on car seats fit behind the head. They are padded to protect the driver and passengers against a neck injury called *whiplash*, which can occur when the vehicle is hit from behind. To get the maximum benefit from head restraints, make sure that they are properly adjusted. Head restraints should be close to the back of the head and at least as high as the head's center of gravity, or about 3.5 inches below the top of the head.

AIR BAG SUPPLEMENTAL RESTRAINT SYSTEM

Air bags are very effective in preventing injuries, but they do not eliminate the need to wear a safety belt. **Air bags** are balloon-like devices that inflate automatically in a frontal crash, and then deflate again in a fraction of a second. Air bags reduce the chance of serious chest and facial injuries during head-on collisions by providing a cushion that reduces the force of impact (see **Figure 4.5** on page 78). Some vehicles also have air bags that inflate during a side collision. All 1998 and newer passenger cars have air bags on both the driver and passenger side, called *dual air bags*. Since 1999, all light trucks also have dual air bags.

All new cars equipped with air bags carry a warning label under the sun visor. Labels explain proper seating position, the placement of infant seats, and the risk of placing or mounting objects near the air-bag cover. Failure to follow these important safety warnings may increase the risk of personal injury in the event of a crash. If your vehicle is equipped with dual air bags, the steering wheel and passenger-side dash is labeled SRS (supplemental restraint system) or with the words *air bag*.

Driver Ed Online

Topic: Air bags and safety belts

For a link to more information on air bags and safety belts, go to **drivered .glencoe.com**.

Activity: Using the information provided at this link, write a letter to the editor of your local newspaper. In your letter, remind parents and caregivers about the importance of making sure that all vehicle passengers are buckled up and provide tips for keeping children safe while riding in a car.

FYI

In 2003, auto manufacturers began installing "smart" air bags in some vehicles. With smart air bags, the size and weight of an individual determine whether and how the air bag deploys during a crash.

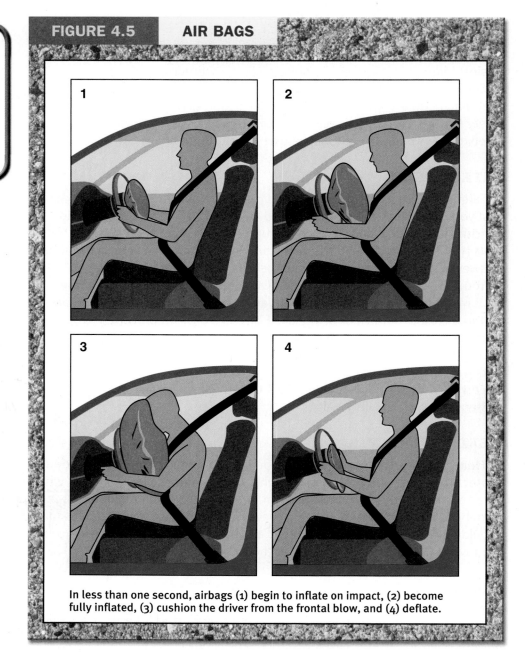

| FIGURE 4.5 | AIR BAGS |

In less than one second, airbags (1) begin to inflate on impact, (2) become fully inflated, (3) cushion the driver from the frontal blow, and (4) deflate.

DOOR LOCKS

When you're in the car, keep vehicle doors locked. Locked doors are unlikely to open in a crash, and they help prevent uninvited people from opening your car door when you're stopped. In addition, they keep young children from accidentally opening the car door. Some doors automatically lock when the vehicle begins moving.

OTHER SAFETY FEATURES

Automobile manufacturers build many safety features into their vehicles that are designed to minimize injuries in case of a crash. These safety features include tempered safety-glass windows, energy-absorbing steering columns, and protective padding on the dashboard and interior roof. Other safety features include impact-resistant bumpers and childproof door locks that are controlled by the driver. Each vehicle's size and weight can determine which safety features manufacturers include as standard equipment.

What Devices Guard Against Vehicle Theft?

Vehicle theft is a nationwide problem. Various types of locks and alarms help protect your vehicle against thieves and vandals.

IGNITION BUZZER

Leaving your key in the ignition makes it easy to steal your car or to lock yourself out. However, when your key is in the ignition switch and you open the driver's door, you will hear a buzz or other sound to remind you to take your key with you when you leave the vehicle.

LOCKS

Vehicles are equipped with several types of protective locks. These can include door locks, steering-column locks, and locks on the trunk, hood, and gas tank.

ALARMS AND OTHER ANTITHEFT DEVICES

Antitheft devices help discourage and ward off car, truck, and motorcycle thieves. These devices include elaborate and expensive alarm systems and disabling devices that keep the vehicle from starting or prevent the steering wheel from turning for unauthorized drivers. Many vehicle-security systems can be turned on or off by remote control using a key-chain transmitter.

WHAT WOULD YOU DO?
What is the driver doing wrong? What would you tell him?

Lesson 2 Review

❶ What vehicle devices aid your ability to see and be seen?

❷ What features help protect you and your passengers from injury in the event of a collision?

❸ What devices might prevent the theft of a vehicle?

Information and Communication Systems

As you drive, you need information about your car and other vehicles. You get information about the workings of your own vehicle by checking the instruments, gauges, and lights on the dashboard. You gather information about other roadway users and the roadway itself by searching in all directions. Some of your vehicle's mechanical devices help you communicate with other drivers, so you can let them know where you are and what you intend to do. Similar devices in other vehicles let other drivers do the same for you.

What Devices Provide Information About Your Vehicle?

When you drive, you need to know how fast you are going, how far you have gone, and whether your vehicle has any serious mechanical problems. The instruments, gauges, and lights on your dashboard can give you this information.

SPEEDOMETER AND ODOMETER

The **speedometer** is a device in front of the steering wheel that shows how fast your vehicle is moving. Your speed is shown in both miles per hour and kilometers per hour.

The **odometer** is often a small mileage counter of numbers at the bottom of the speedometer. The odometer keeps track of the total number of miles the vehicle has been driven. Some vehicles also have a separate trip odometer, which can be reset to zero by the driver at any time.

FUEL GAUGE

How much gas do you have? It's not fun to run out of fuel. You can determine how close to full—or empty—your fuel tank is by checking your fuel gauge (see **Figure 4.6**). Your owner's manual tells you how many gallons of fuel your tank holds.

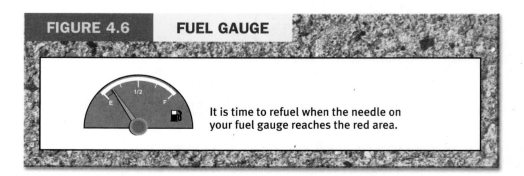

FIGURE 4.6   **FUEL GAUGE**

It is time to refuel when the needle on your fuel gauge reaches the red area.

Dealing with the UNEXPECTED

FLASHING WARNING LIGHT

What should you do if a warning light on your dashboard suddenly starts to flash? A flashing warning light alerts you to a problem, but it does not tell you what is wrong. Take your vehicle to a mechanic as soon as possible. Do not drive any farther than you absolutely must.

ALTERNATOR GAUGE OR WARNING LIGHT

Each vehicle's **alternator** provides electricity to keep the engine running, recharge the battery, and operate the lights and radio. If there is a problem with the alternator, a red warning light will come on or the alternator gauge will indicate "discharge." If the alternator is not working properly, it does not produce enough power and will drain away the vital electricity stored in your battery, which is necessary to start the car.

When the alternator is not working properly, the first thing to do is to turn off unnecessary electrical devices such as the radio. Check with a mechanic as soon as possible. If you delay, your battery will be drained, the engine will stop, and you won't be able to start your vehicle.

TEMPERATURE GAUGE OR WARNING LIGHT

The temperature gauge or temperature warning light lets you know if your engine temperature is too high. Overheating can damage or ruin your engine, one of the most expensive and necessary parts of the vehicle. Get off the road, turn off your car, and let the engine cool down. Have the problem checked as soon as possible.

OIL-PRESSURE GAUGE OR WARNING LIGHT

The oil-pressure gauge or warning light alerts you when the pressure at which oil is being pumped to the engine is low (see **Figure 4.7**). Low oil pressure means that the engine is not being lubricated properly. To avoid serious

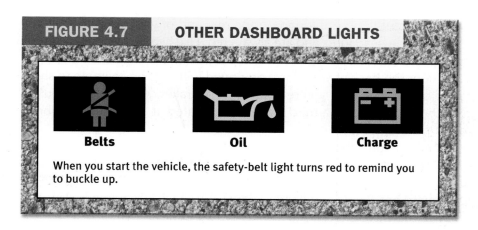

| FIGURE 4.7 | OTHER DASHBOARD LIGHTS |

Belts   **Oil**   **Charge**

When you start the vehicle, the safety-belt light turns red to remind you to buckle up.

engine damage, stop driving immediately and consult a mechanic. Note that the oil-pressure gauge or light does not indicate how much oil is in the engine. You need to check the oil dipstick for that information.

BRAKE WARNING LIGHT

Most vehicles have a brake warning light. It goes on when there is a problem with the brakes. The vehicle might be low on brake fluid, the fluid might be leaking, or the brakes might not work properly. Check with a mechanic immediately.

OTHER DASHBOARD LIGHTS

Several other lights on the dashboard indicate less-serious problems or remind drivers to do certain things. Your parking-brake light reminds you to release the parking brake before moving the vehicle. A safety-belt warning light and buzzer remind you to fasten your safety belt. A door-ajar warning message means one of the car's doors is not closed securely. Many cars have an air-bag light and an antilock brake system (ABS) light. A high-beam indicator light shows when the headlights are on high beams, and a daytime running light indicator shows when the daytime running lights are on. Figure 4.7 on page 81 provides you with a few examples.

How Do You Communicate with Other Roadway Users?

Other drivers need to know where you are and what you are planning to do. You can't shout out this information to other drivers, but your vehicle does have a number of devices to help you communicate with them including
- taillights,
- directional (turn) signals,
- emergency flashers (hazard lights),
- parking lights, and
- horn.

TAILLIGHTS

Several different lights are found on the rear end of your vehicle. Taillights come on with the headlights and are always red. Like headlights, taillights help others see your vehicle.

In addition, the back of your car is equipped with red brake lights to show the driver behind you that you're applying the brakes. All vehicles manufactured since 1986 also have a third brake light, located at the bottom or above the top of the rear window.

White backup lights indicate your car has been shifted into reverse and will back up. These lights also help you see behind you when you are backing up.

The last light on the back of your vehicle is the license-plate light, which comes on with headlights and parking lights. This light is required by law and helps the police and other drivers identify particular vehicles.

DIRECTIONAL (TURN) SIGNALS

Flashing red or amber **directional signals** are sometimes called *turn signals* or *blinkers*. Located in both the front and back of the vehicle, they show other drivers that you plan to turn or change lanes. Directional-signal lights flash in the front and back on either the left or the right side of the car.

To operate the signal, move the turn-indicator arm on the left side of the steering column up for right and down for left. Normally, the turn-signal lever clicks into position, then clicks off when you straighten the wheel. If the signal doesn't stop flashing after your turn, move the lever back manually.

EMERGENCY FLASHERS (HAZARD LIGHTS)

Emergency flashers or hazard lights make all four turn-signal lights flash at the same time. Use your flashers to warn other drivers that your vehicle is stopped on or near the roadway or that you are moving very slowly. The emergency-flasher switch is usually located on the steering column or dashboard.

PARKING LIGHTS

In addition to its headlights, every vehicle is also equipped with parking lights. Parking lights may be used to help other drivers see you when your car is stopped along the side of the road. Parking lights are not headlights, so they're not designed to light the roadway when your vehicle is in motion. In some states it is actually illegal to drive with the parking lights on.

HORN

If another roadway user doesn't see you, they might hear you. Use your vehicle's horn to alert drivers, pedestrians, or cyclists to your presence or to warn them of danger. The horn is generally located on the steering wheel.

Before driving any vehicle, it is wise to locate the horn and make sure it works.

> **WHAT WOULD YOU DO?**
> *You want to turn left and then pull over to the right side of the road. How will you communicate to others what you plan to do?*

Lesson 3 Review

❶ What devices provide information about your vehicle?

❷ What devices enable you to communicate with other roadway users?

❸ What should you do if a warning light on your dashboard suddenly starts to flash?

Checking Your Vehicle Before Driving

OBJECTIVES

1. **Describe** four checks you should make before entering your vehicle.
2. **Describe** six checks you should make after entering your vehicle.

If you were a pilot, you wouldn't dream of taking off without thoroughly checking your airplane first. Safety and equipment checks are also important when you drive. The best time to discover a problem or potential problem is before your vehicle is moving so that you can deal with it before you drive.

What Should You Check Before Entering Your Vehicle?

Before you enter your vehicle, inspect the outside of your vehicle and the area around it. Make the following checks of the area surrounding the vehicle, the wheels, the body, and under the hood before you drive.

SURROUNDING AREA

- Look for children playing nearby. Each year about 200 children under the age of six are killed while playing in the family driveway.
- Look for animals that may be hiding under or walking or sleeping near the vehicle.
- Look for objects in the area of the vehicle and on the roadway that may interfere with safe movement or that could damage the tires.
- Look under the vehicle for fresh stains that could indicate fluid leaks.

WHEELS

- Check for underinflated tires, excessive wear, or tire damage.
- Note which way your front wheels are turned. This is the direction in which your vehicle will go as soon as it begins moving forward.

Check under your vehicle for leaks, objects, and animals every time you plan to drive. *Why is it important to check under your vehicle before driving?*

CAR BODY

- Check for damaged or missing parts.
- Make sure that all lights and windows are clean and undamaged.
- In winter, scrape off snow and ice from car windows.

UNDER THE HOOD

- At least once a week or when you stop for gas, check the engine oil, radiator coolant, brake fluid, transmission fluid, and windshield-washer-fluid levels.
- Check the battery connections and make sure they're tight and that the battery terminals are free from corrosion.

GETTING INTO THE VEHICLE

Having checked the outside of the vehicle, you are ready to get into your vehicle. Enter the vehicle safely, with an eye to the following guidelines:

- Load packages and passengers from the curbside.
- Look carefully for approaching traffic before stepping into the roadway. Have your keys in hand before you start.
- Walk around the front of the vehicle, facing oncoming traffic so that you can see it.
- Wait for a break in traffic before opening the door, and open it only far enough and long enough to allow you to get into the vehicle.

FYI

On a warm day, condensation from a vehicle's air-conditioning unit may form a puddle under the vehicle. It is important to be able to distinguish this puddle from those formed by fluid leaks.

What Should You Check After Entering the Vehicle?

Get into the habit of making safety checks and adjustments as soon as you get into the vehicle. Make any adjustments when traffic and roadway conditions do not pose a threat. Here are some safety checks and procedures to follow inside the vehicle:

- Close and lock all doors.
- Adjust the seat so that you can clearly see the roadway and comfortably reach the floor pedals and other vehicle controls.
- Adjust the head restraint. Have other passengers adjust theirs.

Adjust seats, head restraints, and mirrors; fasten your safety belt; and lock the doors before you move into traffic. *Why are these steps so important?*

Leanna Depue

Director, Missouri Safety Center, Central Missouri State University, Warrensburg, MO

Advice FROM THE EXPERTS

Safety begins before you put your vehicle into Drive. Knowing how to efficiently use your vehicle's controls and safety devices helps you manage risk. A properly adjusted seat, steering wheel, and mirrors improve your visibility and aid in controlling your vehicle. Buckling up is a must for everyone before the ignition is turned on. Good risk managers always take time to know their vehicle and how to best protect its occupants.

Why is it important for you to know your vehicle and how to best protect its occupants?

- Adjust the rearview mirror so that you can use it by moving just your eyes. Adjust the left and right sideview mirrors for the best vision with the least head movement.
- Check the inside of the windows. Clean, defog, or defrost the windows as necessary.
- Make sure there are no objects inside the vehicle that will block your view or tumble about as you drive.
- Familiarize yourself with the controls for any devices you may need to use, such as the horn or headlights. While moving, this minimizes the time you take to use any of these devices.
- Fasten your safety belt and make sure all passengers have fastened theirs.

In addition to the guidelines listed above, consult your owner's manual for further information on the safe operation of your vehicle.

WHAT WOULD YOU DO?
You have never driven this vehicle before. What checks and procedures will you use before entering and driving it?

Lesson 4 Review

❶ What should you check before getting into your vehicle?

❷ What should you check once you are inside the vehicle?

❸ Why is it important to check the surrounding area before entering your vehicle?

MAKING A CIRCLE GRAPH

A poll is a way of finding out what a group of people think about a certain topic. You've probably seen or heard of polls showing what people think about political events, celebrities, and economic situations.

Conduct a poll to find out what members of your class think are their chances of being involved in a collision.

TRY IT YOURSELF

Follow these steps.

❶ Count the number of people in your class. This number represents 100 percent of the class.

❷ Ask each person this question: What do you think the chances are of your being in a collision in any given year? Then ask each person to choose one of the following as a response:

a. 1 in 5　　　**b.** 1 in 9　　　**c.** 1 in 50　　　**d.** 1 in 100
e. 1 in 500　　**f.** 1 in 1,000　　**g.** don't know

❸ Tally the number of responses to each choice.

❹ Divide the number of responses to a choice by the total number of people in the class to get the percentage of people who responded to that choice. For example, if four people said "1 in 10" and there are 27 people in the class, the fraction would be 4/27, or about 15 percent.

❺ Make a circle graph to show the results. A full circle represents the whole class, or 100 percent. First divide the circle into fourths. Each fourth represents 25 percent. Then mark segments of the circle to show the approximate percentage of people who responded to each choice.

❻ Your finished graph might look something like the one below.

The chances of being in a traffic collision in any given year are actually 1 in 5. In a poll of 1,506 people, only 1 person out of 10 chose that rate. How does your class compare?

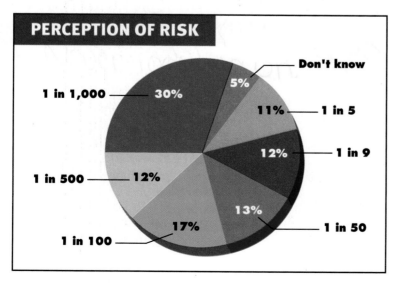

PERCEPTION OF RISK

Don't know 5%
1 in 1,000 — 30%
1 in 5 — 11%
1 in 9 — 12%
1 in 500 — 12%
1 in 50 — 13%
1 in 100 — 17%

Key Points

Lesson 1

1 Devices that help make you comfortable in a vehicle include seat-position controls, adjustable steering wheel, air conditioner and heater, and air vents. (Pages 68–69)

2 Devices that enable you to control a vehicle include the ignition switch, the accelerator, the brake pedal, the steering wheel, the gear selector lever for an automatic transmission, the clutch and gear selector lever for a manual transmission, the parking brake, and cruise control. (Pages 69–73)

WHAT WOULD YOU DO?
You are driving in the right lane at 50 mph. What actions will you take to minimize risk? What vehicle controls will come into play?

Lesson 2

1 Devices that aid visibility include lights, rearview and sideview mirrors, windshield wipers and washer, sun visors, and defroster. (Pages 74–76)

2 Car features that protect you and your passengers from injury include safety belts, head restraints, air bags, and door locks. (Pages 77–78)

3 Devices that guard against vehicle theft are ignition buzzers, locks, and alarms and other antitheft devices. (Page 79)

Lesson 3

1 The speedometer, odometer, fuel gauge, alternator gauge, temperature gauge, oil-pressure gauge, and brake warning lights provide information about your vehicle. (Pages 80–82)

2 Taillights, directional signals, emergency flashers, parking lights, and horns let you communicate with other drivers and pedestrians. (Pages 82–83)

WHAT WOULD YOU DO?
You want to turn left and then pull over to the right side of the road. How will you communicate to others what you plan to do?

Lesson 4

1 Before entering your vehicle, you should check the surrounding area for children, animals, objects, or fluid leaks; check the condition and direction of the tires; inspect the body of the vehicle for damage and clean the lights and windows; and regularly check the fluid levels and battery connections under the hood. (Pages 84–85)

2 After entering the vehicle, lock the doors; adjust the seat, head restraints, and mirrors; clear the windows; reposition any objects inside the car that may block your view or tumble about; familiarize yourself with all controls; and fasten your safety belt, and make sure passengers have fastened theirs. (Pages 85–86)

On a separate sheet of paper, write the letter of the answer that best completes each sentence.

1 Before entering your vehicle,
  a. load packages from the street side.
  b. walk around from the back of the vehicle.
  c. wait for a break in traffic before opening your door.

2 An odometer indicates
  a. the total miles a vehicle has been driven.
  b. the speed at which a vehicle is traveling.
  c. the amount of current in your battery.

3 Three devices that control the speed and direction of your vehicle are the
  a. gearshift, brake pedal, and steering wheel.
  b. engine, battery, and accelerator.
  c. tires, air conditioner, and ignition switch.

4 Ice has formed on your windshield. You should
  a. pull the sun visor into the "up" position.
  b. turn on the air conditioner.
  c. turn on the defroster.

5 Taillights and emergency flashers
  a. are parts of a vehicle's communications system.
  b. cannot be activated when the ignition is off.
  c. are parts of a vehicle's information system.

6 Using a safety belt will
  a. protect you from getting whiplash.
  b. increase your chances of surviving a collision.
  c. decrease your chances of surviving a collision.

On a separate sheet of paper, write the word or phrase that best completes each sentence.

safety checks   air bags

blind spots   manual

7 You should look over your shoulder when turning to detect anything in your _blind spot_.

8 Vehicles that have a(n) _manual_ transmission require you to use a clutch pedal.

9 _Airbags_ are considered passive safety devices because they operate automatically.

10 Get into the habit of making _safety checks_ and adjustments as soon as you get into the vehicle.

Writing

Driver's Log

When you become a driver, what will you do to be sure that you do not forget to make these checks—even if you feel you're in too much of a hurry to take the time? Write a paragraph describing what you will do.

Projects

❶ Obtain a vehicle owner's manual. Find the sections that deal with the various kinds of systems you've just read about. What information can you obtain from an owner's manual that you won't find in a textbook?

❷ Research and report on the comparative safety of different makes and models of motor vehicles. Try to find out specific reasons why some vehicles are safer than others.

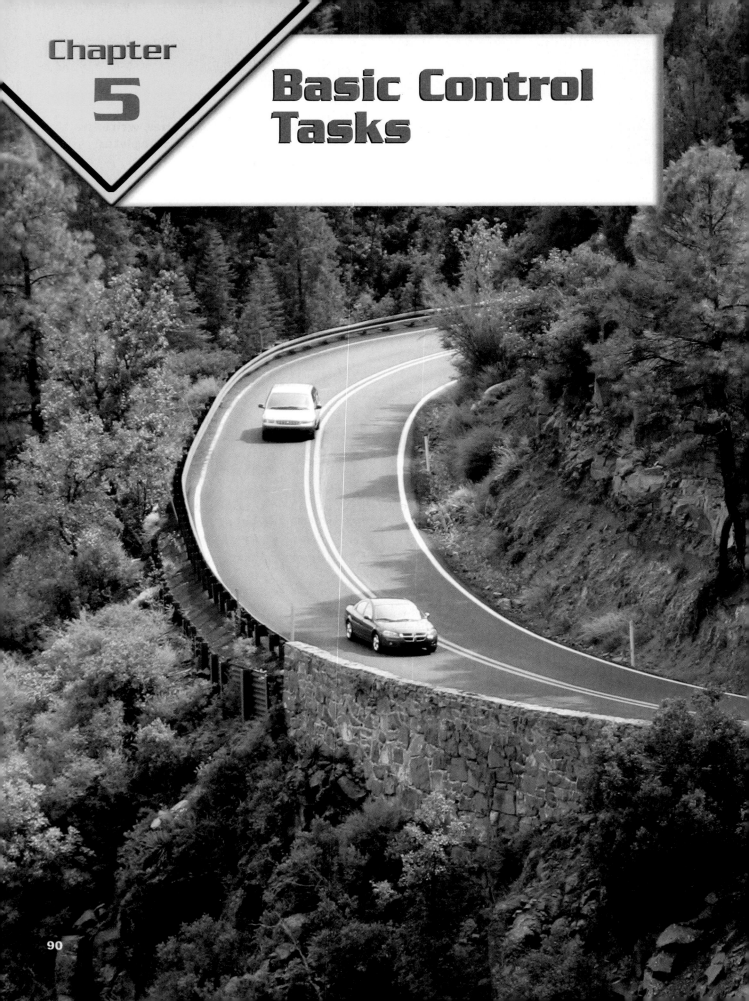

Chapter 5

Basic Control Tasks

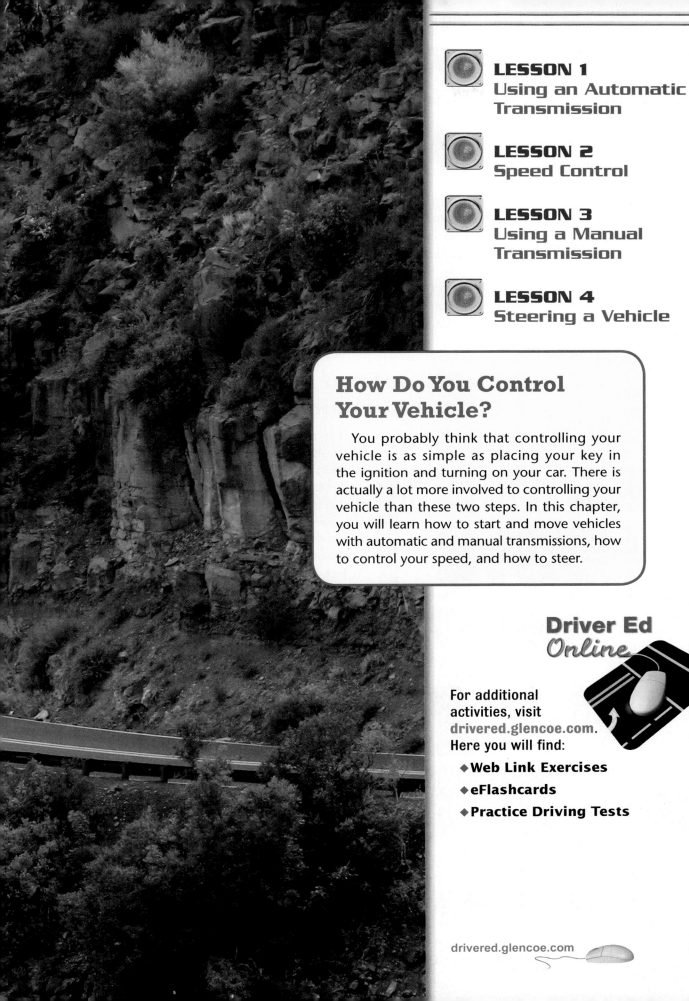

How Do You Control Your Vehicle?

You probably think that controlling your vehicle is as simple as placing your key in the ignition and turning on your car. There is actually a lot more involved to controlling your vehicle than these two steps. In this chapter, you will learn how to start and move vehicles with automatic and manual transmissions, how to control your speed, and how to steer.

Driver Ed
Online

For additional activities, visit drivered.glencoe.com. Here you will find:

◆ **Web Link Exercises**

◆ **eFlashcards**

◆ **Practice Driving Tests**

LESSON 1

Using an Automatic Transmission

OBJECTIVES

1. **Describe** how to start a vehicle with an automatic transmission.
2. **Describe** how to put a vehicle with an automatic transmission in motion.

KEY TERMS

◆ transmission
◆ idle

To begin driving, you need to be able to start, move, and control your vehicle. You move the vehicle using a set of gears called a **transmission**. The transmission takes the energy from the engine and moves it to the wheels, enabling the vehicle to move forward or backward.

All vehicles have either an automatic transmission or a manual transmission. In most driving situations, an automatic transmission is simpler and easier to use. As in all driving tasks, practice is the key to starting and driving a vehicle with an automatic transmission. Manual transmissions are covered in Lesson 3.

How Do You Start and Move a Vehicle with an Automatic Transmission?

It is important to start your vehicle's engine properly to avoid damaging the starter system or wasting fuel.

To start the engine of a vehicle with an automatic transmission, follow the steps below. Practice these steps one at a time, until they become habit. **Figure 5.1** provides you with some of the steps involved in starting your vehicle.

1. Put your right hand on the gear selector lever, and make sure it's in Park. Vehicles with automatic transmissions will only start in Park or Neutral. If the selector lever is in Neutral, however, the car may roll if a brake is not applied to stop it. Apply the brake pedal.
2. Make sure the parking brake is set.
   Note: Most vehicles have an electronic fuel-injection (EFI) system. Do not press down on the accelerator before or during starting. However, if your car does not have EFI, the following two steps may be necessary:
3. Set the automatic choke by pressing the accelerator (gas pedal) once to the floor and releasing it.
4. On most vehicles, press the accelerator lightly with your right foot and hold it steady.
5. Turn the ignition key to the Start position, and start the vehicle. Release the key as soon as the engine starts.

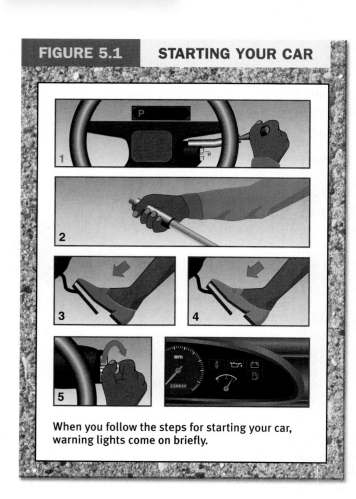

FIGURE 5.1 STARTING YOUR CAR

When you follow the steps for starting your car, warning lights come on briefly.

FIGURE 5.2   ACCELERATING

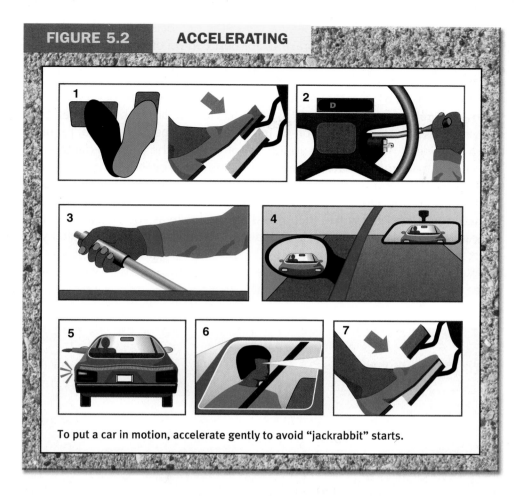

To put a car in motion, accelerate gently to avoid "jackrabbit" starts.

a. Release the accelerator and let the engine **idle**, or run by itself.

b. While the engine idles, check the gauges and warning lights to be sure all the vehicle's systems are working properly.

PUTTING THE VEHICLE IN MOTION

After your engine is running and you've checked the gauges, you are ready to put the vehicle in motion. Follow these steps (see **Figure 5.2**).

1. Press down firmly on the brake pedal. Most drivers use their right foot to brake. Follow the advice of your driving instructor.

2. Use your right hand to shift the gear selector lever to Drive or Reverse, depending on which way you want to move.

3. Release the parking brake.

4. Before you move, check for traffic in your rearview and sideview mirrors. If you're backing up, look back over your right shoulder to check traffic out the rear window.

5. Turn on your directional signal to indicate the direction you plan to move.

6. Look over your shoulder in the direction you plan to move to check blind spots.

7. Be prepared to accelerate into the desired lane once the roadway is clear. Remove your foot from the brake, and gradually apply pressure to the accelerator to move the vehicle.

Did You Know

In 1904, Henry Leland created the Cadillac Motor Car Company. After the wife of a friend was killed crank-starting her car, Leland began putting electrical starters in the 1912 model Cadillacs.

Working the accelerator properly takes a little practice if you use your right foot for both accelerating and braking. For best control of both the accelerator and brake pedals, rest the heel of your right foot on the floor in a position that lets you keep it there while pivoting back and forth between the two pedals. The forward part of your foot should fall comfortably on both pedals.

In nearly all situations, you will use the accelerator or the brake separately. Moving forward after stopping on an uphill grade is a special case that requires extra practice. If necessary, use your left foot to press the brake pedal to keep the vehicle from rolling back. When you're ready to proceed, gently press the accelerator with your right foot. As soon as the vehicle starts to pull forward, take your left foot off the brake. (An alternative is to hold the vehicle in place by setting the parking brake, then releasing the brake as you accelerate.) The procedure is the same in a vehicle with a manual transmission, except that you must also press down and release the clutch.

After you stop the vehicle, turn off the engine, set the emergency brake, and place the gearshift in Park.

?

WHAT WOULD YOU DO?
How can you enter the flow of traffic safely and smoothly?

Lesson 1 Review

❶ What steps would you follow to start a vehicle with an automatic transmission?

❷ What steps would you follow to move a vehicle with an automatic transmission?

❸ What will happen if you allow your vehicle to run unnecessarily while stopped or parked?

Speed Control

OBJECTIVES

1. **Describe** the different ways of controlling speed.
2. **Explain** how acceleration and deceleration are related to speed.

KEY TERMS

◆ acceleration
◆ rate of acceleration
◆ deceleration
◆ rate of deceleration
◆ threshold braking
◆ antilock brake system (ABS)

To drive safely, you must be able to maneuver your vehicle properly. You can do so by knowing your vehicle's limits. When changing lanes or passing, for example, you need to have an idea of how much time and distance your vehicle requires to move ahead of other vehicles. Learning to judge the time and space each maneuver takes will minimize your risk, as will adjusting your speed based on visibility, traffic, and road conditions.

There are several ways to adjust the speed of your vehicle. You can go faster, maintain a constant speed, or slow down by changing the pressure you put on the accelerator or brake pedal. Depending on the amount of pressure on the brake pedal, you can brake lightly, brake harder, lock the brakes, or engage the antilock brake system (ABS) function.

How Are Acceleration, Deceleration, and Speed Related?

Your ability to drive safely and effectively depends in large part on your knowledge of your vehicle's acceleration. When drivers say their vehicle has good **acceleration** (or "good pickup"), they mean their vehicle is able to increase speed relatively quickly. Several factors affect a vehicle's acceleration, including the power of the engine, the transmission and differential gear ratios, adhesion between the drive wheels and the road surface, and the weight the engine is pulling. The amount of time it takes to accelerate from one speed to another is the **rate of acceleration**.

Deceleration, on the other hand, is a word that means decreasing speed, or slowing down. The time it takes to decelerate from one speed to another is the **rate of deceleration**.

ACCELERATION AND DECELERATION RATES VARY

Speed and acceleration are closely linked, since the rate of acceleration varies with speed. At higher speeds, for example, a vehicle's rate of acceleration will be lower. It generally takes more time to accelerate from 45 mph to 55 mph than from 20 mph to 30 mph.

Understanding this principle is important for risk management. For example, you must allow more time to pass another vehicle when you're traveling at 50 mph than you do when moving at 30 mph because it will take you longer to accelerate.

Equally important to keep in mind is that deceleration rates, like acceleration rates, vary with speed. At higher speeds, your vehicle's rate of deceleration is lower. So a vehicle traveling at 60 mph needs a lot more time and space to slow and brake to a stop than the same vehicle traveling at 30 mph (see **Figure 5.3**).

FYI

A speedometer tells you how fast you're traveling at a given moment, but to find out your average speed for a particular distance, a little math is required. Your average speed equals the total distance traveled divided by the total time traveled.

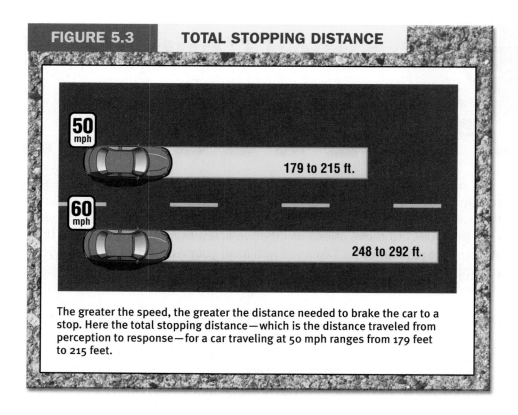

FIGURE 5.3 — **TOTAL STOPPING DISTANCE**

50 mph 179 to 215 ft.

60 mph 248 to 292 ft.

The greater the speed, the greater the distance needed to brake the car to a stop. Here the total stopping distance—which is the distance traveled from perception to response—for a car traveling at 50 mph ranges from 179 feet to 215 feet.

The weight of a vehicle also affects its rate of acceleration and deceleration. A heavy truck, for example, needs much more time and distance to accelerate or decelerate than does a passenger vehicle. In contrast, a motorcycle, which weighs much less than a vehicle, takes less time and distance to accelerate or decelerate.

MAINTAINING A CONSTANT SPEED

It's easy to maintain your speed on a flat, straight road, but the ability of vehicles to maintain a given speed when challenged by terrain varies greatly. Large passenger vehicles with high-horsepower 6- or 8-cylinder engines and midsize and sport sedans with turbo-charged small engines generally have good

Tips for New Drivers

ACCELERATING

▶ For best control when accelerating, rest the heel of your foot on the floor, and press the pedal gently with your toes.

▶ As a general rule, accelerate gradually. Beginning drivers sometimes make errors when they increase speed quickly. Accelerating gradually also saves fuel.

▶ No two cars accelerate exactly the same way. When driving an unfamiliar vehicle, allow yourself time to get used to the feel of the gas pedal and to the vehicle's acceleration capability.

New drivers often increase speed without realizing it. **How can you prevent this from happening?**

acceleration and can maintain their speed climbing a hill. An underpowered subcompact vehicle, however, may not be able to hold its speed because of its small 4-cylinder engine.

Very large vehicles also have difficulty maintaining their speed. Tractor-trailer rigs and interstate buses have huge engines, but these large vehicles accelerate very slowly because they weigh a lot.

MONITORING YOUR SPEED

Most of the time, it is safe to drive at the posted speed limit. As a new driver, you may find it difficult to control the speed of your vehicle simply by observing the speed of traffic around you. As a result, you should frequently check the speedometer. Such checks should be made with quick glances, and only occasionally, as traffic conditions permit.

With experience, you'll become more aware of how fast you are going. You'll pick up on various clues to your vehicle's performance and speed. You will notice, for example, that as speed varies, there's a difference in the vehicle's vibration. You'll also hear a change in the level of sound from the tires, the wind, and the engine. In the next lesson, you will learn that when driving a vehicle with a manual transmission, you must make a special effort to learn to judge speed because you often have to shift gears when you increase or reduce speed.

Your perception of how fast you are going can be wrong. For instance, it is harder to estimate your vehicle's speed immediately after you've made a sharp change in speed. If you have been driving at 20 mph and rapidly accelerate to 45 mph, you will feel as though you're moving faster than 45 mph.

On the other hand, if you have been traveling at highway speeds and suddenly enter a 25-mph zone, your tendency may be to slow down less than you should because you have become accustomed to moving at higher speeds. The best way to prevent yourself from speeding in such an instance is to check your speedometer.

SPEED CONTROL BY BRAKING

Putting on the brakes reduces your speed and allows you to stop. As a driver, you will have to slow down and stop your vehicle many times, under

both planned and unexpected circumstances. Red lights, stop signs, right or left turns, pedestrians running across streets, vehicles cutting in front of you—these and countless other situations will require you to apply your brakes.

SMOOTH BRAKING

For smooth braking, you need to develop a sense of timing. Whenever possible, you want to stop your vehicle gradually, not abruptly. As you drive a particular vehicle, you will get a feel for applying the right amount of pressure on the brake pedal when you need to stop. Your goal is to stop just at the right spot, neither overshooting nor undershooting your desired stopping point. This makes for a safer, smoother ride for you and your passengers.

Identify in advance the need to stop. *How can you identify in advance the need to stop?*

The amount of foot pressure required to brake to a stop depends mainly on your speed. If you are going fast, you will have to brake longer to stop. Other factors include the size and weight of the vehicle, the type of brakes on your vehicle, your maneuvering space, and the road surface. As you practice driving and become more experienced, you'll get better at judging the distance needed to bring your vehicle to a smooth stop.

For effective control of brake pressure, position the heel of your foot between and in front of the accelerator and brake pedal. This way, you'll be able to apply pressure to the brakes with your toes, which are more sensitive than the ball of your foot, so you can easily increase or decrease pressure in small amounts as needed.

BRAKING TO A STOP

Follow these steps when preparing to brake to a stop.
1. Check your mirrors for any vehicles that may be following you. If a vehicle is following you, lightly tap the brake pedal: your flashing brake lights will warn other drivers that you intend to stop.
2. Apply smooth, steady, firm pressure to the brake pedal, easing up slightly as you come to a halt. If your vehicle has a manual transmission, you will need to press down the clutch as you stop.
3. If your car has an automatic transmission, leave the transmission in Drive if you plan to move ahead within a minute or so, as when you're stopped for a red light.

EMERGENCY BRAKING

If a driver or pedestrian suddenly enters your path of travel, you'll need to stop the vehicle as quickly as possible. However, you don't want to slam on the brakes so hard that the wheels lock, or stop turning, which is possible to do with vehicles that are not equipped with antilock brakes. Locked wheels can increase your stopping distance and can also cause you to lose steering control and, when road friction is uneven, can cause loss of stability if the vehicle begins to spin. To prevent the wheels from locking, press, or "squeeze," the brake pedal firmly to a point just before the wheels lock, and hold it there. This is called **threshold braking**, and it's the safest way to stop the car quickly.

If the vehicle starts to skid, reduce pressure very slightly, and then add pressure again as needed. Release pressure as the vehicle comes to a stop. For additional guidelines on braking and skid control, see Chapter 14.

Most new vehicles are sold with an **antilock brake system (ABS)**. On these vehicles, the wheels will not lock and slide even when you press down hard on the brake pedal. Antilock brakes shouldn't make much difference in stopping distances on dry roads, but they do help drivers maintain control of the vehicle during sudden emergency stops, even on wet or slippery roads. Antilock brakes work with your car's normal service brakes; they have speed sensors mounted at each wheel and a secondary electro-hydraulic braking circuit. Antilock brakes prevent tires from locking by monitoring the speed of each wheel and automatically pulsing the brake pressure (up to 20 times per second) on any wheels where locking is detected.

With antilock brakes, you will feel a pulsing against your foot on the brake pedal when applying hard, constant pressure to the brake. This is normal and indicates that the ABS is working.

On many vehicles, you can increase the brake pressure by pressing down a few times on the brake pedal. However, do not pump the brake pedal on vehicles equipped with antilock brakes.

Driver Ed
Online

Topic: Antilock brake system (ABS)

For a link to more information on driving with an antilock brake system, go to **drivered.glencoe.com**.

Activity: Use the information provided at this link to compile your own list of do's and don'ts for driving with an antilock brake system.

WHAT WOULD YOU DO?
Which vehicle probably needs more time and distance to accelerate: the truck or the car? How would knowing this help you manage time and space to reduce risk?

Lesson 2 Review

❶ What is acceleration? How are acceleration and speed related?

❷ What is deceleration? How are deceleration and speed related?

❸ What are some of the different ways of braking in a vehicle?

❹ What is ABS, and how does the system work?

Using a Manual Transmission

OBJECTIVES

1. **Explain** how manual and automatic transmissions differ.
2. **Describe** how to start and move a vehicle with a manual transmission.
3. **Explain** how to use each forward gear.

KEY TERMS

- stick shift
- clutch
- friction point
- downshift

Manual transmissions are more difficult to operate than automatic transmissions, but many drivers prefer them. Some drivers like manual transmissions because they enjoy shifting gears. Others prefer manual transmissions because it's usually cheaper to buy a car with a manual transmission, and repair costs are usually less. In addition, manual transmissions use less fuel than automatic transmissions when properly driven.

How Do Manual and Automatic Transmissions Differ?

With an automatic transmission, the driver doesn't have to pay much attention to the transmission once the car is in motion. An automatic transmission set in Drive will shift the forward gears for you. This is not true if the vehicle has a manual transmission, because the driver needs to shift gears and use the clutch while driving.

When you operate a manual transmission, or **stick shift**, you must shift the gears by manually moving the gearshift (or stick) from place to place (see **Figure 5.4**). Using your right hand, you start in low, or First, gear and shift to higher gears such as Second or Third gear as you pick up speed. As you slow down, you shift back down from higher to lower gears. The choice of the forward gear determines the power delivered by the engine to the wheels. In manual transmissions, there are usually three to five forward gears but only one reverse gear.

The **clutch** is a third foot pedal, to the left of the brake pedal. You always use your left foot to press it down. To change gears, you break the connection between the engine and the transmission by pressing the clutch pedal to the floor. When you let the clutch pedal up, the clutch is engaged and power moves to the wheels.

How Do You Operate a Vehicle with a Manual Transmission?

Learning to drive a vehicle equipped with a manual transmission is easier if you already know how to operate an automatic transmission. The gearshift and clutch are the only things that are different. The keys to driving a stick-shift vehicle include using the clutch, which you press down each time you manually shift gears, and coordinating the gearshift with the clutch.

FIGURE 5.4

GEARSHIFT POSITIONS

4 Speed   5 Speed

Above are the gearshift positions for 4-speed and 5-speed manual transmissions.

STARTING THE ENGINE

To start the engine, you will need to use both feet. First, make sure the parking brake is set. Then press the clutch pedal to the floor with your left foot, press the brake pedal with your right foot, and shift into Neutral. (There is no Park position on a vehicle with a manual transmission.) Now turn the ignition key to start. Release the key as soon as the engine starts.

COORDINATING THE CLUTCH AND GEARSHIFT

To make a manual-shift vehicle move, you must coordinate the clutch with the gearshift and the accelerator. You do the same thing to keep the vehicle moving. To stop the vehicle, press down both the brake and the clutch.

The forward-speed positions are located a short distance from each other, in a particular pattern. The driver must press the clutch and move the gearshift every time a new speed position is desired. Clutching and shifting actions should come to feel so natural to you that you scarcely need to think about them.

The key to smooth clutch operation is learning to sense the **friction point**. This is the point where the engine and the transmission engage. You can feel this happen as you lift the clutch pedal. The easiest way to get a feel for the friction point is to practice by using the Reverse gear. Because Reverse is a lower gear than First, you'll find it easier to sense the friction point. As you continue to let up the clutch, you must coordinate the forward (or backward) motion of the vehicle with increased acceleration, simultaneously using the gas pedal. Once the clutch is engaged, take your foot off the clutch pedal until you need to use it again.

It takes plenty of practice to use the clutch pedal to shift smoothly. *How can you practice using the clutch pedal?*

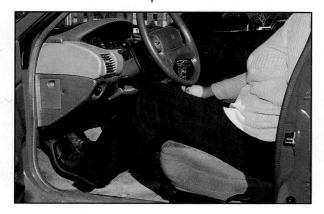

PUTTING THE VEHICLE IN MOTION

Follow these steps to put the vehicle in motion (see **Figure 5.5**).
1. Press the brake pedal with your right foot. Press the clutch pedal to the floor with your left foot.
2. Move the gearshift into First gear or Reverse, depending on which way you intend to move.
3. Release the parking brake.
4. Before you move, check for traffic in your rearview and sideview mirrors. If you're backing up, look back over your right shoulder to check traffic out the rear window.
5. Turn on your directional signal to indicate the direction you plan to move.
6. Look over your shoulder in the direction you plan to move to check blind spots.
7. With your right foot on the brake, slowly let the clutch up to the friction point. Look at the roadway, not down at your feet or hands! Move your right foot from the brake to the accelerator.
8. Pressing down gently on the accelerator, slowly let the clutch pedal up.

If the car stops, or jerks forward, you made a mistake. You either released the clutch too abruptly, or you pressed too hard on the gas pedal. If the vehicle lurches and the engine stalls, you have not given the engine enough gas.

FIGURE 5.5   ACCELERATING

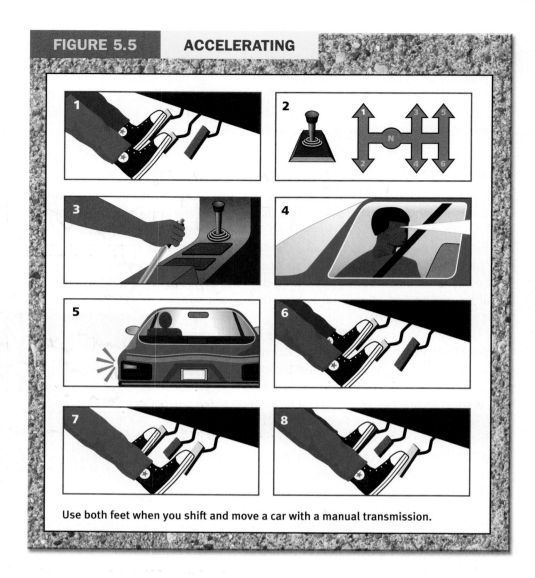

Use both feet when you shift and move a car with a manual transmission.

How Do You Use Each Forward Gear?

Your selection of gears depends on the power and speed you need for various driving tasks. The lower gears provide more power, while the upper gears allow more speed. Normally you move up one gear at a time. Most vehicles have four to six forward gears.

Low gear, or First gear, gives the power needed to set a vehicle in motion.

Second gear lets you go as fast as 15 to 25 mph, depending on the horsepower of the engine and how many gears it has. You can also use Second gear to start on ice or to drive in heavy snow.

In vehicles with 3-speed transmissions, Third gear is used for all speeds over 25 mph. If a vehicle has a 4- or 5-speed transmission and a small engine, Third gear is used at speeds up to 30 or 40 mph.

Use Fourth gear for driving above 35 mph on flat roadways. When you are driving uphill, you may have to go 40 mph or faster before shifting into Fourth or Fifth gear, which allows the greatest speed.

Keep in mind that the gear in use is strictly related to both power and speed. The power of an engine is greater in lower gear. For example, when starting up a steep grade, you generally shift to a lower gear to maintain power. When the roadway levels out, you can shift to a higher gear and keep up the same speed with less power.

SHIFTING TO A HIGHER GEAR

As you begin driving faster, you will want to shift into a higher gear. To shift to a higher gear, follow these steps (see **Figure 5.6**).

1. Accelerate to an appropriate speed.
2. Press the clutch pedal to the floor.
3. Release the accelerator.
4. Shift to the next higher gear.
5. Press on the accelerator. Release the clutch pedal slowly through the friction point.
6. Let the clutch pedal up all the way.

DOWNSHIFTING

There are sometimes reasons to **downshift**, or to shift down from a higher to a lower gear. Down-shifting may help you gain power when driving up a hill, help you brake and control the vehicle on a downslope (except when the road is slippery), or allow you to slow down or stop with good control.

To shift into a lower gear, follow these steps (see **Figure 5.7**).

1. Release the accelerator. (If you want to slow down faster, also press the brake pedal.)
2. Press the clutch pedal to the floor.
3. Shift to the next lower gear. (Sudden decrease in speed may require shifting to an even lower gear—as when braking sharply and downshifting from Fourth gear to Second.)
4. Release the clutch pedal to the friction point. Press down on the accelerator as necessary.

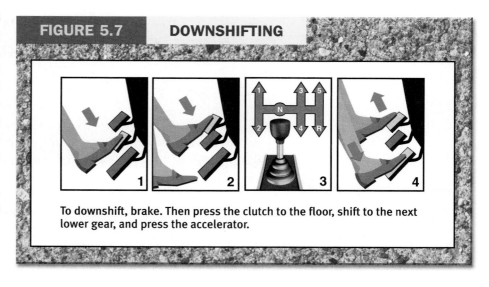

FIGURE 5.6   SHIFTING GEARS

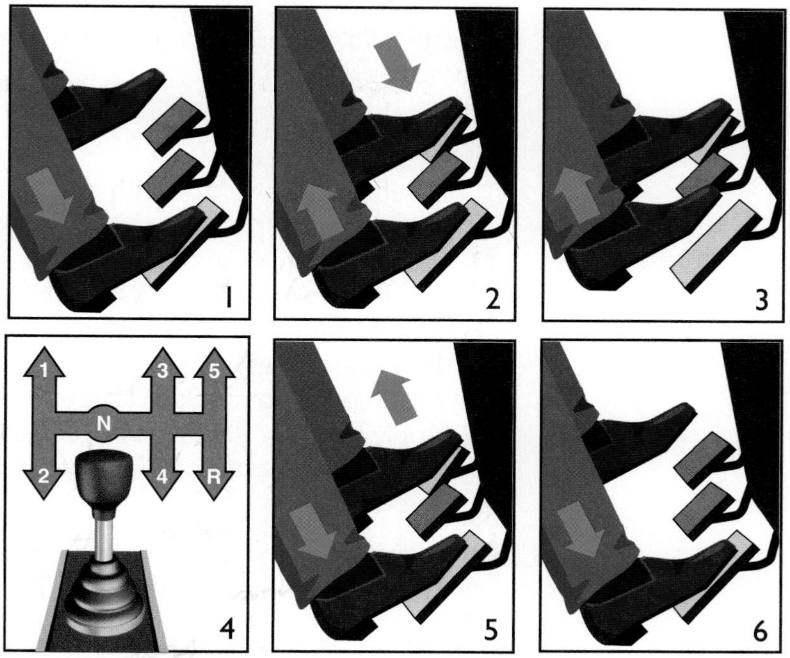

Coordinate using the clutch, gearshift, and gas pedal to shift gears.

FIGURE 5.7   DOWNSHIFTING

To downshift, brake. Then press the clutch to the floor, shift to the next lower gear, and press the accelerator.

You don't have to downshift as you slow down or stop. In fact, routinely downshifting to stop will cause unnecessary wear on the clutch.

It is fairly easy to downshift from Fifth, Fourth, and Third gears to lower gears, but it is very difficult to shift from Second to First without damaging the transmission. To downshift to First gear, you have to bring the vehicle almost to a complete stop.

STOPPING

To safely stop a vehicle with a manual transmission from a low gear, follow these steps.

1. Check your rearview and sideview mirrors for traffic behind you.
2. Tap the brake pedal to flash your brake lights and signal to drivers behind you that you intend to stop.
3. Press the brake pedal to reduce speed to 10 to 15 mph. Then press the clutch pedal to the floor to keep the vehicle from stalling.
4. Apply smooth, steady brake pressure to bring the vehicle to a stop.
5. Keep your foot on the brake pedal, and shift to Neutral before releasing the clutch.

To make an emergency stop, apply the brakes as quickly and safely as possible, and press the clutch pedal to the floor before you stop.

WHAT WOULD YOU DO?
What actions will you take with the brake, the clutch, and the gearshift as you approach and then pass through this intersection?

Lesson 3 Review

❶ How is a manual transmission different from an automatic transmission?

❷ What steps would you follow to start and move a vehicle with a manual transmission?

❸ How would you use the forward gears of a vehicle that has a manual transmission?

Steering a Vehicle

OBJECTIVES
1. **Describe** the procedures for steering straight ahead.
2. **Describe** the two methods for steering to turn.

KEY TERMS
- tracking
- hand-over-hand steering
- push-pull-feed steering

A motor vehicle has a great deal of power independent of your own efforts. This tremendous power affects what it takes to keep you on course and how quickly or easily you can turn. Moreover, steering is not simply a matter of pointing the vehicle in the direction you want to travel. Steering can be a means of risk management.

How Can You Control Your Risk Through Steering?

Steering plays a particularly important role in risk management when you're traveling at speeds over 25 or 30 mph. At such speeds, steering is often your only way to avoid a collision, because the distance and time needed to stop the vehicle are greater at higher speeds.

Of course, to avoid a collision by steering, you must have previously identified an area into which you can safely turn. You don't want to steer into another vehicle, a pedestrian, or another object. But it often takes less time and space to steer away from an object than to brake to a stop.

HOLDING THE STEERING WHEEL

Most of the time, use both hands when you drive. When steering in a straight line or through a moderate curve, grasp the steering wheel firmly with your fingers. Your thumbs should always rest on the wheel, too. Many experienced drivers place their hands at 9 o'clock and 3 o'clock, or at 8 o'clock and 4 o'clock positions (see **Figure 5.8** on page 106). Others position their hands on the lower part of the wheel, in the 7 o'clock and 5 o'clock positions. Follow the recommendations of your instructor when you are beginning to drive.

TRACKING AND STEERING

Steering a vehicle can be challenging. This is particularly true when traveling on winding roads. Keeping your vehicle moving on the path of travel that you have chosen is called **tracking**. You must make steering adjustments to hold a desired course or to keep your car on track.

To keep your vehicle on track and to drive smoothly, direct your attention ahead of your vehicle to a point or points 20 to 30 seconds ahead along your intended path of travel. Choose these points on the basis of where you want to go and on traffic conditions.

Your vehicle does not stay on the road by itself, so you must make frequent steering adjustments. Making adjustments while you look ahead on the road requires practice. However, as you practice and gain confidence, you'll learn to look 20 to 30 seconds ahead of your vehicle along your path of travel. You'll

Did You Know?

Francis W. Davis invented power steering in 1925. It was first used successfully in World War II military vehicles. In 1951, power steering became available in commercial automobiles.

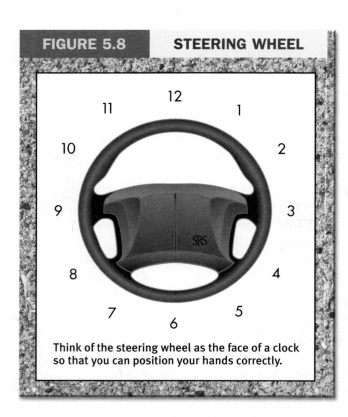

FIGURE 5.8 — STEERING WHEEL

12
11 1
10 2
9 3
8 4
7 5
6

Think of the steering wheel as the face of a clock so that you can position your hands correctly.

soon be able to keep your vehicle on track with minor steering adjustments.

STEERING IN A STRAIGHT LINE

To steer in a straight line, steer toward a point in the center of your path of travel or where you want your vehicle to go as seen in **Figure 5.9**. Look well ahead as you drive. When you look to the point where you will steer, you will automatically steer in the proper direction.

The steering adjustments you must make on a straight road are small but critical. Be on the alert for gradual changes in the position of your vehicle. It should not "wander" in its lane.

As you drive, check your mirrors whenever you spot anything along your intended path of travel that could cause you to change speed or position. You want to know what other vehicles are doing behind you if you have to stop, slow down, or turn. To look in your rearview mirror, move just your eyes. To look in your sideview mirror, turn your head only slightly.

STEERING TO TURN

Making a turn requires you to turn the steering wheel more than you would to drive straight. To turn corners smoothly and safely, you need to develop a good sense of timing and make a habit of searching a wider area.

When steering through a turn, allow some room for the back of your vehicle. Keep in mind that your vehicle's rear wheels do not follow the same path as the front wheels. They have a smaller turning radius, so you must allow some additional space for them inside the curve you're making. Without this space, your rear wheels may hit the curb or other objects as you turn.

There are two techniques to steer through a turn: hand-over-hand and push-pull-feed.

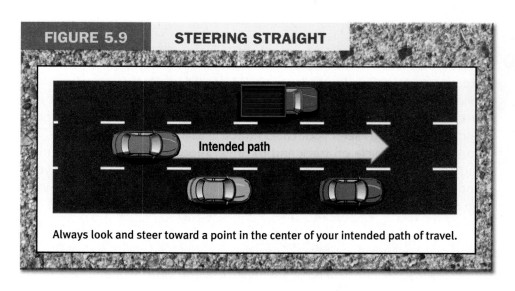

FIGURE 5.9 — STEERING STRAIGHT

Intended path

Always look and steer toward a point in the center of your intended path of travel.

Hand-over-hand steering. To turn right using **hand-over-hand steering**, turn the steering wheel clockwise. Use your left hand to push the steering wheel up, around, and down. At the same time, bring your right hand across your left forearm to grip the wheel on the far side. Then use your right hand to pull the side of the wheel up, around, and down (see **Figure 5.10**). Repeat these movements as often as needed to complete the turn, making steering corrections as required.

To turn left, reverse the procedure, push up and around with your right hand, and cross over with the left, while turning the wheel counterclockwise.

Hand-over-hand steering provides effective vehicle control when you're steering through tight-radius turns, such as hard turns and hairpin turns.

Push-pull-feed steering. You may also turn by pushing the steering wheel up with one hand and then pulling down with the other. This type of steering is known as **push-pull-feed steering**. To try this, grasp the steering wheel with the right hand resting between 3 o'clock and 5 o'clock and the left hand between 7 o'clock and 9 o'clock. One hand pushes the wheel up toward 12 o'clock. (Use the left hand for right turns and vice versa.) At the same time, the other hand slides up to 1 o'clock for the right turn (or 11 o'clock for the left turn). The second hand grasps the wheel, and pulls it down. While the pulling hand goes down, the pushing hand releases its grip and returns to its original position to continue the process as needed (see **Figure 5.10**).

Push-pull-feed steering gives you a little more control of the vehicle because you keep both hands on the steering wheel. The position of your hands causes less fatigue on longer drives and is a good way to make gentle turning maneuvers. Also, using push-pull-feed steering, you can sit farther from the steering wheel. Since your arms never cross over the face of the steering wheel, there is also less chance of injury if the driver's side air bag deploys.

FIGURE 5.10   STEERING METHODS

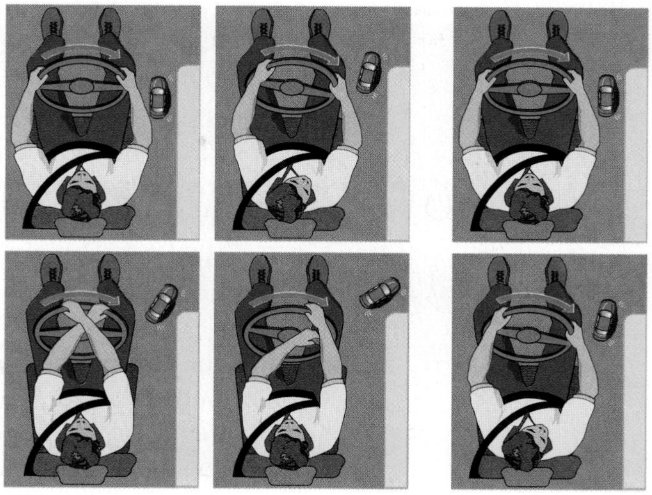

Hand-over-hand steering   Push-pull-feed steering

If you are not too tall or somewhat stout, you may find push-pull-feed steering more comfortable.

GUIDELINES FOR MAKING A TURN

Whichever steering method you choose, use the following guidelines when making a turn:

1. Look beyond the turn to the point you want to reach. Identify this point before you start to turn.
2. Always use your directional signal. Check the roadway ahead and both mirrors before starting to turn.
3. On a hard turn, slow down to maintain control as you enter the turn. Accelerate gently about halfway through to pull out of the turn.

Lindsey Townsend

Mount Mansfield Union High School
Fairfax, VT

When preparing to stop, always check your inside mirror for vehicles that are following you. Maintaining adequate space around your vehicle is very important, and knowing what is behind you is critical to your safety and that of your passengers.

When stopping behind another vehicle, maintain an adequate space cushion in front of your vehicle. The best way to do this is to make sure that from the driver's seated position, the rear tires of the vehicle ahead and a small portion of the roadway are completely visible to you.

Why is an adequate amount of space around your vehicle important?

4. With your eyes on the point you want to reach, start to steer back to the straight-ahead position when you're about midway through the turn. Do this by reversing the hand-over-hand or push-pull-feed movements.
5. Check the mirrors again after completing the turn, waiting if possible until you've straightened the wheels.

?

WHAT WOULD YOU DO?
What procedures would you follow to steer through this curve?

Lesson 4 Review

❶ What procedures would you follow to steer a vehicle straight ahead and when turning?

❷ Describe the procedure you would follow to turn right using hand-over-hand steering.

❸ Describe the procedure you would follow to turn right using the push-pull-feed method.

UNDERSTANDING ROADWAY CLASSIFICATIONS

Maps help you get where you are going. They also tell about the kinds of roads you can use to get there. Most maps have a key such as this one. Find 91 at coordinates D, 5 on the map. The map key indicates that this is a no-toll, limited-access highway. See the dots along Route 2? The key tells you that this is a scenic route. Find Route 9. The key tells you that Route 9 is a paved secondary road that is not divided.

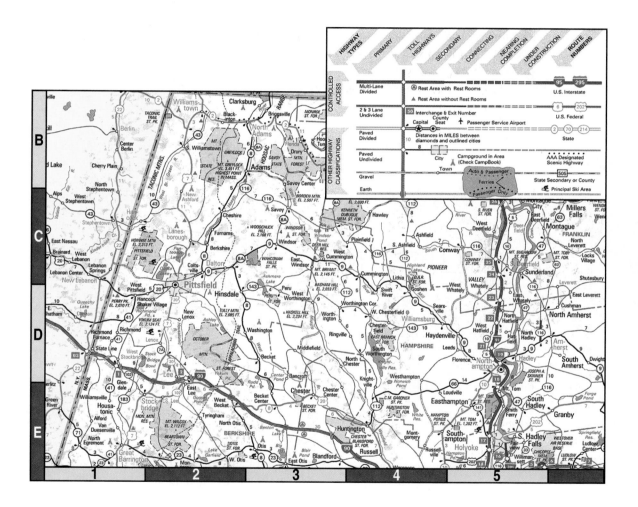

TRY IT YOURSELF

❶ What can you tell about Route 7 between Pittsfield and Stockbridge?
❷ What kind of road connects Adams and Savoy Center?
❸ Describe the different kinds of roads you can take from Southampton to Pittsfield.

Key Points

Lesson 1

1. To start a vehicle with an automatic transmission, put the gear selector in Park. Set the automatic choke if it applies to your car. Press the accelerator and turn the key. Release the parking brake and let the engine idle. (Page 93)

2. To put a vehicle with an automatic transmission in motion, check for traffic in your rearview and sideview mirrors. Turn on your directional signal to the direction you plan to move. Look over your shoulder in the direction you plan to move. Remove your foot from the brake and gradually apply pressure to the accelerator to move your vehicle once the roadway is clear. (Page 94)

Lesson 2

WHAT WOULD YOU DO?
How can you enter the flow of traffic safely and smoothly?

1. To control the speed of your vehicle, you can go faster, maintain a constant speed, or slow down by changing the pressure you put on the accelerator or brake pedal. (Page 95)

2. Speed is related to acceleration and deceleration since the rate of acceleration and deceleration vary with speed. (Pages 95–96)

Lesson 3

1. An automatic transmission set in Drive will shift the forward gears for you. A manual transmission on the other hand requires the driver to shift gears and use the clutch while driving. (Page 100)

2. To start a vehicle with a manual transmission, set the parking brake. Press the clutch to the floor, step on the brake, shift into Neutral, and turn the key. To move the vehicle, shift into First gear or Reverse and release the parking brake. Slowly let the clutch up, move your right foot from the brake to the accelerator, and press gently on the accelerator. (Pages 101–102)

3. First gear sets the vehicle in motion. Second gear is used for speeds up to 15 to 25 mph or to start on ice or to drive in heavy snow. Third gear is used for speeds over 25 mph (3-speed transmissions) or speeds up to 30 or 40 mph (4- or 5-speed transmissions). Fourth or Fifth gear is used for driving at higher speeds. (Page 103)

Lesson 4

1. To steer your vehicle straight ahead, steer toward a point in the center of your path of travel or where you want your vehicle to go. Look 20 to 30 seconds ahead as you drive. (Page 106)

2. To turn right hand-over-hand, turn the steering wheel clockwise. Use your left hand to push the steering wheel up, around, and down. At the same time, bring your right hand across your left forearm to grip the wheel on the far side. To turn left, reverse the procedure. To turn push-pull-feed, turn by pushing the steering wheel up with one hand and then pulling down with the other. (Pages 107–108)

On a separate sheet of paper, write the letter of the answer that best completes each sentence.

1 At higher speeds, a vehicle's rate of acceleration will be
  a. lower.
  b. higher.
  c. the same.

2 With a manual transmission, the speed of the vehicle determines
  a. the tightness of the vehicle's turning radius.
  b. the choice of forward gear.
  c. the need for an occasional fuel injection.

3 To avoid rolling backward when starting on an uphill grade, you should
  a. use your left foot to press the brake pedal.
  b. lock the brakes.
  c. start the engine in Third gear.

4 As you drive, you will develop the ability to estimate your speed by
  a. sensing the vehicle's friction point.
  b. riding the clutch.
  c. sensing a difference in the vehicle's vibrations.

5 If your vehicle has an EFI system,
  a. press down on the accelerator before starting your engine.
  b. press down on the accelerator while starting your engine.
  c. do not press down on the accelerator before or during starting your engin

6 When driving around a curve, you should focus
  a. through the curve well ahead of your vehicle, along your path of travel.
  b. on the road directly in front of you.
  c. on objects in your rearview mirror.

On a separate sheet of paper, write the word or phrase that best completes each sentence.

acceleration   idle
clutch   deceleration

7 _____ means an increase of speed.
8 After you start your ignition, release the accelerator and let the engine _____.
9 The key to smooth _____ operation is sensing the friction point.
10 _____ means a decrease of speed.

Writing
Driver's Log
Write at least two paragraphs giving your ideas about why these procedures are almost second nature to experienced drivers and why they should become second nature to you.

Projects

❶ Talk to someone who has been driving for several years. Ask what lessons this driver has learned through experience and what tips he or she might offer you as a beginning driver.

❷ Demonstrate the difference between the hand-over-hand and push-pull-feed steering. Which technique seems easier to you? Why? Survey several drivers to find out which method they use and why.

Basic Maneuvers

LESSON 1
Moving into and out of Traffic

LESSON 2
Right and Left Turns

LESSON 3
Steering in Reverse and Making Turnabouts

LESSON 4
Parking

LESSON 5
Safe Driving Procedures for Passing and Being Passed

How Do You Change Lanes?

Think about the various steps involved in changing lanes. You probably included using your turn signal. This is just one step in changing lanes. You will learn about changing lanes in this chapter, as well as other basic driving maneuvers.

Driver Ed
Online

For additional activities, visit **drivered.glencoe.com**. Here you will find:

- ◆ **Web Link Exercises**
- ◆ **eFlashcards**
- ◆ **Practice Driving Tests**

Moving into and out of Traffic

OBJECTIVES

1. **Describe** the procedures for moving into traffic.
2. **Describe** the procedures for leaving traffic.
3. **Explain** the steps involved in making a lane change.

Basic driving skills include entering and leaving the roadway. When you want to travel in your vehicle, you usually begin by moving your vehicle away from the side of the roadway and into traffic. When you arrive at your destination, you must steer your car out of traffic and toward the side of the road. Both these actions involve moving into or out of a lane of traffic. They also require planning in advance, before you actually proceed.

What Judgments Do You Make Entering or Leaving Traffic?

As with any driving maneuver, you must plan ahead before leaving a curb and entering traffic. *How can you plan ahead?*

When you enter the roadway, you are going into motion from a stopped position. Traffic is always moving faster than you are. Entering the roadway involves planning how and when you will move and then actually making the move.

As a driver, you face increased risks anytime you move into or out of the flow of traffic. As part of this process, you must have adequate visibility and make judgments about time and space. Can you see well enough to make this move safely? How fast are other vehicles moving? Is there enough time and space to make your move safely now, or should you wait a bit? These are judgments that you will make routinely.

MOVING INTO TRAFFIC

The first thing to do when moving your vehicle into traffic is to plan your move. Visibility, time, and space are crucial considerations in planning to make this maneuver.

Visibility. Take a look at oncoming traffic and the roadway itself. Notice other roadway users ahead and behind you. Can you see clearly? Notice any relevant traffic signals, signs, and road markings nearby.

Time. Will you have enough time to move into your lane given the traffic? Will vehicles behind you have to slow down or stop when you merge into traffic? Be aware of the speed limit on the roadway. Get a sense of how fast the vehicles in the lane into which you want to move and the lanes next to it are moving. You will need adequate time to move your vehicle into traffic.

Space. Make sure you have room to enter the roadway while keeping a safe distance between your vehicle and the one parked in front of you. First, check the space in front of and behind your vehicle. Decide if you have enough room to pull out of your parked position in one smooth move or if you will have to maneuver back and forth to clear the vehicle parked in front of you as you move onto the roadway. Position your vehicle to move into traffic in one move.

MAKING THE MOVE

Before you move into traffic, have your car running, have your foot on the brake, and have the parking brake released. With an automatic transmission, put your vehicle in Drive. With a manual transmission, use First gear. Once you've made your plan to enter traffic, follow these steps. You will usually enter traffic from the right.

1. Check the traffic all around you. Look through the front windshield to check ahead and the side and rearview mirrors to check to the rear.
2. Once it is safe to move into traffic, signal your intention to move left into traffic, either by sticking your left arm straight out of the window, turning on your left turn signals, or both.
3. Look over your left shoulder to check for traffic in your blind spot.
4. If the roadway is clear, immediately turn forward, glancing in your sideview mirror to make sure it is still safe to enter traffic.
5. Steer left, clearing parked cars, and enter the nearest lane of traffic, accelerating moderately. When you have completed your move, turn off your turn signal.

LEAVING TRAFFIC

You need to make plans in advance when moving your vehicle out of traffic, too. Usually, you will move out of traffic to the right.

As with moving into traffic, visibility, time, and space are key factors as you move toward the side of the roadway and park.

Once you have prepared in advance, you are ready to move into the traffic flow. *What steps should you take to make the move?*

Dealing with the UNEXPECTED

PARKING BEYOND AN INTERSECTION

Be especially careful if you need to park in a space or make a turn just beyond an intersection. Follow these steps.

▲ Do not signal right or left as you approach the intersection. Other drivers may think you're going to turn at the intersection.
▲ If other vehicles are near the intersection, move carefully into the correct lane and slow down.
▲ Use your signals only after you have entered the intersection.

Visibility. As you approach your destination, scan the traffic scene in front of you. Use your mirrors to check traffic behind you and to your sides. Pick out the spot where you want to stop.

Time. You'll need a little time to slow down and stop or to park. Note the speed of the traffic you're in. Consider how much time you'll have to slow down to make your move.

Space. Make sure you have adequate space to get to your destination and stop. Notice the amount of room available for you to move into another lane, and if you need to make a lane change prior to parking. Is there space to move your vehicle directly into the parking place, or will you need to maneuver to parallel park?

MAKING THE MOVE

After you have planned your move and decided it is safe to move out of traffic, follow these steps:

1. Signal your intent to move using your turn signals, hand signals, or both.
2. Tap your brakes lightly, signaling drivers behind you that you are going to stop.
3. Apply gradual pressure on the brakes to reduce speed.
4. Steer out of the traffic lane to where you want to go. Use a reference point to make sure you stop with your vehicle out of the traffic lane. Use your brakes as needed to stop the vehicle.
5. Make sure your car is parallel to the edge of the roadway and is legally parked.
6. Turn off your turn signal, put your parking brake on, and then shift your vehicle to Park or Neutral.

You hear an emergency vehicle approaching as you are about to pull away from the curb. *What steps would you take?*

What Is the Safest Way to Change Lanes?

You have probably seen drivers who are constantly changing lanes, swooping and weaving between other vehicles on the highway. Chances are those drivers are exceeding the speed limit. Many of them are driving recklessly and endangering lives. They change lanes too frequently. They are not safe drivers.

There are times, however, when you really do need to change lanes. You can minimize your risk by learning the right way to do it. You can build on the information you learned when entering and leaving traffic, which also involves changing lanes.

As with other safe-driving procedures, changing lanes involves two steps: planning in advance and executing your maneuver.

PLANNING IN ADVANCE

There are a lot of good reasons for changing lanes. You may need to change lanes to make a turn, pass another vehicle, or avoid an obstacle in your lane. Whatever the reason for changing lanes, you need to plan ahead in order to make the move safely.

Planning includes knowing where your vehicle is now, where you want it to go, and what the road and traffic conditions are likely to be between the two.

Check the following as you plan your move.

Visibility. Look around. What is the path of travel in the lane you want to enter? What is the path of travel in the lane you are in? Note if there are vehicles in the path ahead and what they are doing. Use your mirrors to check for vehicles behind you. Search ahead 20 to 30 seconds and to the sides and rear.

If other vehicles are signaling to move into the lane you want, wait until the other vehicles have changed lanes, then check again.

Time. You'll need a few seconds to change lanes. You may need to increase or decrease speed. How fast will you need to go to make the change?

Space. Do you have room to make the move safely? Make sure there is a 4-second gap between vehicles to give you time and space to change lanes.

CHANGING LANES

After you have planned your move and are ready to change lanes, follow these steps.

1. Check your mirrors again.
2. Signal your intent to move right or left.
3. Check over your shoulder on the side next to the lane you want to enter for vehicles in your blind spot.
4. Speed up or slow down as necessary.
5. Move only when you have the time and space to do so.
6. Steer smoothly into the next lane. After you have moved into the next lane, turn off your turn signal.

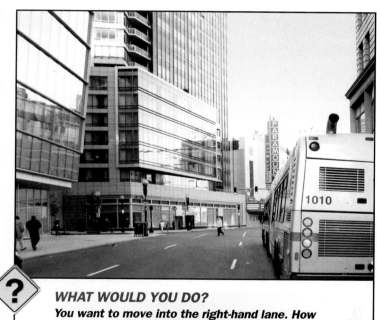

? WHAT WOULD YOU DO?
You want to move into the right-hand lane. How will you manage visibility, time, and space?

Lesson 1 Review

❶ What are the steps for planning and actually moving your vehicle into traffic?

❷ List the steps for planning and actually moving your vehicle out of traffic.

❸ What are the steps for planning and actually changing lanes?

LESSON 2

Right and Left Turns

OBJECTIVES

1. **List** the procedures to follow when preparing to turn right at an intersection.
2. **Describe** the steps needed to execute a right turn.
3. **Describe** how to prepare for a left turn.
4. **Describe** how to make a left turn from a one-way street and from a two-way street.

As a driver, there will be many times when you will want to turn right or left. How should you proceed? To answer that question, you need to know how to perform basic vehicle control maneuvers. Then you need to make a visual search and make good use of time and space as you turn.

How Do You Prepare to Make a Right Turn?

Before you make a turn, you need to check the roadway and choose the correct lane. Then you need to communicate your intentions and position the vehicle correctly. Prepare for the turn before you make it, approximately 8 to 12 seconds in advance of reaching the intersection. Traveling between 30 mph and 45 mph, 8 to 12 seconds equals a distance of about 500 feet or one city block. Remember to reduce speed before making your turn (see **Figure 6.1**).

CHECK

Check for signs and markings that control your movement at the intersection you want to turn. Do you see a traffic signal, a yield sign, or a stop sign? Are turns allowed? Are turns restricted to certain times of day or to certain types of vehicles? Are there special turning lanes? Look through the turn on your intended path of travel. Be sure no one is about to pass you on your left or right side.

FYI

Manage risk. Be aware that more than one-fourth of all collisions occur at intersections.

●- - - - - - - →

You want to turn right at the intersection. *How will you proceed?*

CHOOSE

There is a correct lane to begin the turn. This is normally the lane farthest to the right when making a right turn and the farthest to the left for a left turn. If you're not already in the correct lane, make sure it is clear, signal first, and then move into it. Reduce your speed. Stop behind the stop line if there is one. Keep your wheels straight until you actually begin the turn.

COMMUNICATE

To let other drivers know what you intend to do, tap the brake pedal to flash your brake lights and signal before you turn. Use your turn signal 3 to 4 seconds, or at least 150 to 200 feet, in advance of a turn in urban areas. On rural roads, when vehicles are traveling at higher speeds, signal your intentions several hundred feet ahead of a turn. Be careful not to signal so early that other drivers will be confused.

POSITION THE VEHICLE FOR A RIGHT TURN

Before you execute a right turn, position your vehicle to the right side of the right lane, 3 to 5 feet from the curb or shoulder. Check approaching traffic as well as traffic at and in the intersection. Make sure there are no cyclists to your right. If you are at a stop sign or red traffic signal, stop before the crosswalk. If you are at a stop sign, slowly move up to a point where you can see cross traffic. Always yield the right-of-way to pedestrians and cyclists (see **Figure 6.2**).

How Do You Execute a Right Turn?

The steps for executing a right turn are the same whether you are turning onto a one-way or a two-way street. After you have positioned yourself correctly and signaled your intentions, check again for cross traffic. Then follow these steps.

1. Wait until there is an 8- to 11-second gap in traffic approaching from your left. Just before turning, search the intersection again to the left.
2. Look through the turn along your intended path of travel to the right. When your front bumper reaches the point where the curb begins to curve, begin the right turn.
3. Follow the general curve of the curb as you turn, if there is a curb. Stay in the right lane by looking and driving through the turn along the intended driving path.
4. Reverse your steering and straighten the car as you accelerate and complete the turn. Make sure the turn signal is off.

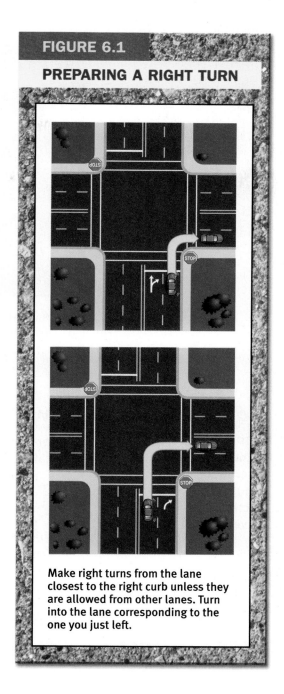

FIGURE 6.1

PREPARING A RIGHT TURN

Make right turns from the lane closest to the right curb unless they are allowed from other lanes. Turn into the lane corresponding to the one you just left.

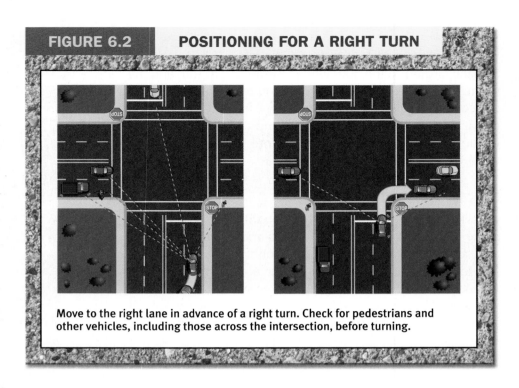

Move to the right lane in advance of a right turn. Check for pedestrians and other vehicles, including those across the intersection, before turning.

Did You Know ?

In 1938, Buick became the first automobile manufacturer to offer electric turn signals on vehicles.

How Do You Prepare for a Left Turn?

To prepare for a left turn, check the roadway, choose the correct lane, communicate your intentions by signaling, and position your vehicle correctly. Always reduce speed before making a turn (see **Figure 6.3**).

CHECK

Check for traffic signs and signals as you approach. Look for traffic ahead and to the left and right. Look through the turn on your intended path of travel to the left. Be sure no one is about to pass you on your left side before you begin your turn.

CHOOSE THE CORRECT LANE

Get your vehicle into the correct lane. This is usually the farthest left lane for traffic moving in your direction. Stop behind the stop line if there is one, or wait for the red light to change. If you stop, keep your wheels straight until you begin the turn.

SAFETY TIP

When you are turning either right or left at an intersection, be very careful not to signal too early if there are other places to turn before the intersection. A driver on another roadway who believes you intend to turn somewhere else could pull out in front of you.

COMMUNICATE YOUR INTENTIONS

Let other drivers know you intend to turn using your turn signal. Signal your intentions to turn 3 to 4 seconds or at least 150 feet in advance. Flash your brake lights by tapping the brake pedal before slowing. **Figure 6.4** shows you how to communicate using hand signals.

POSITION THE VEHICLE FOR A LEFT TURN

Position your vehicle just to the right of the center line on a two-way street or, on a one-way street, in the left lane. Signal and move into the turn.

FIGURE 6.3   **PREPARING A LEFT TURN**

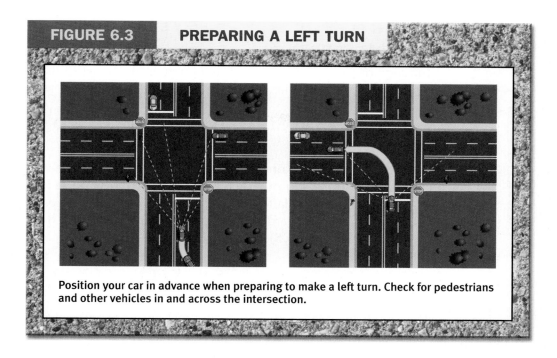

Position your car in advance when preparing to make a left turn. Check for pedestrians and other vehicles in and across the intersection.

How Do You Execute a Left Turn?

When you make a left turn, you follow many of the same procedures you use to make a right turn. One important difference is that a driver turning left must yield the right-of-way to any cross traffic and to vehicles approaching from the opposite direction. In making any turn, you should always be alert for cyclists and pedestrians and be prepared to yield to anyone in the crosswalks or on foot.

The steps for executing a left turn depend on the type of street you are on and the type of street you are turning onto.

TURNING LEFT FROM A TWO-WAY STREET ONTO A TWO-WAY STREET

Turning from one two-way street onto another is probably the most common type of left turn you will make. Of course, yield the right-of-way to other vehicles, pedestrians, or other obstacles in your intended path of travel before you proceed. Here are the steps to follow when safely executing the turn:

1. Find an 11- to 14-second gap in cross traffic to your right and an 8- to 11-second gap to your left.
2. Keep your wheels straight when checking traffic to the left, then center, then right, and then left again. Make sure you check ahead as you scan from left to right and left again. Yield to any approaching traffic and pedestrians in the intersection.
3. Look through the turn along your intended path of travel. Begin to turn the steering wheel just before your front bumper reaches the center of the intersection.
4. Follow the path of travel so that you arrive in the lane just to the right of the center line. Complete the turn by reversing your steering as you accelerate. Afterward, be sure the turn signal is off.

FIGURE 6.4

HAND SIGNALS

Left turn

Right turn

Stop

Use an arm (or hand) signal to communicate better with drivers behind you.

FIGURE 6.5

LEFT TURNS

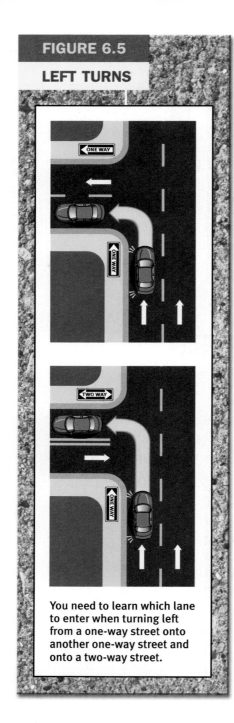

You need to learn which lane to enter when turning left from a one-way street onto another one-way street and onto a two-way street.

TURNING LEFT FROM A TWO-WAY STREET ONTO A ONE-WAY STREET

Turning onto a one-way street is like turning onto a two-way street except that you enter the lane of traffic closest to you.

TURNING LEFT FROM A ONE-WAY STREET ONTO A ONE-WAY STREET

Making a left turn from one one-way street onto another one-way street is similar to making other left turns. You begin from the left-hand lane and end in the left-hand lane. You will not have to cross a lane of traffic coming toward you, although you must still watch for pedestrians (see **Figure 6.5**).

TURNING LEFT FROM A ONE-WAY STREET ONTO A TWO-WAY STREET

If you are turning left from a one-way street onto a two-way street, position your vehicle in the far left-hand lane. Turn into the first left lane of traffic going in your direction (see Figure 6.5).

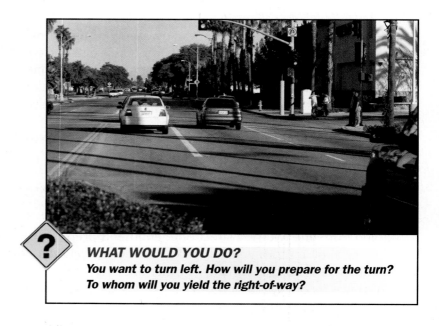

?

WHAT WOULD YOU DO?
You want to turn left. How will you prepare for the turn?
To whom will you yield the right-of-way?

Lesson 2 Review

❶ What should you do before you turn right at an intersection?

❷ How do you make a right turn?

❸ What should you do before you make a left turn?

❹ How would you make a left turn from a two-way street onto another two-way street?

Steering in Reverse and Making Turnabouts

Steering and turning in Reverse gear is a different sensation than driving forward. Reverse gear is only used once in a while. With a little practice, you'll be able to drive in Reverse gear on the occasions when you need it, such as backing out of a driveway, a garage, or a parking space.

How Do You Steer in Reverse?

Always back up slowly, since driving in Reverse gear is more difficult than driving forward. When steering in Reverse gear, you have to learn where you should look and how to control your direction and speed. When you steer either left or right while backing up, the vehicle's movements are more abrupt.

When you are backing up, you must look behind your vehicle. Visibility through the rear window is limited. Head restraints and passengers may further block your view. Don't back up while looking only into the rearview mirror, since this restricts your view even more than turning your body and looking behind you.

To maximize your ability to see, turn your head and shoulders so that you can look back in the direction you want to move. When you move backward, the vehicle turns in a different way than it does when moving forward. The rear of your vehicle moves in the direction that you turn the steering wheel, while the front swings in the opposite direction. When backing up your vehicle, the two points most likely to hit something are the rear side of the vehicle in the direction in which you are turning and the front side of the vehicle opposite the direction in which you are turning.

STEERING IN REVERSE

Before you put the car in Reverse gear, it must be stopped. Then follow these steps (see **Figure 6.6** on page 124).

1. With your foot on the brake, shift into Reverse gear. If you are backing straight, place your left hand on the top of the steering wheel and your right arm across the top of the seat. Turn your body to the right and look through the rear window so you can see behind the vehicle. If you are backing to the right or left, keep both hands on the wheel and look over the shoulder in the direction you want to move.
2. Ease your foot off the brake very slowly. Give yourself plenty of time to monitor the rear and front of your vehicle. Since you don't want to go fast in reverse, apply only slight pressure, if any, to the accelerator.
3. Look at the point where you want to go so that you can identify and correct steering errors early. Turn the wheel as needed.

OBJECTIVES
1. **Explain** how to steer in Reverse gear.
2. **Describe** how to prepare to make a turnabout.
3. **Describe** four ways to make a turnabout.

KEY TERMS
- **turnabout**
- **two-point turn**
- **three-point turn**
- **U-turn**

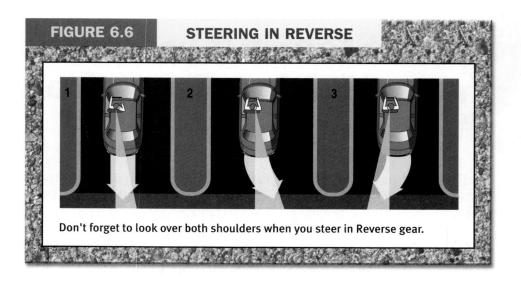

FIGURE 6.6 **STEERING IN REVERSE**

Don't forget to look over both shoulders when you steer in Reverse gear.

4. Look out the rear window, with quick, repeated glances to the front. Keep alert to ensure that the vehicle is moving in the right direction and that the front end is not about to strike anything.

5. Continue to look out the rear window as you bring the vehicle to a stop.

How Should You Prepare to Make a Turnabout?

No matter how skillful a driver you are, you may miss a street or building you are looking for. If so, you may have no choice but to turn around, or make a **turnabout**, in which you turn around and reverse directions. As in all maneuvers you make with your vehicle, careful preparation helps manage risk. Before you make a turnabout, consider the following.

1. Are there signs that prohibit the turnabout?

2. If no signs are visible, are there specific laws that prohibit the turnabout?

3. Is there at least 500 feet of visibility in each direction?

4. Are you near hills, curves, or within 200 feet of an intersection?

5. Is there heavy traffic?

6. Do you have enough space to complete the maneuver?

7. Are other vehicles or pedestrians in your path?

How Can You Make a Turnabout?

SAFETY TIP

By backing into a driveway rather than heading in, you can see in both directions to better assess risk when you prepare to reenter traffic.

You can make a turnabout in one of four ways: driving around the block, two-point turns, three-point turns, and U-turns. Use the method that best suits traffic conditions, the street, and local traffic laws.

DRIVING AROUND THE BLOCK

Driving around the block is the easiest and safest method to use when making a turnabout. It requires making a few turns, but this is not particularly difficult in most places. It does not require driving in Reverse.

TWO-POINT TURNS

The **two-point turn** is another method to use when making a turnabout. Either back into or head into a driveway to reverse your direction.

Backing into a driveway. Back into a driveway when there is no traffic close behind you in your lane and there is a clear driveway on the right side of the roadway (see **Figure 6.7**).

Follow these steps:

1. Signal early. Flash your brake lights to alert drivers behind you. Check for objects or children in or near the driveway as you drive a little past the driveway.
2. Stop about 3 feet from the curb, with your rear bumper just beyond the driveway you will enter. With your foot on the brake, shift into Reverse. Check again for obstacles in your intended path.
3. When it is clear, look over your right shoulder. Back up slowly, turning the wheel rapidly all the way to the right. As the rear of the vehicle enters the driveway, turn the wheel to the left, centering the vehicle in the driveway. Stop when the front of the vehicle is clear of the curb.
4. Shift to Drive or First gear, signal, check traffic, and leave the driveway when it is safe to do so.

Heading into a driveway on the left. When you head into a driveway, you will have to back into the street and possibly into traffic. Select a driveway on the left that affords good visibility. Make sure there are no hedges or other objects along the driveway that will obscure your view of the road (see **Figure 6.8** on page 126).

Follow these steps:

1. Signal a left turn. Check for traffic, flash your brake lights, and stop if necessary. When the driveway is clear, turn into it as close to the right side as you can. This allows more room for the front of the vehicle to swing left as you back out to the right.
2. When the rear bumper clears the edge of the roadway, stop with your front wheels straight. With your foot on the brake, shift into Reverse gear.
3. Look in all directions for pedestrians and over your right shoulder for traffic in your planned path. Back up slowly, rechecking traffic.
4. While slowly moving the vehicle back, turn the wheel quickly all the way to the right. Keep your vehicle in the first lane of traffic. Halfway through the turn, start to straighten the vehicle on the roadway.
5. Stop when the front wheels are straight. Check mirrors and over your shoulder, signal, shift to Drive or First gear, and accelerate to traffic speed.

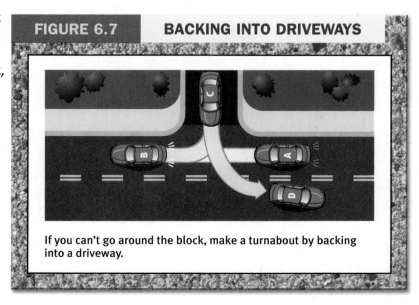

FIGURE 6.7 BACKING INTO DRIVEWAYS

If you can't go around the block, make a turnabout by backing into a driveway.

Heading into a driveway on the right. Heading into a driveway on the right in order to make a turnabout is very dangerous because on a typical street, the driver must back across at least two lanes of traffic before moving forward. You should make this maneuver only in low-speed, low-traffic residential areas. The basic steps are the same, except that you should signal a right turn, look over your left shoulder, and turn the steering wheel to the left as you begin backing out (see Figure 6.8).

THREE-POINT TURNS

One of the hardest turnabouts for a new driver is the **three-point turn**. Two-point turns are simpler and usually safer. To minimize risk, make a three-point turn only when the street is narrow, there are no driveways to turn into, you have very good visibility, traffic is very light, and you cannot drive around the block.

To make a three-point turn, follow these steps (see **Figure 6.9** on page 127).

1. Stop as close to the right edge of the curb as possible. Check for traffic in both directions. Wait until you have a 20- to 30-second gap to complete the turn.
2. Signal a left turn. Look over your left shoulder for any vehicles in your blind spot. Then move the vehicle while turning the steering wheel rapidly to the left to bring the vehicle into the opposite lane. Hold this position.
3. When the front wheels are almost to the curb (about 4 feet away), turn the steering wheel rapidly to the right. Then, stop the vehicle just short of the curb.

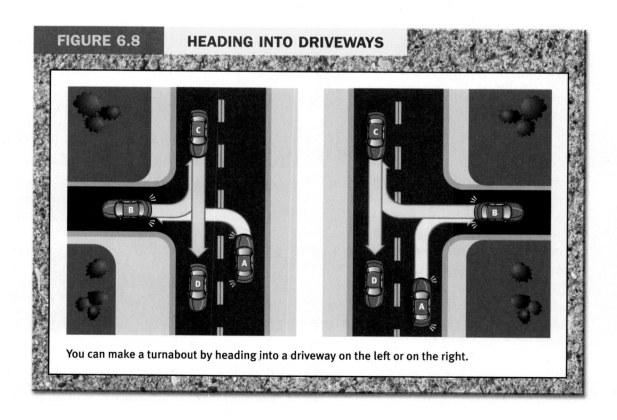

FIGURE 6.8   **HEADING INTO DRIVEWAYS**

You can make a turnabout by heading into a driveway on the left or on the right.

FIGURE 6.9 **THREE-POINT TURN**

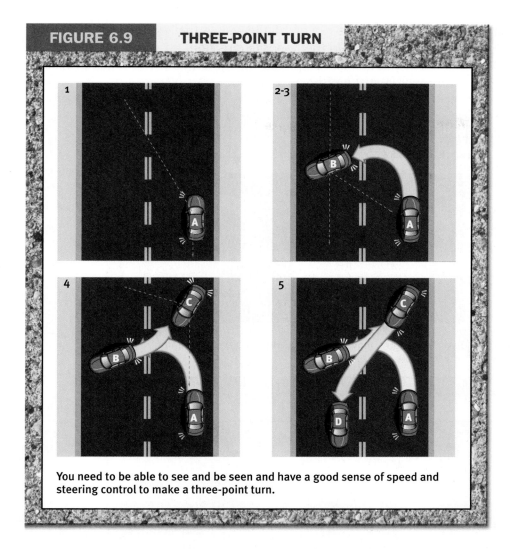

You need to be able to see and be seen and have a good sense of speed and steering control to make a three-point turn.

4. Check traffic to your left, then over your right shoulder. Shift into Reverse. When you have room, back up slowly, turning the wheel to the extreme right position. About 4 feet before stopping, turn the wheel quickly to the left. Keep looking back until you have stopped the vehicle.
5. Shift into Drive, or First gear. Check traffic. Signal, move into the proper lane, and accelerate to a normal speed.

U-TURNS

To make a **U-turn**, you reverse directions in one sweeping turn to the left. You never back up, so you need a wide street in which to make the turn. Most U-turns should be made in intersections, where it is usually legal to make a U-turn, or in places where there is little traffic. Be aware that U-turns are illegal in some states and at some intersections. For instance, it is illegal to make a U-turn on a one-way street (see **Figure 6.10** on page 128).

After first making sure a U-turn is legal, here are the basic steps for making a U-turn on a two-lane road.

1. Stop your vehicle close to the right edge of the curb. Check for traffic in both directions. Signal a left turn. Check over your left shoulder again before starting the turn. Do not start the turn if you will interfere with traffic.

Never make a three-point turn near the top of a hill, on a curve, near an intersection, or near trees, hydrants, or other such objects near the edge of the road.

2. Turn the steering wheel rapidly all the way to the left, moving the vehicle slowly until it is facing in the opposite direction.

3. When the turn is almost completed, straighten the wheels, and proceed in the proper lane at a normal speed.

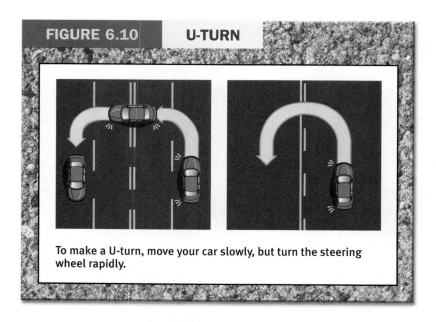

FIGURE 6.10   **U-TURN**

To make a U-turn, move your car slowly, but turn the steering wheel rapidly.

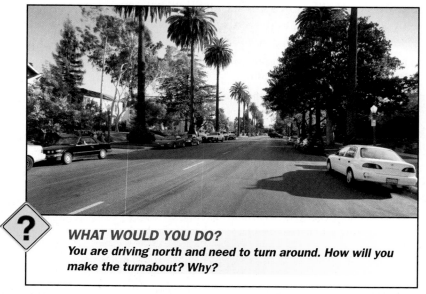

WHAT WOULD YOU DO?
You are driving north and need to turn around. How will you make the turnabout? Why?

Lesson 3 Review

❶ What procedures would you follow to back a vehicle in a straight line?

❷ How do you maximize your ability to see while backing?

❸ What should you consider before making a turnabout?

❹ How can you reverse your vehicle's direction?

LESSON 4

Parking

Parking can be one of the most exasperating experiences of driving. Sometimes you feel the only way you can get into a space is by bumping nearby vehicles out of the way. This is illegal. So how can you park easily?

Parking is more an art than a science. To park quickly and safely, you need to combine several aspects of driving. These include a good control of your vehicle, an accurate judgment of space, and a good understanding of steering. And of course, you need a lot of actual practice parking.

There are several ways to park. These include angle parking, perpendicular parking, and parallel parking.

How Do You Angle Park and Perpendicular Park?

Many parking lots and streets have angular or perpendicular parking. When you park at an angle, you have little room to maneuver. Your visibility is often poor. You must therefore be very careful when entering and leaving angled and perpendicular parking spaces.

RIGHT- OR LEFT-ANGLE PARKING

You may have seen angled parking spaces in parking lots or along the sides of streets of towns and smaller cities. These types of spaces require **angle parking**—parking so that a vehicle is positioned at a 30- to 90-degree angle with a curb or boundary. Angled parking spaces can be set on the right or left (see **Figure 6.11**).

To execute angle parking on the right, follow these steps.

1. Observe traffic in all directions and be alert for vehicles about to leave nearby spaces. Stay 5 or 6 feet from parked vehicles to give yourself room to see and maneuver.
2. When you find an empty space, signal for a right turn.
3. Proceed until you can see along the left side of the vehicle to the right of the space you will enter. Steer sharply right.
4. Creep ahead at 3 to 5 mph into the space midway between the lines.

OBJECTIVES

1. **Describe** how to angle park and perpendicular park.
2. **Describe** how to parallel park.
3. **Describe** how to park in a driveway and in a garage.
4. **Describe** how to park on a hill.

KEY TERMS

◆ **angle parking**
◆ **perpendicular parking**
◆ **parallel parking**

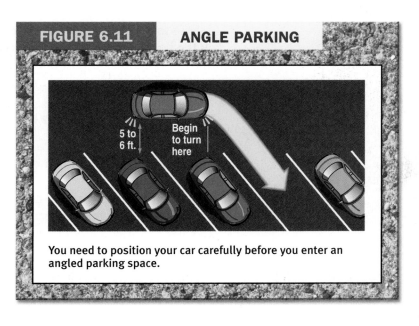

FIGURE 6.11   ANGLE PARKING

5 to 6 ft.

Begin to turn here

You need to position your car carefully before you enter an angled parking space.

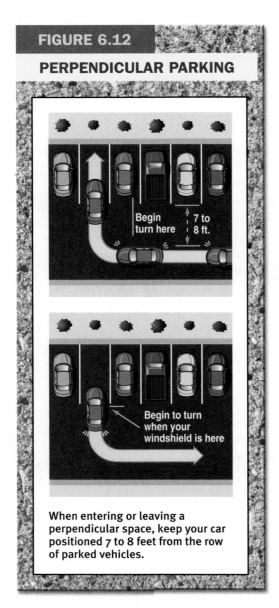

FIGURE 6.12

PERPENDICULAR PARKING

Begin turn here

7 to 8 ft.

Begin to turn when your windshield is here

When entering or leaving a perpendicular space, keep your car positioned 7 to 8 feet from the row of parked vehicles.

Check the left front and right rear of your vehicle to make sure you have clearance on both sides.

5. As you straighten the wheels, move forward until the front of your vehicle is aligned with those on both sides.

Angle parking on the left is similar to that on the right. In this case, start turning the steering wheel to the left when you can see along the right side of the vehicle parked to the left of your chosen space. Proceed slowly, and keep track of the right front bumper and the left rear fender as you park.

PERPENDICULAR PARKING

Many parking lots have parking spaces that are marked at a 90-degree angle (or right angle) to the curb or line. These are spaces for **perpendicular parking**. Perpendicular parking is a little riskier than angle parking because it is hard to see at this angle and there is very little room for maneuvering. If possible, select a perpendicular parking spot that allows you to drive out forward rather than backing out (see **Figure 6.12**).

To enter a perpendicular parking space on the right, follow these steps.

1. Stay 7 to 8 feet from parked cars for best visibility. Observe all traffic conditions, and check for vehicles about to back out of other spaces.

2. When you find an empty space, signal for a right turn.

3. Slow to 3 to 5 mph. Start turning right when you can look down the right side of the vehicle parked to the right of your chosen space.

4. Steer the wheel sharply to turn right. Proceed slowly, checking for clearance of your left front bumper. Check your right rear fender to see that it does not scrape the rear of the vehicle on your right.

5. As you straighten the wheels and center in your space, move forward slowly. Stop just short of the curb or in line with the vehicles parked beside you.

Entering a perpendicular parking space on the left is similar to entering one on the right except that the turn is reversed. In this case, turn the steering wheel to the left and keep track of the right front bumper and the left rear fender as you enter the parking space.

EXITING AN ANGLED OR A PERPENDICULAR PARKING SPACE

To back out of an angled or a perpendicular space, follow these rules (see **Figure 6.13**).

1. Turn on your turn signal and tap your brake with your foot to alert other drivers of your intentions. With your foot on the brake, shift into Reverse.

2. Check all traffic around you. Back very slowly with your wheels straight, looking to your left and over your right shoulder. Yield to any oncoming traffic. Keep checking the back and sides for obstacles as you back out.

3. To exit an angled space on the right, backing to the right, turn the steering wheel sharply to the right after your front bumper clears the rear of the vehicle on your left.
4. When you exit a perpendicular parking space, turn the steering wheel slightly right or left when your windshield lines up with the rear bumpers of the vehicles on both sides. Make sure your front fender clears the rear of any adjacent vehicles.
5. As your vehicle enters the traffic lane, quickly turn the steering wheel in the opposite direction to straighten the front wheels. Keep looking out the rear window until you stop.
6. Shift into Drive or First gear, accelerate, and move into traffic.

How Do You Parallel Park?

You parallel park most often along the side of a street. **Parallel parking**, or parking parallel with the street, may seem hard to you as a new driver. Do it slowly at first, because you'll have to practice to become skillful. You use the steering wheel frequently when you parallel park. To begin, you will need to find a parking space at least 5 feet longer than the length of your vehicle.

PARALLEL PARK

Follow these steps to parallel park (see **Figure 6.14** on page 132).
1. When you locate an empty space, approach it in the lane next to the space. Check traffic behind you. Signal in the direction of the curb and flash your brake lights to alert following drivers of your intention to stop.

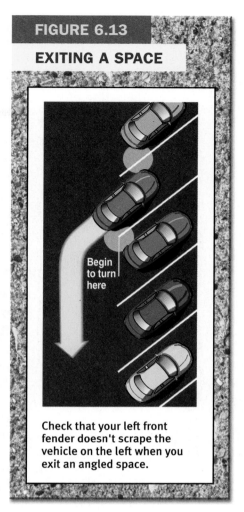

FIGURE 6.13

EXITING A SPACE

Begin to turn here

Check that your left front fender doesn't scrape the vehicle on the left when you exit an angled space.

✓ *Tips for New Drivers*

LEAVING A VEHICLE SAFELY

Be careful. Learn the safe way to leave your vehicle.

▶ With your foot firmly on the brake pedal, set the parking brake. Then shift into Park (automatic) or Reverse (manual).

▶ Turn the key to the lock position, and remove it from the ignition switch. Turn your steering wheel slightly to lock it too.

▶ Check for approaching traffic. Look in your mirrors and check your blind spots.

▶ Wait for a break in traffic before opening the door. Then open it only far enough and long enough to get out of the vehicle.

▶ Lock the door. Then, keeping an eye on traffic, move quickly around the rear of the vehicle toward the curb.

▶ Whenever possible, have passengers exit from the curb side of the vehicle.

Energy Tip

Remember to adjust the driver's seat and all mirrors, lock the doors, and fasten your safety belt before you start your car in order to save fuel.

2. Stop parallel to the vehicle in front of the space, leaving about 3 feet between vehicles. Stop when the center doorposts or the backs of the front seats of the vehicles are even.
3. Keeping your foot on the brake, shift into Reverse.
4. Back up, turning the wheel sharply to the right. Align the back of the front seat with the rear bumper of the vehicle in front. Continue backing slowly, straightening your front wheels.
5. When your front bumper lines up with the rear bumper of the vehicle in front of you, steer rapidly to the left. Check your rearview mirror, and stop before making contact with the vehicle behind you.
6. With your foot on the brake, shift into Drive or First gear. Move forward slowly, centering your vehicle in the parking space. Stop and set the parking brake.

EXITING A PARALLEL PARKING SPACE

For most drivers, it's easier to leave a parallel parking space than it is to park in it. To exit a parallel parking space on the right, follow these steps.
1. Shift into Reverse. Back slowly, with your wheels straight. When your vehicle is about 1 foot from the vehicle behind you, turn the steering wheel rapidly to the left and stop.
2. With your foot on the brake, shift into Drive or First gear. Check your rearview and sideview mirrors. Signal a left turn. Move forward slowly, steering rapidly the rest of the way to the left until you can clear the vehicle ahead of you.
3. Look over your shoulder to check your blind spot. Yield to approaching traffic.
4. When traffic is clear, move forward slowly. When your center doorpost is even with the rear bumper of the vehicle in front of you, turn the steering wheel right until the front wheels point straight ahead.
5. Check the position of the vehicle parked ahead of you, being careful not to scrape it. When your rear bumper is opposite its rear bumper, accelerate gently and steer right as necessary into traffic.

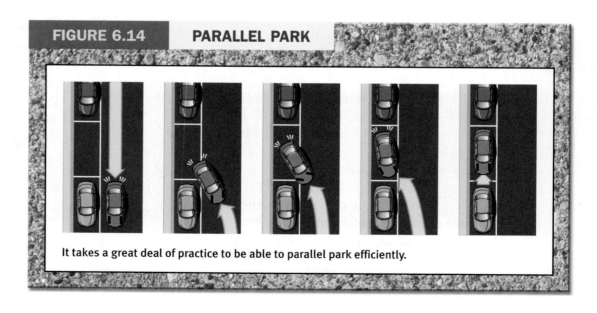

FIGURE 6.14   **PARALLEL PARK**

It takes a great deal of practice to be able to parallel park efficiently.

How Would You Park in Other Areas?

Parking lots and city streets are not the only areas where you park. You might also have to park in a driveway, in a garage, or on a hill.

PARKING IN A DRIVEWAY

You'll often have to park in a driveway, which is similar to perpendicular parking. Driveways may have trees and shrubbery or fences and buildings on either side, making visibility difficult. Centering your vehicle is especially important when parking in a narrow one-car driveway. Furthermore, you should make sure to set your parking brake because many driveways slope downward.

PARKING IN A GARAGE

Parking in a garage is also similar to perpendicular parking. Good positioning and the ability to judge space to your sides are important when parking in a garage. You must make sure to center your vehicle in the proper space, either between the walls of the garage, if it's a one-car garage, or between the sides of the garage-door opening. Before driving out of a garage, walk behind the vehicle to check for objects or children near or behind the vehicle. Remember to check both fenders for clearance as you slowly back out.

PARKING ON A HILL

Parking on a hill is mostly the same as parking on a flat surface. However, you must make sure your vehicle will not roll into traffic after you leave it. To do this, turn your front tires toward the curb (see **Figure 6.15**). The procedures described here are for parking on the right side of the street. To park on the left side, make appropriate right-left adjustments.

Parking downhill with a curb. To make sure your vehicle does not roll, park so that the front wheels turn into the curb. Hilly streets will usually have a curb. There are two additional steps to follow, after bringing the vehicle to its normal parallel-parked position:

1. Turn the steering wheel sharply right, and move slowly forward.
2. Stop the vehicle when the front right wheel touches the curb. Set the parking brake. Put the vehicle in Park. If your vehicle has a manual transmission, shift into Reverse before releasing the clutch.

Parking downhill without a curb. You may need to park facing downhill on a roadway that has no curb. Follow the same procedure for parking downhill with a curb, but move as close to the inner edge of the shoulder as possible.

Driver Ed Online

Topic: Parking

For a link to more information on parking a vehicle, go to **drivered .glencoe.com**.

Activity: Using the information provided at this link, work with two or three other students to create a pamphlet that provides tips for safe parking.

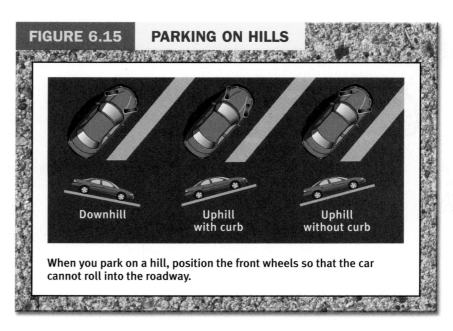

FIGURE 6.15   PARKING ON HILLS

Downhill

Uphill with curb

Uphill without curb

When you park on a hill, position the front wheels so that the car cannot roll into the roadway.

Parking uphill with a curb. Follow these guidelines to park facing uphill when there is a curb at the edge of the roadway, after bringing the vehicle to a normal parallel-parked position.

1. Move forward slowly, turning the wheels sharply left as far as they will go. Move about 2 feet and stop.

2. In Neutral, with your foot covering the brake, allow the vehicle to roll back slowly with the wheels "cramped" left until the rear of the right front tire touches the curb. Put the car in Park. If your vehicle has a manual transmission, shift to First gear before releasing the clutch. Set the parking brake, and stop the car.

Parking uphill without a curb. To park uphill on a road without a curb, follow the procedure for uphill parking with a curb. However, center the vehicle in the space with the front wheels turned to the right so that if the vehicle begins to roll, it will move off the roadway.

?

WHAT WOULD YOU DO?
What procedures will you follow in order to park on the hill?

RESTRICTIONS ON PARKING

Before you decide to park your vehicle anywhere, make sure that you will be parked legally. Every state has its own parking restrictions, and parking laws differ from state to state. However, in most states it is illegal to park in the following areas:

- at a bus stop
- in a loading zone
- in the traffic lane beside another vehicle (double parking)
- on a sidewalk
- half in, half out of a driveway
- across someone else's driveway
- too close to a fire hydrant
- in the fire zone in front of schools and in front of other public and private buildings
- in a no-stopping or no-standing zone

Lesson 4 Review

❶ What should you do when entering an angled parking space? A perpendicular parking space?

❷ How would you parallel park?

❸ What should you do when parking on a downhill with a curb?

❹ What should you do when parking on an uphill without a curb?

Safe Driving Procedures for Passing and Being Passed

Learning the procedures for passing and being passed will help you pass and drive safely.

What Conditions Will Help You Decide Whether You Should or Should Not Pass?

You are driving on a road with one lane of traffic in either direction. Should you pass the vehicle in front of you? To determine if passing is safe and legal, you will need to look at road signs, pavement markings, weather conditions, and the speed of your vehicle and other vehicles.

ROAD SIGNS AND PAVEMENT MARKINGS

To determine if passing is legal, read the signs. "No-Passing" signs mean passing is illegal. Warning signs and roadway markings will tell you whether passing is allowed in the area in which you are driving.

WEATHER CONDITIONS

Passing safely is more difficult in bad weather. Bright sunlight, rain, snow, sleet, hail, and fog add to the danger of passing. If you're driving under these conditions, it is wiser to slow down and to proceed with caution. If the weather is very bad and visibility is poor, the best choice might be to avoid trying to pass at all, even if road signs and markings indicate that passing is allowed.

Nighttime visibility and the condition of the road surface can also add to the danger of passing. At night, if you cannot see ahead to the place where you will reenter the lane after passing, as on a hill or curve, do not attempt to pass. If the road surface seems rough or in poor condition, avoid passing.

YOUR SPEED AND THE OTHER VEHICLE'S SPEED

Before you pass, check the speed limit on the roadway. You will probably need to accelerate to 10 to 15 mph faster than the vehicle in front of you in order to pass it, but you cannot legally exceed the speed limit.

OBJECTIVES
1. **Describe** the procedures for passing another vehicle.
2. **Describe** the procedures for being passed by another vehicle.

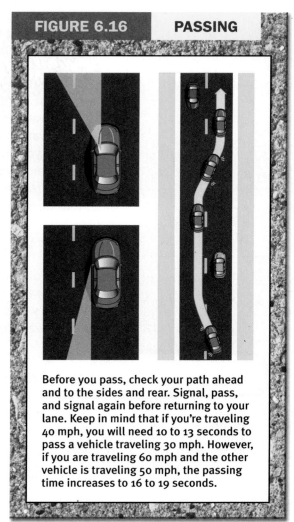

FIGURE 6.16 **PASSING**

Before you pass, check your path ahead and to the sides and rear. Signal, pass, and signal again before returning to your lane. Keep in mind that if you're traveling 40 mph, you will need 10 to 13 seconds to pass a vehicle traveling 30 mph. However, if you are traveling 60 mph and the other vehicle is traveling 50 mph, the passing time increases to 16 to 19 seconds.

Robyn Bordner

Traffic Safety
Sturgis, MI

Basic on-road maneuvers—such as moving to and from the curb, changing lanes, and making right and left turns—never change. The better you perform these maneuvers, the more predictable you are. A good driver is very predictable. Once you have perfected basic on-road maneuvers, you need to tell other drivers what you are doing.

How can you become a predictable driver?

As you approach a vehicle in front of you, note your speed. You may have to slow down. If the other vehicle is going 5 to 10 mph more slowly than you were before you began to slow down, you might decide to pass.

How Do You Pass Another Vehicle?

If it is legal and safe to pass, follow this procedure (see **Figure 6.16** on page 135).

1. Check the path ahead, the off-road areas, behind you, and the lane you want to enter. Make sure no other vehicles are trying to pass you. If you are on a two-lane, two-way road, check that there are no oncoming vehicles. If you have any doubt that you can make it, do not pass.
2. If the way is clear, signal your intent to pass. Use your left turn signal.
3. Glance over your left shoulder for vehicles in your blind spot one last time. Accelerate as necessary, then steer smoothly into the passing lane.
4. Accelerate firmly. If you are on a road with a single lane in each direction, keep watching for oncoming traffic.
5. Check your rearview mirror quickly. When you see both headlights of the vehicle you've passed in the rearview mirror, signal your intent to return to the right lane, maintain your speed, and steer gradually in that direction. Turn off your signal, and be on your way.

What If You Are Being Passed?

When you see that you're being passed, stay to the right in your lane. Do not speed up when you are being passed: this is illegal. Do not accelerate unless it is necessary to give the vehicle more room to get back behind you. Sometimes a passing vehicle will decide to drop back rather than complete the pass.

Lesson 5 Review

❶ What conditions help you when passing another vehicle?

❷ What should you do when being passed?

❸ What steps should you take when passing another vehicle?

BUILDING Skills

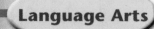

USING PREFIXES AND COMBINING FORMS

The vocabulary describing vehicles and roadways is full of interesting words. Several of these words are formed by using a prefix and a root word.

A prefix is a word part that has a meaning of its own but cannot stand alone as a word. Here are some examples of prefixes and their meanings:

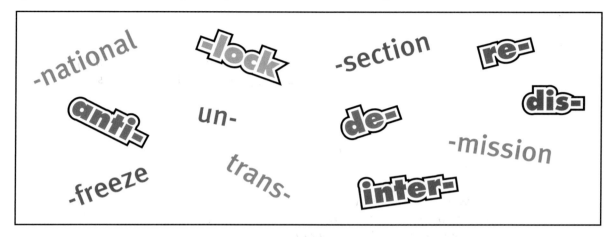

anti—not, against
de—removed, reversed
dis—apart, away from
un—not

inter—between, among
re—again
trans—across, beyond, or through

The vocabulary of driving also includes words that begin with a combining form. This is a word part that can act like a prefix, but it can also join another combining form to make a word, such as **photo** + **graphy**. Two common combining forms are **auto**, meaning "self," and **semi**, meaning "half" or "partly."

Knowing the meanings and uses of prefixes and combining forms can help you figure out the meanings of new words.

TRY IT YOURSELF

Choose a prefix or combining form from those above in order to complete each word or term below. Define the words and terms, using what you already know and what you've learned about prefixes and combining forms. If you don't know what a word or term means, ask someone or look it up.

1. _____ celeration
2. _____ preciation
3. _____ national symbols
4. _____ action time
5. _____ abled
6. _____ protected left turn
7. _____ change
8. _____ section

9. _____ alignment
10. _____ lock brakes
11. _____ freeze
12. _____ fogger
13. _____ theft device
14. _____ tread
15. _____ mission

CHAPTER 6 REVIEW

Key Points

Lesson 1

1. After you have planned to move your vehicle into traffic, check traffic all around you, signal your intention to move into traffic, check your blind spot, immediately turn forward if traffic is clear, and enter the nearest lane of traffic. (Page 115)

2. After you have planned to move your vehicle out of traffic, signal your intention to move, apply gradual pressure to your brakes, steer out of the traffic lane to where you want to go, secure your parking brake, and shift your vehicle to Park or Neutral. (Page 116)

3. After you have planned to make a lane change, check your mirrors again, signal your intent to other drivers, check your blind spot, adjust your speed as necessary, and steer smoothly into the next lane. (Page 117)

Lesson 2

1. To prepare for a right turn, check the roadway, choose the correct lane, and communicate by signaling well in advance of the turn. Position your vehicle to the right side of the right lane. (Pages 118–119)

2. To execute a right turn, find a gap in traffic to your left, look along your intended path of travel, and turn the vehicle, following the curve of the curb. (Page 119)

3. To prepare for a left turn at an intersection, check the roadway, choose the correct lane, and communicate your intentions. Position your vehicle just to the right of the center line or, on a one-way street, the left lane. (Page 120)

4. When turning left from a two-way street, look for an 11- to 14-second gap in cross traffic to your right and an 8- to 11-second gap to your left. Look through the turn along your intended path of travel, and turn your vehicle. When turning left from a one-way street, follow the same procedures, except position your car in the far left-hand lane. (Pages 121–122)

Lesson 3

1. When steering in Reverse, make sure your car is stopped. Shift into Reverse gear. When backing straight or to the right, turn your body to the right to see behind you. When backing to the left, look over your left shoulder. Ease your foot off the brake slowly. Turn the wheel as needed. Make sure your vehicle is moving in the right direction. (Page 124)

2. To prepare to make a turnabout, consider its legality, the amount of visibility, the amount and position of traffic, and the space available. Also consider if you are near hills, curves, or within 200 feet of an intersection. (Pages 124–125)

3. To turn your vehicle around, you can make a two-point turn by heading into or backing into a driveway, make a three-point turn, make a U-turn, or drive around the block. (Page 125)

Lesson 4

1. To perform a perpendicular- or angle-parking maneuver, position your car correctly for best visibility; check for traffic and obstructions and signal; turn into the space when you have clearance on all sides. (Pages 129–130)

2. To parallel park, move parallel to the vehicle in front of the space; back slowly into the space; and center your vehicle in the space. (Pages 131–132)

3. Be aware of objects on either side when you park in a driveway or garage. Centering your vehicle is especially important. (Page 133)

4. To park on a hill, position the front wheels in such a way that your vehicle cannot roll onto the roadway. To do this, turn your front tires toward the curb. (Page 133)

Lesson 5

1. To pass another vehicle, look around you. If the way is clear, signal your intent to pass. Look at your blind spot one last time. Accelerate as necessary, and then steer smoothly into the passing lane. (Page 136)

2. When being passed, stay to the right in your lane. Do not speed up. (Page 136)

On a separate sheet of paper, write the letter of the answer that best completes each sentence.

1 When changing lanes,
a. turn off the radio.
b. make sure you are not on a one-way street.
c. speed up or slow down as necessary.

2 You should signal for a right or left turn
a. 200 to 300 feet in advance.
b. 7 to 8 feet in advance.
c. at least 150 to 200 feet in advance.

3 To parallel park, move your vehicle parallel to the vehicle in front of the space, at a distance of
a. 1 to 2 feet.
b. about 3 feet.
c. about 5 feet.

4 The first thing you should do when passing another vehicle is
a. look around you.
b. signal your intent to pass.
c. accelerate as necessary.

5 To make a two-point turn, you
a. drive around the block.
b. head into or back into a driveway.
c. shift to Neutral.

6 If you park downhill in a vehicle with a manual transmission,
a. shift into Reverse.
b. shift into Neutral.
c. shift into First gear.

On a separate sheet of paper, write the word or phrase that best completes each sentence.

1 passing   2 turnabout
3 perpendicular   4 right turn

7 A _____3_____ parking space is set at an angle of 90 degrees to the curb.

8 To make a _____4_____, position your car to the right side of the right lane.

9 Bright sunlight, rain, snow, sleet, hail, and fog add to the danger of _____1_____.

10 One example of a _____2_____ is the U-turn.

Writing

Driver's Log

In this chapter, you have learned about moving to and from a curb, changing lanes, and making right and left turns and turnabouts and parking. Which do you think will be hardest for you? Write two paragraphs explaining why and how you can gain confidence in executing the maneuver.

Projects

1 Take a ride as a passenger, and record the different forms of communication you notice between drivers. Include communication by mechanical or electronic signals and by body signals. What kinds of information do drivers communicate by each method?

2 Observe several vehicles parked uphill and downhill. Record how each vehicle's front wheels are positioned. Make a diagram showing how each vehicle would move if it started to roll. Determine which vehicles had their wheels positioned correctly.

This review tests your knowledge of the material in Chapters 4–6 and will help you review for your state driving test. On a separate sheet of paper, select the answer that best completes each statement.

1 Adjust the driver's seat so you can
   a. access the vehicle's controls.
   b. see blind spots.
   c. be closer to the steering wheel.

2 Cruise control
   a. should be used on wet, snowy roads.
   b. helps your car operate more efficiently.
   c. should be used primarily in the city when you need to control your speed.

3 Rearview and sideview mirrors
   a. can be used to eliminate all blind spots.
   b. are useful for helping you change lanes safely.
   c. should be adjusted 30 degrees outward.

4 Air bags
   a. can cause personal injury if you fail to follow safety warnings.
   b. eliminate the need to use safety belts.
   c. inflate when a button is depressed.

5 The device that alerts you to an electrical problem is the
   a. alternator light.
   b. speedometer.
   c. odometer.

6 If the temperature gauge rises or warning light displays,
   a. open the car window to let in cooler air.
   b. reduce your speed.
   c. let the engine cool down.

7 You should be aware of stopping traffic when a vehicle's
   a. amber directional signal flashes.
   b. red brake light displays.
   c. white backup lights display.

8 You should use your hazard lights when
   a. the headlights won't come on.
   b. your vehicle is moving very slowly.
   c. you want to move to another lane.

9 If you need to stop your car quickly and safely,
   a. press the brake pedal firmly without locking the brakes, and hold it there.
   b. lock your brakes to keep them from spinning.
   c. pump the brake pedal, especially if you have antilock brakes.

10 Manual transmissions, when compared to automatic transmissions, usually
   a. use less fuel.
   b. operate more easily.
   c. cost more to repair.

11 If your vehicle has a 4-speed transmission, you should use Third gear for speeds
   a. up to 20 or 30 mph.
   b. up to 30 or 40 mph.
   c. over 40 mph.

12 When driving a car with a manual transmission, you may need to downshift when
   a. you are getting ready to parallel park.
   b. you need a higher gear.
   c. you are driving up a hill.

13 Tracking occurs when you
   a. cause your car to zigzag while steering through curves in the road.
   b. keep your vehicle on a chosen track with minor steering adjustments.
   c. make frequent steering adjustments that cause you to overcorrect.

14 The type of vehicle most likely to maintain speed when climbing a hill is a
   a. small vehicle with a 4-cylinder engine.
   b. large passenger vehicle with an 8-cylinder engine.
   c. tractor-trailer rig with a huge engine.

15 To monitor your speed,
   a. always drive as fast as the traffic around you.
   b. check your speedometer when traffic conditions permit.
   c. listen for approaching traffic.

16 To stop your vehicle smoothly for a stoplight,
  a. apply the right amount of pressure on the brake pedal with your toes.
  b. press down on the clutch and then ease up to stop.
  c. use the ball of your foot to apply more pressure on the brake pedal.

17 A vehicle's rates of acceleration and deceleration are dependent on
  a. the make and model of the vehicle.
  b. speed and weight of the vehicle.
  c. amount of pressure in the tires.

18 When you want to merge your vehicle into traffic,
  a. glance in your rearview mirror to check your blind spots.
  b. steer to the nearest traffic lane if clear.
  c. quickly accelerate to get out of the way of oncoming traffic.

19 When you want to move out of traffic,
  a. use your mirrors to scan the traffic in front of and beside you before slowing down.
  b. make sure you have enough space to maneuver to the place you want to move.
  c. apply your brakes firmly to signal you want to move to another lane.

20 When you want to change lanes,
  a. allow a 10-second gap between vehicles.
  b. check the traffic ahead, to the sides, and behind you before you move.
  c. increase your speed.

21 When you are preparing to make a right turn,
  a. reduce your speed as you approach the intersection before making the turn.
  b. turn on the signal as you make your turn so you won't confuse other drivers.
  c. make the turn only if the lane is restricted.

22 When you prepare to make a left turn,
  a. yield the right-of-way to oncoming traffic, pedestrians, and road obstacles.
  b. check traffic to your right and proceed when clear.
  c. make sure no one is about to pass you on your right side before you begin your turn.

23 When you use the Reverse gear,
  a. steer left or right to avoid abrupt movements.
  b. back up slowly and control your direction and speed.
  c. look in your rearview mirror as you back to clearly see what's behind you.

24 When you need to make a turnabout,
  a. back into a driveway on the left side of the roadway.
  b. try a three-point turn when possible.
  c. use the method that best suits traffic conditions and local traffic laws.

25 When you are preparing to pass a vehicle on a two-lane, two-way road,
  a. check to see that the center lines of the roadway are solid yellow.
  b. make sure you are driving the speed limit.
  c. make sure you can clearly see oncoming traffic.

Challenge Questions

1 Before you enter your car,
  a. check the car for paint scratches.
  b. look for children playing nearby and for objects in the road.
  c. make sure the wheels are not turned to either side.

2 The driver of a passenger vehicle
  a. uses more distance to accelerate than a truck driver.
  b. uses less time to decelerate than a motorcycle driver.
  c. uses more time and distance to decelerate than a motorcyclist.

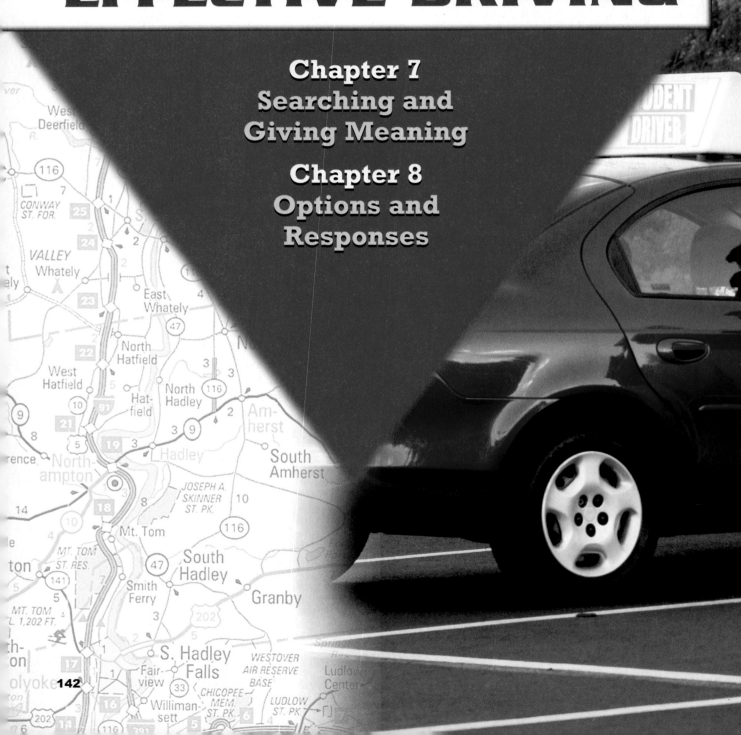

FOUNDATIONS OF EFFECTIVE DRIVING

Chapter 7
Searching and Giving Meaning

Chapter 8
Options and Responses

What are the foundations of effective driving?

The foundations of effective driving are skills in searching, giving meaning to what you have sensed, developing options, and responding in a manner that increases your chances for achieving your goals. These skills help you drive responsibly. This unit will help you identify the skills needed for establishing the foundations of effective driving.

Chapter 7

Searching and Giving Meaning

 LESSON 1
Sight

 LESSON 2
Sound, Balance,
and Touch

 LESSON 3
Scanning, Searching,
and Sensing

 LESSON 4
Giving Meaning

How Do You Use Your Senses When Driving?

Since driving is a mental, social, and physical activity, you need to look and listen for clues in the driving environment. Driving requires the active use of your senses of sight, hearing, feeling, touch, and smell. You can see a pedestrian crossing the street ahead. You can hear the whistle of a train or another driver's honking horn. You can feel the wind blowing against your car. You can smell burning oil or a burning wire. These are just a few ways in which you use your senses while driving. In this chapter, you learn how your senses impact your driving.

Driver Ed *Online*

For additional activities, visit drivered.glencoe.com. Here you will find:

◆ **Web Link Exercises**

◆ **eFlashcards**

◆ **Practice Driving Tests**

Sight

OBJECTIVES

1. **Explain** why vision is considered the most important of your senses in driving.
2. **Describe** the task of the visual system.
3. **List** and describe the nine visual abilities important in driving.

KEY TERMS

- ◆ visual acuity
- ◆ distance vision
- ◆ depth perception
- ◆ central vision
- ◆ peripheral (fringe) vision
- ◆ color vision
- ◆ night vision
- ◆ glare vision
- ◆ glare recovery

●------------➤

Have your vision tested regularly. Good vision is crucial to risk management. Traveling at 30 mph, with 20/20 visual acuity, you can read a 6-inch-high street sign from a distance of about 180 to 225 feet, or 4 to 5 seconds away. With 20/40 vision, you would have to be within 90 to 135 feet, or 2 to 3 seconds away, to read the same sign. **How does this affect driving safety?**

Sight or vision is the most important sense used in driving. Sight is so important that people who are blind cannot legally drive. Vision is the primary way that you gain information about the traffic scene.

What Is the Visual System?

Within your head, the visual system is what allows you to sense what's around you and to give meaning to what you see. It consists of:

- ● the eye, especially the retina.
- ● the optic nerve.
- ● the brain.

The task of the visual system is to search for clues or information about the traffic scene and send images to the brain via the optic nerve. This is how you give meaning to what would otherwise be meaningless shapes, or a two-dimensional image of the world. Your brain lets you perceive the world as moving, multicolored, and three-dimensional.

THE EYE

The eye is a complex mechanism. The eyeball functions remarkably like a camera, taking visible light and converting it into a stream of information that can be transmitted to the brain via the nerves.

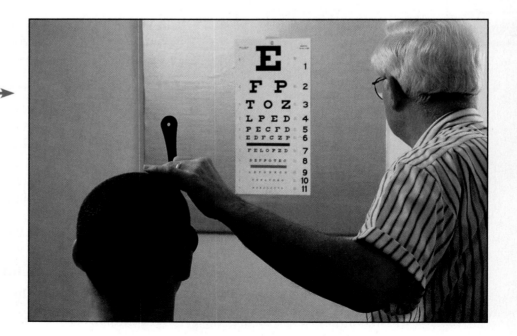

Dealing with the UNEXPECTED

GLARE DANGER

Here are some ways to deal with the danger of nighttime glare.

▲ Do not look directly at the headlights of an oncoming car. Instead, look beyond them and direct your attention to the right edge of the roadway, keeping the approaching car in your peripheral vision.

▲ Reduce your speed if you are momentarily blinded by glare.

▲ Keep alert to possible glare situations that may arise, as on curved or hilly roadways. When you anticipate such a situation, turn your eyes slightly away from it, keeping it in your peripheral vision.

When light enters, it passes through the cornea and a black opening called the *pupil*. The pupil is controlled by the surrounding colored part of the eye, called the *iris*, which is usually blue, brown, or green. Light entering the pupil is refracted by the lens and projected as an image onto the back of the eyeball, called the *retina*.

THE OPTIC NERVE AND BRAIN

Following some rudimentary processing, the information about the image received by the eye is transmitted to the brain via the optic nerve. Every second, some 30 to 40 new images are flashed to the brain via the optic nerve. In humans, the optic nerve is the only sensory nerve that is connected directly to the brain. This is because you need to process visual information quickly.

If the pattern or image is familiar, the brain will understand immediately. However, if the pattern or image is unfamiliar, the brain will have difficulty understanding it. That's why, if you are driving in an unfamiliar environment, interpreting what you see may take longer.

What Visual Abilities Are Necessary for Driving?

Of course you need to see while you drive. Scientists have identified nine aspects of vision necessary for seeing when driving. The primary aspects of vision include visual acuity, distance vision, depth perception, central vision, and peripheral (fringe) vision. Color vision, night vision, glare vision, and glare recovery are important, too.

GENERAL SIGHT

Visual acuity, distance vision, depth perception, central vision, and peripheral vision are important in seeing all the time.

Visual acuity. How well you see determines your **visual acuity**. In relation to driving, visual acuity deals with whether or not objects or hazards in your

Did You Know?

In 1915, a tire on a standard automobile would last for only nine months. By 1930, the life expectancy of a standard car tire had more than tripled to two and a half years.

Driver Ed Online

Topic: Paying attention

For a link to more information on paying attention while driving, go to drivered.glencoe.com.

Activity: Using the information provided in this online brochure, work with two or three other students to create a public service announcement that provides tips for helping drivers avoid distractions while driving.

driving path are sharp and clear, such as letters on a traffic sign or a pedestrian crossing the street. Seeing things clearly is crucial when driving.

Distance vision. Your ability to see in the distance is **distance vision**. If your distance vision is poor, you may not see hazards until it's too late to react safely. Distance vision can also be affected by the condition of your glasses or of your windshield. These should be kept clean and free of dust and scratches, which can greatly reduce vision on bright days and at night. You should not wear scratched sunglasses when you're driving. Poor distance vision and excessive speed increase the risk of making unreliable judgments, with potentially disastrous results.

Depth perception. Your ability to judge the relative distance of objects correctly is **depth perception**, a very important concept, especially in traffic. You need to be able to judge distances accurately to pass other vehicles, change lanes, follow vehicles, pull into traffic, and judge stopping distance.

Central vision. The 3-percent cone at the center of your focus, which is always the same for forward sharp vision, is **central vision**. Focusing on objects is done with the help of central vision. What you focus on is what you see most clearly when you are driving.

Peripheral (fringe) vision. What you can see to the sides is **peripheral (fringe) vision**. It's almost a 180-degree area, about 88.5 degrees on each side of the nose. Peripheral vision detects light, moving objects, and the side ranges of vision. It is the scanning tool that helps the eyes select objects on which to focus.

The faster you drive, the more fringe vision is reduced. Going fast, you naturally have to rely on your central vision. That is one reason why keeping your eyes moving while driving is important.

OTHER IMPORTANT ASPECTS OF VISION

Particularly important at certain times are other aspects of vision, such as color vision, night vision, glare vision, and glare recovery.

✓ Tips for New Drivers

DRIVING AT NIGHT

When driving at night, you need to compensate for reduced visibility. Here are some steps to take.

▶ Drive more slowly than you would during the day.

▶ Keep your eyes moving.

▶ Make sure your windshield and headlights are clean.

▶ Use your headlights wisely.

▶ Avoid driving near your usual bedtime.

Color vision. A crucial aspect in traffic safety is **color vision**. Drivers must instantly recognize traffic signs, signals, and pavement markings, and vehicle turn signals, hazard warning lights, backup lights, and brake lights. People with color-vision defects or colorblindness may react slower to or fail to see the correct light or signal color. Drivers who are colorblind can compensate by knowing the position of the lights in a traffic signal. When you drive, avoid using medium- or dark-blue sunglasses, because they may interfere with your ability to distinguish traffic-signal colors.

Night vision. Your ability to see in low and variable light conditions is **night vision**. Good night vision requires an ability to recover quickly from the glare of oncoming headlights. Glare recovery is best in drivers under the age of 30. Night vision can deteriorate after the age of 40, but drivers over 40 can compensate to some extent for this reduction by driving more slowly or choosing not to drive at night.

Darkness hampers everyone's vision, one way or another. Headlight glare, dark windshields, poorly aimed and dirty headlamps, and dirty windshields and windows all reduce night vision. At night you may not be able to detect objects in your intended path of travel and should scan darkened areas.

Eyes are much slower to adapt to nighttime-light levels after they've been exposed to bright light.

Glare vision. The ability to see when there is a rapid increase in light is **glare vision**. Driving into the sun and sunlight reflecting off bright, shiny surfaces such as other vehicles, oncoming headlights, water, snow, and sand are sources of glare. Sunglasses should be worn during the day to reduce glare. Wearing sunglasses at night is a bad idea, since it reduces overall vision.

Glare recovery. The ability of your eyes to quickly adjust from headlights back to the dark is **glare recovery**. It can take up to 5 seconds for your eyes to adjust to darkness and low-light settings after being exposed to glare.

SAFETY TIP

If you are driving with your high beams on, you can blind drivers coming toward you. Switch to low beams when oncoming traffic is within 500 feet.

WHAT WOULD YOU DO? ?
You must compensate if you are driving at night and have trouble seeing the road. How can you ensure the safety of yourself and your passengers?

Lesson 1 Review

❶ Why is vision the most important sense in driving?

❷ What is the task of the visual system?

❸ What are the nine visual abilities important in driving?

Sound, Balance, and Touch

LESSON 2

OBJECTIVES

1. **Describe** the importance of hearing while driving.
2. **Describe** how balance is important to driving.
3. **Define** pitch, roll, and yaw.
4. **Explain** how touch affects your driving.

KEY TERMS

- ◆ **hearing**
- ◆ **sound**
- ◆ **balance**
- ◆ **pitch**
- ◆ **roll**
- ◆ **yaw**
- ◆ **vibration**

Drivers with a hearing loss may be able to compensate by wearing hearing aids. They can rely more on their vision, frequently searching the roadway and making good use of the rearview and sideview mirrors.

In addition to sight, the senses of hearing and touch frequently come into play when you drive. Listening to the sounds of the road and the vehicle and feeling vibrations and other sensations offer each driver important clues to what's going on inside the vehicle and outside on the roadway and in traffic.

Why Is Good Hearing Critical to Driving Ability?

The sense of **hearing** or listening is important as you drive. Sounds can alert you to where other drivers are located and what they are doing.

The **sound** or noise you hear from an emergency-vehicle siren, for instance, alerts you to such a vehicle and signals you to slow down and pull over to the edge of the roadway. The sound of a horn alerts you that someone is near your vehicle. The sound of an engine revving indicates that another driver is increasing speed. Changes in the sound of tires make you aware that you are leaving the driving path and moving onto a shoulder or center-line rumble strip.

Hearing loss makes drivers less able to hear important cues—emergency sirens, honking horns, engine revving, and screeching tires—while driving. This is a problem especially for people who are unaware of their hearing loss, people who lost their hearing recently, or people whose hearing is constantly changing.

With today's modern air-conditioned vehicle, most people also drive with the windows closed year-round. This reduces the noise in the vehicle, but it also reduces the sounds that can be heard from outside the vehicle. When driving with your windows up, you must utilize your visual skills to compensate for what you cannot hear.

Another sense area relating to the ear that affects your driving is **balance**. Balance is controlled by the inner ear. It helps make you aware of your movement as well as the vehicle's movements. Keep your head up and your eyes to the horizon to assist you in establishing an accurate sense of balance.

What Are Pitch, Roll, and Yaw?

The body responds to movements of the vehicle and changes in its balance while driving, as does the vehicle itself. Vehicle movement actually provides you with a lot of sensual feedback. The various types of feedback are referred to as pitch, roll, and yaw. Pitch, roll, and yaw are the three axes on which a vehicle moves about, and they're all based on the laws of physics to which both people and vehicles respond.

BACKWARD PITCH

When acceleration is applied, weight or center of mass is transferred toward the rear of the vehicle. More rapid acceleration results in greater weight transfer. In accelerating, you'll feel the opposite of braking—the car sits on the rear wheels, and the front of the car comes up. This forward/backward movement of the car is called **pitch**. You may also feel your body pressed back a little into the seat as you accelerate.

FORWARD PITCH

When brakes are applied, weight or center of mass is transferred toward the front of the vehicle. If braking is hard, there is a noticeable drop of the hood and reduced rear-tire traction. Weight transfer is what you feel when you brake hard. The front of the car pitches down, and more weight goes onto the front wheels. In dry conditions, about 70 percent of traction in braking comes from the front wheels. You may also feel your body moving forward due to forward pitch as you apply the brakes.

ROLL

The vehicle can also move from side to side. As you turn corners, you will feel the car lean over to one side. If you go through a left-right combination turn on a corner, you will feel the vehicle rock across from one side to the other between the corners. This is called **roll**. Sudden steering changes or changes in the elevation of the road, or even accelerating and braking, can affect a vehicle's side-to-side balance.

If you begin a turn by violently turning the steering wheel, then the car will immediately roll a lot, and in fact will be unstable. It's better to make turns and other driving actions smoothly and deliberately. There are a few times when you should act quickly, such as hitting the brakes hard (only in straight braking) and depressing the accelerator hard when you need to speed up rapidly. But most of the time, it's better to be gentle and deliberate.

Your sensory organs (eyes, nose, and musculo-skeletal system) provide valuable information about the condition of the vehicle and how it is responding. For example, the senses communicate whether the vehicle is accelerating, decelerating, and in what direction the car is turning. *How is this helpful when you are driving?*

YAW

Sudden steering, braking, or a right or left elevation of the highway affect rear-vehicle balance and results in the loss of tire traction. If a rear tire has less traction than the corresponding front tire, that tire may begin to slide sideways toward the front tire. This spinning action is called **yaw**.

How Does Touch Affect Your Driving?

The sense of touch, which comes into play when a vehicle pitches, rolls, or yaws, also helps you feel other types of movement or pressure. The driver's sense of touch is in contact with the vehicle through the fingers, feet, torso, arms, and legs. The driver can sense changes in steering as the road changes and from various types of movement or vibrations from the vehicle.

The vehicle vibration created by out-of-balance tires not only shortens the life of steering and suspension components but also leads to uneven tire wear and increases fuel consumption. For better gas mileage, make sure that vehicle tires are balanced.

One of the most common sources of vehicle **vibration** or shaking that the driver can sense comes from the tires. Tires that are out of balance can cause vibration. Tires produced today are a tremendous improvement over the tires of 15 years ago, but they still need to be balanced. Out-of-balance tires cause increased wear on all steering and suspension components, and this can be felt. This tire problem starts to be noticeable around 30 miles per hour and will be most noticeable around 50 miles per hour. If the vibration seems to come from the steering wheel, then the front tires should be checked. If the vibration is noticed more in the vehicle seats, then the rear tires should be balanced. If the car pulls to the left or right, the wheels may need to be aligned.

Modern suspension systems are lighter and give the driver a better "feel" of road conditions, but they also transmit vibrations easier into the passenger compartment. Worn or loose universal joints on rear-wheel-drive vehicles can cause a vibration. Vibrations that occur when the brake pedal is pressed indicate a warped brake drum or rotor.

?

WHAT WOULD YOU DO?
You hear the siren from an emergency vehicle approaching from the rear. What action will you take as it approaches and then passes you?

Lesson 2 Review

❶ Why is hearing important while driving?

❷ Why is maintaining vehicle balance important while driving?

❸ What is the meaning of roll, pitch, and yaw?

❹ What role does the sense of touch play in driving?

LESSON 3

Scanning, Searching, Sensing

You discovered in Lesson 1 that vision gives you most of your driving information. The effective and diligent use of vision is necessary for successful sensing and scanning, which goes on all the time as you drive.

What Is Systematic Sensing and Scanning?

When you are driving, you react to what you see. To use visual information quickly and accurately, you must process it into something actionable. This visual process is called *systematic sensing and scanning*. Systematic sensing and scanning will help you identify where to look and what to look for. In addition to vision, of course, you simultaneously use your other senses to help in determining where other drivers are, what other drivers are doing, and what roadway conditions exist.

How Can You Apply Systematic Sensing and Scanning?

You must search and scan with your senses as you drive. **Searching** is focusing and looking at everything in the driving environment. **Scanning** is picking up bits of information quickly, with glances and quick looks. Systematic sensing and scanning involve three important steps:
1. checking the center of the travel path
2. scanning, searching, and listening to what is happening in the traffic scene
3. checking inside and outside mirrors and the instrument panel

When these steps become habit, you can recognize what's important in traffic situations by looking ahead and looking around you. These steps allow you to identify the critical events that affect your driving.

LOOKING AHEAD

Look ahead when you drive. To avoid sudden last-minute moves, you should look down the road 20 to 30 seconds ahead of your vehicle. A driver needs to look that far ahead to react to hazards and potential

OBJECTIVES
1. **List** the steps for systematic sensing and scanning.
2. **Identify** ways you can look ahead while driving.
3. **Identify** situations that require you to look to the side and look behind.

KEY TERMS
◆ searching
◆ scanning
◆ intersection

Ground viewing is a scanning technique. *Why is it important to use this technique while driving?*

Use systematic sensing and scanning to help you judge when to reduce speed or increase following distance and thereby avoid unnecessary stops. Each time you stop and then accelerate again, you burn extra fuel.

hazards. Constantly staring at the road just in front of your car without ever looking to the side is dangerous.

If you look far enough ahead, of course, you will be able to see important situations, such as someone getting into a parked car. In the city, you should look at least two blocks ahead—or about 20 to 30 seconds. On the highway, 20 to 30 seconds is about one half of a mile. Search the roadway and off-road areas 20 to 30 seconds ahead for information that can help you plan a path of travel.

Look for things that could affect your progress. Identify closed or changing visual zones—driving lanes that are available or closed ahead. Listen, too, for engine noises from other vehicles. Are other vehicles accelerating? Do you hear another vehicle braking? Large trucks, construction vehicles, and emergency vehicles will emit an audible and often loud sound when they are backing up.

Take in the whole scene. Looking 20 to 30 seconds ahead does not mean looking only at the middle of the road. It means looking at the side of the road as well. Looking from side to side helps you to see the following:
- cars and people that may be in the road by the time you reach them
- signs that warn of problems ahead
- signs giving you directions

When you are driving, you tend to steer your vehicle in the direction in which you are looking. Where you are looking most of the time should be your target or reference point. Centering your vision on your travel path helps you steer properly so that you stay in your lane. To stay ahead of the game, focus on an area as far ahead on the road as possible and steer toward it.

Remember to keep your eyes moving and scanning the road at the same time. Look near and far, right and left. Anticipate and watch for actions about to happen, such as a ball rolling into the street, a car door opening, a pedestrian suddenly entering your driving path, or a swerving bicycle. Turn your head before changing lanes, too, because mirrors have blind spots that can hide a motorcycle, bicycle, or even a small car.

Your target or reference point varies depending upon the highway setting in which you are driving. Your reference point should be in the middle of your path on a straight road. On curved roads and turns, your reference point should be through the curve or turn to the point where your vehicle will be positioned when you complete the directional change.

Spot possible dangers early. *How can you spot possible dangers?*

Watch for hazards. Look around. Keep your eyes moving. Don't develop a "fixed stare." Look beyond the car ahead of you. Check your rearview mirrors every time you adjust speed or change the position of your vehicle so that you know the position of vehicles behind you.

On the freeway, be ready for changes in traffic conditions. Watch for signals from other drivers. Expect merging vehicles at on ramps and interchanges. On the freeway or in town, be prepared for rapid changes in road conditions and traffic flow.

As you look ahead, think about what might happen ahead. Be alert for vehicles on either side, to the front, and to the rear. Leave enough space between you and the vehicle ahead for safe stops. Always leave yourself an "out." Mistakes cause crashes. To protect yourself, know which lanes are clear so you can use them if you need to. Use your mirrors.

LOOKING TO THE SIDES

At certain points, you must look to the sides and listen for the sound of other vehicles' horns, the sound of an approaching train, or the sound of the crossing bells at a railway crossing. Any time you come to a place where people may cross or enter your path, you should look to the sides to make sure no one is coming. Always look to the sides at intersections, crosswalks, railroad crossings, and other places where people may enter or leave the roadway.

Intersections. Any place where one line of traffic meets another is an **intersection**. It includes:
- cross streets, side streets, and alleys.
- freeway entrances.
- railroad crossings.

Follow these rules at intersections:
1. Make sure you have a good view and that you are listening closely. If your view of a **cross street** is blocked by a building or a row of parked cars, edge forward slowly until you can see. Listen for the sound of other vehicles (horn, brakes, acceleration).
2. Look both ways. Look to the left first, since cars coming from the left are in the lane closest to you. Look to the right. Take one more look to the left before you pull out, just in case there is someone you didn't see the first time.
3. Don't rely on traffic signals. Before you enter an intersection, look left, right, and ahead for approaching traffic. At an intersection, look left, right, and left again even if other traffic has a red light or a stop sign. Remember that some drivers do not obey traffic signals.

Most of the time, threatening objects or conditions that will cause you a problem are going to come from the sides—especially in intersections. *How can you manage this problem?*

Crosswalks. Every intersection where streets with sidewalks meet has a crosswalk for pedestrians. Crosswalks are areas set aside for people to safely cross the street, and they are usually marked. You must always stop and yield to pedestrians in crosswalks and allow them to cross the street. Even when stopping or turning a corner, watch for people who are about to cross the street.

The crosswalk is that part of the pavement where the sidewalk lines would extend across the street. Most crosswalks are at intersections, but some are in the middle of the block. Some crosswalks have flashing traffic signals on a beacon or in the pavement to warn you that pedestrians may be crossing. Whether

SAFETY TIP

Always leave yourself a path of escape—a way to avoid a collision. Position your vehicle so that you always keep a margin of space around it.

or not the lights are flashing, you must always look for pedestrians and be prepared to stop for them. Crosswalks are often marked with white lines. Yellow crosswalk lines may be painted at school crossings. Some crosswalks, especially in residential areas, are not marked but are still legally considered crosswalks, and you must let pedestrians walk across the street.

Remember, if you have a green light, the light is also green for people who are walking in the same direction you are traveling. Drivers should always yield the right-of-way to pedestrians in crosswalks. If you stop in the crosswalk and block the path of a pedestrian, you are violating their right-of-way and placing them in danger.

Roadside areas. Whenever there is activity along the side of the road, there is a good chance someone will cross or enter the road. It is very important to look to the sides of the road when you are near the following:

- railroad crossings
- shopping centers and parking lots
- construction areas
- busy sidewalks
- playgrounds and schoolyards
- vehicles parked or disabled along the side of the roadway

LOOKING BEHIND

It is a good idea to check traffic behind you, especially if you have stopped for a red traffic signal or stop sign. Another vehicle may be coming up behind you too fast. If you see it early, you have time to get out of the way before it hits your vehicle from the rear. Sometimes, too, the sound of squealing tires coming from behind you will alert you to someone driving too fast and suddenly realizing that they need to stop because you are stopped. This can help you to reduce risk.

Use your rearview and sideview mirrors while driving. **How can these mirrors help you with your driving?**

It is very important to check behind you before you drive down a long or steep hill or slow down quickly. Another vehicle may be tailgating you or following you too closely, and you need to know this before you react. It's very important to look behind you when you change lanes or back up.

Changing lanes. This can include changing from one lane to another, entering or exiting the freeway from an on- or off-ramp, or entering or exiting traffic from a curb or the road shoulder. Whenever you change lanes, check behind you to make sure you are not getting in the way of cars in the lane where you want to go.

Before changing lanes, signal and always check traffic behind and beside you by:

1. checking all mirrors.
2. glancing over your left or right shoulder to make sure the lane you want is clear. If you use only your rearview mirrors, you may not see vehicles near the rear of your car because of a blind spot.

You should also check your mirrors when you increase or decrease speed: for example, if you are passing a slow-moving vehicle, preparing to turn into a side road or driveway, following a slow-moving vehicle, stopping to pull into a parking space, or slowing down suddenly.

Backing up. It is always dangerous to back up because it is hard to see what is behind your vehicle. Whenever you need to back up or back out of a parking space, follow these rules:

1. Check behind the car before you get in. Children and pets are smaller than adults and hard to see from the driver's seat.
2. Do not depend only on your mirrors or only looking out a side window. Turn and look over your right shoulder through the rear window if you are backing straight or to the right and over your left shoulder if you are backing to the left.
3. Always back up slowly to avoid collisions.

On long, steep downgrades, keep a lookout for large vehicles behind you that can gather speed very quickly.

Remember that using your senses to search and scan helps you gather information about what is happening around your vehicle. As a driver, this is information you need to know.

WHAT WOULD YOU DO? ?
What are the threatening objects or conditions in this situation?

Lesson 3 Review

❶ What is systematic sensing and scanning?

❷ What are the steps for systematic sensing and scanning?

❸ How can you look ahead while driving?

❹ What situations require you to look to the side and look behind while driving?

Giving Meaning

When driving, you use all your senses to detect what is occurring around you. You also use your brain to give meaning to the information you perceive.

What Is Giving Meaning?

As a skillful driver, it is important that you become adept in giving meaning to what you see, feel, and hear. If you hear a siren and see drivers ahead slowing down and pulling to the edge of the road, you give meaning to this situation by concluding that an emergency vehicle is approaching. If you understand the situation, you may then take appropriate action, such as pulling to the side of the road to let the emergency vehicle pass.

Giving meaning, a mental process that has to do with understanding what you perceive, relies heavily on sensing. You must be in good physical and mental condition to give meaning to what you sense. Such mistakes as driving while you are tired or driving under the influence of alcohol will result in the senses not being able to supply the brain with appropriate information. If you're exhausted or under the influence, you won't be able to give meaning to what is happening in the traffic scene.

Any traffic situation in which you drive will change constantly. You will have to continuously give meaning to new events that occur. With each piece of new information that is recognized, you must do the following:

1. Give meaning to the information for what it is (for example, a stop sign, a vehicle).
2. Identify the information for what it is (for example, a traffic sign controlling four-way traffic, a vehicle making a right turn).
3. Recognize the relationships and interaction between the information (for example, a vehicle making a right turn at a four-way-stop intersection).

All three steps are important if you are going to give the correct meaning to what you sense.

What Factors Help You Give Meaning?

Several different factors help you give meaning to events on the road. Giving meaning to any traffic scene is affected by the following:

- your alertness
- the amount of time taken to give meaning to the traffic situation
- the traffic event and distractions
- your previous experience
- the expectations of the happenings in traffic

Paying attention or being alert to what is happening, both inside and outside the vehicle, will help you give meaning to traffic events. If you are not paying attention, you'll miss things. If you are looking at unimportant events in the traffic scene, such as at friends in a passing vehicle, the entire driving picture will not be seen. You will not be able to give meaning to what is important and are more likely to make a driving mistake.

ATTENTION LEVELS CAN VARY

People are human. Different drivers have different attention levels at different times. A person driving in a very familiar area, such as the same route he or she drives every day, is probably less alert than the same person in an unfamiliar driving environment. Unfamiliar happenings should increase your attention level. Your attention level increases when faced with sudden maneuvers by other drivers, such as another car or truck quickly swerving in front of you, because you need to react.

It is important that you recognize that traffic conflicts, hazards, and snafus can occur at any time. If you recognize such possibilities, you can try to remain alert in any traffic situation. You must also pick and choose to what you will react. Only process those clues that relate to a safe travel path, such as brake lights, reverse driving lights, lane positioning, turn-signal lights, angle of front wheels, and work zones. You must be very selective about what you are giving meaning to and react only when necessary.

YOUR PLAN FOR GIVING MEANING

You must develop your own plan for giving meaning to traffic events. Your plan for giving meaning should include how to look, where to look, and what to look for.

By giving meaning to the information provided, you will know whether there are events that require a change in what you are doing.

With your driving instructor, you might consider using commentary driving to help you in giving meaning. **Commentary driving** is "saying" aloud what you sense in real-world traffic situations. Use one- or two-word phrases to identify important clues and potential hazards along the travel path as well as to the sides and rear.

> Driving is a complex mental task. It requires your full, undivided attention. *What would you risk by not paying attention while driving?*

Do Expectations and Experience Help You Give Meaning?

Giving meaning to what you see in traffic can be enhanced by expectancy. Anticipating what might be ahead can save you time. Generally, you should first identify traffic events that you expect to see. When you've had a little driving experience, your expectations can help you give meaning to traffic scenes quickly and easily.

Dr. Dale O. Ritzel

Health Education and Recreation
Southern Illinois University Carbondale
Carbondale, IL

Driving is more than a physical task. Paying attention and developing a seeing and scanning system are important to crash-free driving. Developing a system of "seeing" helps the driver know what is ahead, behind, and to the side. Also developing the skill of moving your eyes on a regular basis (every few seconds) will keep you from getting fatigued.

How can you develop a seeing and scanning system?

Sometimes expectations can hinder giving meaning when your expectations are not met. You have to recognize and react to this as it happens.

Experienced drivers group important traffic clues together to give meaning to traffic events. They use the results of their searching to create a total mental picture of traffic events. Creating these mental pictures of events makes it easier to give meaning and remember the event. Stored memories from previous traffic events help all drivers give meaning to new traffic scenes.

? WHAT WOULD YOU DO?
You are driving and encounter this traffic scene. What does this situation mean, and what actions would you take to get through the area safely?

Lesson 4 Review

❶ How does giving meaning to the driving scene help you manage risk?

❷ What factors affect your ability to give meaning to any traffic scene?

❸ What three steps are critical to giving meaning to a traffic situation?

BUILDING Skills — Geography

UNDERSTANDING MAP SYMBOLS

Look at the symbols and the legend on a map to learn about the area you are traveling through.

You can see that there is an airport near Great Falls, Montana, at D, 7, and a campground near Choteau at C, 6.

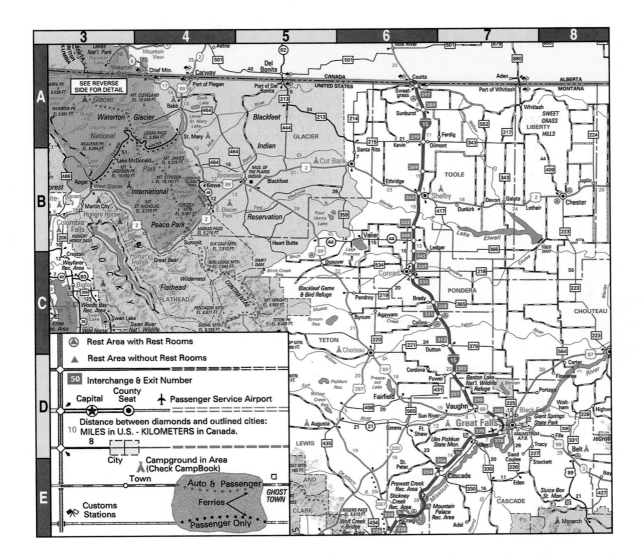

TRY IT YOURSELF

1. At what coordinates can ski areas be found?
2. How many campgrounds can you find in the Blackfeet Indian Reservation?
3. What does ⟨✈⟩ stand for at A, 4?

Key Points

Lesson 1

1. Vision is the primary way that you gain information about the traffic scene. (Pages 146–147)
2. The visual system lets you search for clues about the traffic scene and sends images to the brain. (Page 147)
3. The nine visual abilities important in driving are visual acuity, distance vision, depth perception, central vision, peripheral vision, color vision, night vision, glare vision, and glare recovery. (Pages 147–149)

? WHAT WOULD YOU DO?
You hear the siren from an emergency vehicle approaching from the rear. What action will you take as it approaches and then passes you?

Lesson 2

1. Hearing sounds alerts you to where other drivers are located and what they are doing. (Page 150)
2. Balance helps improve sensitivity to your movement as well as to the vehicle's movements. (Page 150)

3. Pitch is the forward/backward movement of your car when acceleration or brakes are applied. Roll is what you feel when some of your vehicle's weight transfers from one side to the other while turning. Yaw is the spinning action that occurs when the vehicle begins to slide sideways toward the front tire if a rear tire has less traction than the corresponding front. (Page 151)
4. Touch helps you feel different types of movement or pressure. (Pages 151–152)

Lesson 3

1. The three steps for systematic sensing and scanning are checking the center of the travel path; scanning, searching, and listening to what is happening in the traffic scene; and checking the inside and outside mirrors and the instrument panel. (Page 153)
2. When looking ahead, you should take in the whole scene and watch for hazards. (Pages 153–154)
3. Look to the sides at intersections, crosswalks, and roadside areas. Look behind when you change the direction or speed of your vehicle. (Pages 155–157)

Lesson 4

1. Giving meaning is a mental process that has to do with understanding what you perceive. It relies heavily on sensing, a physical process. (Page 158)
2. Giving meaning to a traffic scene is affected by the following: your alertness, the amount of time taken to give meaning to the traffic situation, the traffic event and distractions, your previous experience, and the expectation of the happenings in traffic. (Pages 158–159)
3. Expectancy enhances giving meaning to what you see in traffic. It saves you time, helps you prepare for appropriate action when you get there, and helps you give meaning to traffic scenes quickly and easily. Expectancy can sometimes hinder giving meaning as well. (Pages 159–160)

On a separate sheet of paper, write the letter of the answer that best completes each sentence.

1 When acceleration is applied, weight is transferred to the
   a. rear of the vehicle.
   b. front of the vehicle.
   c. center of the vehicle.

2 Unfamiliar happenings should
   a. keep your attention level the same.
   b. increase your attention level.
   c. decrease your attention level.

3 When watching for hazards, you should not
   a. look around.
   b. develop a fixed stare.
   c. keep your eyes moving.

4 Most crosswalks are marked with
   a. white lines.
   b. yellow lines.
   c. nothing.

5 After you have been exposed to bright lights, your eyes
   a. adapt to nighttime light levels slower.
   b. adapt to nighttime light levels faster.
   c. adapt to nighttime light levels at a constant rate.

6 What you can see to the sides is
   a. central vision.
   b. visual acuity.
   c. peripheral vision.

On a separate sheet of paper, write the word or phrase that best completes each sentence.

glare recovery

hearing loss

giving meaning

crosswalk

7 The _____ is the part of the pavement where the sidewalk lines would extend across the street.

8 _____ is a mental process that has to do with understanding what you perceive.

9 _____ is the ability of your eyes to quickly adjust from extreme bright light back to the dark.

10 _____ makes drivers less able to hear important cues.

Writing

Driver's Log

In this chapter, you have learned about ways to use your senses while driving. Write a paragraph on each of the senses discussed in this chapter, and indicate the one sense that is the most important to use while driving.

Project

As a passenger, identify objects in the area ahead of the vehicle in which you are riding for 1 mile in a residential or business district. What meaning would you give to these objects along the roadway?

What might other drivers do in relation to these objects? Compare what meaning you gave to these objects in relation to what actually happens. Write a one- to two-page paper on these results.

Options and Responses

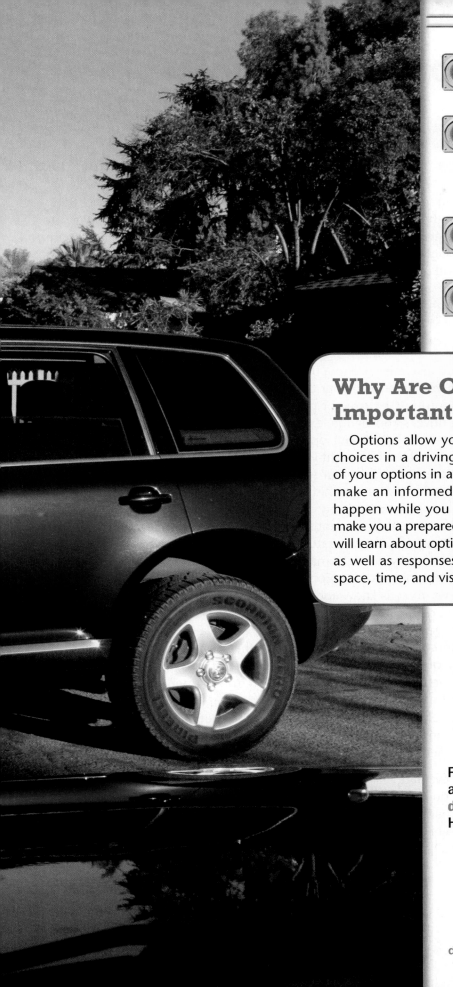

 LESSON 1
Options and Choice

 LESSON 2
Responses to
Manage Space
and Time

 LESSON 3
Managing Visibility

 LESSON 4
Margins of Safety

Why Are Options Important?

Options allow you to understand potential choices in a driving situation. By knowing all of your options in any given situation, you can make an informed guess about what might happen while you are driving. Doing so will make you a prepared driver. In this chapter, you will learn about options as they apply to driving as well as responses and rules for maintaining space, time, and visibility.

Driver Ed *Online*

For additional
activities, visit
drivered.glencoe.com.
Here you will find:

- ◆ **Web Link Exercises**
- ◆ **eFlashcards**
- ◆ **Practice Driving Tests**

Options and Choice

OBJECTIVES

1. **Define** options and explain their role in the driving process.
2. **Describe** the role of assumptions in the driving process.
3. **Explain** the importance of choices in the driving process.

KEY TERMS

- option
- comparison
- assumption
- choice

Like giving meaning, determining options is a mental link that involves thinking through the meaning that results from searching. The meaning you give to a situation determines your options and, ultimately, the response you choose. After you weigh your options, go beyond what is actually happening in a traffic situation, and make an informed guess as to what might happen next.

What Is the Role of Options in the Driving Process?

When you give meaning to a traffic scene, you are determining what to do now. When you determine your options, you forecast how events may affect you in the future. **Options**, or potential choices in a driving situation, are based on a driver's knowledge, experiences, and skills. In the driving process, you want to know all of your options in order to make the best and safest choice possible. Remember that you only have a moment or two to do so.

Your options depend on your situation. For the fullest possible understanding of your options, your searching process must be complete and accurate. If you have been realistic in giving meaning to the situation, the best option for the situation will be easy to identify and select. If what you give meaning to in the traffic situation is not accurate or realistic, the selection of the best option will be difficult and you might make a driving mistake.

When determining your options, you make **comparisons** of the information you have. You will know about or will have experienced certain situations while driving or watching other drivers. There are also certain actions you can take as a driver. First you assess, interpret, and evaluate all the information. Then, you forecast the potential for hazards that may affect you. Here are some examples of questions you can ask that enable you to select various options:

- What if a vehicle slows or stops directly in front of me?
- What if a traffic signal changes?
- What if a vehicle moves into one of my blind spots?
- What if I move into another vehicle's blind spot?
- What if a pedestrian enters the roadway?

You can evaluate a situation and select the best option by asking yourself three basic questions:

1. What is happening here?
2. What do I believe will happen next?
3. What can I do to increase the chance that nothing bad will happen to me?

INFORMED ASSUMPTIONS

As a driver who looks ahead, you often must make assumptions as to what other vehicles might do. **Assumptions** are events you think or assume might happen. For example, if you see the brake lights on the car ahead of you, you make an assumption that the car might stop. Assumptions are used when determining available options and making your final choice of which option has the greatest potential to make something good happen.

If you did not make assumptions, it would take longer to come to conclusions or decisions while driving. For example, if you are approaching a warning sign indicating a sharp 90-degree turn to the left and a recommended speed of 25 mph, you would make the assumption that 25 mph or less would be a good speed to travel around the curve. You assumed that the posted advisory speed was correct and that the 25 mph was the maximum safe speed for the turn.

You also make comparisons between the current situation and your previous experiences. When you make comparisons, you ask yourself questions such as:

1. Is this situation like others I have been in?
2. What happened in the other situation(s)?
3. Could the same thing happen again in this situation?

Making informed assumptions is an essential ability related to determining options.

In this situation, you should respond by using an option that increases space and time between the oncoming traffic and the pedestrian and you and the oncoming traffic. *What type of option might you choose?*

CHOOSING AN OPTION

As a driver, you make many choices. A **choice** is the selection between two or more possible options. Some driving choices, such as selecting a route for travel, can be made before you start driving. Others, such as adjusting speed, selecting a safe travel path, and choosing how and when to communicate with others, are more difficult. Choices that occur as you drive are more difficult because they are made while the vehicle is moving and the traffic situation is changing. By making correct choices, you are able to reduce the risk that an unsafe event will occur, such as death or physical injury, and increase the chance that you will remain safe. As a driver, you constantly choose between your options and try to select the option that is best.

Driving choices must be made quickly, in real time, and usually without anyone's help. In any driving situation, you choose from five basic options: steering, braking, accelerating, signaling, and combinations of the first four. Your best choices help you cope with changing roadway conditions or sudden vehicle failures. Making good choices allows you to successfully manage space, time, and visibility and to drive safely.

WHAT WOULD YOU DO?
You are driving and encounter this traffic scene. What options are available to help you minimize the risk in this situation?

Lesson 1 Review

❶ What role do options play in the driving process?

❷ How do assumptions play a role in the driving process?

❸ Why are choices an important aspect of the driving process?

Responses to Manage Space and Time

OBJECTIVES

1. **Identify** highway conditions that determine a need for speed adjustment.
2. **Describe** how signaling helps you manage time and space.

KEY TERMS

♦ **human-perception time**
♦ **vehicle-reaction time**

Before you can successfully respond to a driving event, you must have adequate visibility and mastery of the skills to sense and search. You must give meaning to what is important in the driving scene. Then you must determine your options and make a choice. After you make a choice, you must also realize that it takes a little time for your choice to be translated into action. To respond properly, you must have the physical skills and the necessary space and time to complete the task. An awareness of how much time and space it actually takes for you and your vehicle to react is an important aspect of responsible driving.

What Happens After You Make a Choice?

In the split second after you have made a choice from your options, a set of mental instructions is sent to different parts of your body to respond as instructed. At that point, perception time ends and reaction time begins. It takes a little time for your muscles to respond and to carry out your choice to steer, brake, accelerate, or signal. During that time, the vehicle is moving. Once the action has been started, reaction time ends and vehicle-reaction time begins.

Controlling a vehicle takes a certain amount of time after an option is selected. The total time needed for a human being to determine his or her options and choose one is known as **human-perception time**. The time it takes a vehicle to respond is known as **vehicle-reaction time**. The four components of the total time and space needed to complete a controlling action are:

1. Human-Perception Time/Space
2. Human-Reaction Time/Space
3. Vehicle-Reaction Time/Space
4. Vehicle-Braking, -Steering, -Accelerating, or -Signaling Time/Space

ADJUSTING SPEED AND MANAGING TIME AND SPACE

As a driver, you will constantly have to adjust your speed. A change in highway conditions is one factor that determines whether a speed adjustment is necessary. Changes in visibility, traction, and space are the three most common highway conditions that require you to adjust speed.

The key idea of basic speed laws is to drive at a reasonable and proper speed for particular road and traffic conditions. This means you should be aware of conditions and drive accordingly. Both time and space are considerations. Every driver should allow a clear distance ahead to stop if necessary, because stopping takes a certain amount of time. If you travel too fast for conditions, it is more difficult for other drivers and pedestrians to predict your probable actions.

Visibility. You need to be able to see a certain distance ahead. A safe speed to drive is affected by the distance you can see ahead along your path of travel. For example, imagine that you can only see 200 feet ahead of your vehicle because of road or inclement weather conditions. Assume that you are traveling at a speed of 55 mph, a speed that requires 300 or so feet to stop. With such poor visibility, you could not stop your car in time to avoid hitting a stationary object in your path.

Stopping distance. Driving too fast is a major cause of crashes, injuries, and fatalities. It takes a while to stop a moving vehicle. Many persons drive too fast in the false belief that if the car in front suddenly started braking, they would react and brake and end up stopped the same distance apart. To recognize and react to a problem takes time. You must adjust your speed to suit visibility (weather conditions), the road (such as hills and curves), and the amount of traffic. Recall from Chapter 5 that the total stopping distance of a vehicle is made up of human perception, human-reaction time, vehicle-reaction time, and vehicle-braking distance.

Here are some useful rules of thumb involving total stopping distance:

- When you double your speed, it takes four times the distance to stop your vehicle.
- When you double your speed, your vehicle will have four times the destructive power in a crash.
- Wet roads can double stopping distance. Reduce your speed by about one-third on a wet road. For example, slow down from 55 mph to 35 mph.
- On packed snow, which reduces traction, reduce your speed by one-half or more.
- If the road is icy, reduce your speed to a crawl. Stop driving as soon as you can.
- Empty trucks require greater stopping distance. An empty vehicle has less traction. The brakes are designed to control the maximum weight of the unit; therefore, the brakes lock up more readily when the trailer is empty or lightly loaded. This can cause skidding and loss of control.

 Tips for New Drivers

MANAGING TIME

Effective time management begins before you get behind the wheel. Here are some tips:

▶ Make a conscious effort to understand and learn to judge time and speed factors. Try to develop a sense, for example, of how much longer it takes a vehicle to slow down and stop when moving at 50 mph than at 20 mph.

▶ Plan your route in advance, and always allow yourself plenty of time to reach your destination.

▶ Get traffic information from the radio or other sources to help you plan the best route of travel.

STEERING TO MANAGE TIME AND SPACE

One of the most-used driving techniques is steering. Steering helps you manage time and space. For instance, you manage time and space every time you make a lane change, because it takes you a few seconds of time and a certain amount of roadway distance to make the lane change. Lane changing can be a difficult and dangerous maneuver if you do not check your blind spots, but usually it is routine.

Under most circumstances, changing lanes involves gradual steering into the next lane. A gradual adjustment in steering should help other drivers who may not see your turn signal or drivers you don't see. Usually you should try to maintain speed and gradually steer to another lane. Turn the steering wheel gradually in the direction of the lane change and use a gradual steering recovery to straighten the vehicle when you're there.

ACCELERATING TO MANAGE TIME AND SPACE

In situations where other vehicles are moving toward the same space as your vehicle, acceleration is sometimes the best way to respond. Another situation when acceleration might help is where you need to clear crossing lanes where cross traffic does not have to stop. If you are stopped at an intersection on a side street and attempting to move across a busy 30-foot wide street, you need to have 6 to 8 seconds to cross this street.

SIGNALING TO MANAGE TIME AND SPACE

Signaling other drivers helps you manage time and space. Use the turn signal to alert other drivers about your intent to change lanes while entering or exiting traffic, to change lanes, to pass, or to enter or exit an expressway. When you signal other drivers, they can make their own adjustments to allow you to make these lane changes.

The use of the horn is another way to alert other highway users to your presence. The horn is used to call attention to the presence of your vehicle when you want to manage time and space with other drivers, when you want to warn them you're coming, or ask them to safely share the road. Be certain that you use your horn when necessary and that you do not abuse the use of your horn.

ADJUSTING SPEED AND VEHICLE POSITION ON CURVES

If you take a curve too fast, your tires lose traction with the road. Losing traction and going into a skid could cause your vehicle to veer off the road or roll over. Trucks and some recreational vehicles with a high center of gravity can roll over even at the posted speed limit for a curve.

At speeds above 30 mph, it takes less time (distance) to steer around an obstacle than to stop for it. But you must have identified an escape route in advance. **How can you identify an escape route in advance?**

Here are some tips for adjusting your speed on a curve:

- Slow to a safe speed before you enter a curve.
- Braking in a curve is dangerous because you can lock the wheels and cause a skid.
- Never exceed the posted speed limit for a curve.
- If the curved road is wet, reduce your speed by at least a third.

SLOWING ON DOWNGRADES

Going down hills requires you to adjust your speed, too. It's a good idea to slow down on downgrades because as you go downhill, your vehicle's speed increases.

- Never exceed the maximum safe speed on a downgrade.
- Check you rearview mirror for following traffic.
- Pick a lane where traffic is traveling about the same speed you are.
- Use your brakes periodically to control your speed.

WHAT WOULD YOU DO?
How would you respond to this situation? What action or actions do you take to minimize risk?

Lesson 2 Review

❶ Which highway conditions determine the need for speed adjustment?

❷ How does signaling help you manage time and space?

❸ How can effective time management help you reduce risk?

Managing Visibility

The best way to avoid collisions is to maintain adequate space all around your vehicle. Maintaining good visibility gives you adequate time to search, give meaning, determine options, decide on choices, and respond. Adequate space gives you room and time to take evasive action in the event of a probable crash.

How Do Time and Space Margins Relate to Your Intended Path of Travel?

The distance or margins of time you maintain between yourself and other vehicles on the road are important for safety purposes. It's important to understand these margins, which involve what you can see ahead. As a driver, you always need lead time to react, and during the time you react, your vehicle is moving forward in space.

Five margins that involve both time and space are important to your intended path of travel. From the most distant to the closest, these include:
- the visual lead margin
- the visual control zone margin
- the response zone
- the following interval
- the potential immediate crash zone

VISUAL LEAD MARGIN

Your **visual lead** is the distance you can see ahead of your vehicle. Visual lead margin is how far down the road you need to look for closed or changing visual signs. Search the roadway and off-road areas 20 to 30 seconds ahead for information that can help you plan a safe path of travel. Looking ahead this far gives you a big cushion of reaction time and distance and an opportunity to gently adjust speed or position your vehicle to handle a threatening situation.

VISUAL CONTROL ZONE

The **visual control zone** is where you identify objects/conditions that may require a response or continuous attention. It is the area in which you can see ahead and safely control your vehicle. This zone is 12 to 20 seconds ahead of you. Actions in this area could interfere with your planned path of travel or line of sight. But if you can see what's coming, you can control your vehicle in plenty of time.

OBJECTIVES
1. **Describe** five margins that are important on your intended path of travel.
2. **Identify** the rules for maintaining a safe margin between your vehicle and what you can see on the road ahead.

KEY TERMS
- visual lead
- visual control zone
- response zone
- following interval
- potential immediate crash zone

FYI

Dirty headlights limit visibility. Road grime on headlights can reduce illumination as much as 90 percent.

By adjusting speed, you can maneuver around the parked car after encountering the oncoming vehicle. *In what other types of situations should you adjust your speed?*

RESPONSE ZONE

In the **response zone**, immediate risk to your vehicle comes into play. This is the zone where you begin to respond to what you perceive, if necessary by taking the action or actions you need to take control or reduce risk. While you're driving, one of the following scenarios occurs:

- A car in front of you suddenly stops.
- A child or animal runs from between two cars.
- A traffic light suddenly changes from green to yellow.
- An object, such as a tree, falls across the road.

How long will it take to determine your response time? The response zone is 8 to 12 seconds ahead of you.

FOLLOWING INTERVAL

The **following interval** is the safe amount of time you should allow when following another vehicle or when being followed. The following zone is the same for either situation, expressed in terms of the distance or space you should allow to react safely. Under ideal conditions, always try to maintain a 4-second following interval between your vehicle and the vehicle ahead. Four to 8 seconds should be the minimum interval for stationary and moving objects crossing your path of travel, because it usually takes a vehicle at least 4 seconds to stop.

POTENTIAL IMMEDIATE CRASH ZONE

If an object suddenly appears in front of your vehicle, you may not be able to avoid it if you only have a few seconds to see it and to react. The **potential immediate crash zone** is that area directly in front and to the rear of your vehicle that will likely cause you to crash when a potential hazard becomes a real hazard. This zone is 0 to 4 seconds ahead of you.

Did You Know?

In 1903, Mary Anderson invented the first windshield wiper for automobiles. She wanted to improve visibility for drivers during bad weather.

SPEED AND VISIBILITY

Always try to maintain a safe margin between your vehicle and what you can see on the road ahead. There is an important relationship between safe driving visibility. Here are two general rules:

- You should always be able to stop within the distance you can see ahead.
- Fog, rain, or other conditions that impede your visibility require you to slow down.

In addition, you should slow down at night when you change to the low beams of your headlights, because you can't see as far ahead with low beams as you can with high beams.

?

WHAT WOULD YOU DO?
What options are available to help you minimize the risk in this situation?

Lesson 3 Review

❶ What are the five margins that are important on your intended path of travel?

❷ What are the rules for maintaining a safe margin between your vehicle and what you can see on the road ahead?

❸ What is the potential immediate crash zone?

Margins of Safety

OBJECTIVES

1. **Explain** how maintaining a margin of safety relates to minimizing risk.

2. **Describe** the rules for maintaining a space margin for safe driving.

3. **Describe** the rules for maintaining a visibility margin for safe driving.

4. **Describe** the rules for maintaining a time margin for safe driving.

KEY TERMS

◆ margin of safety
◆ space margin
◆ space cushion

To make any driving maneuver, you must allow a margin of safety. **Margins of safety** are areas of roadway large enough to allow you the space, time, and visibility you need for safe movement at any time. Keeping a margin of safety will help you become a more effective driver.

Why Do Drivers Need Margins of Safety?

You need a certain amount of distance for routine accelerating, decelerating, braking, and steering maneuvers. You need adequate space and even a little extra space to allow for mistakes that you or others make while completing a maneuver. This margin of space should provide room for quick lane changes, swerves, or a way out of an emergency situation. The size of the space margin will vary with weather, highway, and traffic conditions. In addition, you need margins of safety for managing visibility and time.

AN ADEQUATE SPACE MARGIN

As you drive, you must constantly deal with objects and vehicles that are close to your intended path of travel. You can minimize your risk by allowing a **space margin**, or an adequate amount of space between your vehicle and another. A safe space margin is called a **space cushion**. Adequate space margins allow a safe and appropriate amount of space to the front, sides, and back of the vehicle.

Here are three guidelines for maintaining adequate space margins.

Following distance. Under normal conditions, you should maintain a minimum 4-second following distance behind other vehicles. Following closer than this restricts your field of vision and doesn't allow you time to react safely to unexpected driving events. When following large vehicles or motorcycles, allow a 5- to 6-second following distance. As a matter of course, identify alternate escape paths in case of emergency.

Space behind. Controlling the space behind you is more difficult than controlling following distance. Avoid driving too slowly for conditions. When a car follows too closely (tailgating), encourage the tailgater to pass by slowing gradually and moving to the right side of the lane or roadway. As a precaution, allow more distance ahead and an escape route to at least one side. If you must stop suddenly, make every effort to signal. Be prepared to drive onto the shoulder of the road to avoid a crash, if necessary. When you find yourself in a long line of cars, change lanes or adjust your speed. Then get out of the situation as soon as is practical.

Dealing with the UNEXPECTED

INCREASING SPACE MARGINS

In certain circumstances, it is wise to increase your space margins. Increase your following distance to more than the normal 4 seconds in any of these situations:

▲ when weather or road conditions are poor
▲ when driving at night
▲ when driving at high speed
▲ when the driver behind you is following too closely
▲ when your vision of the road is impaired by a large vehicle in front of you

Driver Ed Online

Topic: Space cushion

For a link to more information on the importance of a space cushion, go to **drivered .glencoe.com**.

Activity: Using the information provided at this link, create a quiz about maintaining a space cushion around a vehicle when driving. Exchange quizzes with a partner to test each other's knowledge.

Space to the sides. The distance to your sides should be great enough to provide for errors in judgment and an escape path or way out. Therefore, you should try to have at least one car width of space to one side of your car. When feasible, it is best to have a space of at least 8 feet on both sides. If you must drive through areas of reduced space (less than one car width on either side), allow more space in front.

DETERMINING SPACE MARGINS

The space margin you maintain will depend on where you are going and what you intend to do. Lanes in the road are typically wider than the vehicles using them. There are normally at least five basic locations for a car in each lane. The center of the lane is the normal driving position and usually the safest and best place to be. When making a turn, one-half car width to the right of the lane is where you should be to prepare to make a right turn. Conversely, position your vehicle one-half car width to the left of the lane when preparing to make a left turn. At other times, you will straddle the lane line to the left (in the process of changing lanes to the left) or straddle the lane line to the right (in the process of changing lanes to the right). Other drivers may be expected to do the same.

SPACE MARGINS FOR WHAT YOU CANNOT SEE

You won't be able to anticipate every problem you encounter as a driver. Vehicles can pull into your path suddenly from concealed areas. For example, a car or bicycle you can't see could shoot out of a driveway. Therefore, try to leave an increased space margin for people or objects you cannot see.

Provide a little extra space when you pass driveways or intersections blocked from view by shrubbery, embankments, or buildings. If a left lane is available and free of traffic, move over one car width as you approach an area of reduced visibility. If a left lane is not available, move at least one-half car width or as close to the center of the roadway as possible.

Make sure the oncoming travel lane is clear before you pass. *How can you see if the oncoming travel lane ahead is clear to pass?*

Energy Tip

Although a scenic route may be more enjoyable, a limited-access highway tends to be much safer and more energy efficient. You will have fewer stops, starts, curves, and hills, and you will be able to maintain a steady speed for longer periods of time.

AN ADEQUATE VISIBILITY MARGIN

Selecting a path of travel is a continual process of deciding which options are best. Usually, a safe path of travel is where you want to go safely. Selecting a safe travel path depends to a great extent on margins you can see to either side. Under extraordinary circumstances, the shoulder of the roadway may sometimes be the best choice. Consider the following questions to help you in determining a good path of travel:

Which path best enhances visibility? Always try to position your vehicle so you have the best view for the situation. Hills, curves, obstructions, and other vehicles in the traffic stream often limit visibility. Positioning your vehicle where you can see well also allows others to see you more readily, particularly if you drive with your low-beam headlights or running lights on during the daytime.

Which path provides the clearest space to the sides? You need space to the sides to minimize risk from objects that could enter your path. You also need enough space to provide an escape path and extra space for possible errors.

Which path provides the smoothest flow of traffic? Going with the flow of traffic is a good idea in most situations. The path where all vehicles are moving at a reasonable speed for existing conditions provides the smoothest flow of traffic. Furthermore, the path with the smoothest traffic flow typically provides the best space visibility.

Dr. Francis C. Kenel

Staff Director of Safety (Retired), AAA

Risk means the chance of injury, damage, or loss. You must develop the knowledge, skills, and habits that will enable you to determine options and respond to risk.

The most important skill of good driving is positioning the vehicle so that you can see others and others can see you. When a vehicle is positioned properly, adjusting speed becomes easier. Equally important is using safety belts and restricting driving if you are not in top physical condition.

How can you position your vehicle properly?

AN ADEQUATE TIME MARGIN

Good timing may involve adjusting vehicle speed. An adequate time margin is critical for safe driving. To maintain it, you may have to adjust your path of travel, change speed, or both. Your first concern should be objects in your 4- to 8-second response zone. Making adjustments is especially important if an object is coming toward you or there is increased chance for error. For example, a motorist changing a flat tire near the road represents a higher level of risk that calls for a greater space margin as you approach.

When an object moves into your immediate 4- to 8-second path of travel, you must choose how much to decrease or increase speed and whether any adjustment to your space margin to either side is needed. Your decision depends on your ability to judge when and where other objects might enter your path of travel.

Timing is most important for situations involving multiple moving objects. This is especially true when you must deal with two or more objects at the same time and place, such as meeting traffic on a narrow bridge. Good timing allows you to deal with each object separately. It also provides you a chance to meet a moving object at a place with better space margins or visibility. Try to avoid meeting fast-moving vehicles in areas of reduced visibility.

TIME MARGINS IN EMERGENCY SITUATIONS

When any driving crisis occurs, the driver has limited time to interpret and react to it. The timing of driver response can be critical. Many collisions caused by inattention happen because drivers don't pay attention to the right thing at the right time and respond too late or not at all.

Allowing adequate time and space margins helps you drive safely. The driver must have an idea of how much time it takes to turn, change lanes, and complete most maneuvers. When you are busy with a maneuver, avoid spending time on any actions that are not part of the maneuver. The middle of a turn is not the time to downshift a manual transmission or to adjust the sun visor. You should plan and perform such actions before the actual turning process. If you forget or misjudge an action, recover from your mistake before you do anything else.

Many drivers don't pick the best times or places to perform maneuvers. Pick the best possible roadway and traffic conditions for what you want to do. For example, avoid passing or changing lanes in areas of reduced visibility. Avoid passing a big truck where there may be strong crosswinds. Remember that holes, bumps, and patches of wet leaves, ice, or water on the road can cause you to lose control.

Compromise. If you are faced with two dangerous situations, try to give the most room to the one with the greatest consequences and chance of happening.

TIME MARGINS AND TRAFFIC CONDITIONS

Traffic conditions can be more favorable at one time than another. Try to time your maneuvers for maximum safety. For instance, time a sharp turn into a narrow side road or driveway so that you can avoid meeting another car at the same moment you make a hard steering movement. Do not pass or change lanes when another vehicle is in your blind spot or when your vehicle is in another driver's blind spot. Proper timing of turn signals also is helpful. Time turning or other maneuvers so you can make them smoothly and gradually and also give other roadway users adequate time to react.

Missed turns. If you miss a turn, do not inconvenience other traffic because of your mistake. Simply go the next intersection, and turn there. Going around the block is much safer than a sudden or poorly positioned turn.

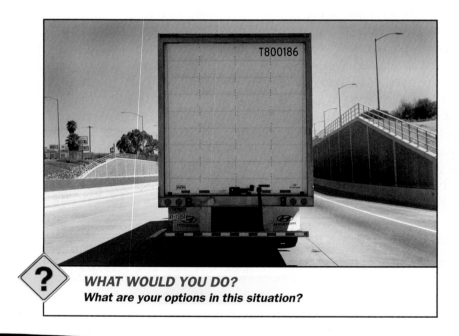

? **WHAT WOULD YOU DO?**
What are your options in this situation?

Lesson 4 Review

❶ How does maintaining a margin of safety relate to minimizing risk?

❷ What are the rules for maintaining a space margin for safe driving?

❸ What are the rules for maintaining a visibility margin for safe driving?

❹ What are the rules for maintaining a time margin for safe driving?

DRIVING RISKS

Some drivers take many unnecessary risks. By doing so, they are sources of danger to themselves and other road users. Study the picture below. Answer the following questions.

- How is the driver in the teal car taking a risk?
- How effective is the driver in maintaining space, time, and visibility?
- In what way is the driver in the teal car a danger to the truck driver?
- If you were the driver in the truck, how would you handle this situation?

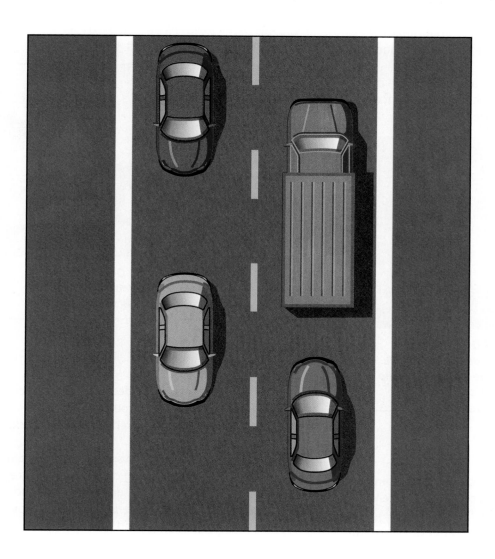

Key Points

Lesson 1

1. Options are potential choices in a driving situation. In the driving process, options are important because they help you make the best and safest choice possible. (Page 166)
2. In the driving process, assumptions are used when determining available options and making your final choice of which option has the greatest potential to make something good happen. (Page 167)
3. Correct choices enable you to reduce the risk of an unsafe situation and increase the chance that you will remain safe. (Page 168)

WHAT WOULD YOU DO?
You are driving and encounter this traffic scene. What options are available to help you minimize the risk in this situation?

Lesson 2

1. Changes in visibility, traction, and space are common highway conditions that require you to adjust speed. (Page 169)
2. Using your turn signal alerts other drivers about your intent to change lanes while entering or exiting traffic, changing lanes, passing, or entering or exiting an expressway. The use of the horn calls attention to the presence of your vehicle. (Page 171)

Lesson 3

1. Five margins that are important on your intended path of travel are the visual lead margin, the visual control zone margin, the response zone, the following interval, and the potential immediate crash zone. (Pages 173–175)
2. To maintain a safe margin between your vehicle and what you can see on the road, slow down in conditions that impede your visibility and always be able to stop within the distance that you can see ahead. (Page 175)

WHAT WOULD YOU DO?
What options are available to help you minimize the risk in this situation?

Lesson 4

1. A margin of safety provides you the distance, time, and visibility that you need for safe movement anytime, thereby minimizing risk. (Page 176)
2. To maintain an adequate space margin, maintain a 3-second following distance, be aware of the space behind you, and make sure the distance behind you is great enough to provide for errors in judgment and an escape path. (Pages 176–177)
3. In establishing an adequate visibility margin, consider which path best enhances your visibility, provides the clearest space to the sides, and provides the smoothest traffic flow. (Page 178)
4. To maintain an adequate time margin, you must be prepared to adjust your path of travel, change speed, or both. (Page 179)

On a separate sheet of paper, write the letter of the answer that best completes each sentence.

On a separate sheet of paper, write the word or phrase that best completes each sentence.

choice

human-perception time

visual lead

space cushion

1 The minimum following interval you should maintain under ideal conditions is
   a. 1 second.
   b. 3 seconds.
   c. 8 seconds.

2 When a vehicle is tailgating, you should
   a. speed up gradually.
   b. keep a constant speed and remain in the lane in which you are driving.
   c. slow gradually and move to the right side of the lane or roadway.

3 On a wet road, you should reduce your speed by
   a. one-third.
   b. one-fourth.
   c. one-fifth.

4 When you miss a turn,
   a. make a U-turn the minute you realize your mistake.
   b. stop your car and put it in Reverse as soon as traffic is clear.
   c. go the next intersection and turn there.

5 Events that you think might happen are
   a. options.
   b. comparisons.
   c. assumptions.

6 In fog and rain, you should
   a. speed up.
   b. slow down.
   c. do nothing.

7 A safe space margin is a _____.

8 _____ is the distance you can see ahead.

9 A _____ is the selection between two or more possible options.

10 The total time needed for a human being to determine his or her options and choose one is _____.

Writing

Driver's Log

In this chapter, you learned about options and choices and managing visibility, time, and space. Write two paragraphs in response to these questions:
1. In which driving environment do you think you will have the most difficulty managing visibility, time, and space?
2. What steps would you take to overcome these difficulties?

Project

Compare and contrast your responses to managing visibility, time, and space in urban and suburban driving to driving on a rural highway. As a motor-vehicle passenger, observe the differences in road surfaces, vehicle density, traffic signs, signals, and roadway markings, visibility, traveling speeds, etc. Write a one- to two-page paper on these results.

UNIT 3 CUMULATIVE REVIEW

This review tests your knowledge of the material in Chapters 7–8, and will help you review for your state driving test. On a separate sheet of paper, select the answer that best completes each statement.

1 Which is most important for driving?
a. sense of vision
b. sense of direction
c. sense of smell

2 Your visual system consists of your
a. eyes, perception, and central vision.
b. color vision, glare vision, and night vision.
c. retina, brain, and optic nerve.

3 Distance vision can be impaired if you
a. fail to react to a potential hazard.
b. wear scratched sunglasses.
c. drive very slowly in heavy traffic.

4 Depth perception is important for
a. judging the stopping distance of the vehicle in front of you.
b. focusing on oncoming traffic.
c. focusing while facing the sun's glare.

5 Good hearing is critical to your driving ability because
a. you need to hear the center-line rumble strip.
b. you use traffic sounds to alert you to situations around you.
c. you need to respond to your vehicle's pitch.

6 A forward/backward movement of your vehicle occurs when you
a. accelerate.
b. turn the steering wheel back and forth rapidly.
c. lose tire traction on the road.

7 When you can feel a vibration in your vehicle, you should
a. accelerate gently.
b. hit the brakes hard.
c. have your tires checked for balance.

8 As you drive, you need to look 20 to 30 seconds ahead so you can
a. react to potential roadway hazards.
b. move with traffic.
c. quickly change lanes.

9 When you approach an intersection with a traffic sign, you should
a. rely on the traffic sign to determine who has the right-of-way.
b. look first in the direction where you want to turn.
c. look to your left, right, and back to your left before you proceed.

10 When you use a ramp to enter or exit the freeway, you should
a. increase your speed gradually.
b. glance over your shoulder to be sure the road is clear where you want to go.
c. use your rearview mirrors to see vehicles in your blind spot.

11 When you are driving, your attention level should increase
a. when the vehicle in front of you makes a sudden move.
b. when you drive on a familiar road.
c. when you have been daydreaming.

12 Commentary driving can help a new driver by
a. providing feedback about your vehicle's safety features.
b. requiring a change in driving time.
c. identifying important traffic clues.

13 To make the best possible choices in a driving situation, you should
a. take as much time as you need to evaluate the situation.
b. choose your first option.
c. assess, interpret, and evaluate the available information.

14 If the road on which you are traveling has a posted recommended speed of 25 mph,
a. assume all drivers will drive at 25 mph.
b. see how fast other vehicles are moving.
c. assume the posted recommended speed is the maximum safe speed for this part of the road.

15 A driving choice that you might make as the traffic situation changes is
a. yelling out your window.
b. selecting the most direct travel route.
c. adjusting your speed for road conditions.

16 To drive at a reasonable speed, consider
a. how close you are traveling to the vehicle in front of you.
b. the time at which you need to arrive at your destination.
c. the posted highway markers.

17 When driving on a road with limited visibility,
a. allow at least a car length between your vehicle and the vehicle in front of you.
b. adjust your speed downward.
c. travel just slightly above the posted speed limit.

18 The distance required to stop your vehicle
a. increases as your speed increases.
b. decreases when roads are wet.
c. decreases when traction decreases.

19 When changing lanes,
a. signal and slow down.
b. try to maintain your speed as you gradually steer into the other lane.
c. signal and quickly accelerate into the lane.

20 To safely drive through a curve,
a. reduce your speed if the road is wet.
b. maintain your speed in curves.
c. brake in curves to avoid locking wheels.

21 For safety purposes,
a. allow a visual lead of 20 to 30 seconds.
b. maintain your speed when you change from high beams to low beams.
c. allow a larger interval of time between your vehicle and the vehicle ahead than the vehicle behind you.

22 Margins of safety are
a. needed to allow adequate visibility, time, and space to maneuver your vehicle.
b. not affected by traffic conditions.
c. needed to correct defective vehicle equipment.

23 To maintain an adequate space margin,
a. allow a 4- to 5-second following distance when following motorcycles.
b. signal tailgaters to pass you.
c. drive onto the shoulder to stop quickly.

24 You can maintain an adequate time margin by
a. avoiding oncoming traffic on narrow bridges.
b. adjusting your space margin for wide vehicles.
c. increasing or decreasing your speed as needed.

25 You may avoid a driving crisis by
a. changing lanes during poor visibility.
b. turning around immediately if you miss a turn.
c. scanning for patches of water on the road.

Challenge Question

Drivers who are adept at giving meaning may conclude that
a. an emergency vehicle is approaching when other vehicles slow and pull to the side of the road.
b. the first vehicle to arrive at an intersection always has the right-of-way.
c. flashing lights on the roadway indicate you should brake quickly.

UNIT 4
APPLYING EFFECTIVE DRIVING

How can you apply the foundations of driving?

You will apply the foundations of driving such as accelerating, steering, and braking, time and time again, in a few basic situations. The foundations of effective driving will be constantly applied on several types of streets and through various types of intersections. You will deal regularly not only with other vehicles but also with pedestrians, cyclists, and even animals on the roadway. Knowing how to handle these common situations allows you to become a responsible driver. This unit will help you to apply the foundations you have learned in the previous units.

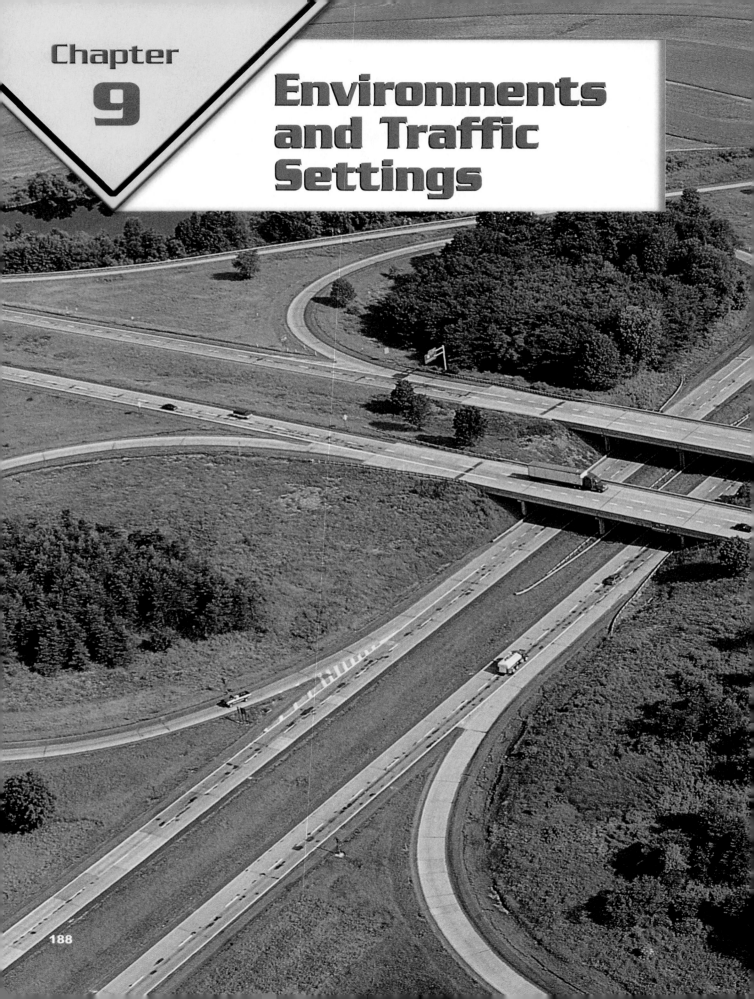

Chapter
9
Environments and Traffic Settings

How Should You Drive in Different Traffic Settings?

Whether you drive on a busy multiple-lane expressway or a quiet country road, you must be alert to the factors that will affect your driving. Learning how to manage visibility, time, and space in different traffic settings will help you build driving expertise. There are many situations and hazards to watch out for on residential streets, on urban and busy suburban streets, on multiple-lane highways, and even on country roads. Knowing how to watch for potential hazards helps you manage risk.

Driver Ed *Online*

For additional activities, visit **drivered.glencoe.com**. Here you will find:

◆ **Web Link Exercises**
◆ **eFlashcards**
◆ **Practice Driving Tests**

Residential Streets

OBJECTIVE

1. **Describe** the special factors that affect driving on residential streets.

KEY TERM

♦ judgment call

What Factors Affect Driving on Residential Streets?

Residential streets run through neighborhoods in which people live and feel at home. Traffic usually moves both ways, and residential streets are relatively narrow. Traffic is light on these streets, compared to driving in downtown urban areas or on superhighways. However, driving on residential streets presents special hazards to the driver. For one thing, people (especially children) don't always watch for oncoming vehicles.

DRIVING PATTERNS ON RESIDENTIAL STREETS

When driving on residential streets, you need to change your driving patterns because the streets are not as empty as they appear. If you think so, try to adopt a different attitude! You should expect surprises on residential streets. It may not be your fault if you have a collision, but imagine the pain you would live with if you hit a child, a beloved family pet, or an elderly pedestrian who suddenly moved out in front of your vehicle.

SPEED ON RESIDENTIAL STREETS

Driving at slower speeds is essential on residential streets because it allows you more time to react to threats, such as a child darting out from behind a parked car. Make a conscious effort to drive 25 mph or slower on all residential streets. Remember that the legal speed limit on residential streets is usually 25 mph, unless otherwise posted.

Kids can be easily distracted. *How can you prepare and adjust your driving for kids?*

PEDESTRIANS AND RESIDENTIAL STREETS

Pedestrians have the right-of-way at intersections, whether or not crosswalks are painted on the street. Always yield to pedestrians.

Be aware that children are the primary pedestrians on neighborhood streets and that they are the most likely victims of careless drivers. Most young children—especially those under nine years of age—have great difficulty in making good judgments about traffic dangers. Children may be playing and not paying attention to traffic. A child may chase a baseball out into the street. When your visibility is poor, slow down more than usual and prepare to take evasive action if necessary.

RESIDENTIAL STREETS WITH PARKED CARS

Approaching oncoming traffic on a narrow residential street with parked cars on one or both sides of the street can be a tricky situation.

If you are on the side with parked cars, you are not required to pull in behind those cars and wait for traffic to pass. The vehicles traveling in opposite directions should share the remaining lane if there's room. There may be times when there isn't room for both cars to squeeze by each other in that single lane. When this happens, you must pull over and wait behind the parked vehicles.

The proper procedure is to slow down and signal that you're going to pull out. The oncoming driver may then have to move over and make room for you to pass.

Driving on residential streets where cars are parked along the side of the roadway is a **judgment call**, a situation in which the driver should size up the situation and then use good judgment. If you think there's enough room, communicate to the other driver by signaling and proceed.

RESIDENTIAL STREETS AS SHORTCUTS

You should avoid using residential streets as shortcuts to save distance and time. The more that you use residential streets of a particular neighborhood as shortcuts, the more you disrupt that area's quality of life by increasing the area's noise and pollution and threatening the safety of children.

TRAFFIC LAWS

Remember that most collisions occur close to home. Therefore, it's very important to drive safely near your residence. Do not take chances, even on short local trips to the shopping mall or when running errands or going to or from school in your own neighborhood. Always observe all rules of the road.

Driver Ed Online

Topic: Pedestrian safety

For a link to more information on pedestrian safety in residential areas, go to **drivered.glencoe.com**.

Activity: Using the information provided at this link, work in small groups to create two checklists of safety tips—one for drivers and one for pedestrians.

? WHAT WOULD YOU DO?
How would you manage risk in this situation?

Lesson 1 Review

❶ What special factors affect driving on residential streets?

❷ Why should you avoid using residential streets as shortcuts?

❸ Typically, what is the speed limit on residential streets?

Urban and Suburban Streets

OBJECTIVES

1. **Describe** the special factors that affect driving on urban and suburban streets.
2. **List** ways to manage visibility, time, and space when driving in urban and suburban settings.

Urban and busy suburban streets can make driving a real challenge, especially for new drivers. Some of the challenges include heavy traffic, large numbers of businesses and pedestrians, and many traffic signals. By anticipating the possibilities, you can manage visibility, time, and space effectively in urban and suburban driving.

What Special Factors Affect Urban and Suburban Driving?

Cities and suburbs can be hectic, crowded places. Cars, buses, trucks, and other vehicles crowd the streets. For much of the day, pedestrians may fill the sidewalks. People can cross the street at any time. Double-parked vehicles often block visibility, and potholes may interrupt traffic flow.

TRAFFIC DENSITY

Traffic is often very dense in urban areas and in crowded suburban areas such as around businesses and shopping malls. Here you will generally drive among more vehicles than you will in residential or rural driving. The traffic is not only dense, it's often slow moving or constantly stopping and starting. Threatening situations can occur more frequently. Maintaining a margin of space around your vehicle can be difficult when other vehicles are crowding around.

NUMBER OF PEDESTRIANS

Pay attention to pedestrians in crowded areas. At certain times of the day, for instance, business districts and malls seem to overflow with people: workers, shoppers, children, and others constantly move in and out of buildings. Expect to encounter pedestrians anywhere. Never assume that pedestrians will see you or even that they will obey traffic rules or signals. Watch for people on foot, and be prepared to yield the right-of-way to them, even if they are jaywalking.

City streets, crowded with vehicles and pedestrians, demand an extra degree of driver alertness. *How can you ensure that you remain alert while driving in city streets?*

INTERSECTIONS

Busy streets are filled with intersections. Urban and suburban intersections are frequently jammed with both vehicles and pedestrians moving in all directions. You may have to wait to cross a crowded intersection, even when the traffic light is green. When approaching or crossing any intersection, use maximum care.

Congested city streets severely limit your ability to search ahead and manage time and space. *How do these limitations affect your ability to drive?*

SLOW OR IRREGULAR TRAFFIC FLOW

On crowded streets, vehicles often move in packs or lines. This movement may be steady or with frequent starts and stops. As a driver, you'll usually have to move with the flow of traffic.

Several things can stop or slow traffic. Vehicles stopping to park or parked vehicles pulling away from the curb may interrupt the flow of traffic. Roadwork or construction can also slow traffic.

While you may move more slowly than you'd like to in congested areas, it is usually dangerous to try to move any faster than the flow of traffic.

POTHOLES AND OTHER ROAD DEFECTS

In cities and suburbs with heavy traffic and winter weather, roads become worn and can develop potholes and rough surfaces. These kinds of road defects slow traffic, damage vehicles, and pose a potential danger.

How Can You Manage Visibility, Time, and Space in Urban and Suburban Driving?

Crowded areas and heavy traffic place many demands on you as a driver. Several factors tend to limit visibility in urban and suburban driving. Double-parked vehicles, as well as parked vehicles, can partially block your view, as can buses, trucks, and vans when parked or moving. By knowing the special factors to be alert for when driving in cities and suburbs, you can minimize your own driving risk while managing the factors of visibility, time, and space.

GUIDELINES FOR MANAGING VISIBILITY IN CITIES AND SUBURBS

Here are some tips to help you manage visibility on urban and suburban streets:

- Search 1 to 2 blocks (or 20 to 30 seconds) ahead and from one side of the street to the other. Do not focus on just one object in your driving path.
- Check your rearview and sideview mirrors to monitor traffic every time you approach an intersection or when you intend to change position or speed.

Energy Tip

Avoid "jackrabbit" starts when traffic signals first turn green. Search the intersection before proceeding on a fresh green light. Accelerating gradually saves fuel—and it is safer.

PROBLEM BEHAVIOR

When you search the roadway, observe the behavior of other drivers for clues to potential problems. Watch for drivers:

▶ talking with others in the car or on a cell phone.

▶ smoking, eating, reading, or looking at a map.

▶ with unusual postures at the wheel, which may indicate intoxication.

▶ signaling late or not at all.

▶ moving too slowly or too rapidly or following too closely.

▶ drifting from side to side in their lane.

▶ whose view may be obstructed.

● Keep alert to the movement of vehicles four or more vehicles ahead of you so that you can anticipate when other drivers are braking or planning to turn. However, always be prepared for stopping or turning vehicles at all times.

● Be alert for pedestrians darting out from between parked vehicles or crossing streets illegally.

● Be on the lookout for warning signs and signals. Also be alert for the sirens and flashing lights of police vehicles, fire engines, ambulances, and other emergency vehicles.

● Use good sense when passing entrances and exits for apartment buildings, parking lots, and the like because of vehicles entering and leaving such areas. Often they are not visible until the last moment.

GUIDELINES FOR MANAGING TIME IN CITIES AND SUBURBS

Paying attention to how long it might take you to react to situations you encounter is particularly important. Follow these guidelines for managing time while driving in cities and suburbs:

● Drive at a moderate speed. Use the searching, giving meaning, options, choosing, and responding processes to help you identify objects or conditions that could increase the level of risk, particularly as you approach intersections (see **Figure 9.1**).

● Always be ready to stop or steer to avoid a collision. Dense traffic makes some drivers tense, impatient, and sometimes reckless.

● Understand that braking is often the only response you can make in city and suburban traffic to avoid a collision. When you spot a possible threatening condition, take your foot off the accelerator and place it just over the brake pedal without pushing down. By "covering your brake" in this manner, you reduce reaction time if you need to slow down or stop.

FYI

Rear-end crashes are more common than any other kind. Too often, drivers follow more closely than they should and are unable to stop in time. The increased chance of being struck in the rear while driving in the city makes it all the more important to monitor your mirrors effectively.

- Give other drivers and pedestrians maximum time to see and react to you. Drive with your low-beam headlights on, and always signal your intentions well in advance.
- When planning to drive, give yourself extra time for driving in city and suburban traffic, particularly during rush hours and other busy periods. Know what route you will be traveling, and listen to the radio for traffic information before setting out.

GUIDELINES FOR MANAGING SPACE IN CITIES AND SUBURBS

Keep a margin of space around your vehicle, although this is difficult in crowded driving conditions. Use these guidelines to manage space in city and suburban traffic:

- Do not follow other vehicles too closely, even in bumper-to-bumper traffic. Never follow less than 3 seconds behind.
- When stopping behind a vehicle, stop well back (20 to 30 feet) and watch the rearview mirror until two or three vehicles have stopped behind you. Then you can move up slightly, making sure that you can see the tires on the vehicle in front of your vehicle touch the road. Wait for the vehicle ahead to move before you start moving forward.
- When possible, keep a wide margin of space between your vehicle and parked vehicles. Watch for people leaving parked vehicles and for vehicles pulling out suddenly.
- Avoid driving in the blind spots of other drivers on multiple-lane streets. Either move ahead of the other vehicles or drop back.
- Keep as much space as you can between your vehicle and vehicles in the oncoming lanes. Identify an escape path to which you can steer.

FIGURE 9.1

URBAN AND SUBURBAN SEARCHING

In urban and suburban areas, search carefully for pedestrians, cyclists, and other vehicles at or approaching intersections. Before entering an intersection, make sure nothing is blocking your intended path of travel.

WHAT WOULD YOU DO?
You are driving through the city during rush hour. What steps will you take to manage visibility, time, and space?

Lesson 2 Review

❶ What are some special factors that affect urban and suburban driving?

❷ What actions can you take to manage visibility, time, and space when you are driving in urban and suburban settings?

❸ What problem behavior might you observe in other drivers?

Multiple-Lane Expressways

OBJECTIVES

1. **Describe** the special factors that affect driving on multiple-lane expressways.
2. **List** ways to manage visibility, time, and space when driving on multiple-lane expressways.

KEY TERMS

- ◆ interchange
- ◆ merging traffic
- ◆ entrance ramp
- ◆ limited-access expressway
- ◆ controlled-access expressway

Traveling on multiple-lane, high-speed highways poses special challenges for drivers. **What types of challenges do these highways pose?**

Traveling on multiple-lane expressways is usually safer and faster than traveling on local roads. Driving at higher speeds is demanding, however. You need to concentrate fully in order to manage visibility, time, and space.

What Special Factors Affect Driving on Multiple-Lane Expressways?

Driving on a multiple-lane expressway is quite different from driving on urban streets or rural roads. You almost never need to stop. There are usually two or more lanes of traffic moving quickly in the same direction. Cars, trucks, buses, and other vehicles pass you at high speeds, and passing is sometimes quite frequent. The scenery seems to whiz by, along with route markers and other road signs containing all sorts of information. You may enter and leave the roadway only at certain points, and you can usually connect to an intersecting limited-access expressway without stopping.

LIMITED ENTRANCES AND EXITS

Entrance and exit ramps on multiple-lane expressways may be many miles or just a mile apart. Entrances and exits are usually made from the extreme right lane, although there are a few entrance and exit ramps located in the extreme left lane.

Large, well-lit signs posted along the expressway tell you when you are approaching an exit or interchange some distance in advance. **Interchanges** are points where two highways cross, such as large nonstop intersections where you can enter or leave the expressway or connect with a highway going in another direction.

Merging traffic means that traffic is entering the expressway, usually from an interchange. Interchanges are composed of through lanes, ramps, and speed-change lanes. Through lanes are nonstop lanes that continue through interchanges. Ramps are short, one-way roads connecting two expressways. **Entrance ramps** allow you to enter another expressway. Speed limits on ramps typically range from 25 to 45 miles per hour (see **Figure 9.2**). Speed-change lanes are short lanes next to the main travel lanes of an expressway. A deceleration lane allows vehicles to reduce speed to exit; an acceleration lane lets vehicles increase speed to merge with traffic.

HIGHER SPEED LIMITS

Expressway speed limits are always higher than those on city streets and most rural roads. Many allow speeds of 55 miles per hour, 65 miles per hour, or higher. Higher speeds mean that drivers must manage time and space with particular care when following and passing vehicles, changing lanes, and reducing speed. High-speed collisions result in more damage and serious injuries than those occurring at lower speeds.

FREQUENT PASSING

Passing other vehicles and having other vehicles pass you is an integral part of driving on multiple-lane expressways. Depending on the roadway and on your lane position and speed, you may find yourself being passed on your left, on your right, or on both sides simultaneously. Traffic is one way, so at least you don't have to worry about vehicles approaching from the opposite direction.

CARPOOL LANES

Many urban and suburban areas have placed special carpool lanes on freeways or expressways for buses and carpool drivers. These lanes were created as an incentive to people who are saving gasoline and reducing overall traffic on the road. A carpool is usually a car containing the driver and at least one passenger, often one sharing a ride on the way to work. These special lanes are referred to as high occupancy vehicle (HOV) lanes. HOV lanes cannot be used by people driving alone, by single drivers passing vehicles in adjacent lanes, or by trucks with three or more axles, regardless of the number of passengers in the truck.

PHYSICAL BARRIERS

Many states today have built four-lane or wider divided roads with some type of physical barrier, such as a guardrail, a median strip, or a barrier in some places. Multiple-lane roadways with the barrier protection allow for safety from oncoming traffic. However, such barriers have their own potential problems since you can run into them.

TRUCKS AND OTHER LARGE VEHICLES

Trucks, tractor-trailers, buses, and other large vehicles add special challenges to driving on multiple-lane expressways because they hamper visibility. Large vehicles can buffet smaller vehicles with wind gusts as they pass, pushing them a bit off their course.

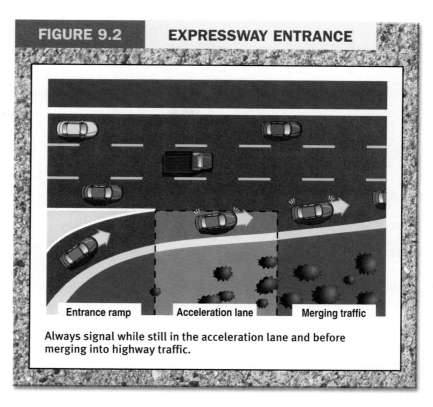

FIGURE 9.2   EXPRESSWAY ENTRANCE

Entrance ramp   Acceleration lane   Merging traffic

Always signal while still in the acceleration lane and before merging into highway traffic.

SAFETY TIP

When passing a vehicle in the center lane of a highway that has three or more lanes of traffic traveling in the same direction, be careful of other vehicles passing on that vehicle's other side. They may wind up in your intended travel path.

You need considerably more time to pass a truck or bus than to pass another vehicle because of their larger size and length. If you are traveling at 60 mph, it takes you 5 to 7 seconds longer to pass a tractor-trailer truck traveling at 50 mph than it would to pass a car.

How Can You Manage Driving on Multiple-Lane Expressways?

Understanding the guidelines for managing visibility, time, and space on expressways is crucial in reducing your risk of a collision or other mishaps.

Managing visibility, time, and space is very difficult when traveling on today's high-speed, high-density urban expressways. *How can you try to manage visibility, time, and space on urban expressways?*

GUIDELINES FOR MANAGING VISIBILITY ON MULTIPLE-LANE EXPRESSWAYS

- Drive with your low beams on at all times. Use your high beams on very dark expressways with no vehicles.
- Search 20 to 30 seconds ahead for vehicles, objects, animals, and even pedestrians on or near the roadway.
- Watch for danger at entrances and exits.
- Position your vehicle so that large vehicles do not block your view of the roadway.
- Check your rearview and sideview mirrors frequently to monitor the position of traffic around you.
- Always signal your intention to change lanes, merge, or exit well in advance.
- Check several vehicles ahead to know when other drivers are slowing down or planning to pass or change lanes.
- Look for road signs to learn what the speed limit is and to know when your exit is approaching and which side it is on.

GUIDELINES FOR MANAGING TIME ON MULTIPLE-LANE EXPRESSWAYS

- Plan your route ahead of time.
- When you merge into traffic, try to enter the stream of vehicles at the speed they are traveling.
- Use the searching, giving meaning, options, choosing, and responding processes to help you identify nearby threatening conditions.
- Always adjust your speed and following distance so that you have at least 4 seconds to stop or steer evasively in case of an emergency. Adjust your speed to avoid traveling in packs of vehicles.
- Adjust for vehicles that may have trouble keeping up with the flow of traffic.
- When an exit lane is available, move over toward the exit lane as soon as you can. Reduce your speed in the exit lane.
- Avoid driving on congested highways during peak traffic periods or in bad weather. Allow extra time if you must drive.

GUIDELINES FOR MANAGING SPACE ON MULTIPLE-LANE EXPRESSWAYS

- Allow a gap of at least 4 seconds when merging with other traffic, changing lanes, or entering an expressway from an entrance lane.
- Adjust your vehicle's position for the prevailing traffic speed and for road and weather conditions. Allow yourself a margin of space to accelerate, brake, and steer. Identify an escape path to which you can steer.
- Make room for vehicles entering the expressway.
- If you must cross several lanes, move over one lane at a time, signaling each time.
- Never cut in too soon in front of a vehicle you are passing.
- If a vehicle is tailgating you, change lanes when it is safe to let the vehicle pass.
- Be alert for places where highways may narrow, and reduce your speed.

Energy Tip

When traveling on the highway, use overdrive gears. Overdrive decreases the car's engine speed, which saves gas and reduces engine wear.

What Special Factors Affect Limited-Access-Expressway Driving?

Some multiple-lane roadways severely limit the places where they may be accessed. **Limited-access expressways** include freeways, interstate highways, expressways, toll roads, parkways, and turnpikes. Limited-access or **controlled-access expressways** allow vehicles to enter and exit only at specific places, usually a mile or so apart. On a limited-access highway, vehicles can enter and leave the roadway only at interchanges. This allows traffic on these expressways to move faster than traffic on local roads.

WHAT WOULD YOU DO?
You are in the left-lane of a crowded multiple-lane highway. Suddenly you realize you are approaching your exit, which is all the way over on the right. How will you handle this?

Lesson 3 Review

❶ What factors affect driving on multiple-lane expressways?

❷ What actions can a driver take to manage visibility, time, and space on an expressway?

❸ What factors affect driving on limited-access expressways?

Rural Roads

OBJECTIVES

1. **Describe** the special factors that affect driving on rural roads.
2. **List** ways to manage visibility, time, and space when driving on rural roads.

Country, or rural, driving often seems easier than either city or suburban driving. Traffic is usually much lighter. There are few pedestrians and not as many human distractions. However, driving in rural areas does pose a number of challenges. More than half all occupant fatalities occur on rural roads.

What Special Factors Affect Driving on Rural Roads?

When driving on rural roads, be especially alert for off-road conditions that limit your ability to see or maneuver. These conditions can include the condition of the roadway, high speeds, slow-moving vehicles, unusual sight obstructions, and even animals darting out onto the roadway.

ROAD CONDITIONS

Drivers on rural roads must exercise special care when passing other vehicles and when driving on loose, low-traction road surfaces. Most rural roads are narrow, and many are somewhat rough. Most rural roads are two-lane, two-way roadways. Curves may be sharper and hills may be steeper than on city streets. Rural roads may be concrete, asphalt, or gravel. They may even be dirt roads, with or without a shoulder. Some rural roads may even have drainage ditches close to both sides. At night, almost all rural roads are poorly lit—or not lit at all.

Snow on the road and a ditch along the side make maneuvering on this roadway difficult. *How do these conditions make maneuvering difficult?*

You may encounter slow-moving vehicles more frequently in rural areas. *How should you respond to these vehicles?*

HIGHER SPEED, FEWER CONTROLS

Sound judgment is more important than ever when driving in rural areas. Roads in these areas typically have higher speed limits than city streets. You will encounter fewer traffic lights, intersections, and stop signs. At railroad crossings, there may be no signs, signals, or gates. Drivers must remain alert for traffic crossing the roadway every now and then.

SLOW-MOVING VEHICLES

Watch for vehicles moving much slower than the flow of traffic. Tractors and other farm equipment creep along the road at much slower speeds than other vehicles. As a result, drivers on rural roads often have to pass such slow-moving vehicles. Doing so can be dangerous because the roads are not always well marked. Some types of farm equipment, such as harvesters, are very wide, limiting the visibility of following drivers and making passing extremely difficult.

SIGHT OBSTRUCTIONS

Different kinds of sight obstructions exist in rural areas than in the city. Trees, bushes, and orchards or tall crops growing near the road all limit visibility for drivers on country roads. These obstructions can make driving even more challenging on narrow, winding, or sharply curving roads.

Dealing with the UNEXPECTED

HORSEBACK RIDERS

When driving on rural roads, search the roadway and off-road area ahead. Here are tips to follow if you see a rider on horseback.

▲ Reduce your speed and pass slowly.
▲ Give the horse and rider as much leeway as possible.
▲ Never sound your horn to warn of your approach.

When driving on low-traction roadways, lower your speed. **Why is it important to lower your speed on these roadways?**

Hills and curves reduce forward visibility. As you near the top of a hill or the apex of a curve, your view of the road ahead will be limited. The steeper the grade or the sharper the curve, the less you can see.

ANIMALS AND OBJECTS ON THE ROAD

Watch for animals near or on the road. Deer, dogs, raccoons, ground squirrels, cows, and other animals—both wild and domestic—frequently are on or near rural roads. Dogs sometimes chase cars.

Dangerous objects to look out for on rural roads can include fallen rocks, tree branches, and wet leaves.

How Can You Manage Visibility, Time, and Space in Rural Driving?

Do not underestimate the risks of rural driving. In cities and suburbs, there is a greater danger of colliding with another vehicle. In the country, there is a greater chance of your losing control and colliding with a fixed object or overturning. Drive cautiously at all times. Use low-beam headlights during daylight hours to make it easier for other vehicles to see you when trees and brush block visibility.

Because there is less traffic, many drivers are not very attentive when driving on rural roads. More than 50 percent of occupant fatalities on rural roads and highways involve only one vehicle. In most of these deaths, the driver drifts or steers off the road and loses control. You must remain fully attentive at all times. Just as you would while driving on city streets, use the searching, giving meaning, options, choosing, and responding processes. Be ready to deal with the unexpected.

GUIDELINES FOR MANAGING VISIBILITY IN RURAL AREAS

Make sure you can see and be seen on rural roads. Here are some guidelines to help you manage visibility on country roads (see **Figure 9.3**):

- During the day, always drive with low-beam headlights on. Use high beams at night on very dark roads when there are no other vehicles around.
- Search ahead 20 to 30 seconds, looking for vehicles, pedestrians, animals, and objects on or near the roadway. If road or weather conditions reduce your visibility, reduce your speed.

FIGURE 9.3 RURAL VISIBILITY

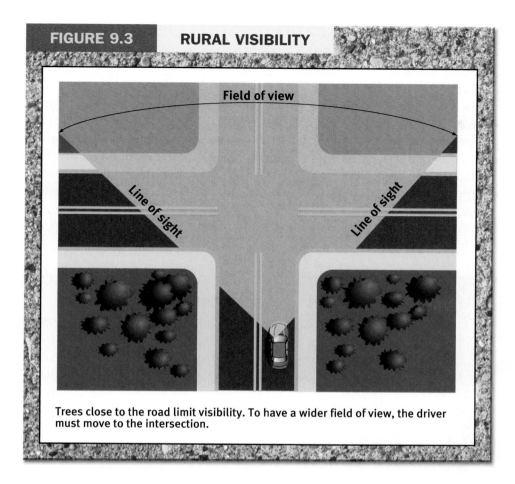

Field of view

Line of sight

Line of sight

Trees close to the road limit visibility. To have a wider field of view, the driver must move to the intersection.

- Identify objects or conditions within 12 to 15 seconds ahead that may pose a danger. If you cannot see that far, slow down until you can.
- Drive at a speed that will let you respond safely to threatening conditions that may be just over a hill or around a curve.
- When driving behind large vehicles, leave enough space so that they do not block your view of potential dangers.
- Always signal your intention to turn, to pull over, to pass, and to get back into your lane.

Bill Wen

Safety/Security Officer, LYNX
Central Florida Regional Transportation Authority
Orlando, FL

Advice FROM THE EXPERTS

Ask yourself three questions while driving: (1) What can I do to reduce the probability of a dangerous event? (2) How can I increase my opportunity to manage a dangerous event should one occur? (3) If a collision is unavoidable, how can I reduce its consequences?

Regardless of the driving environment, the first objective is to prevent a high-risk situation from developing by improving your visibility to others and by giving yourself enough time and space.

What steps can you take to improve your visibility to others?

GUIDELINES FOR MANAGING TIME IN RURAL AREAS

Since road and traffic conditions are different in the country, make allowances for where you are. Use these guidelines to help you manage time on rural roads.

- Watch for slow-moving vehicles. Adjust your speed as needed.
- Reduce your speed as you approach intersections, particularly those without stop signs or stoplights. Be prepared to slow down further or even stop.
- Reduce your speed when driving on gravel, dirt, or other low-traction road surfaces.
- When approaching or passing an animal on or near the road, drive slowly in case the animal bolts across your path.
- Allow extra time for driving on unfamiliar roads. Plan your route in advance.

GUIDELINES FOR MANAGING SPACE IN RURAL AREAS

Space considerations in rural areas are different than in city and suburban areas. Follow these guidelines for managing space on rural roads.

- Search the road for vehicles, animals, or objects that could threaten your safety, and weigh the consequences of acting to avoid the threat against the danger of collision.
- Adjust your following distance for speed, traffic, roadway, and off-road conditions that affect your ability to see. Identify an escape path to which you can steer.
- On two-lane roads, keep as much space as possible between your vehicle and oncoming traffic. If a vehicle is tailgating you, give it as much space as possible to pass and pull in front of you. If there is a vehicle ahead of you, increase your following distance to 4 seconds or longer.
- Never pass on curves or hills when you do not have a clear path ahead on which to complete the pass.

?

WHAT WOULD YOU DO?
You are traveling on a two-way hilly road that has many sharp curves. What special factors affect visibility? What are some ways to manage time and space?

Lesson 4 Review

❶ What are some special factors that affect rural driving?

❷ What actions can you take to manage visibility, time, and space when you drive on rural roads?

❸ How do rural roads differ from roads in cities or suburbs?

NAMES AND MEANINGS OF ROADWAYS

A route in a rural area is generally described as a *road*. A roadway within an urban area is usually called a *street*. Streets are usually paved and have more traffic, while rural routes are usually less traveled.

The roadways that connect cities and towns have many names, which vary somewhat in meaning. A highway is a main public roadway, especially one that runs between cities. An expressway is a high-speed divided highway with limited access that has more than one lane running in each direction. A freeway, sometimes called a *superhighway*, is generally a synonym for expressway, but usually refers to a highway that has no tolls.

A turnpike is a road, usually an expressway, where drivers are expected to pay a toll. The word *turnpike* comes from early days when travelers on a road stopped at gates made of logs or pikes. When a toll was paid, the pike was opened or turned, allowing the travelers to pass through. A toll road may also be called a *tollway*.

A beltway is a highway that goes around an urban area. A parkway is a wide, landscaped highway that may be limited to noncommercial vehicles. Except for occasional rest stops, there may be few or no commercial establishments, such as stores or office buildings, on a parkway.

WHAT DO YOU THINK NOW?

What do names and meanings of roadways tell you about the road systems in the United States?

Key Points

Lesson 1

1 Special factors that affect driving in residential areas include narrow streets, different driving patterns, reduced speeds, pedestrians on the streets, and the presence of parked cars. (Pages 190–191)

Lesson 2

1 Special factors that affect driving in urban and suburban areas are traffic density, multiple-lane streets, number of pedestrians, number of intersections, slow or irregular traffic flow, lower speed limits, sight obstructions, and potholes and other road defects. (Pages 192–193)

2 Some ways to manage visibility, time, and space on city streets are to search 1 to 2 blocks ahead, use your mirrors to monitor traffic, signal early, be ready for pedestrians and hidden exits, always be prepared to steer or stop, and keep a margin of space around your vehicle. (Pages 193–194)

Lesson 3

1 Special factors that affect driving on multiple-lane highways are higher speed limits, limited entrances and exits, frequent passing, and the presence of trucks and other large vehicles. (Pages 196–198)

2 Some ways to manage visibility, time, and space on multiple-lane expressways are to signal when changing lanes, position your vehicle so that you can see and be seen, adjust your speed to avoid traveling in packs, and plan your route ahead of time. (Pages 198–199)

Lesson 4

1 Factors that affect driving on rural roads are road conditions, higher speeds, fewer traffic controls, slow-moving vehicles, sight obstructions, and animals and objects on the road. (Pages 200–201)

2 Among the ways to manage visibility, time, and space on rural roads are to identify dangerous objects 12 to 15 seconds ahead, drive slowly if an animal is nearby, and avoid passing if your view is not clear. (Page 202)

WHAT WOULD YOU DO?
You are driving through the city during rush hour. What steps will you take to manage visibility, time, and space?

WHAT WOULD YOU DO?
You are traveling on a two-way hilly road that has many sharp curves. What special factors affect visibility? What are some ways to manage time and space?

On a separate piece of paper, write the letter of the answer that best completes each sentence.

1 A limited-access expressway
   a. allows vehicles to enter or exit only at certain places.
   b. does not permit trucks or buses.
   c. has no shoulders.

2 On residential streets, you should try to drive
   a. at least 35 mph.
   b. 30 to 35 mph.
   c. no more than 25 mph.

3 Speed limits on country roads are typically
   a. lower than those on city streets.
   b. higher than those on city streets.
   c. between 15 and 30 miles per hour.

4 When driving on a dirt road, you should
   a. pull over to the right side.
   b. increase your speed.
   c. reduce your speed.

5 During urban and suburban driving, you should
   a. look at least 1 to 2 blocks ahead.
   b. look at least 4 to 6 blocks ahead.
   c. use your high-beam headlights.

6 On multiple-lane expressways, passing other vehicles
   a. should be avoided.
   b. is an integral part of driving.
   c. is a method of staying alert.

On a separate piece of paper, write the word or phrase that best completes each sentence.

expressway

rural road

residential streets

urban streets

7 On _____, you may encounter double-parked vehicles that block your view.

8 A(n) _____ may have drainage ditches alongside of it.

9 A freeway is one example of a(n) _____.

10 Driving at slower speeds is essential on _____.

Writing

Driver's Log

In this chapter, you have learned about managing visibility, time, and space in different driving environments. Write two paragraphs in response to these questions: In which driving environment do you think you will have the most difficulty managing visibility, time, and space? What steps will you take to overcome this difficulty?

Projects

❶ Use a road map to plan a trip from one city to another. List the highways you would travel on and the numbers of the exits you would use. Take the trip as a driver or passenger, and compare the accuracy of your plan to what you actually experience on the trip.

❷ Compare city driving and driving on a rural road. Observe differences in road surfaces, traffic signs and signals, density of traffic, and visibility.

How Do Intersections Affect Driving?

Intersections are places where one road meets or crosses another. They are designed with controls to keep vehicles traveling in one direction from crashing into vehicles traveling from another. There are several types of intersections. Most are marked with traffic-control devices, but some are unmarked. Some require you to stop, and some do not. Learning how to drive safely through these different types of intersections will help you manage risk.

Driver Ed
Online

For additional activities, visit **drivered.glencoe.com**. Here you will find:

◆ **Web Link Exercises**

◆ **eFlashcards**

◆ **Practice Driving Tests**

LESSON 1

Basic Intersections

OBJECTIVES

1. **Explain** how you can manage visibility, time, and space in an intersection.

2. **Describe** the characteristics of intersections with traffic control devices, T-intersections, and four-way intersections.

KEY TERM

◆ **T-intersection**

Intersections are places where one road meets or crosses another. There are several types of intersections. Most have traffic-control devices, but some do not. Regardless of where you are driving, there is one safe way to approach an intersection. It is important to be in the correct position in the proper lane. As you approach an intersection, adjust your speed to allow more time to search the area and make a smooth stop if necessary.

How Can You Manage Visibility, Time, and Space at Intersections?

Intersections have different designs and controls that require you to search differently. Traffic on one road may have different traffic controls than traffic on an intersecting road.

Energy Tip

Don't rev the engine when you are stopped at a stop sign or red light or while you are stopped in traffic. Revving the engine wastes fuel and may annoy other drivers.

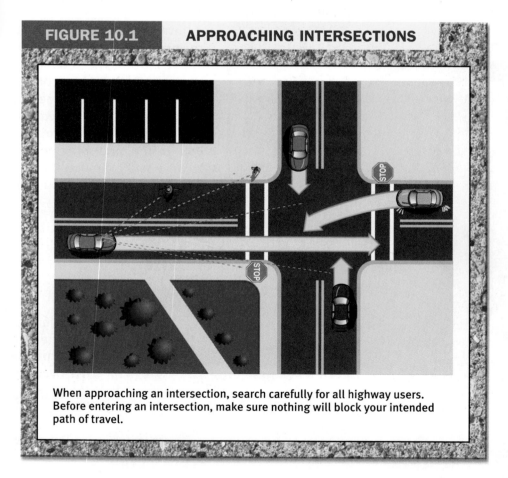

FIGURE 10.1　　**APPROACHING INTERSECTIONS**

When approaching an intersection, search carefully for all highway users. Before entering an intersection, make sure nothing will block your intended path of travel.

Dealing with the UNEXPECTED

TOLL PLAZAS

Here are some tips for navigating toll plazas that you may encounter at some interchanges:

▲ Make sure that you keep change in an easily accessible location. Do not search for change while you're driving.

▲ Read the signs as you approach the toll plaza. Some tollbooths may require exact change or a prepaid pass, so choose a lane accordingly.

▲ Be sure to choose an open lane by looking for a green signal well in advance. Once you have chosen a lane, stay in it.

▲ Be especially alert to drivers ahead of you who switch lanes suddenly.

▲ After you have paid the toll, wait for the go-ahead signal (typically a green light) before exiting the tollbooth.

You can manage visibility by scanning all four corners for signs, signals, markings, roadway features, motorized vehicles, and nonmotorized highway users. When approaching an intersection, always scan for areas of blocked vision. The shape or sharpness of the curbing will provide clues—that is, if the turn is a 90-degree turn, the curbing will be at a 90-degree angle, too (see **Figure 10.1** on page 210).

From a stop, you need about 6 seconds to cross a typical intersection that is about 30 feet wide with cross traffic traveling at 30 mph. For maximum safety, you should wait for an 8-second gap to ensure you can cross without interrupting traffic. As the width of the street increases, the size of the traffic gap must be increased. You may use the counting method—one, one thousand; two, one thousand, etc.—to mark seconds and to judge correct distances and times when you begin.

You need adequate space to cross an intersection. Once you reach the intersection, you will need to decide when it is safe to start across or turn. You need to find room to make your maneuver safely. To do this, you will have to judge a safe gap in traffic. A gap in traffic is the distance or time between the back of one vehicle and the front of the next vehicle in line. The size of the gap needed depends upon the time required to cross the intersection or to make a turn. If cars are moving faster, you will need a bigger gap to safely enter traffic.

You must yield to all traffic on the cross street. *Why is it important to yield to all traffic on the cross street?*

SIGNED INTERSECTIONS

Intersections at low-traffic areas that have stoplights or stop signs are easy to navigate. Just follow the signs, while staying aware of other drivers and pedestrians. On intersections with stoplights, go forward on green lights and stop on red lights. If your street has a stop sign, stop first, then proceed when it is safe. When you meet another driver at intersections with multiple stop signs at the same time, you must give way to the driver on your right. Always keep an eye out for other drivers who misunderstand or don't notice the signs.

T-INTERSECTIONS

A **T-intersection** is one in which one road ends and forms a "T" with a crossroad. The "give-way-to-the-right" rule does not apply to T-intersections. At T-intersections, the vehicle traveling on the road that ends must give way to any vehicle traveling on the road that continues unless a posted sign advises otherwise.

FOUR-WAY INTERSECTIONS

Junctions with a stop sign and a sign saying "4-Way Stop" (or "3-Way" or "All Way") require all traffic to come to a complete stop when reaching the intersection. At these intersections, vehicles then take turns to proceed through the junction in the order in which they reached the intersection. In other words, the first car to stop in the intersection should proceed first. Watch out—there can be stop signs on main thoroughfares in places you would not expect them!

WHAT WOULD YOU DO?
All three vehicles arrive at this intersection at the same time. What action will you take as you approach, then pass through this intersection?

Lesson 1 Review

❶ How can you manage visibility, time, and space in intersections?

❷ What are the characteristics of intersections with traffic control devices, T-intersections, and four-way intersections?

❸ What do you look for when managing visibility at an intersection?

Railroad Crossings

Railroad trains are big and powerful, and they can demolish a vehicle or seriously injure or kill a person if a crash occurs. Trains must stay on their tracks, but drivers can easily avoid them by staying out of their path. Pay attention to signs and lights at railroad crossings, and use common sense at all times.

How Can You Drive Through a Railroad Crossing Safely?

Despite warning signs, crossing gates, and signals, many collisions occur at railroad crossings each year. Among the causes of these crashes are driver impatience, driver inattention, and poor judgment.

It is not safe to drive through a railroad crossing when a train is approaching. Too many drivers forget or ignore safe-driving procedures at railroad crossings, often with fatal consequences. If you have patience, pay attention, and use good judgment at railroad crossings, you won't collide with a train.

FYI

The railroad advance-warning sign is the only highway sign that is round.

Be very cautious at railroad crossings. Never attempt to drive around lowered gates or cross a track if the warning lights are flashing. *How can crossing a track during this time be dangerous?*

DETERMINE WHEN IT IS SAFE TO CROSS

Scanning and searching will help you get across railroad crossings safely. Here are some basic rules to help you determine when it's safe to cross:

1. Slow down as you approach a railroad crossing. Look for warning lights or signals or lowered crossing gates. Even if warning lights are not flashing, look both ways and listen to make sure no train is coming before you cross a railroad track. Never rely solely on mechanical warning equipment—it could be broken.

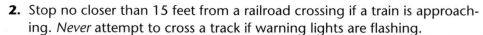
2. Stop no closer than 15 feet from a railroad crossing if a train is approaching. *Never* attempt to cross a track if warning lights are flashing.

3. If there are no lights or crossing gates present at a railroad crossing, proceed with extra caution. If there is any question about safety, then stop, look, and listen for approaching trains before moving ahead.

4. Always wait for the vehicle ahead of you to clear the tracks before you start across. Never stop on the railroad tracks.

5. After a train has passed, check in both directions to see that no other trains are coming, especially before you start across multiple tracks.

STAY ALERT

Even if you cross a set of railroad tracks every day at about the same time, do not take familiar crossings for granted. Never assume the track is clear.

Drivers who travel the same route day after day tend to pay less attention to their surroundings. Such inattention can have tragic consequences.

VEHICLE STALLS

Never stop your vehicle on railroad tracks for any reason whatsoever. This is a good way to lose your vehicle and perhaps your life.

In the rare event that your vehicle stalls on the tracks, do not panic. Immediately check in both directions for approaching trains. If no train is approaching and you have a clear view of the tracks in both directions, calmly try to restart your engine. Continue to check for trains. If you see a train coming, leave your vehicle at once and move away from the tracks.

If you cannot start your vehicle and you are sure no trains are coming, try to push your vehicle off and well away from the tracks.

WHAT WOULD YOU DO?
The train has just about passed. Describe the procedures you would use to resume movement.

Lesson 2 Review

❶ How can you determine if a railroad crossing is safe to travel over?

❷ What would you do if your vehicle stalled on railroad tracks?

❸ What steps will you take when crossing railroad tracks?

Roundabouts

Traffic circles, or **roundabouts**, control traffic through certain intersections. All traffic is routed in one direction around a circle, and drivers exit where they like. Roundabouts can effectively move traffic through neighborhood intersections where traffic volume isn't high enough for placement of a traffic signal.

How Can You Drive Through a Roundabout Safely?

Roundabouts keep traffic moving through intersections at a slow, safer pace. Traffic in circulating lanes moves counterclockwise, so you will make a right turn to enter.

If you follow a few simple rules, driving a roundabout is safe and easy. When approaching a roundabout, which may be either one or two lanes in width, follow these rules (see **Figure 10.2** on page 216):

1. Slow down as you approach the traffic circle. Turn on your right turn signal.
2. If other vehicles are in the roundabout, yield to traffic until there's enough room for you to merge into the circle.
3. Once you're in the roundabout, go in the direction of traffic, and exit where you like.

As many places continue to grow, expect to see more roundabouts.

ONE-LANE ROUNDABOUTS

Some roundabouts have only one lane. At the entry lane to the roundabout, there will be a yield sign and a dashed yield line at the roundabout intersection. As you approach, slow down. Watch for pedestrians and bicyclists. Be prepared to stop if necessary. When you enter with a right turn, yield to circulating traffic from the left. Do not stop if the way is clear.

The roundabout will have "One-Way" signs mounted in the center island. One street before your exit, turn on your right turn signal. Watch for pedestrians and bicyclists as you enter and exit. Left turns are completed by traveling around the center island, then making a right turn into the street you want.

TWO-LANE ROUNDABOUTS

Some roundabouts have two lanes, which allow for a greater volume of traffic than one lane. Similar rules apply to the use of these lanes as with one-lane roundabouts.

1. Vehicles approaching the roundabout are required to yield to vehicles in the circulating lanes.

OBJECTIVES

1. **List** the rules for driving in a roundabout.
2. **Explain** how to navigate a roundabout that has one lane.
3. **Describe** how to navigate a roundabout that has two lanes.

KEY TERM

◆ **roundabout**

FYI

The maximum volume for a single-lane roundabout is between 20,000 and 26,000 vehicles per day. For a double-lane roundabout, the maximum is between 40,000 and 50,000 vehicles per day.

FIGURE 10.2

ENTERING A ROUNDABOUT

The driver of a vehicle entering the circle should yield to vehicles already in the circle.

2. Vehicles in the circulating lanes have the right-of-way. Traffic movement in the roundabout is always counterclockwise.
3. All vehicles are required to yield to pedestrians in the crosswalks.
4. If you are in the inside lane, you should enter the inside circulating lane and exit on the inside lane.
5. If you are in the outside lane, you should enter the outside circulating lane and exit into the outside lane.
6. Drivers should be aware of traffic in the neighboring lane.
7. Never change lanes once you enter into the circulating lanes.
8. Speed should be 20 mph or less as posted.

WHAT WOULD YOU DO?
Describe the process you will use to enter the circle, travel half way around, and exit the circle onto the third roadway.

Lesson 3 Review

❶ What are the general rules for driving in a roundabout?

❷ How do you navigate a roundabout that has one lane?

❸ How do you navigate a roundabout that has two lanes?

Complex Intersections

A complex intersection is one where two major roadways cross paths. Such intersections generally contain five to six lanes traveling in one direction. In addition there are multiple turning lanes, and a turn-arrow signal may be necessary for two or more turning lanes. In complex intersections, there are at least 64 intersecting points where vehicles can make contact with one another.

Because of their setup, complex intersections are areas of highways and streets that produce conflicts among vehicles and pedestrians (see **Figure 10.3**). In contrast to roundabouts, where all drivers generally are doing the same thing, complex intersections are those where drivers and pedestrians may be obeying different signs or lights.

OBJECTIVES
1. **Describe** the major problems you will encounter in a complex intersection.
2. **Describe** the best strategies for dealing with pedestrians at complex intersections.

What Problems Exist at Complex Intersections?

Although traffic usually slows down at intersections, there is usually more traffic here. A large number of collisions occur in complex intersections. In a typical year in the United States, almost 1 million crashes with injuries occur at or within an intersection. In the year 2000, more than 2.8 million intersection-related crashes occurred, some without injuries. This is 44 percent of all reported crashes. About 8,500 fatalities occurred, accounting for 23 percent of all highway deaths. The financial cost to society for intersection-related crashes has been estimated at approximately $40 billion a year.

CRASHES AT COMPLEX INTERSECTIONS

Since many people use complex intersections, crashes may be side impact, rear-end, or those involving pedestrians. Elderly drivers tend to have more problems than younger drivers at complex intersections.

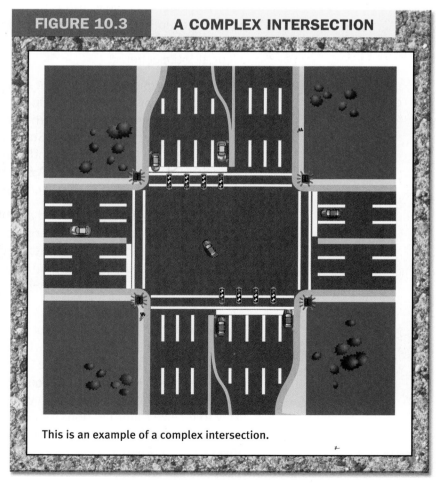

FIGURE 10.3   A COMPLEX INTERSECTION

This is an example of a complex intersection.

Side impact. Each year, more than one-third of all deaths to vehicle occupants occur in side-impact crashes, when a vehicle is hit by another vehicle from the side. These are the most serious kind of collisions, and most of them occur at intersections.

Rear-end. Seventy-five percent of all rear-end crashes involve a vehicle that is either stopping or has already stopped. More than half of these kinds of crashes occur at or near intersections. Both human and property damage losses from rear-end crashes cost the United States billions of dollars each year in medical expenses, lost productive time, and numerous property insurance claims. The National Highway Traffic Safety Association estimates that the cost resulting from injuries suffered in rear-end crashes exceeds $5 billion per year.

Pedestrians. When a person and a vehicle collide, the person loses. Intersections are disproportionately responsible for pedestrian deaths and injuries. Almost 50 percent of combined fatal and nonfatal injuries to pedestrians occur at or near intersections. Pedestrian deaths from crashes are most frequent in densely populated urban areas where more than two-thirds of pedestrian injuries also occur.

The elderly. Elderly drivers do not deal with complex traffic situations as well as younger drivers do. This is particularly evident in multiple-vehicle crash statistics at intersections. People 65 years and older have a higher probability of causing a fatal crash at an intersection, and about one-half of these fatal crashes involve drivers who are 80 years and older. Older drivers are also more likely to receive traffic citations for failing to yield, turning improperly, and running stop signs and red lights. This is another reason to keep an eye on other drivers as you drive.

SAFETY WITH PEDESTRIANS

Pedestrians are vulnerable to injury in a collision with a motor vehicle. Drivers must always watch for pedestrians. Persons with disabilities or older pedestrians may take longer to cross the street—give them enough time.

Drivers must always yield the right-of-way to pedestrians in a crosswalk. Never pass another vehicle yielding to a pedestrian at a crosswalk.

Pedestrians don't always act as you expect—expect the unexpected. Be alert. When you are entering the roadway or backing out of a parking space, remember that pedestrians can be hidden in one of the many vehicle blind spots. You may not be able to see pedestrians who are walking behind your rear-view mirror, beside your door pillars, or to any side of your vehicle.

DESIGNATED LEFT- AND RIGHT-TURN LANES

At many complex intersections, there are special marked lanes for making left and right turns. Signs usually designate these lanes and sometimes indicate what times of day they may be used.

With left turns, there may be one or more special left-turn lanes. It is important to stay in one lane when making and completing the left turn. Most of the time, these left-turn lanes are controlled by a green left-turn arrow, which signals you to make the turn. On some occasions, left-turn lanes are signed to inform the driver to "yield to oncoming traffic." Make sure you use good visual information to make your turn.

Special right-turn lanes are also used at many intersections. When making a turn at such an intersection, make sure you obey the traffic signal. If a right turn is permitted on a red traffic signal, make a complete stop. Then check crossing traffic and oncoming left-turning traffic, and make your turn when it is clear.

If pedestrians are attempting to cross the street while you are making a left or right turn, make sure you yield to them.

WHAT WOULD YOU DO?
You want to make a right turn at this intersection. What action will you take as you approach and then pass through this intersection?

Lesson 4 Review

❶ What major problems could you encounter in a complex intersection?

❷ What are the best strategies for dealing with pedestrians at complex intersections?

❸ What two ways can you use to communicate with other drivers?

LESSON 5

Interchanges

OBJECTIVES

1. **Define** each component of an interchange.
2. **Describe** the different types of interchanges.

KEY TERMS

◆ interchange
◆ diamond interchange
◆ cloverleaf interchange
◆ trumpet interchange

An interchange is similar to an intersection on the freeway or turnpike, usually without stop signs. Engineers look at an interchange as a grade-separated intersection, where one road passes over another, connected by ramps. Basically, interchanges allow through traffic on the freeway to pass from one road to another without much stopping. Even if traffic signals are installed at the ends of the ramps, traffic on the surface street flows smoother when it doesn't have to deal with all the traffic from the interstate. Through traffic does not have to stop.

What Is an Interchange?

Interchanges are places where one major freeway crosses another road. Interchanges usually consist of through lanes, speed-change lanes, and ramps.

THROUGH LANES

Through lanes are lanes continuing straight through an interchange, designed for drivers staying on the same turnpike or interstate highway. Drivers in through lanes don't have to adjust their speed when passing through an interchange.

SPEED-CHANGE LANES

Speed-change lanes are special lanes alongside the main travel lanes of the highway that allow a vehicle to reduce speed to exit or to increase speed to merge into moving traffic. Engineers call these lanes *deceleration* and *acceleration* lanes.

RAMPS

Ramps move vehicles from one road to another. An exit ramp leaves the main roadway for another road; an entrance ramp brings traffic onto the main roadway. Entrance or exit ramps usually are designed for speeds of 25 to 45 mph, although in a few cases drivers must slow to as much as 15 mph. Moving traffic through interchanges at lower speeds allows engineers to make curves sharper and use less land for ramps.

A complete interchange has enough ramps to provide access to and from any direction. Full freeway-to-street access with a conventional interchange requires four ramps in order to get on and off in each direction. A four-way interchange of two freeways requires eight ramps.

SAFETY TIP

Sometimes the same lane is used for both entering and exiting a highway. It may be less risky to let the vehicle getting on the highway go first, but be prepared to yield whether you are the one who is exiting or the one who is entering.

FIGURE 10.4   INTERCHANGE DESIGNS

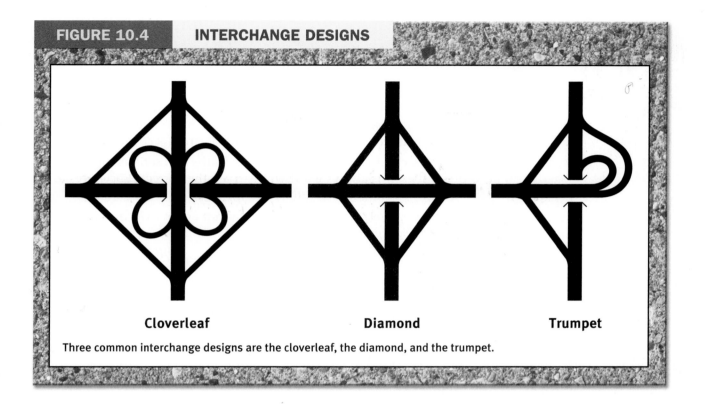

Cloverleaf   Diamond   Trumpet

Three common interchange designs are the cloverleaf, the diamond, and the trumpet.

What Are the Various Types of Interchanges?

Basically, there are three types of interchanges, named for the shape the roads make when viewed from above. These are the diamond interchange, the cloverleaf interchange, and the trumpet interchange (see **Figure 10.4**).

DIAMOND INTERCHANGES

The basic **diamond interchange** is often chosen for lower-traffic interchanges without special constraints. All traffic exits right, forming the shape of a diamond from above. The diamond interchange works well for situations without heavy traffic. Basically, vehicles exit the expressway to the right and stop at an intersecting road before turning right or left. Vehicles also enter on ramps coming into traffic from the right. All ramps function to connect the freeway to the surface street and allow vehicles to transition from low speeds or dead stops to freeway speeds.

The diamond interchange does not perform well when there is heavy traffic on the surface street or ramps or if there is heavy left-turning traffic. Traffic signals can be installed at the two points where the ramps meet the surface street, but very high traffic volumes can cause backups on the street and the ramps—even resulting in stopped traffic on the freeway.

CLOVERLEAF INTERCHANGES

The classic **cloverleaf interchange** looks like a four-leaf clover from above. Cars change directions via "loops" in the roadway. Typically, a cloverleaf

Did You Know

In 1923, the Lincoln Highway, which connected New York City with San Francisco, became the first fully paved road to span North America.

John Popa
Lake Park High School
Bartlett, IL

The maneuvers you can make to enter, exit, and drive through different types of intersections are not always the same. So, you need to understand signs, signals, and pavement markings. You must also practice proper techniques for visual search, steering, speed-control, and space management.

Since intersection crashes result in more deaths and serious injuries than head-on crashes, it is always worthwhile to use the correct procedures to enter, drive through, and exit intersections.

What are some of the differences in how you enter, exit, and drive through different types of intersections?

WHAT WOULD YOU DO?
You are driving and encounter this traffic scene. What does this situation mean and what actions would you take to get through the area safely?

is used where a freeway intersects a busy surface street, although many older freeway-to-freeway interchanges are also cloverleaf.

The cloverleaf interchange allows "nonstop" full access between two busy roads. Traffic merges and weaves but does not cross at-grade. Usually, no stopping is required.

TRUMPET INTERCHANGES

The **trumpet interchange** is a conceptually simple way to end one freeway at another. Similar to a T-intersection, roads loop off either to the right or left to join another roadway. Traffic may sometimes be required to stop. Like a cloverleaf, the trumpet interchange requires only one or two bridges. Designs for higher-speed exits take up more land.

Often an interchange involving a toll freeway to another freeway will be a double trumpet, with all connecting traffic stopping at a toll station between the trumpets. Sometimes more roads join in.

Lesson 5 Review

❶ What are the various components of an interchange? Explain.

❷ What are the different types of interchanges? Explain.

❸ Why might speed limits be lower on ramps?

BUILDING Skills — Geography

USING JUNCTIONS AND INTERCHANGES

Roadways that are numbered routes meet, or intersect, at junctions.

On a map, junctions may be marked by a ○, in the same way that towns are. On an expressway, junctions are interchanges, shown by a ◇ on the map. You need to know about junctions and interchanges to get from one roadway to another.

Suppose you are in Oswego and want to travel to Rome. You might drive south on Routes 81 and 481 until you reach the junction of Routes 481 and 90, at an interchange. Then you would drive east on Route 90 to the interchange that is the junction of Routes 90 and 365. You would drive north on Route 365 to Rome.

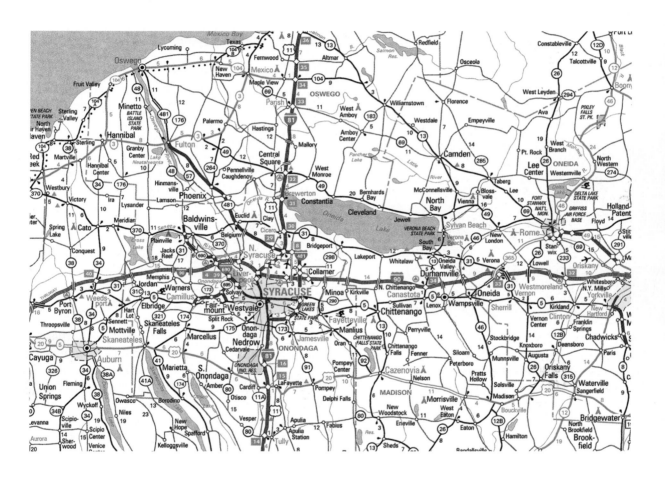

TRY IT YOURSELF

❶ Is there a junction of Routes 20 and 90?

❷ How would you drive from Chittenango to Eaton?

❸ How would you drive from Florence to Parish, stopping in Williamstown? How many junctions are there? Where are they?

❹ Describe the fastest and safest route from Hannibal to Syracuse. How many junctions are there? How many interchanges?

Key Points

Lesson 1

1 You can manage visibility at an intersection by scanning all four corners for signs, signals, pavement markings, roadway features, motorized vehicles, and nonmotorized highway users. You can manage time by leaving 6 seconds to cross a typical intersection. You can manage space by leaving adequate space to cross an intersection. (Pages 210–211)

2 Intersections with traffic control devices are ones that contain signs and signals. T-intersections are ones in which one road forms a "T" with a crossroad. Four-way intersections contain a "4-Way Stop." (Page 212)

WHAT WOULD YOU DO?
All three vehicles arrive at this intersection at the same time. What action will you take as you approach and then pass through this intersection?

Lesson 2

1 To determine when it is safe to cross a railroad track, slow down as you approach a railroad crossing. Stop no closer than 15 feet from a railroad crossing if a train is approaching. If there are no lights or crossing gates present, proceed with extra caution. (Page 214)

2 If your vehicle stalls on railroad tracks, immediately check in both directions for approaching trains. If no train is approaching, calmly try to

restart your engine. If you see a train coming, leave your vehicle at once. (Page 214)

Lesson 3

1 When approaching any roundabout, slow down. Yield to traffic if there is any. Once you enter, go in the direction of traffic and exit where you like. (Page 215)

2 In one-lane roundabouts, watch for pedestrians and cyclists. Be prepared to stop if necessary. When you enter with a right turn, yield to circulating traffic from the left. Do not stop if the way is clear. (Page 215)

3 In two-lane roundabouts, yield to traffic in circulating lanes and to pedestrians in the crosswalks. Enter and exit from the inside lane if you are in the inside lane, or the outside lane if you are in the outside lane. Be aware of traffic in the neighboring lane. Do not change lanes once you enter a circulating lane. Keep your speed at 20 mph or less. (Pages 215–216)

Lesson 4

1 In complex intersections, you are more likely to encounter traffic and are at greater risk of being involved in a crash. You must also have a heightened awareness for pedestrians. (Page 217)

2 The best strategies for dealing with pedestrians at complex intersections include: yielding the right-of-way to pedestrians, never passing a vehicle yielding to a pedestrian, expecting the unexpected from pedestrians, being alert, and being aware of pedestrians in your blind spot. (Page 219)

Lesson 5

1 An interchange consists of through lanes, speed-change lanes, and ramps. (Page 220)

2 A diamond interchange is one that is chosen for lower-traffic interchanges without special constraints. A cloverleaf interchange allows vehicles to change directions via "loops" in the roadway. A trumpet interchange allows roads to loop off either to the right or left to join another roadway. (Pages 221–222)

On a separate sheet of paper, write the letter of the answer that best completes each sentence.

1 The interchange that is often chosen for lower volume traffic is the
  a. trumpet interchange.
  b. cloverleaf interchange.
  c. diamond interchange.

2 When approaching a roundabout, you should
  a. slow down.
  b. drive at a constant speed.
  c. speed up.

3 In 2000, the number of traffic fatalities that occurred at complex intersections was approximately
  a. 850.
  b. 8,500.
  c. 85,000.

4 The portion of all deaths to vehicle occupants that occur in side-impact crashes is
  a. more than ⅓.
  b. less than ¼.
  c. between ¼ and ⅓.

5 To cross a typical intersection that is about 30 feet wide, you need approximately
  a. 2 seconds.
  b. 4 seconds.
  c. 6 seconds.

6 After a train has passed you at a railroad crossing,
  a. proceed as usual.
  b. check in both directions before proceeding.
  c. check only in the direction that the train was traveling before proceeding.

On a separate sheet of paper, write the word or phrase that best completes each sentence.

cloverleaf interchanges

complex intersection

roundabouts

T-intersections

7 _____ control traffic through certain intersections.

8 The give-way rule does not apply to _____.

9 A _____ is used where a freeway intersects a busy surface street.

10 A _____ is one where two major roadways cross paths.

Writing

Driver's Log

In this chapter, you have learned about the risks involved in driving through basic intersections, railroad crossings, roundabouts or traffic circles, and complex intersections and interchanges. Write what you think are the five most important responsibilities a driver has when traveling through intersections.

Project

Observe the interaction between pedestrians and traffic at a busy intersection for about 15 minutes. Make note of unsafe actions taken by both pedestrians and drivers. Discuss your observations with the class.

Sharing the Roadway with Others

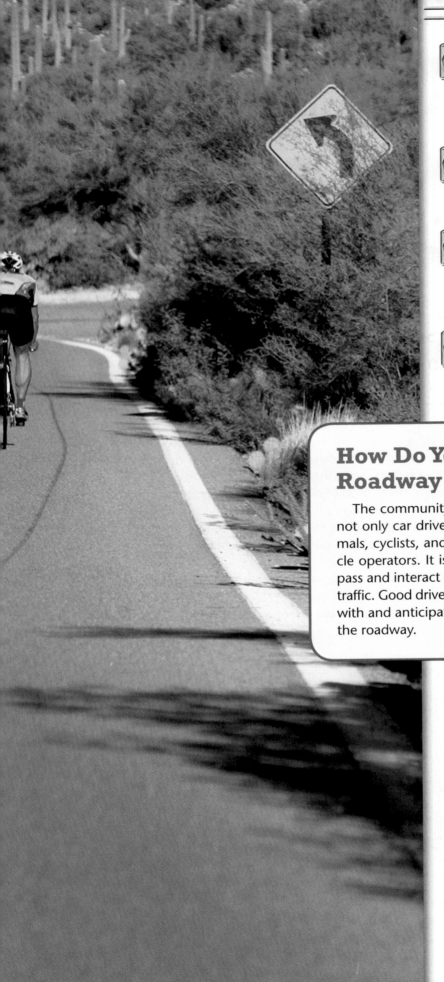

 LESSON 1
Driving with
Pedestrians
and Animals

 LESSON 2
Driving with Bicycles
and Motorcycles

 LESSON 3
Driving with Light
Trucks and Small
Vehicles

LESSON 4
Driving with
Large Vehicles

How Do You Share the Roadway with Others?

The community of roadway users includes not only car drivers but also pedestrians, animals, cyclists, and truck and other large vehicle operators. It is important to learn how to pass and interact safely with different types of traffic. Good drivers do this by communicating with and anticipating the actions of others on the roadway.

Driver Ed
Online

For additional
activities, visit
drivered.glencoe.com.
Here you will find:

◆ **Web Link Exercises**

◆ **eFlashcards**

◆ **Practice Driving Tests**

Driving with Pedestrians and Animals

When driving, you must be alert to all roadway users, not just other motorists. Roadway users such as pedestrians and animals can present special problems. Pedestrians move slowly compared to motor-vehicle operators, and animals darting into the roadway can create a need to react suddenly. Anticipating these problems can help you protect yourself and others.

What Problems Do Pedestrians Pose to Drivers?

Pedestrians pose problems because they are often difficult to see. Adults and children who walk are smaller than cars and trucks, and they don't have headlights or brake lights. Drivers concentrating on traffic, signs, and signals often fail to see pedestrians until it is too late.

Jaywalking, or walking across the street without regard for traffic rules or signals, is a common pedestrian error. Pedestrians do not always use the designated crosswalk or obey the lights or signs that tell them when it's safe to walk across the street. Walking into the street from between parked vehicles is another type of jaywalking.

Pedestrians may be distracted when crossing to the other side of the street. Intersections are the most common sites of fatal collisions with pedestrians who often hurry across streets either against a red light or just as a light is turning red. When traffic is light, pedestrians sometimes cross at places other than intersections because they assume no vehicles are coming. In areas without sidewalks, pedestrians walk in the street or roadway, posing an additional risk to drivers.

Be on the lookout for pedestrians who cross the street illegally or who may need extra time to cross the street. *What can you do to stay on the lookout for pedestrians?*

CHILDREN

Children are at a disadvantage when crossing the street because they're even smaller and less visible than adults to drivers. Children are less capable than adults of judging when it's safe to cross a street, and they're less likely to fully understand the consequences of their actions.

In many urban and suburban areas, children use the street as a playground. When playing on sidewalks, children tend to forget about traffic and dart into the street, often between parked vehicles.

Even when playing on the sidewalk, children or young adults on skateboards, sleds, roller skates, or bicycles sometimes lose control and shoot over the edge of a sidewalk into the street.

ADULTS

Adults often jaywalk, particularly when rushing to get somewhere or to escape harsh weather. Adult pedestrians often assume that drivers will see them and that drivers will grant them the right-of-way. Making either one of these two assumptions can result in a pedestrian fatality.

Be alert for children on bicycles riding in or near the roadway. *What are ways that you can be alert for children on bicycles?*

How Can You Avoid Hitting a Pedestrian?

Never assume a pedestrian can see your vehicle. A pedestrian who is preoccupied, or one who has been drinking, may not notice your approach even if it's night and you have your headlights on. You should always be ready to take evasive action. To warn a pedestrian that you are approaching, tap your horn lightly. Blasting your horn loudly could frighten a pedestrian into doing something dangerous.

Searching is essential to avoid hitting pedestrians. You must watch for them. Search the roadway and sides of the road continuously as you drive. However inconvenient, you should always yield to pedestrians. They have the right-of-way, even if they are crossing the road illegally.

In particular, watch for children on or near the roadway or for clues that children may be present. Playground and school-crossing signs, toys in a front yard, or a tricycle in a driveway are all clues that children may be nearby.

PEDESTRIANS IN RESIDENTIAL AREAS

In residential areas, reduce speed and drive as far away from the curb or parked vehicles as you safely can. Use **ground viewing**, which means searching beneath parked vehicles as much as you can, as you drive, searching for any sign of movement. Be on the alert for children on bicycles in suburban areas.

PEDESTRIANS IN URBAN AND SUBURBAN AREAS

In urban and crowded suburban areas, exercise special care at intersections, particularly when you are making a turn. Be alert for people crossing against the light, stepping off a curb prematurely, or rushing to beat a changing light. Also be alert for adults and children near bus stops, train stations, in school zones, near parks, and in shopping areas.

OTHER PEDESTRIANS

Watch, too, for pedestrians who need more time to cross a street than the "walk" signal allows them. Although not exactly a pedestrian, you must also be careful of someone riding a skateboard or on roller skates, especially near intersections.

FYI

In 2002, more than 4,800 pedestrians were killed and about 71,000 were injured in traffic crashes in the United States. Over 75% of pedestrian fatalities occurred at intersections compared to about 50% of the injuries. The pedestrian fatality rate is highest for persons over 74 years old while persons 10 to 15 years old have the highest injury rate.

Did You Know?

More than 650 bicyclists were killed and about 48,000 were injured in the United States in collisions with motor vehicles in 2002.

BACKING UP

When backing up, never rely on your rearview mirror alone. Before backing up, make certain there is no one behind or next to your vehicle. This is particularly important with regard to children who may be too small for you to see when you are behind the wheel. If you think there may be people behind your vehicle, get out of your car and check the area before backing up.

What Responsibilities Do Pedestrians Have?

Pedestrians have responsibilities, too. Like drivers, pedestrians must pay attention to motor vehicles, signs, signals, and rules. Pedestrians must judge gaps in traffic and cross streets only when and where it is safe—and legal—to do so.

Here are some general rules for pedestrians:

- Never assume that a driver will see you and stop.
- Pause before crossing—look and listen for approaching traffic.
- Cross only at intersections.
- Cross only when the light is green or when a pedestrian signal shows a "walk" symbol.
- Do not step off the curb while waiting for the light to change.
- When walking on or near a roadway, walk facing traffic.
- When walking or jogging on or near a roadway, wear reflective clothing, especially when visibility is reduced. In addition, do not wear headphones.
- When walking with young children, always take them by the hand when crossing streets.

Tips for New Drivers

PEDESTRIANS TO WATCH FOR

Certain pedestrians require drivers to pay special attention.

- ▶ Elderly pedestrians may have impaired eyesight or hearing. They may move and react slowly and require extra time to cross streets.

- ▶ The physically challenged, such as people who are blind and people in wheelchairs, may need extra time to cross streets.

- ▶ Pedestrians with strollers or carriages may need extra time to move onto or off a sidewalk.

- ▶ Joggers running with their backs to traffic can pose a hazard. Many do not wear reflective clothing, which makes them difficult to see when visibility is low.

- ▶ People on the job, such as mail carriers, delivery people, or roadway maintenance workers, may be distracted by their work and step out into the roadway without checking traffic.

- ▶ Umbrellas and hooded parkas may impair pedestrians' ability to notice traffic.

What Problems Do Animals Pose for Drivers?

FYI

Each year, motor vehicles kill thousands of deer, antelope, and other large wild animals.

The dangers posed by animals on the roadway should not be taken lightly. Smashing into a 150-pound deer at 50 miles per hour, for example, will not only kill the animal but will also wreck your vehicle and may well kill the passengers. Colliding with small animals can present problems, too. Small animals can be family pets, and the driver may feel remorseful after hitting them. Small animals also can cause crashes if drivers try to avoid them.

The problem of animals on the roadway is particularly serious during the hours between sunset and sunrise, when it's hard to see them. Fog can also contribute to vehicle-animal collisions.

AVOIDING COLLISIONS WITH ANIMALS

Whether you're driving on city streets or along country roads, keeping an eye out for animals will help you avoid hitting them.

WHAT WOULD YOU DO?
What possible unseen hazards may be present in this situation? How can you manage risk?

Search for movement along the sides of the road. Be especially cautious when driving through farmland or any wooded areas where you are more likely to encounter deer or other large animals alongside or in the road. At night, search for sudden, unusual red spots of light that may be identified as the reflection of your headlights off animals' eyes. In urban and suburban areas, most pets are located around or near homes, so be especially careful there.

As you're driving, think about what you could do if an animal suddenly darted onto the road and into the path of your car. If another car is not following you closely, your best choice could be to apply the brakes.

Lesson 1 Review

❶ What are some pedestrian behaviors that could lead to collisions with vehicles?

❷ What precautions can drivers take to avoid collisions with children?

❸ What are some of the basic safety rules pedestrians should follow?

❹ What steps can you take to minimize the risk of hitting a large animal?

Driving with Bicycles and Motorcycles

OBJECTIVES

1. **Identify** situations involving cyclists, and explain actions that drivers can take to reduce the risk of collision with them.

2. **Describe** the responsibilities of motorcyclists on the roadway.

Bicyclists and motorcyclists present special problems for other traffic. These vehicles have a right to use the roadway, but they are at great risk in a crash. As a driver, you can take precautions to avoid crashing into a cyclist.

How Can You Recognize and Reduce the Risk of Problems Caused by Cyclists?

Cyclists cause problems because they are difficult to see. Drivers have the protection of their vehicles' metal frames and bodies, but cyclists are unprotected. In the event of a collision, skid, or blowout, the risk of serious or fatal injury to the cyclist is very high. In 2002, over 3,900 cyclists (662 bicyclists and 3,244 motorcycle operators and passengers) were killed and more than 112,000 cyclists (65,000 motorcyclists and 47,000 bicyclists) were injured in collisions in the United States.

There are several types of two-wheeled vehicles. Motorcycles and bicycles are most commonly seen on suburban and city streets. Motor scooters are similar to motorcycles, but they have smaller wheels and less power. A moped has even less power and is basically a bicycle with a lawn-mower engine. All these two-wheeled vehicles share the roadway with motor vehicles and present some of the same visibility problems.

Because these vehicles are not as common as cars or trucks, drivers tend not to look for cyclists. If you don't see them right away, you have less time to react to their actions. Motorcycles and bicycles are very maneuverable, but they are smaller, less stable, and less visible than other vehicles. Bicyclists can't go very fast. Two wheels provide less stability than four, making motorcycles and bicycles harder to steer and handle than many people realize. Be aware of cyclists and of how the problems they face are different from yours.

SAFETY TIP

Drivers must be careful when driving close to cyclists. Drivers should allow a minimum of 3 feet of space between the vehicle and bicycle when passing.

WATCHING OUT FOR CYCLISTS

Two-wheeled vehicles are much more difficult to spot than other vehicles for drivers, especially when they approach from behind or from the side (see **Figure 11.1**). Motorcycles and bicycles are easily hidden from drivers' sight by larger vehicles sharing the roadway. On highways, motorcycles do not take up entire lanes, and they are so small they may not be seen, especially when they are straddling the line between two lanes of traffic.

It is difficult for riders of two-wheel vehicles to see to the rear. The small handlebar mirrors on motorcycles and bicycles offer their drivers only a limited view to the rear. Many riders have trouble seeing in the rain. Some motorcycles have no windscreen or windshield wipers to aid visibility in case of a sudden shower, and bicycles never have these visibility aids.

Always make cyclists aware of your intentions and position. Drive with your headlights on, and signal well in advance when turning, changing lanes, or stopping. Tap your horn early to warn a cyclist of your approach.

In addition, you can take specific actions when sharing the road with cyclists. Make a visual check for cyclists when changing lanes or turning. Also increase your following distance with motorcyclists, and remember that motorcycles are entitled to the full lane width.

DANGEROUS ROADWAY CONDITIONS

Road conditions that are minor annoyances to motor vehicles can pose major hazards to motorcyclists. Potholes, gravel, wet or slippery surfaces, pavement seams, railroad crossings, and grooved pavement can cause motorcyclists to slow down or turn suddenly. If you are aware of the effect of these conditions and drive with care and attention, you can help reduce motorcycle collisions, injuries, and fatalities.

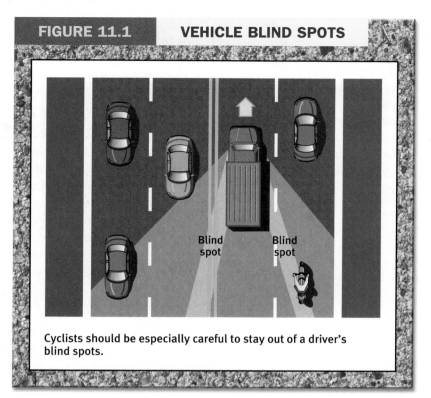

FIGURE 11.1   VEHICLE BLIND SPOTS

Cyclists should be especially careful to stay out of a driver's blind spots.

Be aware of the problems that cyclists face in order to anticipate situations in which a cyclist might have problems. Cyclists can veer or skid into the path of a vehicle. They might suddenly slow down, steer widely left or right, or stop suddenly.

Cyclists must make more adjustments in speed or positions than a driver in situations such as these: encountering a storm drain, a gravel surface, or a pothole; driving on a rain-slicked road or through a large puddle; getting caught in an unexpected rain or snow shower; and being blown by a sudden strong gust of wind.

If a cyclist is carrying a passenger, be especially careful. A passenger leaning the wrong way can throw a motorcycle or bicycle off balance.

What Special Responsibilities Do Motorcyclists Have?

Motorcyclists and motor-scooter operators have the same rights and responsibilities on public roadways as automobile drivers. While everyone must follow the same traffic laws, motorcyclists face unusual dangers because motorcycles require exceptional handling ability.

Motorcycle drivers should not take advantage of the smaller size of their vehicles to weave carelessly in and out of lanes of traffic at high speeds. This behavior is highly dangerous to the cyclist, and it is confusing to other drivers. Motorcyclists should try hard to stay out of other drivers' blind spots. Other drivers might not be as aware as they should be about looking in their mirrors

Did You Know?

Motorcycles have a shorter stopping distance than other motor vehicles. This means you need to increase your following distance when there is a motorcycle in front of you.

for motorcycles to begin with, so it is important that a motorcyclist never be in a spot that is not visible to nearby vehicles.

Consider driving two-wheelers with the headlight on, even during daylight hours, to increase visibility.

FAILURE TO OBEY TRAFFIC LAWS

Human error or ignorance accounts for countless collisions involving cyclists. Careless riding poses a danger not just to the cyclist but to all roadway users.

Motorcycles are subject to the same laws as other motor vehicles. Riding between lanes, weaving in and out of traffic, riding in drivers' blind spots, and failing to signal intentions are dangerous because drivers may not be able to presume a cyclist's actions. Children on bikes may ride the wrong way on one-way streets or sail through intersections with barely a glance to either side.

When you are driving a motor vehicle, be alert to the possibility that cyclists may not follow traffic laws. Be prepared to take evasive action if necessary.

DRIVE RESPONSIBLY

Some cyclists become the victims of careless or inconsiderate drivers. These drivers may tailgate cyclists, cut them off, or pass too close for safety. Such reckless actions put both the driver and cyclist at risk. Many more collisions involving cyclists occur because drivers have difficulty seeing motorcycles and bicycles.

As a driver, follow all traffic laws so that you do not endanger cyclists and other users of the roadway. Keep an eye out for them, too.

? WHAT WOULD YOU DO?
Motorcyclists are approaching you. What can you do to minimize the risk?

Lesson 2 Review

❶ Describe problems that cyclists can cause for a driver. Explain how you would manage risk in each circumstance.

❷ What should motorcyclists do to avoid risks on the roadway?

❸ What roadway conditions pose a special hazard to motorcyclists?

Driving with Light Trucks and Small Vehicles

The most popular vehicles on American roads today are light trucks. These vehicles drive a bit differently than cars. Even if you don't drive one, you will have to share the roadway with these vehicles. Knowing how they differ from cars will be a plus when you encounter them on the road, or even when you are driving a small car.

How Do You Drive a Pickup, Sport Utility Vehicle, or Van?

The category of light trucks includes pickup trucks, vans, and **sport utility vehicles (SUVs)**, which all sit higher off the road than a car and are usually wider, too. SUVs are passenger vehicles built on truck frames that usually have four-wheel drive, and they are considerably less fuel efficient than smaller cars.

Driving a light truck or sharing the road with them requires consideration of their size and limitations. Light trucks start, steer, and stop in much the same way as a car. However, the visibility they offer, their size, and other factors make light trucks and vans more difficult than cars to drive and more difficult with which to share the road. The best way to drive them is with an awareness of their limitations.

FACTORS TO CONSIDER WHEN DRIVING A LIGHT TRUCK

Driving a light truck safely has a lot to do with knowing your vehicle. Light trucks are different types of vehicles than cars. They are usually taller, heavier, and have different tires than cars. If you drive one, be aware of these differences because they affect where the vehicle can go and not go. These differences also influence how well nearby drivers can see and maneuver in traffic.

Because you sit higher in a van or sport utility vehicle, you can see farther ahead than you do in a car. *How can someone driving this vehicle use visibility in planning a driving strategy?*

Look for signs that tell you what the clearance is. **Why is it important to know the clearance?**

Visibility. A taller vehicle allows the driver to see over surrounding traffic and take advantage of that height to search farther down the road for pending problems. This gives the driver an advantage in planning driving strategy.

Vehicle height. Most light trucks are a foot or so taller than most cars. The extra height affects where you can drive and where you can park. When you park, don't forget to check the height of your vehicle, since some do not fit into certain garages or enclosed parking spaces. The extra height means that vehicles sharing the road with you often cannot see through, around, or past you to determine what lies ahead. While you can usually see through the front, side, and rear windshields of a car, the same cannot always be said for these taller vehicles. When following one, stay farther behind to increase your ability to see around it.

Because these vehicles are taller than cars, the bumpers are above the bumpers of most passenger cars. In case of a crash, the bumpers will not match up with those of surrounding vehicles but will more likely strike the cars' bodies above their bumpers. This will result in more damage to the vehicles and increase the possibility of injury to the cars' occupants.

Because headlights are higher, they also cause more glare when approaching or following other traffic. As the driver of the taller vehicle, you should be aware of this and stay farther back from vehicles you are following. Make sure you keep your lights on low beam when approaching other vehicles.

Be alert for wind, too. High winds are more likely to blow these vehicles off the road. The square shape and taller height mean that light trucks present a greater surface to the wind and are more susceptible to it.

Vehicle weight. Because of their construction on truck frames and additional components, light trucks weigh quite a bit more than cars. Weight is the enemy of fuel mileage, handling, and braking. Light trucks usually get poor mileage, sometimes as little as 10 to 12 miles per gallon. Being heavier than cars, these vehicles take longer to stop, turn, or accelerate than do lighter vehicles.

The additional weight also makes pickups handle much less securely than cars in emergency situations. The added bulk causes problems when you are trying to turn or stop suddenly. The center of gravity is higher, and the vehicle will roll to the side or pitch forward more easily than a car.

Tires. Light trucks have larger tires than passenger cars. Like all vehicles, maintaining the tire pressure recommended by the vehicle manufacturer determines how well the vehicle can stop, turn, or accelerate. Tires used on light trucks have a more open and rugged tread design to allow them to deal with off-road use. However, these tires are less efficient on wet or dry pavement because they place less rubber on the road, limiting their ability to stop or turn. On average, a pickup or sport utility vehicle will take between 10 percent and 20 percent more distance to stop from highway speeds than a passenger car.

SHARING THE ROADWAY WITH SMALL VEHICLES

When you drive a light truck, be considerate of other drivers, particularly those in smaller vehicles. Adjust your driving to take into account that you are operating a larger and wider vehicle than many others on the road.

Maintain a greater margin of space around the vehicle. Increase your following distance to give yourself more time to maneuver and stop. Keep in mind that you may be blocking the visibility of other drivers. Take this into consideration when you spot potentially threatening conditions ahead that cars behind you may not see.

Manage the risk to yourself and to others by staying alert and allowing extra time to accomplish driving maneuvers. Keep in mind that the difference in the size, shape, and weight of your vehicle affects its handling ability as well as your visibility.

OTHER KINDS OF LARGER VEHICLES

As a driver, you will encounter other kinds of larger vehicles on the roadway. Keep an eye out for emergency vehicles, maintenance vehicles, ice-cream trucks, or even snowmobiles.

Emergency vehicles. All drivers must yield the right-of-way to a police car, fire engine, ambulance, or other emergency vehicle using a siren and flashing lights. Pull as close to the right edge of the road as possible and stop, then wait for the emergency vehicle to pass. Do not stop in an intersection. Continue through the intersection and then pull to the right as soon as you can. Sometimes emergency vehicles will use the wrong side of the street to continue on their way. Their drivers may also use a loudspeaker to talk to drivers blocking their path.

Don't be a "lookie-loo." You interfere with the essential services of police, firefighters, ambulance crews, or other rescue or emergency personnel when you drive for "sight-seeing" to any emergency call site or when you slow down to gawk when passing by the scene of a collision. It is best that you keep the area clear so that the emergency crew can work effectively. When approaching the scene of an emergency, you must obey any traffic direction, order, or signal by traffic or police officers or firefighters. Obey their orders in emergency or special situations, even if it conflicts with existing signs, signals, or laws.

Maintenance vehicles. Roadwork involves construction and repair vehicles of many sizes and shapes with the potential to disrupt traffic. Be alert for signs and flags that warn of such vehicles working on or near the roadway. Drivers need to be alert to these vehicles and to adjust speed and position to accommodate sudden changes in traffic flow.

Ice-cream trucks. Approach vendors such as ice-cream trucks cautiously, since many of their customers are young children. Watch for children darting into the street and emerging from between parked vehicles to catch the ice-cream truck. In some states, drivers are legally required to stop for an ice-cream

Driver Ed
Online

Topic: Sharing the Road

For a link to more information on sharing the road with trucks, go to **drivered** **.glencoe.com**.

Activity: Using the information provided at this link, write a paragraph discussing a truck's limitations in terms of maneuverability, stopping distances, and blind spots.

truck equipped with flashing red lights and must yield the right-of-way to pedestrians going to and from the truck. Check your state driver's manual.

Snowmobiles. During the winter, snowmobiles are allowed on certain roads in some states. Snowmobiles can come onto the roadway in unexpected places. They are often hard to see and can be difficult for their drivers to handle and to stop. Allow extra time and space to adjust to any maneuver that a snowmobile makes.

How Do You Drive a Small Car?

?
WHAT WOULD YOU DO?
Since you are driving a vehicle larger and wider than many others, how should you adjust your driving to protect other motorists?

Along with larger and heavier vehicles such as SUVs, there are also more small cars on the road today than ever before. Small cars are also lighter than most other cars. These vehicles cost much less to buy and operate than larger vehicles, but they have some drawbacks. In many small cars, for instance, the driver also sits lower and therefore has reduced visibility over the tops of other cars.

Small cars may have less power than larger vehicles. As a result, a small car may take a little longer to pass other vehicles. When driving a small car, allow yourself extra space and time to pass another vehicle. If a small car is passing you, give the driver ample space and time to maneuver. Small cars may also lose speed when climbing a steep hill.

Plan to give small cars extra room when roads are slippery or there are strong winds. Lightweight cars tend to skid more easily than heavier vehicles on slick roadways.

Lesson 3 Review

❶ Describe how vehicle size affects visibility. Explain how you would manage risk when driving a sport utility vehicle and a small compact car.

❷ What are some precautions you can take to protect yourself and other motorists when driving a pickup truck, sport utility vehicle, or van?

❸ What can drivers of small cars do to minimize risk?

Driving with Large Vehicles

Some vehicles on the road are quite large. Trucks today can be up to 120 feet long, about eight times as long as the average car. Big trucks can weigh up to 60 tons, equivalent to the weight of 40 to 60 cars. Buses and farm equipment can be on the road. To manage visibility, time, and space near large vehicles, you need to understand their characteristics and limitations.

How Can You Safely Share the Roadway with Large Vehicles?

It is not difficult to share the roadway with large vehicles if you allow for their differences. You must be aware of problems related to their size and their stopping and turning limitations. To reduce the chance of a collision with a large truck, become more familiar with the physical capabilities of big vehicles and how they maneuver.

Put yourself in the truck driver's place. Being aware of problems he or she faces will help you manage risk.

TRUCKS AND TRACTOR-TRAILERS

Trucks create visibility problems for other drivers. With a truck blocking your view, you can't see other traffic or the roadway ahead. Drivers of trucks have limitations on their own visibility, which includes some large blind spots (see **Figure 11.2**). Trucks also stop more slowly and handle differently than cars. Here are some ways trucks are different:

Visibility. Truck drivers sit high above the roadway and have excellent visibility ahead. However, it is hard for them to see to the side and behind the truck. Despite the use of sideview mirrors, some vehicles may be all but invisible to a truck driver. Your vehicle can get lost in those blind spots. If you drive for a long time in those blind spots, you block the trucker's ability to take evasive action to avoid a dangerous situation.

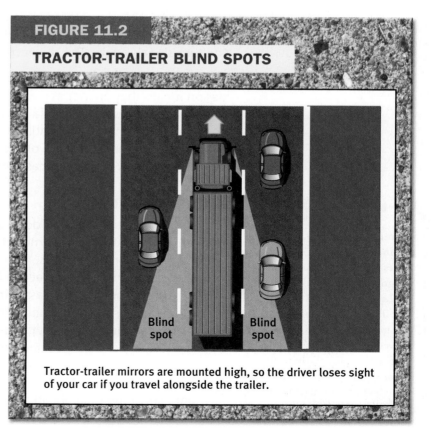

FIGURE 11.2

TRACTOR-TRAILER BLIND SPOTS

Blind spot

Blind spot

Tractor-trailer mirrors are mounted high, so the driver loses sight of your car if you travel alongside the trailer.

Generally speaking, if you can't see the truck driver in his or her side mirror, he or she can't see you. These blind spots are often called the "No Zone."

Time. When you're passing a truck, allow much more time than you'd need in order to pass a car. Not only is the truck longer, its bulk creates a wind factor that you'll also have to be aware of as you steer around the vehicle. Remember that handling a truck is more difficult than handling a car. Weighed down with cargo, a truck accelerates slowly on flat ground and loses speed when climbing an uphill road. Going downhill, however, a truck's momentum causes it to pick up speed. See Chapter 12 for more on momentum.

Space. Trucks take up a lot more room on the roadway than do cars. As a result, it is much harder to see around one when you are following it. Increase your following distance when you're behind a truck. When you approach a truck in an oncoming lane, leave as much space as possible between the truck and your vehicle. Remember that a truck requires a wide turning area and more time and space to stop than a car does.

Braking. Large trucks take longer to stop than a car traveling at the same speed. The average passenger vehicle traveling at 60 mph can stop in about 160 feet once the brakes have been applied. However, a large truck traveling at the same speed takes about 300 feet to stop after the brakes have been applied. That's almost twice as far as passenger vehicles. Don't ever pull in front of a large truck and suddenly slow down or stop. The trucker will not be able to stop quickly enough to avoid crashing into you.

Turning. Truck drivers must often swing wide to complete a turn. For all turning vehicles, the rear wheels follow a shorter path than the front wheels: the longer the vehicle, the greater the distance between the paths of the front and rear wheels. When you follow a big truck, look at its turn signals before you start to pass. If you think the truck is turning right, wait a second and check the turn signals again. The driver may actually be turning left.

Maneuverability. Trucks are designed to transport products. Their bulky design means they are not as maneuverable as passenger vehicles. Large trucks require longer distances to start and stop. They take more space for turns and they weigh more. On multilane highways and freeways, large trucks usually stay in the center portion of the lane to help the flow of traffic. This also increases truckers' options in case they must change lanes to avoid a hazard.

AVOIDING CRASHES

Colliding with a truck can do great damage to a smaller, lighter vehicle. Here are some of the most common mistakes passenger-vehicle drivers make when driving near large trucks.

- Cutting into the open space in front of a truck is dangerous. Slow down and don't speed up to pass a truck so you can exit the roadway. Take a moment to slow down and exit behind a truck—it will only take a few extra seconds, and it's much safer.
- Always pass a large truck on the left side, and after you have passed the truck, move ahead of it. If you linger beside the truck, you make it very difficult, if not impossible, for the trucker to take evasive action if an obstacle appears in the road ahead.

FYI

A truck weighing 80,000 pounds traveling at 55 mph takes about 300 feet, or the length of a football field, to brake to a stop. This does not include the distance covered during the time the driver identifies a need to stop and applies the brakes. A car typically requires less than half this distance.

If a truck is bearing down on you as you drive downhill, move into another lane or pull over to let the truck pass.

- Trucks have blind spots. When you follow behind a truck and you cannot see the truck driver's sideview mirrors, the trucker has no way of knowing you are there. Tailgating a truck or any vehicle is dangerous because you take away your own cushion of safety.
- A large tractor-trailer often appears to be traveling at a slower speed because of its large size. Many collisions have taken place at intersections because a passenger-vehicle driver did not realize how close the truck was or how quickly it was traveling.

BUSES

Buses are also quite large. The same visibility and handling factors that pertain to trucks also apply to buses. Allow buses an equal amount of "elbow room," and follow the same 4-second distance rule when following a bus. If you're driving in town, remember that local buses stop frequently to pick up and discharge passengers, often disrupting traffic flow in the process.

Be especially careful when you approach or pass a stopped bus, whether it's a school bus or not. Reduce speed and keep alert for pedestrians rushing to catch the bus and discharged passengers hurrying across streets in front of the bus. Always be ready to stop.

Always stop for a school bus. Remember, it's a law that drivers traveling in either direction must stop for a school bus with red lights flashing. The flashing lights indicate the bus is picking up or dropping off children.

Allow a wide vehicle more room to maneuver, especially on turns. *Why is it important to allow a wide vehicle more room to maneuver?*

Carol Hardin
Fairfax County Public Schools
Springfield, VA

To safely share the road with a truck or tractor-trailer, be aware of the "No-Zone," allow more time for passing, increase your following distance, do not pull in front of the larger vehicle and then suddenly slow down or stop, and beware of the truck's turn signals when passing.

What tips might you follow when sharing the road with pedestrians, animals, or cyclists?

How Do You Deal with Slow-Moving Vehicles?

Try to spot a slow-moving vehicle as early as possible, because your vehicle will approach it more rapidly than a vehicle traveling at a normal rate of speed. Slow-moving vehicles often, but not always, display special signs identifying them as slow moving. If a vehicle is especially wide, it may carry a "wide-load" sign on the rear. Once you identify such a vehicle, reduce speed immediately and follow at a safe distance.

Since you will want to pass these vehicles, consider the driver's likely actions before passing. If you decide to pass, do so safely and only where it is legal to pass. If you see a slow-moving vehicle traveling in the opposite direction, be alert for oncoming vehicles moving into your path as they pass the vehicle.

 WHAT WOULD YOU DO?
You are passing this truck. What should you do?

Lesson 4 Review

❶ Name three types of large motor vehicles with which you might share the roadway. Explain how you can reduce risk when interacting with these vehicles.

❷ When you are sharing the roadway with a slow-moving vehicle, what are three precautions you should take?

❸ How can you share the roadway safely with large motor vehicles?

FIGURING TRAVEL TIME

Travel involves rate of speed, distance, and time. To find how long it will take you to get somewhere when you know your distance and speed, divide the distance by the speed. (To get an exact answer, you may have to change miles per hour to miles per minute by dividing mph by 60.)

$T = D \div S$, where T = time, D = distance, and S = speed.

For example, suppose you will drive 270 miles at an average speed of 45 mph. How long will the trip take?

$$T = 270 \div 45$$
$$T = 6$$

The trip will take 6 hours.

Figure the time for each distance and speed below.

TIME	DISTANCE	SPEED
(a)	20 miles	30 mph
(b)	40 miles	35 mph
(c)	115 miles	50 mph

To estimate distance when you know speed and time, multiply the speed and the time.

$$D = S \times T$$

How far can you travel in 5 hours at an average speed of 35 mph?

$$D = 35 \times 5$$
$$D = 175$$

You can travel about 175 miles.

Figure the distance for each speed and time below. Round your answer to the nearest whole mile.

DISTANCE	SPEED	TIME
(d)	25 mph	30 minutes
(e)	45 mph	2¼ hours
(f)	30 mph	1 hour 20 minutes

Now look back at each problem. If you wanted an estimate instead of an exact answer, what shortcuts could you take?

TRY IT YOURSELF

❶ Traveling at local speeds, about how many miles away is a location 20 minutes from your home?

❷ Use a map to plan a trip from one city to another. Estimate the amount of time it will take to travel the distance between the two cities.

❸ Use a map to figure out which cities or towns are about 3 hours away from your home.

Key Points

1. Some of the problems posed by pedestrians include jaywalking, crossing the street without looking, and walking in the street or roadway when there is no sidewalk. (Page 228)
2. To avoid collisions with pedestrians, reduce speed, drive as far away from curbs and parked vehicles as you can, use ground viewing, and exercise special care at intersections. (Page 229)
3. Pedestrians should pay attention to rules, signals, and signs; judge gaps in traffic; and cross the street only when it is safe to do so. (Page 230)
4. What steps can you take to avoid hitting large animals? (Page 231)

Lesson 2

WHAT WOULD YOU DO?
Motorcyclists are approaching you. What can you do to minimize the risk?

1. To reduce the risk of collision with cyclists, always make cyclists aware of your intentions and position, make a visual check for cyclists when changing lanes and turning, increase your following distance, and be aware of problems that cyclists face. (Page 232)
2. Motorcycle drivers should not take advantage of the smaller size of their vehicles, should try to stay out of other drivers' blind spots, and consider driving with the headlights on at all times. (Page 233)

Lesson 3

1. Visibility is important when driving a light truck because it enables you to see over surrounding traffic and search farther down the road for pending traffic. Vehicle height affects where you can drive and where you can park, blocks the vision of drivers in smaller vehicles, causes more glare, and creates more problems in the wind. Increased vehicle weight means that light trucks get poor fuel mileage and require special caution for handling and braking. (Page 236)
2. When driving a small vehicle, allow yourself extra space and time to pass another vehicle and when roads are slippery or there are strong winds. (Page 238)

Lesson 4

WHAT WOULD YOU DO?
You are passing this truck. What should you do?

1. To safely share the road with a truck or tractor-trailer, be aware of the "No-Zone," allow more time for passing than you would in order to pass a car, increase your following distance, do not pull in front of the larger vehicle and then suddenly slow down or stop, and beware of the truck's turn signals when passing. For buses, reduce speed and keep alert for pedestrians; you should always be prepared to stop. (Pages 239–240)
2. Try to spot a slow-moving vehicle as early as possible. When you identify such a vehicle, reduce speed immediately and follow at a safe distance. Before passing, consider the driver's likely actions. (Page 242)

On a separate sheet of paper, write the letter of the answer that best completes each sentence.

1 As the use of cycles increases,
   a. collisions with other vehicles will decrease.
   b. air pollution will decrease.
   c. the number of collisions with other vehicles might also increase.

2 Drivers use ground viewing to
   a. search the road for animals.
   b. search beneath parked vehicles for signs of movement.
   c. avoid large puddles.

3 Because truck drivers sit high above the surface of the roadway, they
   a. don't have any blind spots.
   b. have great visibility of the road ahead.
   c. are able to see above fog.

4 If another car is not following you closely and an animal suddenly darts onto the road, your best choice may be to:
   a. apply the brakes.
   b. turn off your vehicle's engine.
   c. steer to strike it at an angle.

5 When driving behind a motorcyclist, you should
   a. increase your following distance.
   b. pass at the first opportunity.
   c. turn on your high beams.

6 Most small cars have
   a. more power than larger cars.
   b. the ability to pass easily.
   c. less power than larger cars.

On a separate sheet of paper, write the word or phrase that best completes each sentence.

traffic flow

emergency vehicle

stability

jaywalking

7 Crossing a street without regard for traffic rules or signals is called _____.

8 Motorcycles are harder to steer than many people realize because two wheels provide less _____ than four.

9 Local buses stop frequently to pick up and discharge passengers, often disrupting _____ in process.

10 When you see an _____ using its siren, pull as close to the right edge of the road as possible and stop.

Writing

Driver's Log

In this chapter, you have learned about the responsibilities and risks of sharing the roadway with motorists, pedestrians, cyclists, and animals. Write what you think are the five most important responsibilities a driver has when sharing the roadway.

Projects

1 Observe the interaction between pedestrians and traffic at a busy intersection for about 15 minutes. Make note of unsafe actions taken by both pedestrians and drivers. Discuss your observations with the class.

2 Visit a bicycle shop or sporting goods store. What products does the store sell to help make cyclists, joggers, and others more visible in dim light?

CUMULATIVE REVIEW

This review tests your knowledge of the material in Chapters 9–11, and will help you review for your state driving test. On a separate sheet of paper, select the answer that best completes each statement.

1 Driving on residential streets often presents special hazards because
  a. the streets usually handle a lot of traffic.
  b. traffic usually moves in only one direction.
  c. pedestrians may move in the path of vehicles.

2 You may need to make a judgment call when
  a. you need to travel on a street with parked cars.
  b. you notice the speed limit is 25 mph.
  c. you take shortcuts through a neighborhood street to save time.

3 When driving on urban and suburban streets that are dense with traffic, you should
  a. assume pedestrians will use crosswalks to cross the street.
  b. be careful to maintain an adequate margin of space.
  c. assume traffic moving in packs or lines will move smoothly without incident.

4 You can minimize your driving risks in cities and suburbs if you
  a. focus on one object in your driving path.
  b. are prepared for stopping and turning vehicles at all times.
  c. drive with your high beams on and signal when you are turning.

5 In order to manage your space when driving on a multiple-lane road in cities and suburbs, you should
  a. keep enough space in front of your vehicle so that you see the rear bumper of the vehicle in front of you.
  b. drive to the side and a little behind the vehicle in the lane to your right.
  c. keep as much space as you can between your vehicle and the vehicles in other lanes.

6 Driving on multiple-lane highways is more complex than driving on rural roads in that
  a. HOV lanes often have reduced visibility when used by large trucks.
  b. entrances and exits are usually made from the extreme left lane.
  c. vehicles often pass on the left or the right.

7 When driving on rural roads, you should
  a. pass slow-moving vehicles that are very wide while on a curve so you will have more room.
  b. be prepared to drive at a higher speed because there are fewer intersections.
  c. use sound judgment when approaching railroad crossings because there may be no signs, signals, or gates.

8 When driving on rural roads that may have limited visibility, you should always
  a. drive with your high beams on so you can be seen.
  b. pass large vehicles so your vision will not be blocked.
  c. signal your intention to turn, to pull over, or to pass.

9 A safe way to approach and cross an intersection is to
  a. look at all four corners for traffic signals, vehicles, and areas of blocked vision.
  b. look for a small gap in the traffic and then accelerate quickly.
  c. count to 10 before you cross the intersection.

10 When you enter a T-intersection, you must
  a. give the right-of-way to the car on the left.
  b. give the right-of-way to the car traveling on the continuing road.
  c. give the right-of-way to the car traveling on the road that ends.

11 Drive through a railroad crossing when
   a. warning lights are not flashing.
   b. crossing gates have not been lowered.
   c. you have looked both ways and do not see or hear an approaching train.

12 When you approach a roundabout,
   a. stop and look both ways before you enter the flow of traffic.
   b. be prepared to drive in a clockwise direction.
   c. yield to the traffic from the left until there is room for you to enter.

13 A side-impact crash occurs when
   a. a vehicle hits another vehicle in the side, sometimes causing death.
   b. a vehicle crashes into the rear of another vehicle, turning the vehicle around.
   c. a vehicle hits a pedestrian who is crossing a side street.

14 When sharing the roadway with cyclists,
   a. expect that cyclists will be more visible when they travel in bike lanes.
   b. drive with headlights on, signal when turning, changing lanes, or stopping.
   c. blow your horn so the cyclist will move.

15 Drivers of SUVs should
   a. be careful when driving in windy conditions.
   b. decrease their following distance.
   c. allow less time than lighter vehicles to stop.

16 To avoid a crash with a truck,
   a. try to pass the truck before you enter a single-lane construction zone.
   b. move ahead to the right lane as soon as you pass the truck on the left side.
   c. assume that the truck is always traveling at a slower rate of speed.

17 Traffic engineers may use a diamond interchange to connect roads that have
   a. light traffic.
   b. heavy traffic wanting to turn left.
   c. special lane constraints.

18 A cloverleaf interchange allows vehicles to
   a. connect to the freeway from a side street.
   b. bypass a toll freeway.
   c. use loops to exit one road and enter another without stopping.

19 Jaywalking occurs when
   a. pedestrians are distracted when crossing a street.
   b. people lose control of their skateboards.
   c. pedestrians walk into the street from between parked vehicles.

20 When driving through a residential area,
   a. yield to pedestrians even if they are crossing the road illegally.
   b. blast your horn loudly so pedestrians will move out of harm's way.
   c. concentrate only on traffic signs and signals.

Challenge Question

Foundations of effective driving are especially important when you drive on
   a. residential streets because you may encounter unexpected obstacles suddenly moving in your path.
   b. multiple-lane highways because you may encounter double-parked vehicles.
   c. rural roads because there are no traffic signs or speed limit restrictions.

UNIT 5

CHALLENGES TO VEHICLE CONTROL

What factors affect vehicle control?

It isn't easy to control a vehicle under every driving situation. For one thing, natural laws affect how a vehicle stops and moves in space. Your ability to see and stop can be challenged by adverse weather and road and driving conditions. Even the environment can challenge your control over the vehicle you are driving, as can a malfunctioning vehicle or certain actions by other drivers that call for an appropriate response. This unit looks at some challenges to vehicle control and suggests ways to cope with them as you drive.

Vehicle Movement

Can Natural Laws Affect Your Driving?

Natural laws include the laws of inertia, friction, gravity, and momentum. While you may have some background knowledge of these laws from your science classes, did you know that natural laws have a major impact on the way you drive your vehicle? In this chapter, you will learn how natural laws help you operate your vehicle and how they can help you manage risk.

Driver Ed *Online*

For additional activities, visit drivered.glencoe.com. Here you will find:

◆ **Web Link Exercises**

◆ **eFlashcards**

◆ **Practice Driving Tests**

LESSON 1

Using Appropriate Speed

OBJECTIVE

1. **Describe** the three major highway conditions that require you to adjust speed.

An appropriate speed is one that keeps the driver traveling safely. This means that you must be aware of conditions and drive accordingly. A reasonable and proper speed provides time and space to brake and steer to a safe alternate path 8 to 12 seconds ahead of any emergency that develops. If you drive too fast for conditions, then you will not be able to stop in time to avoid a collision. Traveling at an inappropriate speed also makes it more difficult for other drivers and pedestrians to predict your probable actions.

How Can You Adjust Speed to Highway Conditions?

It is important to be aware of when a speed adjustment is necessary. One factor that determines whether a speed adjustment is necessary is a change in highway conditions. Changes in visibility, traction, and space are the three major highway conditions that require you to adjust speed.

Energy Tip

When driving on the highway, maintaining a speed of 55 mph will improve your gas mileage by about 20 percent over traveling at 65 mph.

VISIBILITY

Your speed affects the distance you can see ahead along your projected path of travel. For example, imagine you can see only 200 feet ahead of your car because of road or inclement weather conditions (such as rain or snow). Assume you are traveling at 55 mph, a speed that requires about 300 feet to stop. You could not possibly stop your car in time to avoid hitting a stationary object in your path or avoid other emergencies because by the time you see it, there isn't time to stop the vehicle.

You also must be able to see either side of the roadway. You need to see well enough to search intersections, driveways, and other roadside areas where other vehicles or pedestrians may emerge.

TRACTION

Rain, snow, sleet, or hail makes the road's surface slippery and more difficult to drive on. Unfavorable weather reduces traction, so you need more time and distance to stop. On snow or ice, you may need 6 to 8 seconds more to stop the car.

SPACE

Make sure you have adequate distance to stop or maneuver safely. On the highway, always adjust your speed so that your stopping zone is less than the distance you can see ahead.

When Should You Adjust Your Speed?

The location of other vehicles in traffic determines whether you need to speed up or slow down. In many situations, such as changing lanes or accelerating across a gap in traffic, you will need to adjust your speed, or speed up. Allow adequate time to complete the maneuver. Most control actions require about ½ to ¾ of a second, while high-risk maneuvers made under stress and severe space limits may take up to 10 seconds.

When you can't keep a safe distance between your vehicle and other vehicles or objects, slow down. The closer a driver must pass by an object, the slower the speed should be. This is especially true when passing a slow-moving vehicle that might change direction suddenly or stop quickly. Make a greater reduction in speed when the consequences of a possible collision are increased.

WHAT WOULD YOU DO?
What procedures would you follow prior to and after the crest (top) of this hill? What safety precautions should you take to improve your visibility?

Lesson 1 Review

❶ What are the three major highway conditions that require the driver to adjust speed?

❷ When should you adjust your speed?

❸ What is the definition of *appropriate speed*?

Total Stopping Distance

OBJECTIVES

1. **Describe** the three components of total stopping distance.
2. **Determine** the total stopping distance for a vehicle traveling at 60 mph.

KEY TERM

♦ total stopping distance

Driving too fast is a major cause of crashes, injuries, and fatalities because it takes time to stop a vehicle. During that time, a vehicle continues to move. Both the driver's reactions and the vehicle's equipment are factors in stopping distance. Understanding and respecting the concept of total stopping distance may help you prevent a crash.

What Is Total Stopping Distance?

You might think that if the car you were following suddenly started braking, you could brake and end up stopped the same distance apart. This idea is not correct. The distance it takes you to stop any vehicle is called the **total stopping distance** (see **Figure 12.1**). The total stopping distance of a vehicle is made up of three components:

● human-perception distance
● human-reaction distance
● vehicle-braking distance

HUMAN-PERCEPTION DISTANCE

You must see and recognize a problem in order to react to it. Human perception is the distance your vehicle travels from the time your eyes see a hazard until your brain recognizes it. Perception time for an alert driver averages from $1/2$ to $3/4$ second. At 60 mph, you travel 44 to 66 feet in this period of time. Mathematically, a good way to calculate this is to take 1.1 times the speed (in miles per hour) equals perception distance in feet.

HUMAN-REACTION DISTANCE

After you recognize a problem, your body must physically react to it. Human-reaction time is the distance traveled from the time your brain tells your foot to move from the accelerator until the time your foot pushes the brake pedal. An average alert driver reacts within $1/2$ to $3/4$ second. This adds an additional 44 to 66 feet to the distance traveled at 60 mph.

VEHICLE-BRAKING DISTANCE

Once the driver reacts, the vehicle must mechanically react, too. Vehicle-reaction time is the time it takes the vehicle to begin slowing down once the brake pedal is applied. How much time this takes depends on the brake pedal free-play, hydraulic properties of the brake fluid, and how well the brakes work. Vehicle-reaction time usually is from 0 to $1/4$ second, and it can add distance to the time required to stop.

FYI

The average driver takes $1/2$ to $3/4$ of a second to step on the brake after identifying a dangerous situation. Thus, even at 20 mph, your vehicle would travel at least 20 feet before you could step on the brake.

FIGURE 12.1 **STOPPING DISTANCE AT SPEEDS**

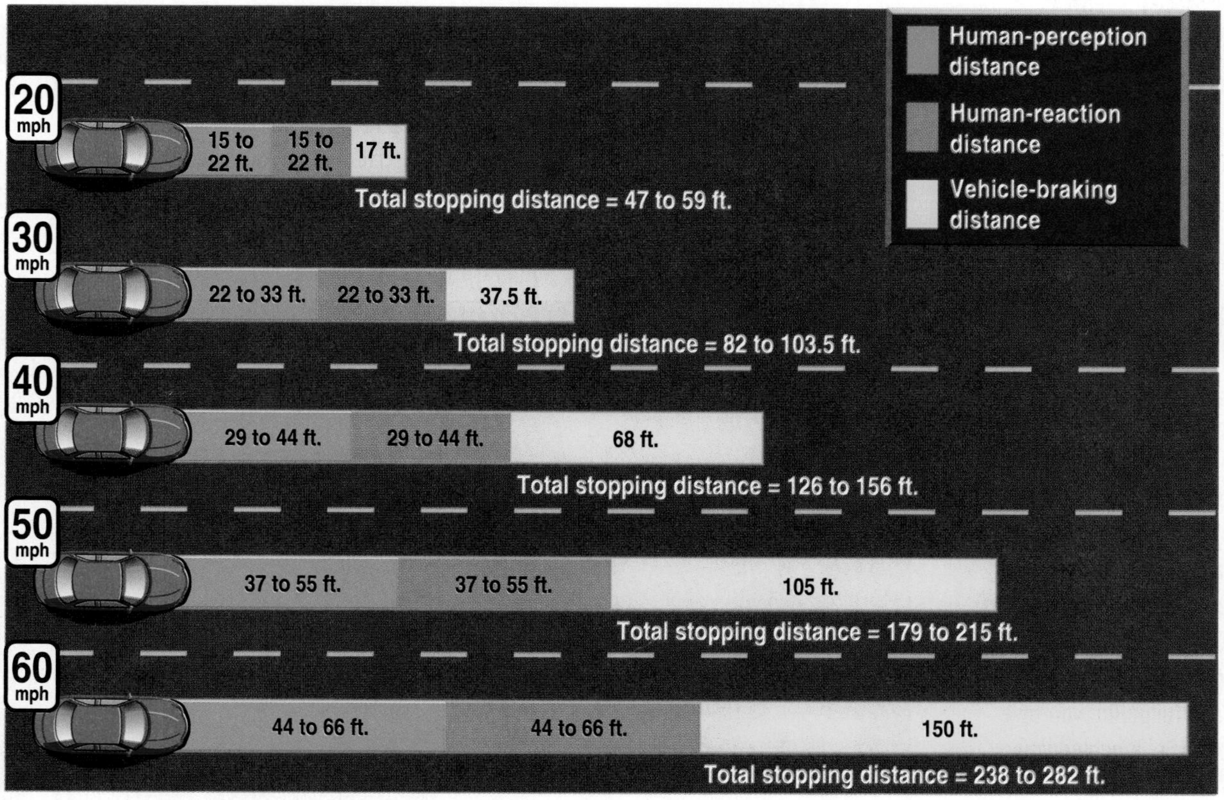

Legend:
- Human-perception distance
- Human-reaction distance
- Vehicle-braking distance

20 mph
15 to 22 ft. | 15 to 22 ft. | 17 ft.
Total stopping distance = 47 to 59 ft.

30 mph
22 to 33 ft. | 22 to 33 ft. | 37.5 ft.
Total stopping distance = 82 to 103.5 ft.

40 mph
29 to 44 ft. | 29 to 44 ft. | 68 ft.
Total stopping distance = 126 to 156 ft.

50 mph
37 to 55 ft. | 37 to 55 ft. | 105 ft.
Total stopping distance = 179 to 215 ft.

60 mph
44 to 66 ft. | 44 to 66 ft. | 150 ft.
Total stopping distance = 238 to 282 ft.

Stopping distance depends on many factors, including the vehicle's weight, speed, condition of the tires and brakes, and road surface conditions.

It takes time for a vehicle to stop even after you hit the brakes. Vehicle-braking distance is the distance it takes the vehicle to stop once you apply the brakes. At 60 mph on dry pavement, it takes a new 3,000-pound vehicle with good brakes about 3½ to 4¼ seconds to stop. Within that time, the vehicle will travel another 160 feet (braking distance equals 0.04 times the speed squared). Braking capability depends on the following factors:

1. the type of braking system
2. the brake pad material
3. the brake alignment
4. the vehicle's tire pressures
5. the tire tread and grip
6. the vehicle weight
7. the suspension system
8. the coefficient of friction of the road surface
9. the wind speed
10. the slope of road
11. the road's surface smoothness
12. the braking technique applied by the driver

Not allowing for total stopping distance is why a car that is following you too closely often cannot stop when your brake lights come on. The driver in the vehicle following you hadn't completed the perception and the human- and vehicle-reaction periods by the time he or she hit the rear end of your car.

How Long Does It Take to Stop a Vehicle Traveling 60 MPH?

For an average, alert driver traveling at 60 mph, it will take a total of about 4 to 6 seconds to stop a 3,000-pound vehicle. During this short time, the vehicle will travel a total stopping distance of approximately 248 to 292 feet before coming to a stop. That is almost the entire length of a football field.

As you drive, keep a safe distance from the car ahead to allow time to stop your vehicle safely. You must always adjust your speed to suit weather conditions, the road (such as hills and curves), visibility, and traffic.

SAFETY TIP

At highway speeds of 40 to 65 mph, you'll need at least 4 to 5 seconds to react to a threatening situation and brake your vehicle to a stop. Therefore, you must be able to see ahead at all times an absolute minimum of 4 to 5 seconds. Furthermore, if a vehicle is tailgating you or a large vehicle is behind you, you should identify an escape path for evasive steering. Too often such vehicles cannot stop in time to avoid rear-ending the vehicle in front of them.

WHAT WOULD YOU DO?
What are some ways you can manage visibility, time, and space in this situation?

Lesson 2 Review

❶ What four components make up total stopping distance?

❷ What are the total stopping distances when traveling at 30 mph, 50 mph, and 60 mph?

❸ What is vehicle-braking distance?

Natural Laws and the Movement of Your Vehicle

Natural laws are always at work. Imagine that you are in a vehicle and the driver applies the brakes. The vehicle stops, but your books on the backseat of the vehicle fall forward onto the floor. Why did this happen? The books were obeying a natural law, the law of inertia. The books weren't attached firmly to the car, so they kept moving forward in space even though the car was slowing down. Then the law of gravity pulled them down to the floor.

What Are Natural Laws?

Natural laws are forces in nature that are always at work. Some of the natural laws that affect you as a driver include the laws of inertia, friction, momentum, kinetic energy, and gravity.

INERTIA

The law of inertia helped cause your books on the backseat to continue moving forward even after the driver braked. All physical objects have inertia. As the vehicle was moving, so were your books. When the driver braked, a force was exerted to make the vehicle stop, but unrestrained, your books kept moving forward in a straight line. Then they fell to the floor.

There are two aspects of the law of **inertia**. One is that moving objects continue to move in a straight line unless some force acts on them. The other is that objects at rest do not move unless some force acts on them. Drivers must manage risk by anticipating how to reduce inertia's effects.

When you drive, you, your passengers, and the objects in your vehicle have inertia. If you brake a vehicle hard, everyone and everything will tend to keep moving forward. One way to manage the effects of inertia is to wear safety belts. These belts provide a force that restrains the force of inertia. If you brake hard and are not wearing a safety belt, you may be thrown forward against the steering wheel, windshield, or dashboard. You can also manage the risk of inertia by securing all loose objects, such as your books, luggage, or boxes. Securing these objects will prevent them from moving around when you brake hard.

FRICTION

Press your foot down hard on a carpeted floor. Keep it pressed down as hard as you can and try to move across the carpet. Does it feel as if some kind of force is trying to stop your foot from moving, almost as if your foot and the carpet are sticking together?

The force that seems to make your shoe "stick" to the carpet's surface is called **friction**. Friction is the force between two surfaces that resists the

OBJECTIVES

1. **Describe** the natural laws of inertia, friction, momentum, kinetic energy, and gravity.
2. **Explain** the relationship of these natural laws to driving.

KEY TERMS

- ◆ inertia
- ◆ friction
- ◆ traction
- ◆ adhesion
- ◆ momentum
- ◆ kinetic energy
- ◆ gravity
- ◆ center of gravity

Driver Ed Online

Topic: Friction and Automobile Tires

For a link to more information on how friction allows a wheel to turn, go to drivered.glencoe.com.

Activity: After you have read the information on this site, take the miniquiz to test your knowledge. Share your results with the class.

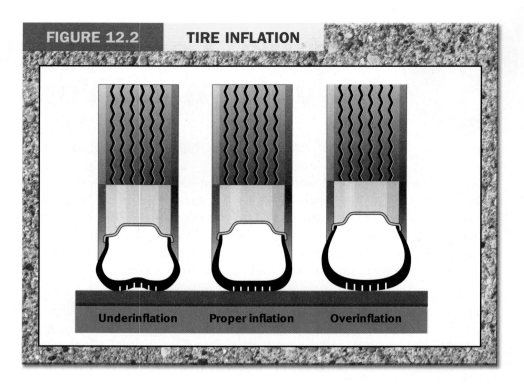

FIGURE 12.2

TIRE INFLATION

Underinflation   **Proper inflation**   **Overinflation**

movement of one surface across the other; it is the force that seems to hold the two surfaces together. Just as friction tries to make your foot stick to the carpet, it helps make the surface of your tires "stick" to the surface of the road. Your vehicle has to overcome friction in order to move. At the same time, your vehicle stays on the road because a certain amount of friction is always present.

Friction between the road and your tires is called **traction**, or **adhesion**, a word that means "sticking together." Traction holds your vehicle on the road. But your vehicle's level of traction can change. Here are some factors affecting your vehicle's traction.

Tire pressure. Tires are made with grooved surface treads that are designed to grip the road in a wide variety of conditions. You should inflate tires to the maximum pressure recommended by the vehicle manufacturer. Properly inflated tires create the best traction because they grip the road evenly. Under- or overinflation reduces traction. If you underinflate your tires, only the outer edges grip the road. If you overinflate them, only the centers tend to make contact with the road. **Figure 12.2** shows you different tire inflation levels.

Tire condition. Would you try to walk on slippery packed snow or ice with plastic bags on your feet? Of course not! You would slide all over. The same concept applies to tires. Bald tires—tires with very little or no tread—provide almost no traction on wet, icy, or snow-covered roads. Even on dry roads, bald tires reduce directional control, particularly if there is sand or debris on the road. Bald tires are also more apt than treaded tires to get punctured.

Rain. When the road is wet, water gets between the surface of the road and the tires and reduces the amount of friction or traction. At 55 mph, tires can lose contact with the road surface if the water is as shallow as $\frac{1}{12}$ inch. Water provides a smooth, nearly frictionless, surface for the tires to move across, and

To check your tires' tread depth, examine the tread-wear bars that are built into the tire. When the tread-wear bars are even with the surface of the tread at more than two spots around the tire, the tire is no longer legal or safe to use. *Why is it important to have proper tread depth on your tires?*

it does not provide good traction. If tires are properly inflated and have good tread, much of the water will go into the grooves between the treads. This means that the treads themselves will maintain contact with the road surface. Problems occur when the treads on the tires that help grip the road are unable to get proper traction. The minimum legal—though not necessarily safe—tread depth for your tires is $1/16$ inch.

Ice and snow. Ice and snow reduce traction even more than rain. Traction is poorest near 32°F, when snow and ice start to melt and become a slippery, watery slush. Any road is dangerous when covered with ice or snow, so increase awareness, reduce speed, increase space margins around the vehicle, and perform maneuvers smoothly and gradually. Snow tires do help increase traction in snow but not necessarily on ice. In states where studded tires are allowed, they can help on ice, but they are not as effective as chains. Chains are helpful in increasing traction on ice, but they provide poor traction on pavement. All-weather tires are a good choice for most drivers.

Snow and ice make a roadway slick, reducing friction between the tires and the road's surface. *What should you do when driving in these conditions?*

Road condition. The condition of the road also affects traction. Rough roads, potholes, and a poor vehicle-suspension system may make your vehicle's tires bounce up and down, reducing traction. Wet leaves on the road also reduce friction, causing the tires to lose traction and slide.

MOMENTUM

If a 60,000-pound Mac truck and a 5,000-pound compact car were rolling toward an object at the same speed, which vehicle would cause more damage? The truck would, because it is heavier and it has greater momentum.

DRYING THE BRAKES

Wet brakes do not work as efficiently as dry brakes. After you have driven through heavy rain or deep puddles, always check for wet brakes. If you apply the brakes lightly and the vehicle pulls to one side or does not slow as quickly as normal, your brakes are probably wet. Dry the brakes by driving slowly and applying light pressure on the brake pedal with your left foot. The friction created will generate heat, which will dry the brakes.

Momentum is the quality of motion in a moving object, a combination of its weight and its speed. Momentum provides an explanation for what seems obvious in the above example. All objects in motion have momentum. The greater the momentum of the vehicle, the greater the damage in a collision will be. If the vehicle's weight or speed doubles, so does the vehicle's momentum. If the weight or speed triples, so does momentum.

As a driver, you need to understand that as your speed increases, so does the likelihood of damage in case of a collision. Lighter vehicles may cause less damage to your car than heavier vehicles because of reduced momentum. However, the lighter your vehicle, the greater the likelihood that it will be damaged when in a collision.

KINETIC ENERGY

All objects in motion have kinetic energy as well as momentum. **Kinetic energy** is the energy of motion, not the motion itself.

Understanding kinetic energy is important because the more kinetic energy a vehicle has, the more time and distance it will take to stop. The faster a vehicle moves, the more energy of motion it has. If a vehicle's speed doubles, the stopping distance increases by an amount equal to the square of the difference in speed.

Here is an example of how kinetic energy and momentum affect you when you are accelerating or braking.

Accelerating. Suppose that you drive a van or sport utility vehicle (SUV) and usually carry one or two passengers and light packages. You know how your vehicle usually accelerates when you enter an expressway. Suddenly, things change. You are now going on a trip with four other people, and the back of the van or SUV is fully packed, so you have increased the weight of your vehicle. It will take more power to build your normal momentum, but once you get moving, your kinetic energy will be greater. On a practical level, the vehicle will not accelerate as quickly, and you will not be able to enter an expressway as quickly as you usually do. With a heavier load and more kinetic energy, you need to manage time and space differently. You will have to press down more on the accelerator to compensate for the extra weight. You will also have to wait for a larger gap in traffic before entering the roadway.

Braking. Once you are moving on the expressway, the van or SUV's momentum and kinetic energy have increased because its weight and speed have been increased. This means that its stopping distance has also increased. Reduce your risk by leaving a greater distance between your vehicle and the one in front of you. You don't have to do the math to realize that the faster you are traveling, the more space you have to leave in front of you in case you have to brake suddenly.

GRAVITY

If you toss a skateboard into the air, it comes down. The skateboard falls because of gravity. **Gravity** is a force that pulls all objects toward the center of the earth. Because gravity affects all objects, it can make a vehicle speed up or slow down.

When you drive uphill, gravity acts to slow your vehicle because the force of gravity is pulling you down as you drive up. To maintain speed, accelerate just before the vehicle begins to climb the hill, and this will give you a little more upward power to compensate for the downward pull of gravity. When you drive downhill, gravity acts with your vehicle, pulling it down the hill faster, so your speed increases. To keep the vehicle from moving downhill too fast, ease up on the accelerator to give your car less power to compensate for the pull of gravity. You may even have to use your brakes or downshift.

CENTER OF GRAVITY

Gravity gives objects their weight. The weight of an object, such as your vehicle, is distributed evenly about a point somewhere in the center of the vehicle, between all four tires. This point is called the object's **center of gravity**. The lower an object's center of gravity, the more stable the object. Small cars that sit low to the ground are therefore more stable than SUVs and vans, which sit

Energy Tip

Do not overload your vehicle. Every 100 miles that you travel with extra weight costs you 1 mile per gallon.

Overpacking can make a vehicle less stable by changing its center of gravity. **Why is this dangerous?**

higher off the ground. Most vehicles are designed to have a relatively low center of gravity in order to handle well in turns and during quick maneuvers.

Changes in a vehicle's center of gravity affect how well the vehicle handles. A roof carrier loaded with heavy objects, such as lumber, camping gear, or luggage, raises the vehicle's center of gravity. Raising the center of gravity makes a vehicle less stable and difficult to control on turns and curves and during sudden changes in braking, acceleration, and direction. Vehicles that have a high center of gravity, such as sport utility vehicles, some types of vans, and pickup trucks, also have these problems.

WHAT WOULD YOU DO?
What would you say to the driver and passenger about wearing safety belts?

Lesson 3 Review

❶ What affects traction? How?

❷ How would changes in a vehicle's center of gravity affect its stability?

❸ What are the natural laws affecting drivers?

Natural Laws and Steering and Braking

Natural laws affect many of the most important factors involved in driving, such as braking and steering. Understanding the relationships between natural laws and driving can help you to be a better and a safer driver.

How Do Natural Laws Influence Braking Distance?

As you learned in Lesson 1, the distance your vehicle takes to stop is its total stopping distance. As previously stated, a combination of perception distance, reaction distance, and braking distance make up total stopping distance. In an emergency, it takes approximately 4 or 5 seconds to stop. This is a three-step process. You must first identify a need to stop, your human-perception distance. Next, you react by moving your foot from the accelerator to the brake, your human-reaction distance. Finally, there is the road space required to stop your vehicle once the brakes are applied, your vehicle-braking distance. All these moves take a little time while the vehicle is slowing to a stop.

FACTORS AFFECTING BRAKING DISTANCE

The laws of friction, momentum, and kinetic energy definitely affect the time it takes you to stop. Braking is a result of friction between the two parts of your brakes. This friction you create by pushing the brake slows the rotation of the wheels and tires. As you brake, the friction you applied is working against your vehicle's momentum and kinetic energy by utilizing friction in the brakes and friction between the tires and the road.

In addition to natural laws, factors such as speed, vehicle condition, and roadway conditions can also increase your braking distance.

Speed. The greater the speed, the greater the momentum, and the longer the braking distance. Therefore, your vehicle requires more braking distance when you are traveling at 55 mph than it would when traveling at 35 mph.

Vehicle condition. The condition of your vehicle can also affect your braking distance. Worn brakes, tires, or shock absorbers reduce the traction needed to stop. Reduced traction increases braking distance. To prevent this from happening, it is important to keep your brakes, tires, and shock absorbers in good condition.

Roadway conditions. Braking distance is greater when roadway friction is reduced, such as by rain, snow, ice, sand, leaves, vehicle fluids, and other debris, or if the road is unpaved. On hills and mountains, gravity adds to the time and space needed to stop a vehicle going downhill because gravity contributes to its inertia, so the braking distance increases.

OBJECTIVES

1. **Explain** how natural laws affect a vehicle's stopping distance.
2. **Identify** the factors that affect steering.
3. **Name** the ways that natural laws affect steering around a curve.
4. **Describe** how gravity and the contour of the road affect steering.

KEY TERMS

- **directional control**
- **centrifugal force**
- **banked curve**
- **crowned road**

FYI

Telephone poles usually are 100 feet apart. Use this measure to help you estimate distance while you are driving.

What Factors and Natural Laws Affect Steering?

Your ability to control a vehicle depends on your ability to steer. Steering is affected by natural laws, including friction and inertia.

Friction helps to keep your vehicle on the road. When a driver turns the steering wheel, the front tires provide the friction, or traction, to turn the vehicle. Because of inertia, a moving vehicle will tend to go in a straight line, although small, regular steering corrections will be necessary.

Directional control is a vehicle's ability to hold a straight line or to continue in a particular direction. You always have an easier time keeping the vehicle moving in the direction in which you steer it. For better control, hold the steering wheel with your fingers rather than the palms of your hands. Keep your thumbs along the face of the steering wheel, not wrapped around it. This provides you a better sense of feel of the interaction between the tires and the roadway and leads to better directional control.

The steering mechanism, tires, and suspension are three mechanical factors that are important in proper steering. Wheel alignment and road conditions are also important in steering, as is the way you load the vehicle if you are carrying extra weight, which can throw off your vehicle's normal center of gravity.

STEERING AROUND A CURVE

Inertia tends to keep a vehicle moving straight. As you enter a curve or turn, you must overcome the effects of inertia by turning the steering wheel. When you turn, you are directing the vehicle out of its straight path. At the same time, you feel as if you are being pulled toward the outer rim of the curve. What you feel is **centrifugal force**, which pushes you in the direction opposite to the way you are turning. Centrifugal force tends to throw a spinning or turning object away from the center of the spin (see **Figure 12.3**).

FIGURE 12.3   **CENTRIFUGAL FORCE**

Turning the steering wheel enables friction to overcome centrifugal force.

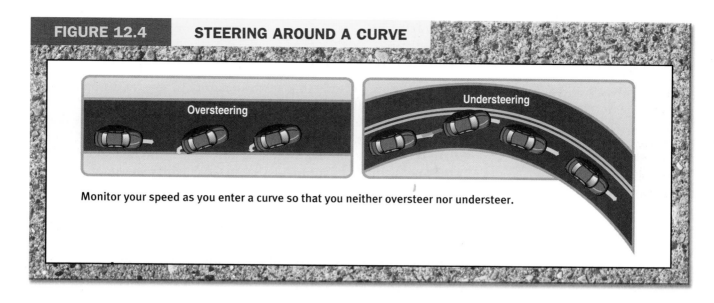

FIGURE 12.4   STEERING AROUND A CURVE

Oversteering

Understeering

Monitor your speed as you enter a curve so that you neither oversteer nor understeer.

Friction between the tires and the road acts against centrifugal force and allows the vehicle to follow a curved path. As long as there is enough friction to overcome centrifugal force, you can make the turn. As you turn the wheel, the front tires provide the traction needed to turn the vehicle.

Generally speaking, slow your vehicle as you approach a curve or turn. The faster you go, the more difficult it is for traction to overcome inertia (see **Figure 12.4**).

GRAVITY AND THE CONTOUR OF THE ROAD

The relationship between gravity and the contour of the road affects how well a vehicle will take a curve, particularly on banked roads and crowned roads (see **Figure 12.5**).

Banked roads. Have you ever seen the Indianapolis 500 auto race? The track contains **banked curves**, that is, they are built much higher on the outside of curves than on the inside. On a properly banked curve, the roadway tilts down toward the inside of the curve so that your vehicle can easily make the curve without running off the road. Since a vehicle tends to move toward the outside of a curve due to centrifugal force, the downward tilt of a banked curve improves steering control by working with the force of gravity to balance the

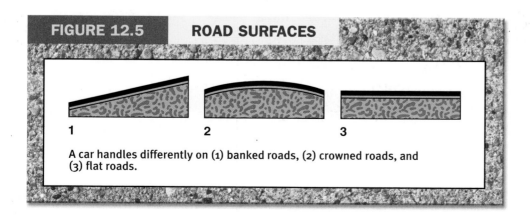

FIGURE 12.5   ROAD SURFACES

1   2   3

A car handles differently on (1) banked roads, (2) crowned roads, and (3) flat roads.

Bill Van Tassel

AAA National Office
Heathrow, FL

Your choice of speed greatly impacts your ability to steer and stop a vehicle. Let's say that after you apply the brakes, your vehicle takes 40 feet to stop from 30 mph. Would you guess that the same vehicle would take double the distance, 80 feet, to stop if it were moving at 60 mph instead? Wrong! Rather than the braking distance doubling at twice the original speed, the braking distance actually quadruples! That means it will take you roughly four times longer (160 feet) to stop at double the original speed. This makes it even more important to drive no faster than conditions allow. Remember, higher speeds require longer seeing distances and larger space margins. So be sure to maintain a safe following distance and watch your speed!

Besides speed, what affects your stopping distance?

WHAT WOULD YOU DO?
You are driving at 30 mph. Explain what you will do before you enter the turn.

effects of centrifugal force. If the bank tilted instead toward the outside of the curve, gravity and inertia would work together to pull the vehicle off the road, making steering more difficult.

Crowned roads. Roads that are higher in the center than at either of the edges are **crowned roads**. These roads facilitate drainage so that water can run off the roadway when it rains. When driving in the right lane on a two-way crowned road, gravity will tend to pull your vehicle to the right, off the roadway. You may have to counteract the effect of gravitational pull by steering slightly toward the center of the highway to keep the vehicle on the road. Slowing down as you drive will give you more control on this type of roadway.

Lesson 4 Review

❶ How do speed, traction, and gravity affect braking distance?

❷ Describe how steering is affected by traction and inertia.

❸ What role do friction and centrifugal force play in steering around a curve?

❹ How does gravity affect steering on a banked or crowned road? How should you respond?

BUILDING Skills

USING THE DISTANCE NUMBERS

The distance numbers shown on a map can give you a more accurate idea than the map scale of how far apart two places are. On this map, distance numbers are either black or red. The numbers indicate the distance in miles between towns, junctions, and interchanges.

Here's an example of how the numbers work. Find Lake Butler and Starke on the road map. Along the highway running between the two cities, you'll see a red number 15. This means that Lake Butler and Starke are 15 miles apart.

Along Route 301 between Starke and Waldo, you'll see the red number 11. It tells you that it is about 11 miles from Starke to Waldo.

If you add the numbers—15 + 11—the sum is 26. The distance by road from Lake Butler to Waldo, going through Starke, is about 26 miles.

In general, you can estimate driving time more accurately by using distance numbers rather than the map scale, especially if the road to be driven has many curves and loops. Keep in mind, though, that distance numbers indicate only the mileage, not the condition of the road. Six miles of travel along a twisting back road can take twice as long as 10 miles of highway driving!

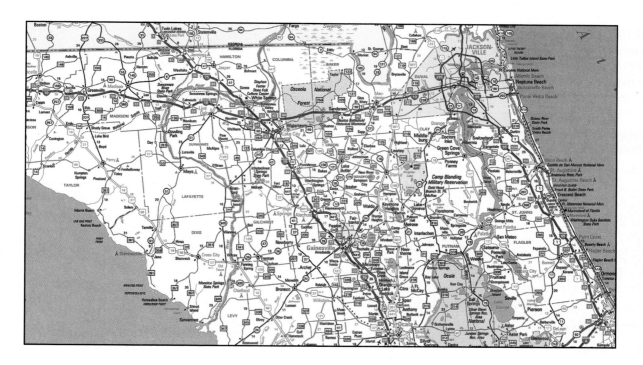

TRY IT YOURSELF

❶ How many miles is it from Otter Creek to Trenton along Routes 98 and 129?

❷ You're going from Jasper to Branford along Route 129. How far is it?

❸ What is the shortest route between Greenville and Branford?

Key Points

Lesson 1

1 Changes in visibility, traction, and space are the three major highway conditions that require you to adjust speed. (Page 252)

? WHAT WOULD YOU DO?
What procedures would you follow prior to and after the crest (top) of this hill? What safety precautions should you take to improve your visibility?

Lesson 2

1 The three components of total stopping distance are human-perception distance, human-reaction distance, and vehicle-braking distance. (Page 254)

2 For an average, alert driver traveling at 60 mph, it will take a total of about 4 to 6 seconds to stop a 3,000-pound vehicle. During this time, a vehicle will travel a total stopping distance of approximately 248 to 292 feet before coming to a stop. (Page 255)

Lesson 3

1 The law of inertia states that moving objects continue to move in a straight line unless some force acts on them. Friction is the force between two surfaces that resists movement. Momentum is a quality of motion in a moving object. Kinetic energy is the energy of motion.

Gravity is a force that pulls all objects toward the center of the earth. (Pages 257–261)

2 Inertia causes passengers and unsecured items to keep moving forward when a vehicle is stopped abruptly. Friction between the road and tires counteracts other natural forces. Momentum determines the extent of damage in a collision. Kinetic energy affects braking and acceleration. Gravity can slow your vehicle or increase its speed on hills. (Pages 257–261)

? WHAT WOULD YOU DO?
What would you say to the driver and passenger about wearing safety belts?

Lesson 4

1 As you brake, the friction applied is working against your vehicle's momentum and kinetic energy by utilizing friction in the brakes and friction between the tires and the road. (Page 263)

2 Steering is affected by natural laws including friction and inertia as well as mechanical factors, such as the steering mechanism, tires, and suspension. (Page 264)

3 As you enter a curve, inertia and centrifugal force can be overcome by the friction between the tires and roadway. (Page 264)

4 Gravity pulls a vehicle into the curve on an inwardly banked curve. If the banking is toward the outer part of the curve, gravity pulls the vehicle away from the curve. (Page 265)

On a separate sheet of paper, write the letter of the answer that best completes each sentence.

1 A vehicle's momentum depends on its
   a. kinetic energy.
   b. speed and weight.
   c. center of gravity.

2 If only the inner and outer edges of a tire grip the road,
   a. the tire is properly inflated.
   b. the tire is overinflated.
   c. the tire is underinflated.

3 Three factors that affect braking distance are
   a. vehicle and roadway conditions and speed.
   b. steering, centrifugal force, and tracking.
   c. tread, controlled recovery, and energy.

4 Vehicle-reaction time is usually
   a. $0 - \frac{1}{4}$ second.
   b. $\frac{1}{2} - \frac{3}{4}$ second.
   c. $3\frac{1}{2} - 4\frac{1}{2}$ seconds.

5 If your vehicle has good directional control,
   a. you can decrease total stopping distance.
   b. you will be able to keep the vehicle moving in the direction in which you steer it.
   c. you can make sharp turns at high speed.

6 How much additional time do you need to stop your car on snow or ice?
   a. $\frac{1}{2} - \frac{3}{4}$ second
   b. $3\frac{1}{2} - 4\frac{1}{2}$ seconds
   c. 6–8 seconds

On a separate piece of paper, write the word or phrase that best completes each sentence.

   traction

   kinetic energy

   center of gravity

   inertia

7 Any object in motion has _____.

8 Safety belts work against _____ to keep you from being thrown forward.

9 A higher _____ makes a vehicle less stable and harder to control on turns and curves.

10 Unfavorable weather reduces _____, so you need more time and distance to stop.

Writing

Driver's Log

In this chapter, you have learned about the effect that natural laws have on a variety of driving situations. Summarize, in a few sentences for each, the meaning of inertia, gravity, and momentum. Explain how these laws help you anticipate and manage risk.

Projects

❶ Make a photo display of potential low-traction areas in your community. Label each photo, and list the potential danger. Return to the area to check out your suspicion. Make sure to position yourself so that you are safe and will not become a danger to traffic.

❷ Check the shoulders and off-road areas of some local highways. Are they well designed and maintained? Do they provide an escape path in an emergency? What dangers do they pose to drivers? How could they be improved?

Light and Weather Conditions

Why Are Different Light and Weather Conditions Important?

Good drivers are prepared for any kind of light or road condition. In poor light and inclement weather conditions, it is important for you to understand how to manage visibility, time, and space in order to minimize risk.

Driver Ed *Online*

For additional activities, visit drivered.glencoe.com. Here you will find:

- ◆ **Web Link Exercises**
- ◆ **eFlashcards**
- ◆ **Practice Driving Tests**

Driving Safely in Low Light and at Night

OBJECTIVES

1. **Describe** how visibility is affected by low-light conditions.
2. **Explain** how to drive safely in low light and at night.

KEY TERM

◆ **overdriving your headlights**

You know you can't see as well at night, but the same is true just before sunrise or after sunset. As visibility decreases, your risk of not being able to see something coming—and getting in a collision—increases. To lessen your own risk, be aware that reduced light limits visibility.

How Do Low-Light Conditions Affect Visibility?

Your ability to see and to be seen diminishes when there is less light. This is obviously true at night, when you absolutely must use your headlights to see the road. But it is equally true during daybreak and at sundown, when traffic going to and from work is sometimes heavier and people don't always use their headlights. Intensifying and diminishing levels of sunlight during the dusk and dawn hours make it more difficult to see the roadway and vehicles traveling on it. Other drivers, as well as pedestrians, will have more difficulty seeing your vehicle at these times, particularly if you don't have your headlights on.

Night driving presents special challenges. At night, darkness limits your view of the road ahead and the surrounding area. Even with your headlights on, your ability to see ahead when turning or driving around a curve is severely reduced although you can often see the beams of the other vehicle's headlights before you can actually see the car. However, sudden glare from another vehicle's headlights can be distracting—or blinding.

How Can You Drive Safely When the Amount of Light Is Low?

FYI

Fifty percent of all teen motor vehicle fatalities occur between 9 P.M. and 6 A.M.

To drive safely in low-light conditions, you must maximize visibility by turning on your headlights. You must also manage time and space wisely.

Use common sense. When your view of the road is limited, slow down. Drive with your headlights on whenever you drive, day or night. Your headlights and taillights help illuminate your vehicle, making it easier for others to see you in all kinds of light. When you suddenly meet another car with its bright lights on, look at the line of the right side of the road for an instant until your eyes adjust.

DUSK AND DAWN DRIVING

Using your headlights makes it easier to see and be seen in the dim light of dusk and dawn. Do not use your parking lights. They are not designed to light the road ahead but only to indicate your position when you are parked.

Tips for New Drivers

NIGHT VISIBILITY

Here are additional tips for dealing with visibility problems at night.

▶ Avoid looking directly into the headlights of oncoming vehicles.

▶ If an approaching driver's high beams are on, quickly switch your own headlights from low to high and back again.

▶ Adjust your rearview mirror to cut glare from other headlights.

In addition to turning on your headlights at dawn or dusk, also try to increase the distance between your vehicle and the one ahead.

NIGHT DRIVING

Night driving requires a greater level of awareness. Since you can't see very well, it is wise to drive more slowly at night than you do during the day and to leave more distance between your vehicle and the vehicle ahead. Use the 3- or 4-second rule you have learned to help you judge a safe following distance in addition to using your headlights correctly.

Use low beams and high beams correctly. Usually you drive with low beams. Use your high beams to increase visibility only on very dark roads with no other vehicles around or on divided highways with no traffic in front of you. Switch back to low beams as soon as you spot a vehicle ahead of you. The glare of your high beams can momentarily blind another driver.

Do not overdrive your headlights. At night, drive at a speed that will allow you to stop within the range of your lights—that is, within the distance you can see. Driving faster than you can safely see is called **overdriving your headlights** and makes you vulnerable to unseen hazards. Look beyond your headlights. Get into the habit of looking for objects just beyond your headlight beams to see possible threatening conditions.

WHAT WOULD YOU DO? *What kinds of visibility problems do you face in this situation? How can you reduce the risk of collision?*

Lesson 1 Review

❶ Describe how visibility is affected by low-light conditions.

❷ What can you do to minimize risk when driving at night?

❸ What does the phrase *overdriving your headlights* mean?

Visibility, Bright Light, and Glare

OBJECTIVES

1. **Describe** the conditions that create glare from the sun.
2. **Explain** how you can drive safely in the glare of the sun.

Think of a bright summer morning, just as the sun rises. The sky is cloudless, and the world is bathed in sunlight. That's a pretty picture for a morning walk, but it is not always so pretty when you are behind the wheel of a vehicle. The beautiful sunlight can turn to dangerous glare.

What Conditions Create Glare from the Sun?

Sunlight increases visibility, but it is possible to get too much of a good thing. Glare is caused when the sun hits your windshield, and glare can act in the opposite way—it can reduce your ability to see. The sun's glare is most dangerous at certain times early and late in the day when you are driving directly into the sun. Glare from sunlight also reflects from other vehicles' windshields or even mirror-surface buildings if the angles are right.

In the morning or late afternoon, when the sun is low on the horizon, glare can make it hard to see the road ahead. With the sun in your face, glare can also reduce your ability to see the brake lights of other vehicles, especially if you're driving toward the sun with a dirty windshield, and the sun's rays are shining directly in your eyes.

How Can You Drive Safely in the Glare of the Sun?

As in all driving situations, advance preparation can help you minimize the risks associated with glare.

As part of your predriving check, make sure that your vehicle's windshield is clean. As part of your overall vehicle maintenance, replace a badly scratched or pitted front windshield. Glare is worse through a dirty or scratched windshield because the dirt and scratches intensify and refract the glare close to your face. So have sunglasses handy. As soon as you begin to squint, slip on the sunglasses to shield your eyes.

When you are dealing with glare, reduce your speed. Give yourself an extra margin of safety by leaving more distance between your vehicle and other vehicles. Adjust your sun visor to block out the sun, but be careful that the visor does not hinder your view of overhead signs and signals.

Glare decreases visibility and causes you to become more easily fatigued. *How can you reduce the effects of glare?*

Even if you have your sunglasses on and can see road signs and signals, keep in mind that others on the roadway may not be able to see as clearly as you. Always be alert for the sudden, careless, or unsafe actions of other drivers and pedestrians. Watch carefully for pedestrians—remember, they may be having trouble seeing because of the glare, too.

OTHER DRIVERS

If you are having trouble seeing, so are the drivers around you. Keep in mind that when the sun is behind you, oncoming drivers have the sun's glare in their eyes and may have trouble seeing you. Drive with your low-beam headlights on to make your vehicle more visible, and signal your intention to turn or change lanes well in advance.

The sun shining on the back of your vehicle may also make it very difficult for the driver behind you to see your brake lights or directional signals. For this reason, it's wise to tap the brake pedal to flash your taillights, to turn on your turn signals well in advance, and to use hand or arm signals as well to communicate your intentions.

The reflection of sunlight off snow and ice causes wide areas of glare. *How can you reduce the effects of glare from sunlight off snow and ice?*

?

WHAT WOULD YOU DO?
The sun is shining behind you. What can you do to minimize risk for both yourself and the drivers behind and ahead of you?

Lesson 2 Review

❶ Describe the circumstances in which the sun's light can create dangerous glare.

❷ What steps would you take to minimize overall risk in a glare situation?

❸ Describe how using your low-beam headlights helps you travel safely when glare is a factor.

Minimizing Risk in Rain and Snow

OBJECTIVES

1. **Explain** how to manage visibility, time, and space in rain and snow.
2. **Explain** how to minimize risk in rain and snow.

KEY TERM

◆ hydroplaning

It's nice to just stay indoors when it's raining or snowing outside. However, if you have to drive somewhere in rainy, icy, or snowy weather, it's not pleasant and can be dangerous. As a driver, you must understand and manage the risk that driving in such weather presents.

How Do Rain and Snow Affect Visibility, Time, and Space?

You won't be able to see very far ahead in heavy rain or snow. You may not even be able to see the edges of the roadway. Snow and sleet collecting on your windshield can produce blind areas that your windshield wipers can't reach. Snowy or rainy weather can also make the roadway slick, reducing the ability of your tires to grip the road. You won't be able to stop and steer as securely as under dry conditions, and the differences in stopping time and space increase your risk of collision unless you allow for them.

Rain and snow decrease your ability to see in every direction. Decreased visibility makes it more difficult than usual for you to judge distances and to manage time and space well. Bad weather conditions also make it much harder for other drivers and pedestrians to see your vehicle.

PRECAUTIONARY MEASURES IN RAIN AND SNOW

Advance preparation and some commonsense precautions will help you drive in rain and snow. Here are some steps you can take to control the level of risk when weather conditions are bad.

1. **Advance preparation.** Prepare in advance by cleaning your vehicle's windows and lights of dirt and snow. Check the tread and pressure of your tires. Check the headlights, windshield wipers, defroster, and other equipment to make sure they are in good working condition.
2. **Margin of safety.** Allow an extra margin of safety by driving more slowly and leaving extra space between your vehicle and other vehicles.
3. **Low-beam headlights.** Keep your low-beam headlights on at all times. This increases the distance you can see and makes your car more visible to other drivers and pedestrians.
4. **Vehicle tracks.** On wet pavement, drive in the tracks of the vehicle ahead of you. Those tracks are drier than the surrounding surface and offer better traction.
5. **Advance notice.** Give other drivers plenty of advance notice. When you intend to slow down or turn, communicate your intentions early by signaling so that other drivers have time to react accordingly.

Driver Ed Online

Topic: Winterizing a Vehicle

For a link to more information on getting a vehicle ready for winter, go to drivered .glencoe.com.

Activity: Using the information provided at this link, work with two or three other students to create a poster that illustrates several important tips for preparing a vehicle for winter weather.

6. **Turns and curves.** Ease your way into turns and curves. Avoid sudden acceleration, starts, or stops, which can cause your vehicle to go into a skid.
7. **Be alert.** Be on the watch for pedestrians dashing for shelter or those with umbrellas restricting their view of traffic.

PULL OFF THE ROAD

If rain becomes so heavy that even your windshield wipers' highest speed cannot keep up with the downpour, signal and then pull well off the road. Go into a protected area if possible, and wait for the storm to calm down. Remember to switch on your emergency flashers so that other drivers can see your vehicle while you're stopped.

You may also need to pull over in snow or sleet. Pull over if your windshield wipers become crusted with ice or if accumulating snow or sleet creates blind areas on your windshield. In this case, use a scraper and brush to remove all of the buildup. Run your defroster to clear the windshield as much as possible before you resume driving.

How Can You Minimize Risk in Rain and Snow?

The best way to reduce the level of risk in snowy or icy conditions is to postpone driving until the weather clears. Whenever possible, wait until the roads are plowed and sanded or salted before venturing out on them.

Unfortunately, sometimes you cannot postpone a trip. If you do have to drive under snowy or icy conditions, keep in mind that you might go into a skid. Drive slowly, with extra caution. Allow yourself an especially large margin of safety with other vehicles when you need to stop or turn. When you do want to slow down, stop, or turn, maneuver the vehicle gently and gradually.

If you live in a snowy area, keep on hand cold-weather items, such as a windshield scraper and brush, a shovel, jumper cables, emergency flares, and gloves during the winter.

PREVENTING BAD-WEATHER SKIDS

Skidding out of control is the biggest worry during bad weather. In Chapter 14, you will learn what to do if your vehicle starts to skid. If you change speed or direction gradually and smoothly rather than abruptly, you will minimize the chance of skidding.

Anticipate situations in which skids are likely, and take steps to maintain control of your vehicle. When you see a stop sign or red signal light ahead on an ice- or snow-packed roadway, press the brake pedal down very gently to avoid a skid.

ANTICIPATE AND PREVENT HYDROPLANING

A sudden shower of rain while you are driving presents an additional hazard. During the first 10 to 15 minutes of rainfall, the roads are at their slickest. This slickness occurs because the rain's moisture mixes with surface dirt and oil to form a slippery film. This film is like driving on an oily surface, and it greatly reduces the ability of your tires to grip the road.

SAFETY TIP

Avoid using your high beams in heavy rain, sleet, or snow. Under such conditions, light is reflected back into your eyes, decreasing your ability to see.

Energy Tip

Even though snow tires may be necessary during winter months, they reduce fuel economy. Remove them as soon as winter is over.

SAFETY TIP

If you are approaching a large vehicle on a slush-covered roadway, turn on your windshield washers and wipers about 2 to 3 seconds before you meet. This gets the glass wet and will help clean the glass quickly after you pass.

Dealing with the UNEXPECTED

STUCK IN THE SNOW?

If you get stuck in snow, you may be able to free your vehicle by "rocking" it. Follow these steps.

▲ Keep your front wheels pointed straight ahead.

▲ Shift back and forth between Drive (or First gear) and Reverse. Accelerate forward slowly and steadily. When the vehicle will move forward no farther, press firmly on the brake to stop and hold the vehicle while you quickly shift into Reverse.

▲ Release the brake and accelerate with gentle pressure as far back as the vehicle will go until the wheels start to spin. Step on the brake again and hold it while shifting to Drive or First gear.

▲ Repeat as necessary. Do not spin your wheels—you'll only dig yourself in more deeply.

WHAT WOULD YOU DO?
How would you get your vehicle out of a snowdrift?

Additionally, even at speeds as low as 35 mph, the tires of a vehicle can begin to skim along the wet surface of the road. The vehicle's tires may completely lose contact with the road and be moving on a thin film of water. This is called **hydroplaning**. Hydroplaning is very dangerous because it severely limits your ability to control your vehicle since your tires have actually lost contact with the road.

To reduce the chance of hydroplaning, reduce your speed by about one-third when driving on wet roadways. Make periodic checks to make sure your tires have plenty of tread and are properly inflated too.

Lesson 3 Review

❶ What strategies can you use to manage visibility, time, and space in rainy or snowy weather?

❷ What risks can you anticipate when driving in rain or snow? What steps can you take to minimize them?

❸ What can you do to prevent bad-weather skids?

Other Hazardous Weather Conditions

Snow and rain are not the only weather-related driving problems. These conditions have additional effects that are not present when it rains or snows. It is also important to be aware of other hazardous weather conditions. Fog, industrial smog, or a sudden dust storm or sandstorm affects visibility. Strong gusts of wind can blow your vehicle off the road. You can manage these conditions if you know what they are and what hazards they present.

OBJECTIVES

1. **Describe** three rain-related weather conditions.
2. **Describe** the risks involved with other hazardous weather conditions.

How Can You Manage Other Rain-Related Conditions?

When driving in other rain-related conditions, you must take the same steps in managing your visibility and minimizing your risk that you do when it rains. In addition, it is important that you know what to do if you are caught in these particular conditions.

THUNDERSTORMS

Thunderstorms can be harsh and unpredictable. Some thunderstorms can be seen approaching, while others hit without any warning. If your visibility becomes impaired from the thunderstorm, pull safely onto the shoulder of the roadway, away from any trees that could fall on your vehicle, and turn on your emergency lights until the heavy rains subside. Make sure you stay in your vehicle with the windows closed to protect yourself from lightning.

What would you do if you encountered a thunderstorm while driving?

HAIL

Hail can be destructive and should be taken seriously. Hailstorms relentlessly pummel everything in their paths, from trees to vehicles. If a hailstorm catches you while driving, you should take extra precautions to protect yourself and your car. To stay safe and avoid damage, stay inside your vehicle. Hail can travel at highway speeds or higher—the larger the hail, the faster it falls.

If possible, stop driving and pull to a safe place so the hail doesn't break your windshield or any windows—driving compounds hail's impact with your car. When you stop, do so under an overpass, and don't forget to pull out of traffic lanes and onto a shoulder. Avoid ditches due to possible high-rising water.

Floods are the number one weather-related killer in the United States. *How can you manage the risk of floods when driving?*

When parking, keep your car angled so the hail is hitting the front of your car. Windshields are reinforced to withstand forward driving and pelting objects. Side windows and back glass are not reinforced, so they are much more susceptible to breakage.

Finally, lie down if possible, and keep your back to the windows. If you have a blanket, cover yourself with it to prevent possible debris from hitting you.

FLOODS

If it is raining hard for several hours or rain is steady for several days, you should be aware of the possibility of floods. Begin by avoiding dips and under-passes. When you come to a flooded area, turn around and go the other way.

If you are caught in a flood, do not drive through flooded areas, even if they look shallow enough to cross. Two feet of water can easily carry away most automobiles. If your car is caught in a flash flood, abandon it immediately and move to higher ground.

How Can You Minimize Risk in Other Hazardous Weather Conditions?

You must understand and learn how to manage risk posed by other weather hazards, including fog, smog, sandstorms, dust storms, winds, and tornadoes.

FOG OR SMOG

Dense fog poses hazards. Scattered patches of fog may suddenly occur, cutting your field of vision without warning. If humidity is too high, moisture can form on the inside and the outside of the windshield, further reducing visibility. Turn on your windshield wipers and defogger as necessary.

Low-beam headlights are also essential when driving in fog. You may want to switch on your emergency flashers to further increase the ability of other highway users to see you. Resist the temptation to put on your high beams. The small droplets of water in fog reflect light back into your eyes, making visibility worse with high beams than with low beams.

To better manage time and space when driving in fog, reduce speed, increase your following distance, and remain alert for sudden movements.

If fog is very dense, the wisest thing to do is to signal, pull off the road, and wait for conditions to improve. Do not stop on the road. Stop outside a guardrail if possible, and turn off all lights.

In some areas, industrial smoke and other kinds of air pollution create smog that decreases drivers' visibility as much as fog. Methods described for driving in fog are equally useful for smog conditions.

SAND AND DUST

In some parts of the country, sandstorms and dust storms cause serious visibility problems.

As you drive, you may encounter various conditions that affect your ability to see and operate your car safely. To reduce risk, use your headlights every time you drive and keep them clean and aligned. Be alert to changing environmental and roadway conditions. When buying a car, consider one whose design limits blind spots and whose color enhances its ability to be seen.

Whenever visibility becomes limited, adjust your speed and position to provide more space between your car and other highway users.

If you are caught in a sandstorm or dust storm, signal, pull off the road, turn on your flashers, and wait for the storm to pass. If you must drive, use your low-beam headlights and proceed slowly and very cautiously.

Never try to out drive a tornado. **What are some of the dangers of out driving a tornado?**

WIND

Depending on the size and weight of the vehicle you are driving, high winds can be a nuisance—or dangerous. A strong gust of wind can actually push a lightweight vehicle right out of its lane!

Under windy conditions, reduce speed and grip the steering wheel firmly to maintain control of your vehicle. Leave extra space between your vehicle and nearby vehicles, especially those that are likely to be affected by the wind, such as vans, recreational vehicles, and vehicles pulling trailers.

Nature is not the only source of wind. Buses, trucks, and tractor-trailers can generate powerful blasts of wind as they pass by you. Always allow as much distance as possible to the side between your vehicle and a passing large vehicle. In this way, you can minimize the force of the resulting wind gust.

Don Krites

Oregon Driver Education Center
Salem, OR

As you drive, you may encounter various conditions that affect your ability to see and operate your car safely. To reduce risk, use your headlights every time you drive and keep them clean and aligned. Be alert to changing environmental and roadway conditions. Whenever visibility becomes limited, adjust your speed and position to provide more space between your car and other highway users.

What are some conditions that might affect your ability to see and operate your car safely?

TORNADOES

Although tornadoes can occur at any time throughout the year, the peak activity period is March through early July according to the National Weather Service. If you encounter a tornado while driving, listen to your car radio and stay alert until you get to safety.

If you spot a tornado, get out of the vehicle and take shelter in a substantial structure. However, if there is no time to get indoors, lie flat in the nearest ditch or depression and use your hands to cover your head and protect yourself from flying debris. Never try to outdrive a tornado. It changes direction quickly and can easily lift and toss a car or truck through the air.

? **WHAT WOULD YOU DO?**
Explain how you would manage risk in this situation.

Lesson 4 Review

❶ What weather conditions other than rain and snow pose dangers for drivers?

❷ What risks would you anticipate in these conditions?

❸ What should you do when caught in a flood?

BUILDING Skills — Geography

USING A TRIPTIK

A TripTik is a continuous series of strip maps in booklet form put out by the American Automobile Association (AAA). A TripTik provides detailed routing from one place to another. All you have to do is flip the strips.

The front page of each strip map shows a section of a through, cross-country route and all necessary highway details (Map A). The centerfold contains an area map (Map B). It shows the area surrounding the major route so that you can deviate from the marked route if you choose. The back page ordinarily shows detailed maps of cities along the marked route (Map C).

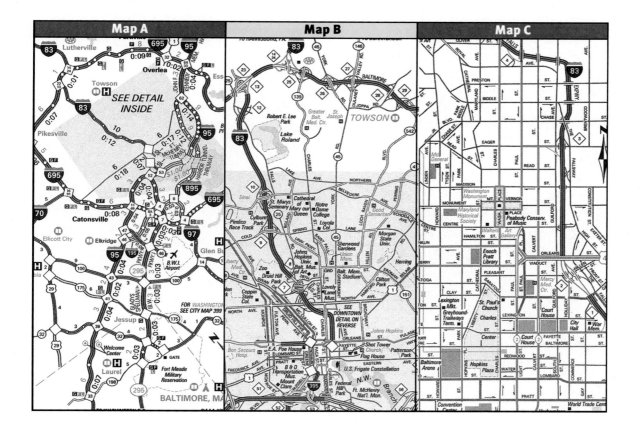

TRY IT YOURSELF

❶ On which map would you find the route highlighted for best travel through Baltimore? What route is this? What else does the map tell you about this route?

❷ You are at the corner of Bentwood Avenue, heading west on Chase Street. Describe how you would get to the Baltimore Arena. Which map would you use?

❸ Suppose you are north of Baltimore, traveling south on Route 83. You want to take Route 45 into the city. Which map would you use? How would you get to Route 45?

Map A   Map B   Map C

Key Points

Lesson 1

1 Reduced light during dusk and dawn and at night makes it harder for you to see and harder for others to see you. At night, your view of the roadway is limited, and you have to cope with glare from the lights of oncoming vehicles. (Page 272)

2 When driving in low light, reduce speed, increase following distance, signal turns well in advance, and use your low or high beams as appropriate. (Pages 272–273)

Lesson 2

? **WHAT WOULD YOU DO?**
The sun is shining behind you. What can you do to minimize risk for both yourself and the drivers behind and ahead of you?

1 When the sun is low on the horizon, glare makes it hard to see the road and the brake lights of other vehicles. (Page 274)

2 To minimize the risk from sun glare, wear sunglasses and use your sun visor. Reduce speed and increase your following distance. (Pages 274–275)

Lesson 3

1 Steps you can take to manage visibility, time, and space in rain or snow are to prepare in advance, leave an extra margin of safety, drive in the tracks of the vehicle ahead of you, signal other drivers early, keep your low-beam headlights on, ease your way into turns and curves, and slow down gradually for stops. (Pages 276–277)

2 To minimize risk in rain or snow, maneuver the vehicle gently and gradually to prevent skids, allow extra time for braking and steering, and drive slowly to avoid hydroplaning. (Pages 277–278)

? **WHAT WOULD YOU DO?**
Explain how you would manage risk in this situation.

Lesson 4

1 In thunderstorms, hail, and floods, you should pull over and avoid driving. (Pages 279–280)

2 Fog and smog decrease visibility. Keep on low-beam headlights, reduce speed, and increase following distance. If necessary, pull off the road and wait for driving conditions to improve. In a sandstorm or dust storm, pull off the road. Use emergency flashers to alert others of your presence. If you must drive, use low-beam headlights and proceed with caution. In heavy winds, reduce speed and grip the steering wheel firmly; increase the distance between your vehicle and other vehicles. (Pages 280–281)

On a separate sheet of paper, write the letter of the answer that best completes each sentence.

1. You can lessen the risk of sun glare by
   a. opening your sunroof.
   b. using your high beams.
   c. wearing sunglasses.

2. As visibility decreases,
   a. your risk of not being able to see something increases.
   b. your risk of not being able to see something decreases.
   c. the barometer rises.

3. Using your high beams in fog can
   a. increase visibility by as much as 250 feet.
   b. decrease your ability to see.
   c. warn other drivers of your approach.

4. A dirty or scratched windshield
   a. can cause you to skid in bad weather.
   b. can worsen the effects of glare.
   c. has no effect on glare.

5. To brake safely on a snow-packed road,
   a. quickly press the brake all the way to the floor.
   b. shift to Overdrive and press the brake.
   c. press the brake gradually.

6. Dense fog can
   a. permanently affect the surface of your windshield.
   b. cause moisture to accumulate on the inside of your windshield.
   c. cause elevated roadways to freeze.

On a separate sheet of paper, write the word or phrase that best completes each sentence.

sun visor

hydroplane

smog

taillights

7. When you _____, your car skims along the surface of water on the roadway.
8. Your headlights and _____ help illuminate your car.
9. One way to avoid glare is to use your _____.
10. Air pollution and smoke can create _____, which decreases drivers' visibility as much as fog does.

Writing

Driver's Log

In this chapter, you have learned how different light and weather conditions affect the driving task. Imagine that the temperature is between 25°F and 35°F and that it is beginning to rain. Write a weather advisory for drivers that gives hints on driving safely in these conditions and what conditions drivers might expect later in the day.

Projects

1. Laws governing the use of headlights and parking lights vary from state to state. Find out what the rules are in your state. Take an informal survey of drivers you know. How many are aware of your state's regulations?

2. Stores sell products designed to help drivers cope with winter driving. Visit a store and evaluate several such products. Which would you buy? Which would you avoid? Why? Discuss your findings with the class.

Environmental Challenges

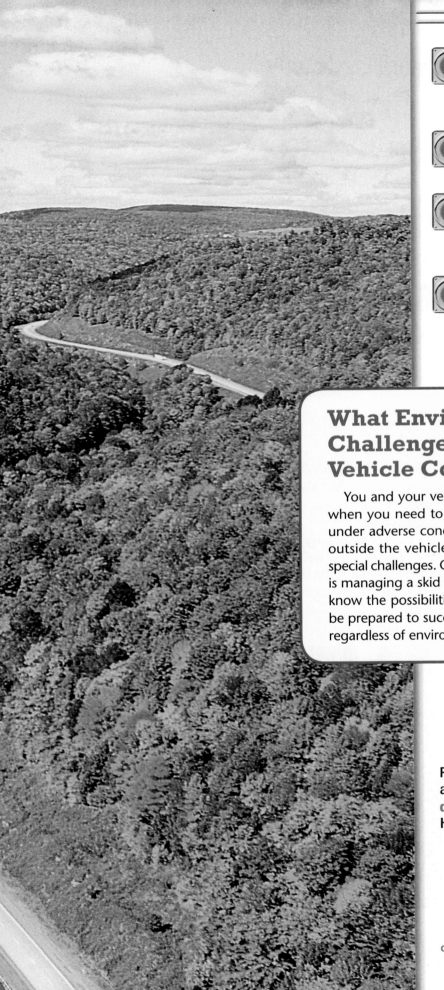

 LESSON 1
Hill and Mountain
Driving

 LESSON 2
Skids

 LESSON 3
Avoiding or Minimiz-
ing Crash Damage

 LESSON 4
Challenging
Environmental
Factors

What Environmental Challenges Can Affect Vehicle Control?

You and your vehicle's limits may be tested when you need to steer, brake, or accelerate under adverse conditions in the environment outside the vehicle. Mountain driving poses special challenges. One of the biggest problems is managing a skid when traction is lost. If you know the possibilities that can occur, you can be prepared to successfully control the vehicle regardless of environmental conditions.

Driver Ed
Online

For additional
activities, visit
drivered.glencoe.com.
Here you will find:

- **Web Link Exercises**
- **eFlashcards**
- **Practice Driving Tests**

LESSON 1

Hill and Mountain Driving

Mountain driving presents special problems for you as a driver. Driving on hills takes extra effort and more concentration on steering and speed control, regardless of whether your vehicle has an automatic transmission or a manual transmission. It is more difficult to control your speed as you go up and down hills, and your visibility and stopping distance are also affected in this driving environment.

How Do You Drive in the Mountains?

Driving on hills or mountain roads isn't easy. Roads are often curved, with reduced visibility, and grades may be steep. Shoulders may only be on one side of the road, with a sharp drop on the other side. Because of the force of gravity, you need to use extra care to be able to control your vehicle under these conditions.

GRAVITY IN THE MOUNTAINS

Whenever you drive, you always have an invisible passenger with you. That passenger is the force of gravity. Gravity works both inside and outside your vehicle at the same time.

When you drive uphill, gravity pulls against your vehicle, so you need to use more power. When you drive downhill, gravity is working with you, pulling you down faster, so you need to use less power, and you may have to use your brakes. For more information about how gravity affects your vehicle, see Chapter 12.

Whether you are driving uphill or downhill, the force of gravity is pulling on your car. **How does gravity affect the power of your vehicle when driving uphill and downhill?**

DRIVING UPHILL

As you drive uphill, your vehicle needs more power in order to keep moving at the same speed. When driving up a mountain, you sometimes encounter steep grades, which require a lot more power. You'll need to push the accelerator pedal harder, of course, but exactly how you provide that power depends on whether your vehicle has an automatic or a manual transmission.

Automatic transmission. Before your vehicle begins to lose speed while moving uphill, slowly increase the amount of pressure you are putting on the gas pedal. Notice your speedometer and pay attention to the feel of the vehicle and the sound of the engine. When you reach the speed you want to maintain, keep your foot at that point until you near the crest of the hill or need to slow down for any reason. If you have been driving in Overdrive, shift to Drive just prior to going uphill; this will give your vehicle more power.

Manual transmission. Before your vehicle begins to lose power and speed, downshift to a lower gear in order to increase the engine's pulling power. With a 5-speed manual transmission, for instance, you may have to downshift from Fifth to Fourth gear to make it up a hill. For more information on downshifting, see Chapter 5.

Listen to your engine. If the engine slows down, the vehicle is slowing down and losing power, too. If the engine revs too slowly, your power will drop dramatically. Know where your engine's best "power band" is (in revolutions per minute). Try to keep the engine near that range by selecting the proper gear.

DRIVING DOWNHILL

As you drive downhill, gravity will cause your vehicle to gain speed, although it does it slowly at first. You will need to decrease the engine power. How you do this depends on whether you have an automatic or a manual transmission.

Automatic transmission. Ease up on the pressure you are applying to the gas pedal. Your vehicle will begin to coast, although your transmission will have a slight braking effect. If your vehicle begins to pick up too much speed, and the hill is small, press the brake pedal lightly to slow down. If you are going to go down a long, steep hill, it is best to move the selector lever to a lower gear before starting down the hill, if possible. Doing so gives you better control of your speed and steering and saves on braking. If you need to use the brake, use periodic light to medium pressure, depending on the size of the hill. Do not ride the brake pedal. When brakes are applied continually down a long hill, the buildup of heat will reduce the efficiency and friction of the materials and "brake fade" will occur. It will feel as if the brakes are failing.

Manual transmission. If you are going to go down a long, steep hill, it is best to downshift to a lower gear before you start down the hill. For instance, with a 5-speed manual transmission, you may need to downshift from Fifth to Fourth gear. Doing so gives you more control over the speed of your vehicle. In a lower gear, taking your foot off the accelerator will slow down the car more than in a higher gear. If you wait to downshift until you are moving downhill and picking up speed, you will gain a little speed while you have the clutch depressed. Therefore, you may need to apply the brakes a little while

Did You Know ?

In the 1400s, the Inca Empire stretched from the border between Colombia and Ecuador to central Chile in South America. From Cuzco, the empire's capital, roads that were well-constructed ran to all parts of the empire. The total length of this road system was about 9,500 miles, and it was designed for people on foot. Relay runners were stationed at posts along the road to carry messages and parcels quickly to and from the capital.

Energy Tip

If your vehicle is equipped with cruise control, do not use it when you are driving uphill or downhill. It wastes gas. Save it for flat, straight roadways.

downshifting. If the hill is steep, a little braking power may not be enough to slow the vehicle. You may need to continue to apply the brakes and to down-shift again. Use your brakes to slow down even more if necessary.

RUN-OFF AREAS

Some steep hills contain run-off areas to help big trucks that are having difficulties in braking come to a stop. These run-off areas usually occur before a curve or at the bottom of a long hill, and they allow high-speed vehicles to continue off the road and then up a hill, using gravity and sometimes a soft road surface to slow down the vehicle. Usually, you will not need to use these areas unless you are driving a tractor-trailer truck or other large vehicle, but they help make you safer because they allow trucks going too fast to safely stop.

How Is Your Visibility Limited in the Mountains?

Some special visibility problems occur in the mountains. Sharp curves, steep grades, and other vehicles limit how much of the road ahead you can see at one time, whether it is day or night.

When you come to a curve where it is difficult to see oncoming traffic, slow down before the curve. If necessary, tap your horn and flash your lights to warn approaching drivers. If you are behind a truck or vehicle with a trailer, increase your following distance, and don't pass until you are positive it is safe to do so. Most mountain roads have passing zones; don't try to pass unless you're in one of these zones. Pay attention to signs and pavement markings.

EFFECTS OF HIGH ALTITUDE

High altitudes in the mountains can affect either the driver or the vehicle. In high altitudes, the air contains less oxygen. Lack of oxygen can cause you to feel short of breath and sleepy. Your heart may beat faster, and you may get a headache. If any of these symptoms occur, change drivers, stop driving, or find a route at a lower altitude, if possible.

Shift to a lower gear to control speed when driving down a long, steep hill. *What is the difference between driving down hill with an automatic transmission and a manual transmission?*

Mountain air also affects your vehicle's engine. The engine gets less oxygen and loses power. The engine heats up faster, and gas may vaporize in the fuel line, causing the engine to sputter and stall. Keep an eye on the temperature gauge. Engines that are not well maintained are prone to overheat under difficult conditions. If your temperature gauge shows red or hot, stop in a safe area and allow the engine to cool.

EFFECTS OF BAD WEATHER

Rain, snow, haze, and fog are especially dangerous when you are driving in the mountains. Try to find out about current weather conditions in the area before you begin a mountain drive. Certain seasons are more likely to have treacherous weather and can cause rock or mud slides. You should know when these times occur in your particular area. Remember that strong gusts of wind are also associated with mountain terrain and can occasionally send your vehicle into a skid.

WHAT WOULD YOU DO?
Your vehicle has an automatic transmission, and you've been using the Drive gear. Describe your procedure as you are about to head up a hill.

Lesson 1 Review

❶ How are procedures for driving uphill different from those for driving downhill?

❷ How can high altitude affect you and your vehicle if you are driving in the mountains?

❸ How can your visibility be limited when you are driving in the mountains?

LESSON 2

Skids

OBJECTIVES

1. **List** factors that can cause your vehicle to skid.
2. **Name** and describe the various kinds of skids.

KEY TERMS

- skid
- braking skid
- power skid
- cornering skid
- blowout skid

When you go into a **skid**, your vehicle careens wildly across the road. You lose control of the direction and speed of the vehicle. Understanding the natural laws that affect the control of your vehicle can help you regain that control when you lose it through skidding. If you skid, you are not helpless. If you think it through, once you understand what causes a skid, you're already on your way to understanding how to respond to it.

What Can Make Your Vehicle Skid?

The cause of a skid is too little traction for the action taken. A loss or reduction in traction can be frightening and dangerous. Even experienced drivers fear this loss of vehicle control. When traction is reduced because of a change in conditions, such as water on the road, your tires can lose their grip on the road's surface, and the vehicle may begin to slide. Momentum and inertia might carry your vehicle in a direction you may not want to go. People call this a skid.

Wet roads or excessive speed on a curve are among the things that can cause your vehicle to go into a skid. When your vehicle goes into a skid, tires spin, slip, and slide because the combination of your actions (braking, steering, or accelerating) requires more traction than is available. One of three basic things may have happened: you tried to change speed too quickly, you tried to change direction too quickly, or you tried to steer and change speed too quickly.

 Tips for New Drivers

DEALING WITH SKIDS

Skidding can be frightening. You can minimize trouble, however, by remembering the following points:

▶ Respond quickly and correctly. Concentrate. Do not panic.

▶ Do not brake. This will only make the skid worse.

▶ Look and steer in the direction you want the front of the vehicle to go.

▶ Make steering corrections quickly but smoothly.

▶ Do not give up. Keep steering.

Accelerate and brake gradually on snowy roadways. *Why should you accelerate and brake gradually on these roads?*

CHANGING SPEED TOO QUICKLY

You are on a slippery road, and you want to slow down. You step firmly on the brake pedal, but your vehicle starts to skid. What happened? You tried to change speed too quickly. Traction could not overcome the vehicle's kinetic energy and momentum as fast as you wanted it to. A skid can also result if you try to change speed too quickly by acceleration.

If you are driving a front-wheel drive vehicle, the front wheels lose traction and spin if you over accelerate. In rear-wheel drive vehicles, the rear wheels lose traction and spin if you over accelerate. And if you are driving an all-wheel drive vehicle, all wheels lose traction if you over accelerate.

How fast is a high speed, and what is changing speed too quickly? It depends on the road and the weather. Look at the speed-limit signs posted to determine the maximum safe speed. If road conditions or weather conditions are bad, slow down below the posted speed limit to stay safe and accelerate slowly to avoid spinning your drive wheels.

CHANGING DIRECTION TOO QUICKLY

Turning a vehicle too quickly is like trying to get a horse to make a sharp turn at a full gallop. Occasionally it works, but usually it doesn't. If you're driving at a high speed, your vehicle has built up a tremendous amount of momentum and kinetic energy. Inertia is also at work, trying to force your vehicle to move in a straight path. Tire traction may not be great enough to compensate for the forces of momentum, kinetic energy, and inertia when you turn or enter a sharp curve, not to mention the centrifugal force pulling your vehicle toward the outer edge of the turn.

Before you negotiate a curve, look at the speed limits posted just below the warning signs as you near a curve. They tell you the maximum safe speed you should use to enter the curve. Remember that centrifugal force will be pulling you toward the edge of the road on curves and that force will be stronger if you have less traction. To remain safe, adjust speed downward according to current conditions.

CHANGING SPEED AND DIRECTION AT THE SAME TIME

When you try to steer and change speed at the same time, you increase the chance that you will lose traction and go into a skid. At any time there is only so much available traction. If you ask your vehicle to do something that needs more traction than is available, you will skid. If you must steer and change speed at the same time, remember the more you steer the less traction is available to change speed.

FIGURE 14.1   **CAUSES OF SKIDS**

Cause	Braking skid	Power skid	Cornering skid	Blowout skid
Reason	The brakes are applied so hard that the front or rear tires lose traction.	The gas pedal is pressed too hard.	A turn made too fast	A tire suddenly loses air pressure.
Conditions	A sudden stop A wet, slippery, or uneven road	A sudden, hard acceleration A slippery road surface	Poor tires or a slippery road surface	A punctured, worn, or overinflated tire An overloaded vehicle
What can happen	Steering control can be lost. If the front tires lock or lose traction (**understeer**), the vehicle skids straight ahead. If the rear tires lock or lose traction (**oversteer**), the rear of the vehicle slides sideways. The vehicle may spin around.	A vehicle with front-wheel drive plows straight ahead. In a vehicle with rear-wheel drive, the rear end can skid to the side. The vehicle may spin around.	Directional control can be lost. All four tires can lose traction simultaneously. The vehicle skids toward the inside or outside of the curve or turn.	There is a strong pull toward the side on which a front tire has blown out. A rear-tire blowout may cause a pull toward the blowout, side-to-side swaying, or fishtailing.
What to do	Take your foot off the brake pedal. Look and steer in the direction you want the front of the vehicle to go. Don't give up. If the rear tires are skidding, continue to steer; you may have to make several steering corrections before you regain directional control. When the tires regain traction, steering control will return.	Ease up on the gas pedal until the tires stop spinning. Look and steer in the direction you want the front of the vehicle to go. Don't give up. If the rear tires are skidding, continue to steer; you may have to make several steering corrections before you regain directional control.	Look and steer in the direction you want the front of the vehicle to go. When the vehicle stops skidding, steer in the direction you want to go.	Do not brake. Make firm, steady steering corrections. Do not change speed suddenly. Slow down gradually, and drive off the road.

What Are the Causes of Skids?

Knowing the cause of the skid you are experiencing will help you manage the risk involved, and it may even help you prevent skidding. Look at **Figure 14.1** for a detailed description of the different causes of skids. Here is a brief summary:

- A **braking skid** occurs when you apply the brakes so hard that the front or rear tires lose traction.
- A **power skid** occurs when you suddenly press on the accelerator too hard.
- A **cornering skid** occurs when all four tires lose traction at the same time.
- A **blowout skid** occurs when a tire suddenly goes flat.

How Do You Respond to a Rear-Wheel Skid?

Suppose you are driving on an ice-covered roadway. Vehicles are parked alongside the road, and traffic is heavy in both directions. Suddenly the rear of your vehicle begins to skid. Here are the steps to manage the risk of a rear-wheel skid, which might help you safely drive out of it:

1. Continue to look well ahead and focus on the direction that you want the front of the vehicle to go.
2. Stay off the brake and steer toward your intended path.
3. If the rear of the vehicle begins to swing in the opposite direction, turn the wheel smoothly and quickly in the direction in which you want the front of the vehicle to go.
4. Keep steering until you are out of the skid.

WHAT WOULD YOU DO? *You have a blowout. What is likely to happen? What should you do? Why?*

Lesson 2 Review

❶ What conditions can make your vehicle skid?

❷ Describe four causes of skids.

❸ Describe how to safely steer out of a skid.

Avoiding or Minimizing Crash Damage

Your main goal as a driver should be to get to where you're going without having a collision and sustaining injuries. Natural laws come into play when you drive during adverse weather or road conditions or when other drivers make mistakes. To be a good driver, you must understand how to use accelerating, braking, and steering to help you minimize risk.

How Can You Use Speed Control or Braking to Avoid a Collision?

Steering away is a natural reaction to avoid a collision. However, this is not always the correct evasive action. Accelerating or braking are sometimes better choices.

ACCELERATING TO AVOID COLLISIONS

Accelerating is sometimes your only means of reducing the risk of a collision. Sometimes, you just have to speed up, using the traction of your tires to increase the momentum and inertia of your vehicle. Such situations occur most often at intersections or in merging traffic. A vehicle may be coming at you from one side (see **Figure 14.2**). Putting on the brakes may stop you in

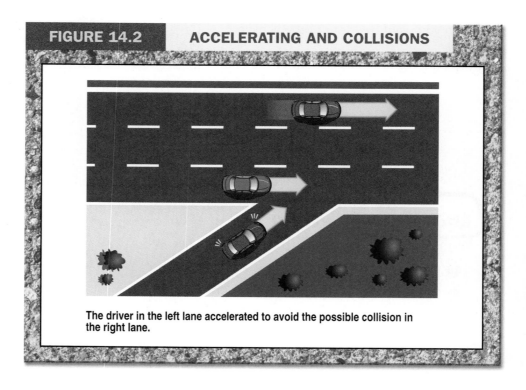

FIGURE 14.2   **ACCELERATING AND COLLISIONS**

The driver in the left lane accelerated to avoid the possible collision in the right lane.

the vehicle's path. Steering to the side may be impossible if there are objects on both sides of your vehicle. If the road ahead is clear, a quick burst of speed could take you to safety, or at least move the point of impact to the rear fender of the vehicle. The same is true if you are merging into traffic and must speed up to avoid getting in the way of another vehicle.

BRAKING TO AVOID COLLISIONS

Braking may be the correct choice when steering to the side or accelerating is not possible. Braking uses friction to slow momentum. Under 25 mph, it actually takes less time and distance to stop than to steer into another lane.

You will only have a few seconds to brake in an emergency when you want to stop quickly without making the wheels lock. Locking the wheels reduces traction, and it will probably throw you into a skid. To brake safely and quickly, use the threshold/squeeze braking method. Use your toes on the brake pedal to sense how much traction exists between the tires and roadway. Keep your heel on the floor and use your toes on the brake pedal. "Squeeze" the pedal down with steady, firm pressure until just before the brakes lock. If the brakes do lock, relax your toes to release brake pressure a little, then immediately "squeeze" the brake pedal again to just short of lockup. Continue this "squeeze" until you reduce to your desired speed or the vehicle comes to a stop. This braking technique allows you to maintain steering control, which you lose in a skid (see **Figure 14.3**).

Most new vehicles are equipped with an **antilock brake system (ABS)**, which eliminates the problem of locked brakes by making it mechanically impossible for locking to occur.

ABS serves the small patch of tire that comes into contact with the road surface. Traction Control technology builds on ABS by adding extra valves to the system's hydraulics. This allows application of the brakes on drive wheels without pressing the brake pedal to minimize wheel spin and improve vehicle control and stability while accelerating.

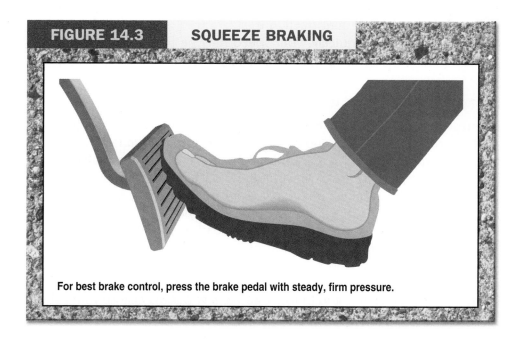

FIGURE 14.3   **SQUEEZE BRAKING**

For best brake control, press the brake pedal with steady, firm pressure.

How Can Knowledge of Natural Laws Help You Avoid a Collision?

Knowledge of natural laws, such as friction, traction, and centrifugal force, are helpful in understanding vehicle control and can help you avoid collisions with vehicles, animals, or other roadway obstructions. Knowing how natural laws work is helpful when thinking ahead to evasive maneuvers, such as steering away from a problem and recovering control of the vehicle when you run off the road. Thinking a problem through before you actually encounter it can help you make a reflex action during a crisis that may save your life. Actions you can take include steering to avoid a collision and controlled off-road recovery.

STEERING TO AVOID A COLLISION

You are driving at 55 mph on a clear day with no glare on the roadway. As you top the hill, you see a disabled vehicle with a flat tire stopped in your lane about 3 seconds ahead of your location. You are going too fast to stop in time. Under normal circumstances and with normal traction, it takes about 4 to 5 seconds to stop your vehicle. You have only 3 seconds. There is traffic in the other direction moving toward you, and that traffic is unable to stop. What can you do?

You should steer to the right road shoulder, if possible. To do that, take the following steps.

1. Turn the steering wheel just enough to get onto the shoulder while keeping your foot off the accelerator and brake.
2. Once you have passed the disabled vehicle, if there is enough space, slow gradually, and then turn the steering wheel to the left to return to the roadway.
3. Once the front wheels are on the road, turn the wheel right to bring your vehicle back into its original path.

Use what you know about traction to steer out of trouble. If you turn the wheel too hard or too quickly, your speed may be too high for traction to overcome centrifugal force.

CONTROLLED OFF-ROAD RECOVERY

You see a passing vehicle coming toward you in your lane on a two-lane road and realize that the passing vehicle cannot return to its lane in time. What should you do? You should steer to the right. The vehicle passes safely on the left, but now your two right wheels are on the unpaved shoulder. You have two wheels on the shoulder and two wheels on the roadway, but you want to get back on the road. How can you return to the road?

Natural laws will affect your return to the road because tires rolling on different surfaces have different amounts of traction. Paved areas give your tires more grip than unpaved dirt or graveled areas. Your vehicle's center of gravity may be slightly off normal because the shoulder is often lower than the road. In this situation, if you panic and brake or accelerate, this may cause your vehicle to lose traction and go into a skid. Turning the wheel too sharply could cause your vehicle to skid, flip over, or shoot back across the roadway.

Still, it's a manageable situation. For a controlled off-road recovery, do the following:

1. Don't panic—stay off the brake and accelerator.
2. Continue to look in the direction you want the front of the vehicle to go.
3. If there is space, let the vehicle slow gradually.
4. Let the vehicle move right until the wheels on the shoulder are about 12 to 18 inches from the road edge.
5. Look for a spot where the road edge appears to be no more than 2 inches higher than the shoulder.
6. Signal your intention to return to the roadway.
7. Move the steering wheel $1/16$ to $1/8$ of a turn to the left. As soon as you feel the right front tire contact the road edge, steer back to the right a little, approximately $1/8$ to $1/4$ of a turn. Accelerate smoothly to prevent a rear-wheel skid.
8. Turn the steering wheel straight.

WHAT WOULD YOU DO?
A driver has lost control of a vehicle, and it is swerving into your lane. What should you do?

Lesson 3 Review

❶ Under what conditions can accelerating or braking help you avoid a collision?

❷ How can traction and steering help you avoid a collision?

❸ How would you use knowledge of force of impact to respond to a head-on or side collision?

LESSON 4

Challenging Environmental Factors

OBJECTIVES

1. **Identify** environmental factors outside the vehicle that affect risk.
2. **Describe** ways you can minimize risk in multiple environmental combinations.

KEY TERM

◆ grip

Drivers deal with what may be seen as three different environments. The first environment is the one outside the vehicle, which is covered in this chapter. This environment includes risks associated with the roads, the weather, the lighting conditions, and other traffic. These factors often overlap. The two other environments, the baggage and the people and equipment inside the vehicle, are covered in Chapters 4 and 17.

Which Environmental Factors Outside the Vehicle Affect Risk?

To become a skillful driver, you must be alert and know how to deal with a wide range of environmental driving situations outside the vehicle. Weather conditions, road conditions, lighting conditions, and traffic all have a direct effect on driving risk and deserve special attention. Problems in these areas often occur simultaneously, posing challenges for you as the driver.

WEATHER AND ROAD CONDITIONS

Bad weather and poor road conditions are probably the most common troublesome combination of environmental factors that contribute to collisions. After a storm, you often hear that the rain caused many crashes. Rain, snow, and fog are commonly encountered weather conditions that demand an adjustment to driving behavior. Add road factors, and potential driving hazards increase significantly. Road factors that affect driving risk include rough pavement, gravel, mud and potholes. Other factors include road design of shoulders, road width, road slope and curve, road lines, curbs, and signs and signals that must be navigated by the driver.

Often the adjustments you must make involve increasing visual search and reducing speed. You can check the weather in the area you plan to visit before you leave.

It is important to manage time and space when driving in fog. *How can you manage time and space when driving in fog?*

Scan for changes in weather that might suddenly occur at that time of year in your area. Be aware of the road surface you are on, and drive accordingly. When in doubt, slow down a little. To be prepared for this combination of factors, your vehicle's tires and suspension should be in optimal shape, since good tires and suspension will give you maximum traction.

ROAD AND LIGHTING

Poor conditions on the road or in lighting can combine to increase risk. The condition of the road you are on is an important factor in driving. How the road is constructed is important, too. It's important to note that getting that kind of road information is dependent on how much you see. How much you see is directly related to how much light is in the environment.

The light you need in order to see while driving comes from two sources—the sun or artificial sources such as streetlights and headlights. Light from the sun is complete and abundant. At times, it overwhelms the senses. Normal sunlight is generally adequate for all of the usual visual search activities that drivers conduct. At certain times, however, the light is so strong and direct that you have to block it or filter it with a sun visor or sunglasses.

Bright light gives you great visibility in your surrounding environment and helps you see edges and detail. During bad weather, the light level is lower, and light is more diffused or scattered. Poor light hides some of the environmental detail outside the vehicle you might normally see and rely on. Poor light also prevents you from seeing well ahead and getting all the information you need in a timely manner—a very important safe-driving skill. When you can't see well, slow down!

At night, you have no sunlight. The vehicle you are driving provides most of the light you use to drive, although streetlights and other vehicles also contribute light. The moon occasionally adds some light to the situation. Avoid the tendency to stare at the light patch your own headlights project. Instead, scan and search the entire driving environment, both inside and outside the glare of your headlights. At night, be sure to look well down the road at and beyond the area illuminated by your vehicle's headlights. Remember that you tend to drive where you look, and you look where there's light. Make sure to turn down your dash lights to increase your sensitivity to the light out on the road. And remember, don't use your high beams in bad weather. High beams only cause more distraction by reflecting light back at you and interfering with your ability to see farther ahead.

In northern climates, low angles of the sun and abundant snow cover can result in bright intense light shining and reflecting directly into your eyes. It's important to not look directly at this bright light. These bright conditions also exist in other areas during morning or evening drives when the sun is low on the horizon. If you drive in these areas, know the times and places these conditions will affect you and try to avoid them or compensate for them by using sunglasses or your vehicle's sun visors.

In all cases, you must make sure your vehicle in good condition and be able to deal with light properly. Keep the windshield clean and in good repair. Cracks and pits cause obstructions and distractions to vision and also reflect and refract light and glare. Keep all lights, but especially the headlights, clean and properly aligned.

Driver Ed Online

Topic: Driving at Night

For a link to more information on driving at night, go to **drivered .glencoe.com**.

Activity: Using the information provided at this link, work in small groups to create two checklists of safety tips—one list of tips to prepare your car for night driving and one list of tips to follow while driving at night.

HANDLING HYDROPLANING

When you are driving in rainy conditions, it is possible that your car will start to hydroplane. If this happens, follow these guidelines.

▲ Avoid braking or turning suddenly because doing so could cause the car to skid.

▲ Ease off the gas pedal until the car slows down and you regain traction.

▲ If you need to brake, gently pump the brake pedal.

▲ If your car has antilock brakes, you should brake as you normally would. The antilock brakes will prevent the wheels from locking.

OTHER TRAFFIC AND LIGHTING

Traffic and lighting are environmental factors that can interact, too. In the case of traffic, how drivers behave and interact with each other on the roads create situations that frequently lead to congestion, close calls, and collisions. The very design of some roads at times causes drivers to become uncertain, confused, frustrated, and occasionally angry. As a driver, you will deal with good and bad traffic. All you can do is learn to avoid places or times where you might expect bad traffic. If you have to be there, learn to be as patient with other drivers as possible.

Poor lighting adds more risk in heavy traffic, too. When it's difficult to see ahead or the lighting is poor, you won't get enough information to help you understand what is happening in traffic. Consequently, you will probably get frustrated. In situations where lighting is poor, use other drivers ahead as a visual extension. Watch other cars and trucks—pay attention to their signal and brake lights, and react accordingly to keep yourself safe. Notice whether other drivers in your path are slowing, turning, or acting confused. This will help you avoid trouble.

MAXIMIZE TRACTION

Traction is the single most important factor in maintaining vehicle control. Your vehicle can only have a certain amount of traction. Like a bank account, you cannot use more than you have. Those who try usually pay a hefty price— loss of vehicle control and a serious crash! Traction is useful when you accelerate, brake, and steer. When you accelerate too quickly, steer too sharply, or brake too hard, you may exceed the available traction and the tires may loose their **grip**—the ability to change the speed or direction of the vehicle. This is especially true of poorly maintained and older vehicles not equipped with antilock brakes and other traction-control systems.

Generally speaking, you need traction to change vehicle speed or direction. When you need to change speed or direction or both, you create additional demands on the vehicle and may exceed the limits of the available traction.

This is usually okay, but when you try to start, stop, and/or turn the vehicle too quickly, your vehicle may go into a skid. This is especially true on a low-traction surface. When your vehicle skids in these conditions, inertia has exceeded the amount of traction available and the tires lose their grip on the road.

To maintain or improve traction while driving, buy the proper tires for your vehicle, inflate them correctly, and ensure that the vehicle's suspension system is working properly. As previously stated, the laws of nature really dictate how much traction exists between the roadway and the tires. Gravity, weight, inertia, centrifugal force, and friction all play a role in determining how much traction—and vehicle control—you will have.

ASSESSING MULTIPLE FACTORS

You may experience a combination of three or more hazardous environmental factors—weather, road conditions, other traffic, or lighting. You may have to deal with these problems simultaneously.

When road conditions, weather conditions, and traffic conditions are poor, you should recognize both the individual danger of each environmental element and the multiple dangers of all these elements that the situation presents. When possible, analyze the risky elements in each environmental factor and assess the risk potential before driving. If you decide to drive, consider what strategies and actions you can take to reduce risks you may encounter.

How Can You Minimize Risk in Multiple Environmental Combinations?

Whenever you get out onto the road, you need to recognize that a multitude of factors affects your ability to drive safely. Some are within your control, such as personal factors, behaviors, attitudes, knowledge, skill, and impairments. Some are beyond your control, such as the traffic, weather, lighting conditions, and road design and condition. But in all cases, you have the choice as to
1. whether to get on the road in the first place.
2. where, when, and how you will go.
3. how you will respond to the constantly changing conditions on the road.

Barry Thayer

Thayer Driver Education Center
Danbury, CT

Hill and mountain driving requires extra effort and concentration on steering and speed control. Use your horn and lights to signal your presence when you cannot see around a sharp curve or over a steep hill. Increase your following distance, and be aware of the effects of low oxygen on your body.

Weather, road, lighting, and traffic conditions are environmental factors that affect risk. You can minimize risk in multiple environmental combinations by knowing what could happen in different situations, looking well ahead while driving, and driving at the appropriate speed.

How does hill and mountain driving differ from driving on an urban street?

Maximizing your vehicle's traction and looking ahead are two good ways to minimize driving risk.

KNOWING WHAT COULD HAPPEN IN DIFFICULT SITUATIONS

Your instincts and driving knowledge can often help you in difficult situations. When you know you are in a difficult situation and know what could possibly go wrong, you feel fear, and your survival instinct increases. You naturally become more cautious and behave much more safely. It's an irony of driving that the less safe you feel, the safer you are likely to be.

When you are driving in difficult situations, knowing what to do in an emergency situation makes it more likely that you will take the right action, take the action in good time, and complete the action properly and with the expected outcome. When you know what to do in emergencies, you react to them with less panic, and they then don't seem as dangerous.

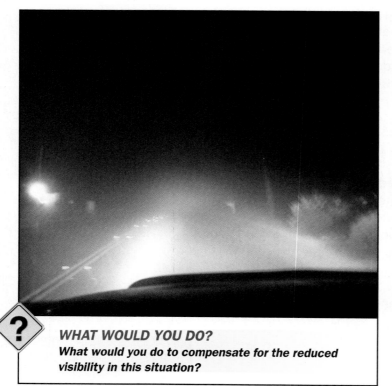

WHAT WOULD YOU DO?
What would you do to compensate for the reduced visibility in this situation?

LOOK WELL AHEAD

Time and space allow you to know how to make driving easier, how to anticipate situations, and how to plan ahead and execute effectively. They also allow you to know what's happening 20 to 30 seconds ahead. Finally, they enable you to select options to deal with the danger 12 to 15 seconds before encountering it.

DRIVE AT APPROPRIATE SPEED FOR SPECIFIC CONDITIONS

No matter what the driving environment, always drive at a safe speed. Speed is directly related to energy, inertia, momentum, stability, and control. When you drive too fast, you lessen your ability to respond to situations and to respond properly. Simple solutions become more complex, and you have to execute them faster. What might have been a simple steering maneuver at 40 mph becomes a crisis brake-and-avoid situation at 60 mph.

Lesson 4 Review

❶ What environmental factors outside the vehicle pose a risk to you while driving?

❷ How can you minimize risk in multiple environmental combinations?

❸ What strategies can you use to assess multiple risk factors?

THE TRANS-ALASKA PIPELINE

Oil, the precious resource that is the source of the gasoline that powers our motor vehicles, has been the cause of a confusing mix of benefits and drawbacks to the Inuits of Alaska. In the 1800s, these native people witnessed the exploration of their homeland by navigators searching for a quick Arctic sea route from the New World to the wealth of Asia. This sea route, the Northwest Passage, was finally traveled in 1903 by the Norwegian explorer Roald Amundsen.

Today the Inuits are affected by another exploration—the search for oil in the waters of the Northwest Passage. With the discovery of oil at Prudhoe Bay on Alaska's north coast, human-made oil-drilling islands have been built amidst the 18,000 islands of the 4,000-mile-long Northwest Passage.

The trans-Alaska pipeline carries the oil from Prudhoe Bay to ports in southern Alaska, where it is transferred to huge ice-breaking tankers that carry the oil to refineries outside of Alaska.

For many Inuits, the frozen-over sea is like the land. Driving a ship through it is like driving a bulldozer across a farmer's field. The tankers also pose a danger to the environment, such as that caused when the *Exxon Valdez* struck a reef and poured 10.9 million gallons of crude oil into Prince William Sound. The oil destroyed wildlife that lived in these waters and was absorbed in the gravel beaches along the shoreline.

The threat to the environment and to the Inuit way of life is somewhat balanced by the increased income that oil has brought to these Native Americans of Alaska. In the Alaskan Native Claims Settlement Act of 1971, the U.S. government gave Alaskans with at least one Native American grandparent a share in the oil-rich lands.

The Inuits are in the forefront of a movement that recognizes the need for oil and its economic benefit yet also recognizes the need to protect the environment. The threat of pollution has been an important topic in the five Inuit Circumpolar Conferences that have been held since 1977 to discuss the future of Arctic peoples.

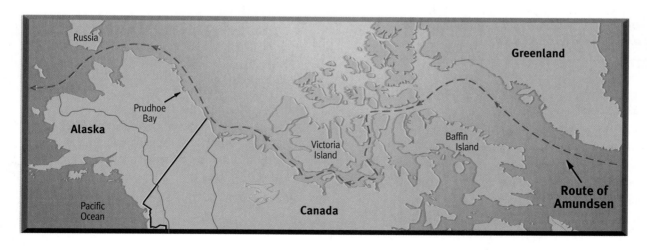

WHAT DO YOU THINK NOW?

How can the need for oil and the economic advantages it brings be balanced by the need to protect and preserve the environment?

Key Points

Lesson 1

1. To drive up or down hills, downshift and accelerate or brake as necessary. (Page 289)
2. Use your horn and lights to signal your presence when you cannot see around a sharp curve ahead. Increase your following distance, and be aware of the effects of low oxygen on your body and your vehicle. (Page 290)

? WHAT WOULD YOU DO?
Your vehicle has an automatic transmission, and you've been using the Drive gear. Describe your procedure as you are about to head up a hill.

Lesson 2

1. Reduced traction and too rapid changes in either speed or direction can cause skidding. (Page 292)
2. A braking skid occurs when you apply the brakes so hard that one or more of the wheels lock. A power skid occurs when you suddenly press on the accelerator too hard. A cornering skid occurs when you lose directional control in a turn, curve, or lane change. A blowout skid occurs when a tire suddenly goes flat. (Page 294)

Lesson 3

1. It is possible to avoid some collisions by accelerating and steering if the roadway is clear. At speeds under 25 mph, braking requires less time and space than steering to avoid a collision. (Pages 296–297)
2. You may be able to avoid a collision by understanding the relationship between steering, speed, and friction. (Page 298)

? WHAT WOULD YOU DO?
A driver has lost control of a vehicle, and it is swerving into your lane. What should you do?

Lesson 4

1. Weather conditions, road conditions, lighting conditions, and traffic conditions are environmental factors outside the vehicle that affect risk. (Pages 300–301)
2. You can minimize risk in multiple environmental combinations by knowing what could happen in different situations, looking well ahead while driving, and driving at an appropriate speed. (Pages 303–304)

On a separate sheet of paper, write the letter of the answer that best completes each sentence.

1 When driving downhill in a vehicle with a manual transmission, you should
 a. downshift to gain more control.
 b. upshift to decrease engine power.
 c. ride the clutch to maintain an even speed.

2 Driving on mountain roads can cause you to
 a. become short of breath and feel sleepy.
 b. lose control of the gears.
 c. lose the effects of gravity.

3 When trying to avoid a collision while traveling under 25 mph, it takes less time and distance to
 a. steer into another lane.
 b. accelerate.
 c. brake.

4 A braking skid occurs when you
 a. apply the brakes too hard.
 b. press the accelerator too hard.
 c. downshift too quickly.

5 The most important factor in maintaining vehicle control is
 a. the condition of the road.
 b. grip.
 c. traction.

6 A power skid occurs when you
 a. apply the brakes too hard.
 b. press the accelerator too hard.
 c. downshift too quickly.

On a separate sheet of paper, write the word or phrase that best completes each sentence.

altitude

braking

grip

skidding

7 _____ is the ability to change the speed or direction of the vehicle.

8 Driving at a high _____ can affect the performance of your vehicle.

9 _____ is loss of control over the direction in which your vehicle is moving because of reduced traction.

10 _____ uses friction to slow momentum.

Writing

Driver's Log

In this chapter, you have learned about the effect that natural laws have on a variety of driving situations. Summarize, in a few sentences for each, the meaning of inertia, gravity, and momentum. Explain how these laws help you anticipate and manage risk.

Projects

❶ Make a photo display of potential low-traction areas in your community. Label each photo, and list the potential danger. Return to the area to check out your suspicion. Make sure to position yourself so that you are safe and will not become a danger to traffic.

❷ Check the shoulders and off-road areas of some local highways. Are they well designed and maintained? Do they provide an escape path in an emergency? What dangers do they pose to drivers? How could they be improved?

Vehicular Emergencies

What Should You Do in an Emergency?

No matter how well you maintain your vehicle, there is always the possibility that a part may break or a system may malfunction. Your brakes, engine, steering, tires, or other systems can fail when you drive. In these types of emergencies, it is important to learn how to assess and respond to emergencies quickly, safely, efficiently, and calmly. When you learn what to do about these problems, an emergency need not turn into a disaster.

Driver Ed
Online

For additional
activities, visit
drivered.glencoe.com.
Here you will find:

◆ **Web Link Exercises**

◆ **eFlashcards**

◆ **Practice Driving Tests**

LESSON 1

Engine, Brake, and Steering Failures

OBJECTIVES

1. **Explain** what to do in case of engine stalling or other engine failure.
2. **Describe** what to do in case of brake failure.
3. **Describe** what to do in case of steering failure.

KEY TERM

◆ stall

You see the stop sign at the intersection ahead and step on the brake. The pedal goes all the way to the floor, but your vehicle doesn't slow down. Two teenagers start across the street. Your mind races: "What should I do?"

Mechanical emergencies can occur suddenly and without warning. Engines can stall, brakes can fail, and steering systems can malfunction. If you are prepared to deal with such emergencies, you can keep a dangerous situation from becoming a tragedy.

Why Prepare for Emergencies?

Thinking through what you might do in an emergency is important. Have you ever surprised someone or seen a person in a situation just freeze? These situations happen because you are caught off-guard and don't have a ready response. Sometimes after a few minutes of thinking, or perhaps an hour or a day later, you have the perfect response, but it's much too late.

Traffic emergencies play out in much the same way. When you don't know how to respond to a situation, you can be caught for a moment or two without a response. In an emergency traffic situation, a hesitation or pause can bring about disaster.

What Causes Engine Failure?

Engine failure occurs more often than any other kind of vehicle failure. Engines fail for many different reasons—a broken timing gear, a broken timing belt or serpentine belt, or a malfunctioning fuel or electrical system. The fuel system can fail from lack of fuel, water in the fuel, plugged fuel filter, and so forth. The electrical system can go down because of a broken wire, water in the electrical system, battery failure, or other problems sometimes caused by extreme heat or cold.

OVERHEATED ENGINE

When the engine temperature is too high, the temperature gauge or warning light on your instrument panel indicates that the engine is overheating. You may see steam or smoke rising from under the hood.

Your engine may overheat for several reasons. Driving in slow-moving traffic during hot weather with the air conditioner running

○ - - - - - - - - ┐
Learn how to deal with emergency-vehicle failures to manage risk.
How can you deal with emergency-vehicle failures?

is a major reason vehicles overheat. Other reasons are driving up long, steep hills; having a loose or broken fan belt; having a broken water pump or hose; having a stuck or broken thermostat; not having enough coolant or antifreeze in the cooling system; or having a clogged radiator.

If your engine overheats on the road, follow these steps.

1. Turn off all unnecessary accessories, especially the air conditioner.
2. If the temperature gauge continues to show hot or if the warning light stays on, signal and pull off the road. If you can't pull off the road immediately, turn on the heater to draw heat from the engine. Turning on the heater will not solve the problem, but it will help while you get off the road safely. Then get off the road and stop.
3. If there is no steam or smoke coming from the engine, carefully open the hood. (Wear gloves to protect your hands.) Look for such problems as a broken hose or belt. Note whether the radiator overflow tank is empty, but do not touch the radiator or the radiator cap.
4. After the engine has cooled completely, check the fluid level in the radiator overflow tank again. If the fluid level is low, you need to add coolant. Most radiator overflow tanks have a fill line imprinted on the side of the tank to help you determine the proper level of fluid. Start the engine, and let it idle as you add the coolant.
5. If you can't solve the problem, get professional help.

ENGINE FIRE

Engine fires are usually fuel-fed or electrical. If your engine is on fire, you'll see and smell smoke coming from under your hood. Follow these steps.

1. Steer off the road to an open space. Turn off the ignition.
2. Get out of the vehicle, and have all passengers get out, too. Move far away from the vehicle. Call for help.
3. Decide how serious the fire is. If it is serious—high heat and flames around the hood—do not attempt to put the fire out yourself. Wait for the fire department.
4. If the fire is not serious and you have a fire extinguisher, you can try to put it out yourself. *Do not use water;* water is not effective against fuel, electrical, or oil fires. If you have a fire extinguisher, protect yourself. Wear gloves, or wrap your hands in cloth. Face away from the vehicle, and crouch down so that your head is at the level of the hood. *Do not open the hood.* Just pull the hood release to create a small space, and spray the engine from this position while looking the other way.

PASSENGER-COMPARTMENT FIRE

Vehicle fires do not occur often, but when they do, prompt action minimizes risk to people and property. A fire in the passenger compartment is usually caused by carelessness of a passenger or the driver. A common cause of such fires is a burning cigarette or match that drops to the floor or gets blown into the backseat.

In an emergency situation, try to stay calm, think clearly, and act quickly. Learning what to do in case of vehicle failure will help you avoid panic.

Let the temperature cool before you check an overheated engine. *What steps should you follow if your engine overheats?*

Get out of the vehicle as soon as you safely can if your car catches fire. **What else should you do if your vehicle catches fire?**

If there's a fire in the passenger compartment, steer off the road and stop clear of traffic. Turn off the ignition. Get out of the vehicle, and have all passengers get out on the side away from traffic. Use a fire extinguisher or water to put out the fire if you are certain it is not a fuel- or oil-based fire.

STALLED ENGINE AND OTHER ENGINE FAILURES

If your vehicle's engine **stalls** or stops suddenly while you are driving along the road, check traffic around you and determine the best point at which to leave the roadway. Keep rolling if you can; do not brake unless traffic conditions force you to slow. Signal, then steer off the road or to the curb as quickly as possible while you still have momentum. Keep in mind that if your engine stalls and you have power brakes and power steering, the brakes and steering will still work, but they will be much harder to operate.

Once you are off the road, shift to Neutral, and try to restart the engine. If the engine starts, shift into Drive or First and continue driving. Don't trade one emergency for another. Remember, you must be able to perform these steps without taking your attention off the road for more than a second at a time!

If the engine won't start, stop your vehicle and make sure your flashers are on. Raise the hood. Place flares or warning triangles 100 feet in front of your vehicle and at least 100 feet behind it, if you have them in the car. Then signal or wait for help.

ENGINE FLOODING

If you pump the accelerator more than once when trying to start your vehicle, too much gas may be supplied to the engine. The result is a "flooded" engine that won't start until some of the extra gas evaporates. When your engine is flooded, you can often smell gas. In vehicles with fuel injection, there is no need to pump the accelerator before starting; if you do, you may flood the engine.

To start a flooded engine, press the accelerator pedal all the way to the floor and hold it there. At the same time, turn on the ignition switch to start, and hold it for 3 to 5 seconds. If the vehicle starts, release the ignition switch and slowly release the accelerator. If the vehicle doesn't start, wait 5 or 10 minutes and try again.

WET ENGINE

If you drive through water, your vehicle's engine may get wet and sputter or stall. Water splashed up into the engine may short out your vehicle's electrical system or be drawn into the combustion chamber by way of the air filter and the carburetor.

If your engine stalls in wet weather, steer off the road and turn off the ignition. Wait a few minutes, keeping the hood closed to let the heat of the engine compartment dry out the moisture. Then try to restart the engine. If it doesn't start, give the engine more time to dry. If it's a hot, sunny day, you may speed up the process by raising the hood.

What Causes Brake Failure?

In a new vehicle, complete brake failure is unlikely. That's because all new vehicles have a dual-service brake system. Some vehicles have separate systems for the front and back wheels. Other vehicles use an "X" brake system, which links each front wheel with its diagonal rear wheel. Total failure of both systems at once is very unlikely, although partial or temporary brake failure happens occasionally. Sometimes a brake line may break or leak, sometimes oil or brake fluid will get on the brake pads, sometimes the brake lining will wear off, and occasionally high heat may cause the brake fluid to boil.

Older cars don't all have these protections. On rare occasions, the brakes on all four wheels go out at the same time, particularly if the car has not been well maintained.

IN CASE OF BRAKE FAILURE

When brake failure occurs, the foot brake may have no resistance. Your brakes won't work. The brake pedal may sink to the floor. The brake warning light may come on.

Here is what to do if you suddenly have no brakes:

1. Shift down to a lower gear to slow the movement of the vehicle.
2. Rapidly pump the brake pedal. Doing so may build up pressure in the brake-fluid lines, providing some braking force. After a few pumps, you will know whether or not you have restored braking power. If power is restored, stop pumping and use the brakes.
3. If pumping the brakes does not work, use the parking brake. In vehicles where the parking brake is a pedal, you may need to push down with your left foot while you pull the release to prevent any locking of the brakes. The parking brake usually affects only the rear wheels, but applying the parking brake too abruptly may lock the rear wheels and send the vehicle into a spin. Use an apply-release-apply-release pattern with the parking brake to slow down the vehicle. Either keep your thumb on the release button or hold the brake handle so that you can alternately apply and release brake pressure.
4. If you still have little or no brake control, look for a way to reduce your speed. Find a place to steer against the curb if there is one, because scraping the tires against a curb can help reduce speed. If not, steer into an open area. If you can bring the vehicle to a stop, put the gear selector in Park to keep the vehicle where it is.

Energy Tip

Power equipment and accessories add to the total weight and energy requirements of a vehicle. This extra weight and load on engine power, in turn, leads to reduced fuel efficiency.

5. If you cannot avoid a collision, steer so that you sideswipe an object rather than hit it head-on. If possible, steer your vehicle into bushes or scrape along a guardrail or even parked vehicles rather than hitting pedestrians or vehicles with passengers.

OTHER BRAKE PROBLEMS

If you apply your brakes hard for a long time, you can experience "brake fade," a kind of temporary brake failure caused by overheated brakes. To help prevent this, shift to a lower gear before starting down the slope. You can also pull off the road to let your brakes cool when they are fading.

Wet brakes can also fade. As a precaution, drive more slowly through puddles. To dry your brakes, drive slowly with your left foot gently on the brake pedal.

If your vehicle has power brakes, engine failure may cause brake malfunction. If that is the case, your brakes will still work, but you'll have to press harder on the pedal. With power brakes, it won't do any good to pump the brakes.

How Does Your Steering Fail?

Two kinds of steering failure are possible: power-assist failure and total steering system failure. The former is far more common than the latter. Both make the car undriveable until the steering is fixed.

Dealing with the UNEXPECTED

EMERGENCY ITEMS

It is wise to keep the following items in the trunk of your vehicle in case of an emergency:

- flashlight with extra batteries
- jumper cables (for starting a dead battery)
- flares, warning triangles, or reflectors
- coolant and windshield-washer fluid
- wiping cloth
- ice scraper, snow brush, and snow shovel
- jack with flat board for soft surfaces
- lug wrench (for changing a flat tire)
- screwdriver, pliers, duct tape, and adjustable wrench (for making simple repairs)
- fire extinguisher
- blanket and heavy gloves
- drinking water
- first-aid kit
- pencil and notebook (for recording information)

POWER STEERING FAILURE

Power-steering failure can occur if your engine stalls or the power-assist mechanism fails. When power steering fails, your steering wheel suddenly becomes very difficult to turn.

If your vehicle's power steering fails, grip the steering wheel firmly and turn it with more force. Check surrounding traffic, signal, and when it's safe to do so, steer off the road as well as you can, and stop. Have a mechanic fix your steering system before you try to drive the vehicle again.

Your car's engine may stall and your brakes may get wet in rainy weather. *How can you manage risk in this weather?*

TOTAL STEERING FAILURE

Sudden and total steering failure is an extremely rare occurrence. However, if a breakdown in either the steering or suspension system does happen, your ability to steer your vehicle will vanish.

In case of total steering failure, bring your vehicle to a stop as quickly and safely as possible. Downshift and take your foot off the accelerator. Use the parking brake, not the foot brake, because using the foot brake might cause your vehicle to pull sharply to one side. Just as when responding to brake failure, keep hold of the parking brake release button or handle to avoid locking the rear wheels and going into a spin.

WHAT WOULD YOU DO? ?
As you prepare to slow your vehicle, you find that the brakes don't work and the vehicle does not slow down. What do you suppose has happened? How will you handle this situation?

Lesson 1 Review

❶ What would you do if your engine stalled while you were driving? What if the engine overheated?

❷ What actions would you take if your vehicle's brakes failed?

❸ What would you do if your vehicle's power steering suddenly failed?

Tire Failure and Other Serious Problems

OBJECTIVES

1. **Explain** what actions to take if your vehicle has a blowout or flat tire.
2. **Explain** how to jump-start a dead battery.
3. **Describe** what to do if the hood flies up.

KEY TERMS

◆ blowout
◆ jump-start

In addition to the major system failures you read about in the previous lesson, you should be prepared to deal with a number of other serious problems, such as tire failure. Mechanical failure can occur in the suspension system, the exhaust system, the lubrication system, the battery, and in other parts of the car.

What Can You Do in Case of a Blowout or Flat Tire?

A tire can go flat either while the vehicle is parked or when it is moving. A **blowout** is an explosion in a tire while the vehicle is in motion. The tire suddenly loses air pressure, and the vehicle may become difficult to control.

A tire can also lose pressure gradually through a slow leak. If you don't detect the leak in time, the tire is likely to go flat. With a slow leak, you may only discover your tire is flat when you are about to enter your car.

The most frequent cause of a flat tire is not sudden major damage to the tire but a very gradual loss of air that goes unnoticed by the driver. Proper tire pressure enhances vehicle responsiveness, fuel economy, and ride quality. Two different methods are used to monitor tire pressure.

The deflation detection system (DDS) uses an indirect means to determine a tire pressure problem and gives a general warning signal when there is a decrease in tire pressure. The direct-measuring tire-pressure monitoring system (TPMS) provides direct measurement of tire pressure. Both systems can provide drivers with information needed to avoid the problems associated with driving on underinflated tires.

GETTING OFF THE ROAD WITH A BLOWOUT OR FLAT TIRE

When a front tire fails while you are driving, you may feel a strong pull to the right or left. The rear of your vehicle may shimmy or swerve back and forth. You may even hear a thumping sound. The effect may be gradual if the tire has a slow leak or sudden if the tire blows out.

If you are driving with a blowout or flat tire, take these steps:

1. Keep a firm grip on the steering wheel with both hands. Look well ahead along your intended path. Maintain or slightly increase pressure on the accelerator until your steering is stable.
2. Release the accelerator slowly. Do not brake—you could make the vehicle swerve out of control.
3. Check the traffic around you. When you find a gap, signal and steer off the road. You will have to change the tire, so move as far off the main roadway as you can.

4. As the vehicle slows, brake gradually and come to a stop on a flat surface.

5. Shift to Park, or to Reverse if you have a manual shift. Then set the parking brake, and put on your emergency flashers.

6. Get out of the vehicle, and have passengers get out, too, on the side away from traffic.

When a tire loses pressure gradually, you will probably sense it through changes in handling and steering. A softness or looseness in handling should become evident. When a front tire is getting low, there will be a delay in normal turning time when you turn a corner. While braking, your vehicle could pull to one side. There may even be some tire noise or squeal. When a rear tire is low, cornering will become loose and sloppy.

HOW TO CHANGE A TIRE

Changing a tire requires caution and may require more strength than some people possess. Don't try it if you don't know how to do it. Between 300 and 400 people are killed yearly while changing tires when the vehicle falls off the jack and onto them, or they are struck by passing vehicles.

For maximum safety while changing a tire, position your vehicle on a flat, hard surface as far from traffic as possible. Turn on your hazard lights or set out flares at least 100 feet around your vehicle to alert other drivers.

Use two rocks, bricks, or pieces of wood (each at least 4 inches by 8 inches by 2 inches) to block the wheel that is diagonally across from the flat tire. Put one block in front of the wheel and another behind it. The blocks will keep the vehicle from rolling when it is jacked up. You can also put on your emergency brake and put your vehicle in Park or Reverse to keep the vehicle from rolling.

You'll find complete instructions for using your jack and changing a tire in your owner's manual or inside the trunk of your vehicle. Here are the basic steps:

1. After the wheel blocks are in place, remove the jack, lug wrench, and spare tire from your vehicle and place them near the flat tire.

2. Assemble the jack, and position it according to instructions in the owner's manual.

3. Jack up the vehicle until the flat tire is just barely in contact with the ground.

4. Locate the special adapter(s) used to remove security locks for hubcaps or lug nuts, if your car has these. Remove the hubcap or wheel cover from the wheel. Use the lug wrench to loosen the lug nuts, turning them counterclockwise, enough so that they'll move easily, but do not completely remove them yet.

5. Jack up the vehicle until the tire clears the ground.

6. Take off all the lug nuts and put them inside the hubcap.

7. Pull off the wheel with the flat tire. Replace it with the spare tire. Put the lug nuts back on by hand, and tighten them slightly with the wrench.

8. Carefully let the vehicle down, and remove the jack. Tighten the lug nuts.

9. Put the flat tire, jack, wrench, and other equipment back in the vehicle, and be on your way.

When you change a tire, get as far from traffic as possible. Then continue to watch for traffic approaching you. ***What are steps for changing a flat tire?***

If the spare is an undersized tire or limited-mileage tire, drive no faster than 50 mph to the nearest service station.

With an undersized tire, especially, have the flat tire repaired or replaced right away because you will not be able to drive many miles on the little tire before it goes bad. With a regular flat, get the tire fixed or repaired as soon as possible, and always make sure you have a usable spare.

What Should You Do If Your Vehicle's Battery Is Dead?

A battery may go dead if you keep your headlights on or play the radio for a long time while the engine is not running. An old battery may no longer have enough power to start a vehicle in very cold weather.

If the battery is dead, you won't be able to start the engine. However, you may be able to restore power to your battery by using jumper cables or a portable battery.

JUMP-STARTING YOUR VEHICLE

The most common way to temporarily start your car is to **jump-start** it, using special cables to "jump" power from another vehicle to yours. To do this, you need another vehicle with a working battery or a portable battery that is the same voltage as yours and a pair of jumper cables.

Before you decide to jump-start your car, make sure the battery fluid is not frozen or the level of fluid low. If this is the case, do not attempt to jump-start your battery because it might explode.

To jump-start your vehicle with jumper cables, follow these steps.

1. Position the vehicle so that the cables can easily reach between the two batteries. Do not let the vehicles touch.
2. Turn off the ignition and electrical equipment in both vehicles. Put on their parking brakes, then shift both vehicles into Park or Neutral.
3. Double-check to make sure both vehicle batteries have the same voltage (usually 12 volts).
4. If either battery has cell or vent caps, remove them. Check again to make sure your dead battery is not frozen (if the weather is not cold, the battery is not frozen).

It's a good idea to keep jumper cables in the trunk of your car. *How do you jump-start your car?*

5. The positive jumper cable is marked red, P, or (+). Attach it to the positive terminal of the good battery. Clamp the positive, or red, end of the same cable to the positive terminal of the dead battery. If it sparks a lot when you try, you have the wrong terminal. You must match positive to positive.
6. The negative jumper cable is marked black, green, N, or (-). Attach it to the negative terminal of the good battery. Be sure the cables do not touch the fan or drive belts.

7. Attach the other end of the negative cable to the negative terminal of the vehicle with the dead battery. Connect as far as possible from moving parts, such as the fan. If the cable sparks a lot when you touch the second battery terminal, you have reversed the cables and need to begin again.

8. Start the engine of the vehicle that has the good battery. Hold down the accelerator so that the engine runs at a high idle for a while.

9. Start the engine of the vehicle with the dead battery, and with the cables still attached, run it for several minutes.

10. With both engines still running, remove the cables in reverse order from the order in which you attached them.

11. Replace battery caps if they've been removed.

If you are using a portable battery, follow the manufacturer's instructions.

What Should You Do If You Experience a Lubrication System Failure?

Whenever you see the oil pressure light come on or the oil pressure gauge register low or no oil pressure, you must turn the engine off immediately. In most cases you should be able to move over to the side of the road and then do this. Check the vehicle's oil level and for any leaks. Get the vehicle towed to a reputable mechanic as soon as possible to fix the problem.

What Can You Do in Case of Suspension Failure?

There are two types of suspension system failure. One variety is annoying, unsafe, and fairly common. The other is rare but catastrophic and potentially life threatening.

Most of the time, the annoying variety of suspension failure means one or more of the following:

- the joints are loose,
- alignment is off, and/or
- the shock absorbers are old and worn out.

These problems are very serious, yet many people continue to drive vehicles with these safety problems. You'll notice these vehicles by their unusual bobbing action as they encounter small bumps or unevenness on the road. You really need to get these problems fixed because if you don't, you will be a candidate for the next category of problems.

When the suspension gives out while driving, it is a catastrophe. The parts of your vehicle that help you steer it down the road and control it over changing road surfaces stop working. At best, you will have some ability to decelerate, and use the brakes and stop. At worst, the front wheels will have a mind of their own and take turns moving your vehicle randomly left and right until you hit something. While rare, this kind of crash happens often to younger, newer drivers in old cars who certainly don't have any experience to deal with this. The best thing you can do to avoid this type of vehicle failure is to have the problem repaired as soon as you know the suspension components no longer do what they are designed to do.

What Should You Do If You Experience an Exhaust System Failure?

Problems with the exhaust system are not a cause for panic but should be repaired. Most leaks in the exhaust system are the result of old, rusting-out pipes, resonators, and mufflers. While loud noise might be the most obvious problem in this case, the most dangerous potential problem is the accumulation of carbon monoxide that can build up in the vehicle when it sits and idles for any period of time. This gas is toxic, odorless, colorless, and deadly; every year it kills scores of people. Carbon monoxide builds up slowly in the bloodstream. It sometimes causes headaches and mostly makes you feel drowsy. Sometimes it accumulates inside the vehicle when the trunk is left open when hauling cargo or when the back windows of a station wagon or SUV are left open. The airflow of moving vehicles creates a low-pressure area at the back of a vehicle that can draw exhaust gases up and into the vehicle—enough to cause drowsiness from carbon monoxide poisoning, which can impair your judgment while driving.

Occasionally, the exhaust system can become plugged through exhaust debris, carbon particle fouling, or foreign matter entering the exhaust system. In any of these cases, the back pressure will cause the engine to run badly and may cause an explosive rupture of pipes and mufflers and/or a leak that may have health and safety implications.

Another exhaust problem is hot spots on the pipes or even sparks coming from the pipes. These have been known to start gas fires or even engine fires where enough combustible oily material is available.

 Tips for New Drivers

15-MINUTE CHECKUP

To keep your vehicle in good working order, follow the suggestions in your owner's manual for checkups and maintenance. In addition, if you drive 10,000 or more miles a year, do a 15-minute check of the following items every month:

- ▶ all lights for burned-out bulbs
- ▶ the battery fluid level or the green battery-charge indicator
- ▶ the engine oil level and transmission-fluid level
- ▶ the brake pedal for firmness and proper operation
- ▶ the brake-fluid level
- ▶ the air pressure in all tires
- ▶ the tires for uneven wear
- ▶ the cooling system
- ▶ the hoses and belts that operate the fan and compressor
- ▶ the windshield washer and wipers
- ▶ the power-steering fluid level

Whenever there is a problem with the exhaust system, have it repaired by a reputable shop. If you suspect your exhaust system is leaking, drive with as much ventilation as possible, keeping at least one or two windows partly open.

What Should You Do If Your Accelerator Pedal Sticks?

As you're driving along, you decide to decrease speed. You lift your foot from the accelerator pedal but nothing changes. You can't slow down. The vehicle keeps moving at the same speed. The problem is a stuck accelerator pedal. The engine does not return to idle when you take your foot off the pedal.

A stuck accelerator pedal may be caused by a broken engine mount, a crumpled floor mat, or ice or snow on the floor around the pedal.

Sometimes tapping the accelerator pedal a couple of times with your foot will unstick it. If not, here's what to do:

1. Apply the brakes, and shift to Neutral. The engine will race, but power will be disengaged from the wheels.
2. Check traffic, and signal a lane change off the road.
3. Choose a safe path, and steer off the road, continuing to apply the brakes.
4. When you are off the roadway, shift to Park, turn off the ignition, and apply the parking brake.
5. Do not attempt to unstick the pedal until after you've steered off the road and come to a stop. Test the pedal before reentering traffic. If the pedal problem is mechanical, have it repaired before driving again.

What Should You Do If the Hood Flies Up?

If the hood of your vehicle suddenly flies up while you're driving, you must take action to avoid a collision and get off the road.

Here's how to handle this emergency:

1. Lean forward and look through the space between the dashboard and the hood. If this view is blocked or limited, roll down your side window and look around the hood. Continue to steer in the direction in which you were moving.
2. Check your mirrors to see what traffic is behind you. Check the traffic to either side of your vehicle.
3. Signal to indicate the direction you want to move. Maintain your lane position while waiting for a gap in traffic. Then steer off the road.

What Should You Do If Your Headlights Fail?

Headlight failure at night is dangerous because without lights your ability to see is reduced and other drivers can't see your vehicle very well.

Rarely do both headlights fail at the same time. However, if one headlight goes out, you may not notice it until the other also goes out. Headlight failure is usually the result of a burned-out, low-beam headlamp.

If you're driving at night and suddenly your lights flicker or die, you have to get off the road without making any sudden, possibly dangerous moves. Here's what to do:

1. Slow down and continue in the same direction you were going. Be aware of the traffic around you.

2. Try switching to high beams. Headlights seldom burn out on both high and low beams at the same time, and this will probably give you enough light to get to your destination.

3. If switching to high beams gives no light, try turning on parking lights, turn indicators, and the emergency flashers. These can give you enough light to help you get off the road.

4. When you see a gap in traffic, steer off the roadway. If you have no lights at all, look for the side-lane markers on the pavement. You can also utilize available light from streetlights or other vehicles on the roadway.

5. If possible, stop your vehicle off the roadway near a lighted place, such as a lighted sign, building, or streetlight. Call for help.

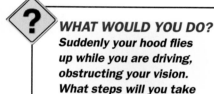

? WHAT WOULD YOU DO?
Suddenly your hood flies up while you are driving, obstructing your vision. What steps will you take to avoid a collision?

Lesson 2 Review

❶ What would you do if one of your vehicle's tires suddenly lost pressure while you were driving?

❷ How would you deal with a stuck accelerator pedal while driving?

❸ What would you do if your vehicle's hood flew up while you were driving?

❹ List the steps for jump-starting a dead battery.

❺ What would you do if your headlights failed while you were driving at night?

Waiting for Help and Protecting the Scene

If your car breaks down, you may need assistance but be miles from a phone. You may be able to correct a minor mechanical problem yourself. You might also choose to call on passing vehicles and pedestrians to get the help you need.

What Should You Do at the Scene of a Vehicle Breakdown or Other Emergency?

If your vehicle breaks down, you may be able to remedy the problem yourself—by changing a flat tire, for example. If you can't fix the problem yourself, you will need to get help and have your car towed if it can't be fixed on the spot.

If you have a breakdown, pull completely out of traffic. Then communicate your situation to passing drivers or pedestrians in a way that keeps you and other roadway users safe.

MAKE OTHERS AWARE OF YOUR PROBLEM

If you have a cellular phone, you'll be able to call for help immediately from your vehicle. If you have no cell phone, there may be a public telephone or a roadside callbox within walking distance. If the public telephone is in an open gas station or mini-mart, you can probably safely wait there for help.

If you can't call for help, you'll need to get the attention of other drivers. Do this safely—in a way that protects you as well as other drivers. Raise the hood of your vehicle, and tie a handkerchief or scarf to the antenna or left-door handle, or wedge it out of a window. Switch on your emergency flashers to alert passing drivers to your situation.

Raising the hood of your car is one action you can take to let others know you need help. *What else can you do?*

If your vehicle breaks down on a highway, your immediate goal is to get the vehicle safely off the roadway and onto the shoulder. Then set out flares or other warning devices to increase your vehicle's visibility to other drivers.

Stay in the vehicle if you have pulled well off the roadway. Otherwise, get as far away from the road as you can.

PROTECT YOURSELF

You can wait inside your vehicle if the weather is bad and you're far enough off the road. Keep the windows open a little bit and the doors locked. Do not sit in a stopped car with all the windows closed, the engine running, and the heater on. You could be putting yourself and your passengers at risk of carbon monoxide poisoning.

It is very dangerous to completely roll down your window or open your vehicle door to strangers. If a stranger does stop to offer help, just ask the person to call for emergency road service.

If your vehicle is not far enough from roadway traffic, or if you think it might be struck from behind by another vehicle, leave your vehicle and walk to a safe place. Proceed carefully—especially at night or in bad weather when visibility is limited.

Never stand behind or directly in front of your vehicle. Other roadway users will have trouble seeing you. Your parked car could be struck by an oncoming vehicle.

? WHAT WOULD YOU DO?
Your vehicle has broken down, and you have moved it to the side of the road. What actions will you take to find assistance?

EMERGENCY ROAD SERVICE

Emergency road service operators can help you in an emergency. They usually can change a flat tire or do minor repairs on the spot. They may also have gasoline or booster cables in case you've run out of gas or have a dead battery.

If you need to be towed to a service garage, you should know whether or not your insurance covers all or part of the towing charge or if you have a private service such as AAA, which pays for the towing charges. Before your vehicle is towed, find out how many miles away the service garage is. Ask for an estimate of the charges for towing before you begin.

If your vehicle is towed, arrange transportation for yourself and your passengers. Passengers are often not allowed to ride in a vehicle when it's being towed, although they may sometimes ride in the tow truck itself.

Lesson 3 Review

❶ What steps would you take to get help if your vehicle broke down?

❷ How would you protect yourself at the scene if your vehicle broke down?

❸ How can you increase your vehicle's visibility if your vehicle breaks down on the roadway?

If You Are Involved in a Collision

No matter how good a driver you are, at some point you will probably be involved in a collision. After a collision, be aware that some people may panic or react in strange ways. Other drivers or passengers may be in a state of shock. Human suffering, loss of time, legal problems, and great expense can result from a collision regardless of who is at fault. Know what you might expect if you are involved in a collision, so that you can act effectively and in your own best interest.

What Should You Do If You Are Involved in a Collision?

If you are in a collision, try to remain calm. Remember that the collision scene is no place to begin arguing with the other driver or with the police. Do not accuse anyone of causing the collision, and do not admit fault yourself. Sign only forms given to you by the police, if any. Do not sign any other statements at the scene of the crash. Remember that you have the legal right to consult an attorney before making any statement, and you should exercise this right.

If you are involved in a collision, stop your vehicle immediately. You may be able to warn other drivers, give aid and medical help to the injured, or call the police. You should also exchange information with other drivers, get the names of witnesses, and wait for help to arrive.

STOP IMMEDIATELY

Drivers who do not stop when involved in a collision are breaking the law. Unless someone was seriously injured or killed, and if you can still drive your vehicle, try to move it off the roadway and out of traffic as soon as you can. Turn off the ignition to prevent the risk of fire. If someone has been seriously injured or killed, leave the vehicle in the road, if possible, and direct traffic around it until emergency vehicles arrive.

WARNING OTHERS

If you cannot move your vehicle out of traffic, you must do everything you can to warn other drivers that there is a problem ahead. Turn on your hazard flashers. If you have flares or reflecting triangles, set them up at least 100 feet ahead of and behind the collision scene. If you don't have this equipment, you might ask someone, possibly another driver who offers to help, to stand at the side of the road out of traffic and wave a flashlight or light-colored cloth to warn oncoming traffic. You can also do this yourself, if you are not injured and there is no one else who needs first aid.

OBJECTIVES

1. **Describe** the actions that you should take if you are involved in a collision.
2. **Understand** the possible legal consequences of a collision.

Driver Ed
Online

Topic: First-aid kits

For a link to more information on first-aid kits, go to drivered.glencoe .com.

Activity: Using the information provided at this link, work with two or three other students to create a bulletin-board display showing items to include in an automobile first-aid kit.

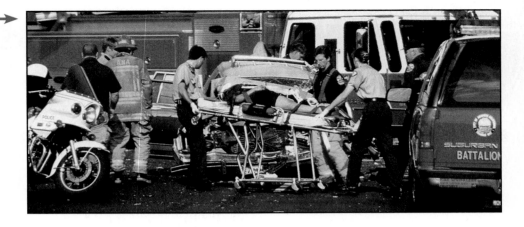

Professional medical personnel are the only ones who should move an injured person. **Why is this the case?**

GIVING AID TO THE INJURED

Check the vehicles involved for injured persons. Try to make them comfortable, but do not move them unless they are in immediate danger of additional injury and you know what you are doing. Moving an injured person, particularly one with neck or back injuries, can result in more serious injury. Do what you can to provide first aid.

CALLING THE POLICE

If you or someone who has stopped to help has a cellular phone, use it to call the police. The police will usually notify other emergency services.

By law, a collision resulting in injury, death, or property damage above a given dollar value must be reported to the police. Some states require reports only for serious crashes, but a few states require that all collisions be reported.

Death rates are higher for occupants of small pickup trucks and small utility vehicles than for any other type of passenger vehicles, including the smallest cars.

MEDICAL HELP

Use 911 or other emergency numbers, if available, to call for an ambulance if someone is seriously injured. If you don't have a cell phone, flag down another driver to contact the appropriate emergency services.

EXCHANGE INFORMATION

If you are involved in a collision, you should exchange information with the other driver and any passengers. You should exchange drivers' and passengers' names and addresses, driver's license information, names of insurance companies, and vehicle registration information. For your records, and for your insurance company, write down a description of the crash including the license number of the vehicle that was struck, plus the date, time, and place. If you are involved in a collision with a parked car, try to locate the owner. If you cannot, leave a note under the windshield wiper blades containing the same information that you would exchange at any other collision scene.

WITNESS INFORMATION

If there are witnesses at the scene, write down their names and addresses, too. You might need them to verify your account of the collision if the other driver comes up with a different version of events.

STAY AT THE SCENE

If you are uninjured, remain at the scene of the collision until your help is no longer needed. If people have been seriously injured or killed, remain at the scene until the police allow you to leave. If an ambulance wants to take you to the hospital, go to receive medical help.

What Should You Do After a Collision?

After a collision occurs, if you have any injuries, or if the crash was serious, make sure you see a doctor. In addition, you should file all appropriate reports. You may have legal consequences to address, depending on the severity of the collision and your role in the crash.

SEE A DOCTOR

Even if you have been treated at the scene of the collision, be sure to see your own doctor. Some injuries do not appear right away.

MAKE COLLISION REPORTS

If someone was injured, make a collision report. Drivers involved in any collision that results in injury should make a written report to the police and to the state department of motor vehicles. If you do not file a required report, your driver's license could be suspended regardless of whether or not the collision was your fault.

States have different laws about reporting property damage under certain amounts. Know what your state law requires. Check your state driver's manual or contact your motor vehicle department to get this information.

Of course, you should also inform your automobile insurance company. Your insurance company can advise you on what reports you need to file. Your insurance company will want to hear your version of events, and they will want you to give them all the pertinent information that you have so that they can represent your interests. In some states, if you are driving a vehicle that is not insured, you are assumed to be at fault and you will have less legal recourse than an insured driver regardless of who was at fault.

DEAL WITH THE LEGAL CONSEQUENCES

Legal consequences of a collision can be very serious. If a collision is the result of your having broken a traffic law, there probably will be consequences for you depending on the severity of the crash and the laws that you broke or the injuries or damage that occurred. Legal consequences can include fines, court costs, suspended or revoked license, or jailtime.

If it is found that you were intoxicated or under the influence of other drugs at the time of a collision, the penalties will probably be more severe. Remember that your insurance company will hire a lawyer to represent you for property damage or injuries to others that resulted from the collision, but not in criminal proceedings. If there are serious criminal charges against you, and if you can afford it, hire a lawyer to represent you.

Did You Know?

Early ambulances were horse-drawn wagons used to transport sick or injured soldiers during wartime. Soon after the introduction of the automobile, ambulance vehicles became motorized.

FYI

A rear-end vehicle collision may cause a whiplash injury, in which the victim's head snaps backward, then abruptly whips forward. Such an injury can cause severe neck damage. Ensuring that your headrest is properly adjusted at all times can minimize this type of injury.

Walter Barta

Manager Driver Education
Alberta Motor Association

Emergencies can occur suddenly and without warning. It is important to prepare for and learn how to assess and respond to emergencies quickly, safely, efficiently, and calmly. In an emergency situation, try to stay calm, think clearly, and act quickly.

The best way to deal with challenges caused by vehicle failure is to prepare for it. Keep your vehicle in good working order and follow the suggestions in your owner's manual for periodic checkups and maintenance. Play the "What If" game. Mental preparation helps you to avoid panic and better prepares you to respond to emergency situations.

What would you do if the brakes fail, one of the front tires blows out, or the hood flies up?

?

WHAT WOULD YOU DO?
You have been involved in a collision with another vehicle. You are uninjured, but the other driver is bleeding. How can you help?

What Should You Do If You Pass a Collision Scene?

Use good judgment and common sense when you pass the scene of a collision. If help appears needed, you may choose to stop well off the roadway and offer whatever assistance you can, such as calling for help. However, if the situation appears under control or looks potentially dangerous, keep going. The presence of police cars, ambulances, or tow trucks with flashing lights indicates the situation is under control. Stopping at the scene when it is unnecessary can cause additional hazards for others who are using the roadway.

Lesson 4 Review

1 What are your responsibilities if you are in a collision?

2 What are the possible legal consequences of a collision?

3 What should you do and not do when passing the scene of a collision?

BENJAMIN BANNEKER

To drivers traveling through the United States, it may seem as though many major cities just grew, without any plan at all. In many cases, this is true. However, our capital city, Washington, D.C., is one of the few cities in this country that was designed before it was built. This is particularly evident in the area surrounding the U.S. Capitol, which is located near the center of Washington, D.C. Like the spokes of a wheel, broad streets extend out from the Capitol in all directions. This roadway pattern can also be seen near Union Station, the Lincoln Memorial, and Mt. Vernon Square.

President George Washington chose Pierre L'Enfant, a French engineer, to draw up the plans for the new capital. Benjamin Banneker helped L'Enfant to work out the city's plan and to survey, or measure, the size, shape, and area of the land. Banneker was the first African American ever to be appointed to work for the government.

L'Enfant left the United States before the building of Washington, D.C., was completed, taking the plans with him. However, Banneker stepped in and finished laying out the city from memory.

Banneker was the son of a free woman and a slave father. He was born free in 1731 on a farm in Maryland. Banneker was educated in a Quaker school, where he became interested in mathematics and science. He later taught himself astronomy.

Banneker used his knowledge to make astronomical and tidal calculations in order to write a yearly almanac predicting weather conditions. He sent a copy of his almanac to Thomas Jefferson along with a letter urging the abolition of slavery. Those against slavery held Banneker up as an example of the talents and abilities of African Americans.

WHAT DO YOU THINK NOW?

What do you think was Benjamin Banneker's most important accomplishment? Why?

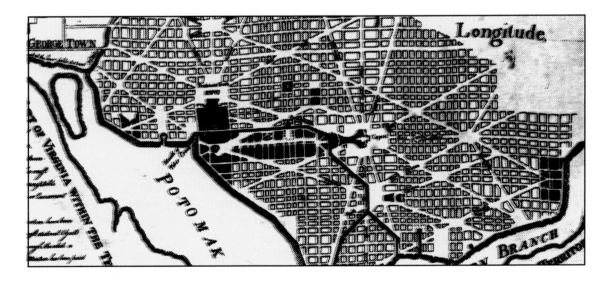

Key Points

Lesson 1

1 If your engine stalls while you're driving, signal and steer off the road. If your vehicle is in motion, shift to Neutral and try to restart the engine. If the engine won't start, steer near the curb or onto the shoulder and stop. (Page 312)

2 In case of brake failure, rapidly pump the brake pedal. If that doesn't work, use the parking brake. Downshift. (Page 313)

3 If your vehicle's power steering fails, grip the steering wheel firmly and turn it with more force than usual. Steer off the road and stop. In case of total steering failure, use the parking brake to stop. (Page 315)

? **WHAT WOULD YOU DO?**
As you prepare to slow your vehicle, you find that the brakes don't work and the vehicle does not slow down. What do you suppose has happened? How will you handle this situation?

Lesson 2

1 If your vehicle has a blowout or flat tire, keep a firm grip on the steering wheel. When steering is stabilized, release the accelerator slowly, but do not brake. Steer off the road. (Page 316)

2 To jump-start a dead battery, turn off the ignition in both vehicles, and shift both into Park. Attach the jumper cables properly. Start the engine of the vehicle with the good battery, then the engine of the other vehicle. (Page 318)

3 If the hood flies up, look through the space between the dashboard and the hood or out of the driver's side window. Continue to steer in the direction in which you were moving until you can leave the road. (Page 321)

Lesson 3

? **WHAT WOULD YOU DO?**
Your vehicle has broken down, and you have moved it to the side of the road. What actions will you take to find assistance?

1 If your vehicle breaks down, get off the road. Let other drivers know you need help. (Page 323)

2 Protect yourself at the scene if your vehicle breaks down. Wait inside your vehicle. Don't open your vehicle to strangers. (Page 324)

Lesson 4

1 Drivers involved in a collision must stop immediately and turn off the ignition, give aid to the injured, try to get medical help, call the police, exchange relevant information, get names and addresses of witnesses, stay at the scene, make collision reports, and see a doctor. (Pages 325–327)

2 The legal consequences of a collision can be serious. If the collision is the result of your having broken a traffic law, you may, depending on the severity of the crash, be fined, have your license suspended or revoked, or be sent to jail. (Pages 327–328)

On a separate sheet of paper, write the letter of the answer that best completes each sentence.

1 If your vehicle breaks down, you should
   a. phone for help or get the attention of passing drivers.
   b. stand in front of your vehicle for help.
   c. stand in the road and wave your arms.

2 If the fluid in your battery is frozen and the engine won't start,
   a. use jumper cables.
   b. do not use jumper cables.
   c. turn on the heater and use jumper cables.

3 If the hood flies up while you're driving,
   a. stop immediately.
   b. honk your horn and move right.
   c. look through the space between the hood and the dashboard.

4 If your foot brake suddenly loses power,
   a. turn the ignition to the lock position.
   b. shift into Reverse.
   c. rapidly pump the brake pedal.

5 Two drivers who have been in a collision should
   a. avoid any contact with each other.
   b. split the cost of any damages.
   c. exchange names and other information.

6 To dry wet brakes,
   a. drive slowly with your left foot pressing gently on the brake pedal.
   b. stamp down on the pedal several times.
   c. drive in low gear.

On a separate sheet of paper, write the word or phrase that best completes each sentence.

cooling system   brake fade

collision report   battery

7 If the _____ is dead, you won't be able to start your vehicle.

8 Applying your brakes hard for a long time may cause _____.

9 Your engine may overheat if there is not enough coolant in the _____.

10 If you are involved in a collision, you should make a _____.

Writing

Driver's Log

In this chapter, you have learned how to deal with emergency situations caused by vehicle failures and those that result in collisions. Write two paragraphs giving your ideas on the most important factors to keep in mind when confronted with both types of emergencies.

Projects

❶ Look over a vehicle owner's manual. What special directions does the manual contain for avoiding and responding to vehicle failures and emergencies? What preventive maintenance tips does the manual offer?

❷ Interview a traffic enforcement officer. Ask what traffic violations and vehicle failures most frequently cause collisions. Also find out what drivers can do to prevent these crashes.

This review tests your knowledge of the material in Chapters 12–15, and will help you review for your state driving test. On a separate sheet of paper, select the answer that best completes each statement.

1 The speed at which you are driving will probably need to be adjusted if you
  a. see another vehicle approaching from the opposite direction.
  b. encounter a slippery road surface.
  c. are moving with the flow of traffic.

2 To avoid colliding with the vehicle in front of you,
  a. allow enough time and space to see and react if a problem occurs.
  b. move to another lane of traffic.
  c. apply your brakes if you see the brake lights of the vehicle in front of you.

3 If you need to brake hard, you can manage the law of inertia if you
  a. place your foot firmly on carpeted floor.
  b. place your hand firmly on the steering wheel.
  c. wear your seat belt properly.

4 To enable your vehicle to hold to the road, you should make sure your tires are
  a. bald, especially on rough roads.
  b. inflated so that they grip the road evenly.
  c. inflated so that only the center edges of the tires grip the road.

5 Compared to driving a compact car, if you are driving a fully packed SUV, you should allow
  a. more time to accelerate and enter the freeway.
  b. a smaller gap between vehicles when changing lanes.
  c. less time to stop in an emergency.

6 To maintain your speed when you drive uphill,
  a. slow down to compensate for the downward pull of gravity.
  b. accelerate just before your vehicle begins to climb the hill.
  c. make sure there are no slow vehicles ahead of or behind you.

7 A vehicle having a low center of gravity usually
  a. sits higher off the ground.
  b. is more stable when carrying a loaded luggage rack.
  c. handles well when you need to make quick maneuvers.

8 You can reduce the risk level of driving in inclement weather by
  a. keeping your high-beam headlights on at all times.
  b. cleaning your vehicle windows and lights before you travel.
  c. avoiding driving in tracks created by another vehicle.

9 Hydroplaning is dangerous because
  a. your tires lose contact with the road.
  b. your tires get stuck in the mud.
  c. your vehicle skids out of control.

10 To minimize your risks while driving during a tornado,
  a. try to drive out of the way of the tornado.
  b. get out of your vehicle and find suitable shelter or a ditch.
  c. reduce your speed and grip the steering wheel firmly to control the vehicle.

11 Mountain driving requires that you
  a. push down on the accelerator as you ascend a steep grade.
  b. always drive in Overdrive if you have an automatic transmission.
  c. shift to a higher gear to decrease the engine's pulling power if you have a manual transmission.

12 If your vehicle picks up too much speed when driving downhill,
  a. press on the brake pedal firmly until you reach the bottom of the hill.
  b. shift to a lower gear if you are going down a long, steep hill.
  c. apply the brakes until you feel your brakes fade.

13 When your vehicle goes into a skid,
  a. you should step firmly on the brake pedal to slow the vehicle quickly.
  b. look and steer in the direction you want the front of the vehicle to go.
  c. accelerate until the tires stop spinning.

14 If you know how natural laws work, you may be able to avoid a collision by
  a. increasing the traction for your tires.
  b. steering your vehicle off the roadway.
  c. making a reflex reaction after thinking through a situation.

15 To safely make an off-road recovery,
  a. turn your steering wheel sharply to return to the roadway.
  b. let your vehicle slow gradually until it is off the roadway and then gradually return to the roadway.
  c. brake to stop the vehicle and then turn back onto the roadway.

16 Environmental factors that cause the most problems for drivers include
  a. poor street lighting.
  b. rain, snow, and fog.
  c. the angle of the sun.

17 Vehicle engines fail most often because of
  a. lack of fuel and water.
  b. broken belts or a malfunctioning fuel or electrical system.
  c. driving too fast or too slow on the roadway.

18 If you notice steam or smoke rising from under the hood of your vehicle,
  a. your engine may have overheated.
  b. you need to add water to the cooling system.
  c. you need to turn on the air conditioner.

19 If you suddenly have no brakes,
  a. slow the movement of the vehicle by running into something head-on.
  b. shift to a higher gear.
  c. rapidly pump the brake pedal unless you have power brakes.

20 When a blowout occurs,
  a. your vehicle's tire suddenly loses pressure, and the car is hard to control.
  b. your vehicle's tire loses pressure through a slow leak.
  c. you should slow the vehicle by braking and moving to the side of the road.

Challenge Questions

1 To control your vehicle in weather-related conditions
  a. drive a vehicle that is equipped with seat belts and air bags.
  b. inflate your tires to the minimum pressure recommended.
  c. drive your vehicle at a reasonable speed that allows you 8 to 12 seconds to react to an emergency.

2 If you are involved in a collision in which someone is injured,
  a. make a written report to the police and the state department of motor vehicles.
  b. report property damage regardless of the amount of damage.
  c. pay court costs and the medical expenses of the persons involved.

UNIT 6

DRIVING READINESS

How does impairment relate to driving?

Impairment is a major problem in driving. If your driving is impaired, you may not be able to drive safely. Impairment can be something as simple as being tired. Driving is impaired by the use and abuse of drugs such as alcohol. Driving can also be impaired by the condition of your vehicle. Since driver readiness is so crucial, the next four chapters discuss several types of impairments and include tips for preventing or overcoming their effects.

LESSON 1
Fatigue and Driving

LESSON 2
Short-Term Physical Conditions and Driving

LESSON 3
Long-Term Physical Factors and Driving

Why Is It Important to Recognize Physical Impairments?

Drivers must be physically ready to drive. Physical impairments impede your ability to drive. Physical impairments can include problems with general health, alertness, sleep, fatigue, illness, chronic disease, injury, and general physical status including declines normally associated with aging. Understanding and compensating for any physical impairment you may have or experience reduce your driving risk.

Driver Ed
Online

For additional activities, visit drivered.glencoe.com. Here you will find:

◆ **Web Link Exercises**

◆ **eFlashcards**

◆ **Practice Driving Tests**

Fatigue and Driving

OBJECTIVES

1. **Define** fatigue and describe how fatigue affects driving ability.
2. **Identify** kinds of fatigue that can negatively impact driving performance.
3. **Describe** how you can deal with fatigue.

KEY TERMS

- fatigue
- repetition
- duration
- recovery time

Imagine you are driving and find your eyes getting extremely heavy as your drive progresses. You are experiencing fatigue. In this lesson, you will learn about what causes fatigue and what you should do if you are experiencing fatigue.

Like all impairments, fatigue affects a driver's ability to perceive or respond to threats on the road. The busy nature of many people's lives leads them to drive while tired, even though they know better. You get tired for a variety of reasons. Conditions such as overwork, a cold, the flu, or even a temporary injury can tire you and affect your ability to make good decisions while driving. In some instances, you can compensate for a limiting physical condition. At other times, your wisest course of action is not to drive at all.

How Does Fatigue Affect Your Driving Ability?

Fatigue is weariness resulting from too much physical or mental exertion. Fatigue is dangerous if you're driving because your senses are impaired. You may not see objects clearly, or it may take you longer to perceive and respond to driving dangers. You may miss critical information—signs, lights, and sounds. You may misjudge speed and distance or take needless risks. You may drift into a state of "highway hypnosis" and fall asleep at the wheel. There are four types of fatigue:

- attention fatigue
- visual fatigue
- muscular fatigue
- sleep fatigue

Attention fatigue and sleep fatigue result from too much mental exertion. Visual fatigue is a combination of mental and physical fatigue. Muscular fatigue comes from too much physical exertion or physical work.

Fatigue does not only come from exertion. The body's natural rhythms cause nearly everyone to be less alert in the late afternoon. Fatigue may be brought on by boredom, illness, stress, or even lack of sleep. Drowsy driving is now recognized as one of the leading causes of traffic collisions—perhaps even ahead of alcohol impaired driving.

When you feel tired, you're clearly in no condition to drive. Driving a motor vehicle is a complicated task that requires you to be in good physical and mental condition. So make sure you are not fatigued before driving.

Avoid overeating, drinking alcoholic beverages, taking drugs, or riding in an overheated vehicle since all these activities compound the effects of fatigue.

Each year, drivers who fall asleep at the wheel cause at least 100,000 automobile crashes, 40,000 injuries, and more than 1,500 deaths. [Source: National Highway Traffic Safety Administration]

SIGNS OF FATIGUE

When you are driving, it is important to pay attention to signs of fatigue. Drivers should look for the following clues to indicate sleepiness, which signals the need to stop driving and rest.

▶ Frequent yawning

▶ Loss of concentration or focus

▶ Reduced awareness of surroundings (for example, a vehicle seems to appear out of nowhere)

▶ Inability to recall anything about the last few miles driven

▶ Driving too fast or too slow, or speed varies

▶ General sluggishness

If you begin to experience any of these symptoms, stop doing whatever you are doing and get some rest. Remember that fatigue is usually temporary and easy to overcome.

How Do You Avoid Fatigue?

There are several ways you can avoid fatigue, but you should always follow one simple rule. To avoid fatigue, understand that more activity requires more rest. Knowing this one simple rule is the key to avoiding fatigue while you drive.

Repetition, duration, and recovery are important aspects of fatigue. **Repetition** refers to the number of times you repeat doing something. Whatever you are doing, more repetitions over a longer period of time make it more likely that you will experience fatigue. **Duration** refers to the length of time you engage in a specific task. The only way to recover from fatigue is to take a break from the activity that created the fatigue, a break called **recovery time**. The length of the break should be directly related to the number of repetitions and the duration of the task. In other words, if you work longer, you should rest longer, too.

Fatigue is usually temporary and easily overcome. To avoid fatigue while driving, give yourself a break from the repetitions and duration of driving. Here are some things you can do to avoid the repetitions and duration of driving:

● stop regularly (at least 10 to 15 minutes every 2 hours)

● breathe deeply

● get out of the car

● walk, jog, or do other light exercises for a few minutes

Remember that the best way to overcome fatigue is to stop doing whatever you are doing and get some rest.

Did You Know?

In 1989, the Pennsylvania Turnpike Commission introduced "rumble strips" designed to help reduce the number of crashes caused by drowsy drivers. When drowsy drivers start to drift off the roadway, their vehicles' tires roll onto the rumble strips along the shoulder. This action creates noise and vibration, which alert drivers and allow them to correct their steering and return safely to the road.

FIGHTING FATIGUE

Fatigue is usually temporary and easily overcome. The best way to overcome fatigue is to stop doing whatever you are doing and get some rest.

Before You Drive
▲ Get plenty of rest.
▲ Avoid heavy, fatty foods.
▲ Do not drink alcoholic beverages.

While You Drive
▲ Make sure there is a good flow of fresh air in your vehicle. If it is overheated or poorly ventilated, you may become sleepy.
▲ Wear sunglasses to cope with glare from sun and snow.
▲ Take turns driving with someone else.
▲ Turn on the radio. Sing, whistle, or talk to yourself.
▲ Stop regularly, get out of the vehicle, and walk, jog, or do other light exercise for a few minutes.

THE NEED TO SLEEP

If you are already on the road and find yourself getting sleepy and not quite able to keep your eyes open, you're better off pulling over and sleeping for a while than trying to continue driving. Although it is usually not a good idea to sleep in your car at the side of the road, there are times when it's the safe choice and better than continuing to drive.

If you are feeling sleepy while driving, you must overcome this feeling. *What is the best way to overcome sleepiness while you are driving?*

Here are some tips if you have no choice but to stop and rest.

1. At night, stop at a well-lit roadside rest area. If you cannot find such an area, make sure you are as far off the highway as possible.
2. Roll down a window just enough so that fresh air enters the vehicle you are driving but not enough that someone might be able to enter it.
3. Turn off the engine to avoid being poisoned by carbon monoxide, a colorless, odorless gas.
4. Lock all the doors.
5. Leave your parking lights on, but turn off all other electrical equipment.
6. Before you begin to drive again, get out of the car if it is safe to do so, and make sure you are fully awake.

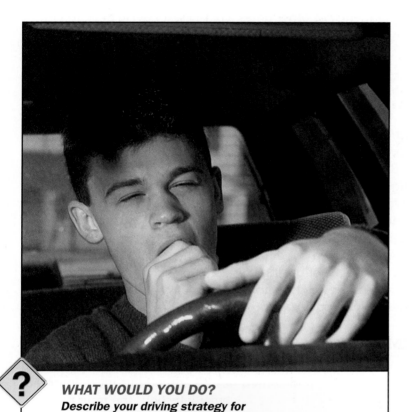

WHAT WOULD YOU DO?
Describe your driving strategy for the next few hours until you reach your destination.

Driver Ed
Online

Topic: Drowsy driving

For a link to more information on ways to avoid driving drowsy, go to **drivered.glencoe.com**.

Activity: Using the information provided in this online brochure, design a bumper sticker that reminds drivers about the importance of avoiding driving drowsy.

Lesson 1 Review

❶ What is fatigue? How does it affect your driving ability?

❷ What are the four types of fatigue?

❸ How can you avoid or recover from fatigue?

Short-Term Physical Conditions and Driving

OBJECTIVES

1. **Explain** the ways that short-term illnesses and injuries may affect driving.
2. **Identify** ways to compensate for your temporary illness or injury.

KEY TERMS

◆ compensate
◆ carbon monoxide

Ask your doctor or the pharmacist if you can drive safely while taking any medication. *What risks can medications cause while you are driving?*

Conditions such as fatigue, a cold, the flu, or an injury are temporary physical impairments, but these conditions can affect your ability to make good decisions while driving. In some instances, you can compensate for these types of temporary impairments. At other times, your wisest course of action is not to drive at all.

How Do Short-Term Illnesses or Injuries Affect Your Driving?

Even short-term illnesses and injuries impair your ability to think clearly or to drive. A temporary illness, such as a cold, the flu, or an allergy, can make it risky for you to drive. A temporary injury, such as a broken bone or a sprain, can make driving more risky and more uncomfortable. The discomfort or pain you experience from either an illness or an injury can distract your attention from the road and lessen your ability to manage visibility, time, and space.

If you cannot avoid driving when you're ill, try to **compensate**, or to make allowances, for your impaired condition. For instance, if it's difficult to drive, try to minimize the amount of driving you do. Allow extra time to get where you're going. Drive more slowly than you normally would, and keep your attention focused on driving, not on how you feel.

SHORT-TERM ILLNESS

You probably get ill from time to time. Sometimes it's a simple, common cold; sometimes it's the flu; and sometimes it's something more involved, such as a bacterial infection, the mumps, measles, chicken pox, or mononucleosis. All of these maladies usually only last a week or two, but they can have a powerful negative effect on your energy and alertness.

Be especially careful about driving if you are taking any medication. Some medications for common illnesses can cause drowsiness, nausea, headache, or dizziness—conditions that are extremely dangerous when you are driving a vehicle. Always read the information that appears on medicine containers. Some labels specifically warn against driving.

The pain, ache, and discomfort that short-term illnesses bring usually prevent you from even wanting to venture out into traffic. However, if

Lynn Silvestro

Community College of Vermont
Rutland, VT

Community College of Vermont
Rutland, VT

Advice FROM THE EXPERTS

Teens and young adults, especially, are susceptible to fatigue. It could cause them to fall asleep while driving, miss critical information, take risks, or misjudge speed and distance. The best way to overcome fatigue is to stop doing whatever you are doing and get some rest. On average, teens need 9 hours of sleep each day.

Short-term illness or injury can cause pain or discomfort and distract your attention from the road and lessen your ability to manage visibility, time, and space. If you cannot avoid driving when you're injured, at least try to minimize the amount of driving you do. Allow extra time to get where you're going, drive more slowly than you normally would, and keep your attention focused on driving, not on how you feel.

Why is it important to understand how to handle fatigue, short-term illnesses, and injuries?

you absolutely must get out, perhaps to pick up medicine, keep in mind that you are driving while impaired. Even the simple act of wiping or blowing your nose is difficult and distracting enough to seriously affect your driving. When you're sick, remember that you are not in the best position to be driving.

CARBON MONOXIDE POISONING

One of the most deadly forms of impairment is carbon monoxide poisoning, which can affect your ability to drive just as much as the most powerful medicine. **Carbon monoxide** is an odorless, colorless gas that can silently surround you as you drive. It is known as the *silent killer*. This gas is produced when your vehicle's engine is running, and it can creep into the passenger compartment if your exhaust system is defective. Headache and sleepiness are two early signs of carbon monoxide poisoning, which can occur when you are driving an old car or one whose exhaust system has not been well maintained.

SAFETY TIP

All vehicles emit carbon monoxide gas. It can make you physically ill or even kill you. Have your vehicle's exhaust system checked regularly. Avoid driving a vehicle that has an exhaust leak or a broken tailpipe. Such defects allow harmful exhaust gases to be trapped beneath the vehicle, even when it is moving. These gases may leak into the vehicle's interior.

A temporary illness, such as a cold, flu, or an allergy, can make it risky for you to drive. ***What are some of the risks?***

When a vehicle is left with the engine idling, it produces pollution in the form of carbon monoxide. It also wastes gas. You can help reduce pollution and also save energy by avoiding excessive idling.

Having a well-maintained vehicle and a steady supply of fresh air entering your vehicle are the best defenses against carbon monoxide poisoning.

TEMPORARY INJURY

Temporary injuries are also driver impairments. A physical injury is a distraction because of the pain or discomfort that it brings. Injuries often reduce your effectiveness as a driver by decreasing the speed, smoothness, strength, or responsiveness of the driver-control functions necessary for safe driving. They can affect the necessary sensitivity with which you handle the pedals and steering wheel and how you move within the vehicle. Most injuries are accompanied by some sort of medication, which can impair perception, too.

Certain types of injuries may affect the range of motion in your arms, legs, torso, head, and neck. Checking over your shoulder before changing lanes is a critical safe-driving behavior, but it's hard to turn your head to check traffic behind you with a back, neck, or shoulder injury.

If you cannot avoid driving when you're injured, at least try to compensate by minimizing the amount of driving you do. Just as you would with an illness, allow extra time to get where you're going. Drive more slowly than you normally would, and keep your attention focused on driving, not on how you feel.

WHAT WOULD YOU DO?
What advice would you give this teen about driving while recovering from a temporary injury?

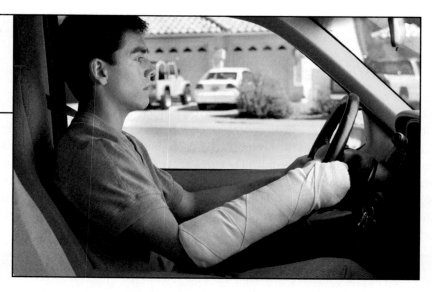

Lesson 2 Review

❶ How can short-term illnesses affect your driving?

❷ What effect can an injury have on your driving?

❸ How can you protect yourself from carbon monoxide poisoning?

Long-Term Physical Factors and Driving

LESSON 3

Chronic diseases, permanent injuries, and physical decline all affect your general health and ability to drive. You might or might not experience pain or discomfort from these conditions. Changes in your body chemistry or changes in your ability to use parts of your body can also distract your attention from the road. For instance, a disease such as diabetes can make it risky for you to drive at certain times, as can a permanent injury, such as spinal-cord damage.

How Do Chronic Diseases Affect Driving Ability?

Disease by definition is a condition of not being at ease. If you have a disease, you are not in perfect health, or you are not experiencing the comfort of physical wellness. A chronic disease is one that is ongoing. Many chronic diseases affect driving ability by impairing certain aspects of the body's normal function. This lessens the ability to manage visibility, time, and space. However, it is still quite possible to drive responsibly with a chronic disease.

Chronic diseases include diabetes, narcolepsy (sudden onset of sleep), epilepsy, glaucoma (a leading cause of blindness), mood disorders, asthma, cancer, and coronary heart disease. Although people with these diseases may have to adjust certain aspects of their behavior in order to compensate for the decline in function that each particular disease brings, it is still possible for them to drive safely.

Diseases such as diabetes and epilepsy often require medication, and people who take certain medications may need a medical doctor's permission to drive. Sometimes, the medication itself can result in side effects that impair driving more than the illness. These effects might include drowsiness, dizziness, headache, and nausea, which can significantly interfere with safe driving. To obtain a driver's license, people with certain chronic illnesses that can impair their driving ability must furnish proof that the illnesses are under control and that the medication they take won't cause side effects that impair driving ability.

How Can Challenges Caused by Physical Disabilities Be Met?

At one time, it would have been virtually impossible for a person with cerebral palsy or a spinal cord injury to drive. Such challenges, called *physical disabilities,* often created obstacles that seemed impossible for potential drivers to overcome. With driving aids and devices developed by modern science and

OBJECTIVES

1. **Describe** how diseases affect driving ability.
2. **Identify** several ways that drivers can compensate for physical disabilities.
3. **Describe** how aging and chronic illnesses can affect driving ability.

KEY TERMS

◆ disease
◆ driver evaluation facility

SAFETY TIP

Be especially careful when you see elderly pedestrians. People 75 years of age and older have the highest pedestrian death rates.

Special devices enable many people to drive who would otherwise be unable to do so. **Discuss some devices that you know of that may help drivers.**

technology, however, such disabilities are no longer permanent barriers. Although the severity of a person's physical disability still has some impact on driving ability, new types of equipment have made it easier for disabled persons to be mobile.

For example, many people who do not have full use of their legs can use vehicles equipped with hand-operated brakes and gas pedals. People without arms can utilize artificial limbs, called *prosthetic devices,* which allow them to drive safely using special rings attached to the steering wheel, dashboard controls, door locks, and radio controls.

Special vans are available for people in wheelchairs. Vans are equipped with wheelchair lifts that can be operated from inside or outside the vehicle, as well as with extra space that permits the driver to smoothly transfer from a wheelchair to a special power seat.

Drivers who can't fully turn their heads or shoulders can install extra-large rearview mirrors to extend their vision over a wider area.

Anyone with a physical disability who wants to drive a car and is able to show that he or she can do so safely can get a license. Usually, such individuals are required to undergo a comprehensive medical assessment that determines their potential to drive. A special center to evaluate drivers with physical disabilities, called a **driver evaluation facility**, may be utilized specifically for this purpose.

HOW DOES PHYSICAL DECLINE AFFECT DRIVING ABILITY?

Physical decline is often associated with growing older. Aging can affect a person's ability to drive. As people age, their bodies change. Reflexes and reaction times decline and become slower. Most importantly, the vision of older people may be a little weaker and hearing a bit impaired, problems that also affect some younger and middle-aged drivers.

FYI

Some states have special driver's license renewal procedures for older drivers to help ensure their driving competency. For example, older drivers may be required to renew their license more often, in person, and to pass a vision test.

VISION

Vision is the most critical sense used in driving. Almost everything you do is in response to what your eyes tell you. Your eyes gather almost 95 percent of all driving information you receive about the driving environment. Vision is at its peak at age 14 and begins to slowly decline for the rest of your life. Your eyes are the most important tool that you have when you drive.

In order to drive safely, you need to have your eyes checked frequently. This is particularly true for older drivers. Vision declines occur so slowly and imperceptibly that you might not be able to tell until you start having noticeable problems.

HEARING

Your sense of hearing is also an important guide to conditions on the roadway and within your own vehicle. The sound of a siren, a horn, or a train signal warns you of possible danger. You may hear the sound of a vehicle before you actually see the vehicle. Sounds from your own vehicle may alert you to engine, muffler, brake, or tire trouble.

Older or younger drivers with a hearing loss may be able to compensate by wearing hearing aids. To compensate for the hearing impairment, these drivers can rely more on their vision, frequently searching the roadway and making good use of the rearview and sideview mirrors.

OLDER PEOPLE CAN COMPENSATE FOR PHYSICAL DECLINES

Older people can drive quite safely, and most of them have learned to compensate for their physical decline. Older people can call on their driving experience to help them reduce risk and anticipate threatening conditions. They can also compensate for possible age-related limitations by allowing more time to get to their destination and by changing the time and travel routes.

SHARING THE ROAD WITH OLDER DRIVERS

As a young person, your reaction time is likely to be faster and your sense of sight keener than that of an older person. As you encounter older drivers

It is estimated that one in five Americans will be over age 65 by 2020 and that most of them will have a driver's license.

Science and medicine, along with advances in technology, have greatly improved the driving potential of people with temporary and permanent injuries. *What are some of the improvements that have been made?*

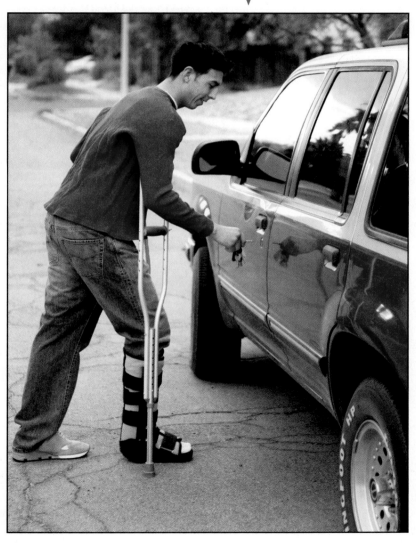

and older pedestrians, be respectful of their age and experience. Remember that older drivers and pedestrians tend to get out during the middle of the day, in better weather, and on quieter roads. Older drivers generally obey the rules of the road, including the speed limit.

When you encounter older drivers or pedestrians, slow down and be patient.

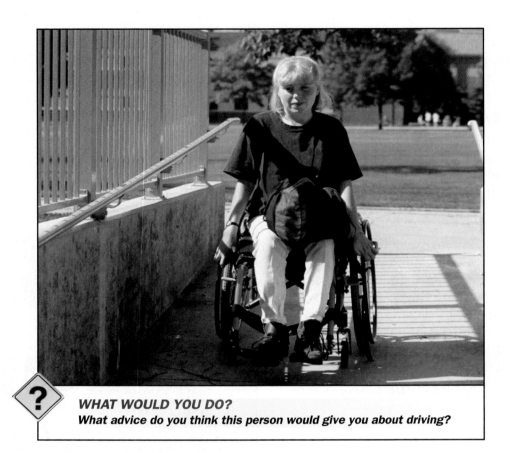

WHAT WOULD YOU DO?
What advice do you think this person would give you about driving?

Lesson 3 Review

❶ How can diseases affect your driving ability?

❷ How can impaired hearing affect your ability to drive?

❸ How can drivers who have a physical disability compensate for that disability?

❹ What effect do aging and chronic illnesses have on driving ability?

KITTY O'NEIL

Kitty O'Neil is 5 feet 3 inches tall and weighs only 98 pounds, but her accomplishments are giant-sized. She has held the women's world land speed-driving record of 512 mph and has gone on to become the second-fastest human, with a land speed of 618 mph. Of course, both of these records were accomplished in specially designed cars driven at test sites and not on highways.

O'Neil has also set records as a champion drag-boat racer and water-skier, and she is a former American Athletic Union national diving champion. She uses the skills that enabled her to set these records in her work as a movie stuntwoman. Among other things, she has jumped off six-story buildings, pretended to be drowning, and been set on fire.

Why does Kitty O'Neil do these things? As she says, one reason is to prove that physically challenged people "can do anything." O'Neil has been deaf since she was 4 months old. She believes that she owes her will to succeed to her mother, a woman of Cherokee descent who died when Kitty was 21 years old. She taught Kitty how to talk and play the cello and the piano and rewarded Kitty whenever she perfected a new skill. O'Neil says that she would like to show others that her mother's encouragement and support "has paid off beyond anyone's hopes."

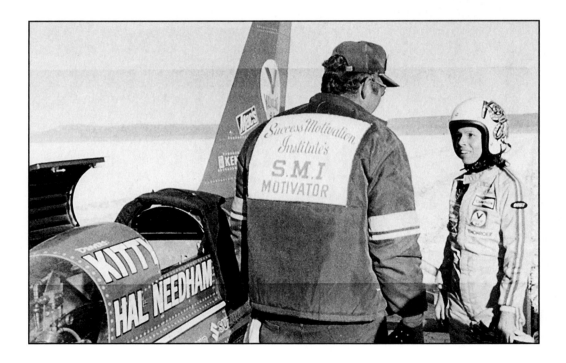

WHAT DO YOU THINK NOW?

Does the story of Kitty O'Neil change or confirm your opinion of the capabilities of people who are physically challenged? Explain your answer.

Key Points

Lesson 1

1 Fatigue is the weariness resulting from too much physical or mental exertion. It could cause you to fall asleep while driving, miss critical information, or prevent or delay you from seeing objects clearly. (Page 338)

2 Attention fatigue, visual fatigue, muscular fatigue, and sleep fatigue are the four types of fatigue that can negatively impact your driving performance. (Page 338)

3 To avoid fatigue while driving, give yourself a break from the repetitions and duration of driving. Stop regularly, breathe deeply, get out of the car, and walk, jog, or do other light exercises for a few minutes. (Page 339)

?

WHAT WOULD YOU DO?
Describe your driving strategy for the next few hours until you reach your destination.

Lesson 2

1 Short-term illness or injury can cause pain or discomfort, which can distract your attention from the road and lessen your ability to manage visibility, time, and space. (Pages 342–343)

2 If you cannot avoid driving when you're injured, at least try to minimize the amount of driving you do. Just as with illness, allow extra time to get where you're going, drive more slowly than you normally would, and keep your attention focused on driving, not on how you feel. (Page 344)

Lesson 3

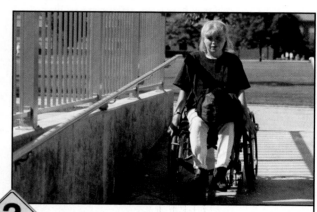

?

WHAT WOULD YOU DO?
What advice do you think this person would give you about driving?

1 Many chronic diseases affect driving ability by impairing certain aspects of the body's normal function. This lessens the ability to manage visibility, time, and space. However, it is still quite possible to drive responsibly with a chronic disease. (Page 345)

2 People with disabilities can drive with the aid of adaptive devices such as hand-operated brakes and accelerators. With the aid of prosthetic devices, people without arms can drive using special rings and dashboard controls. Those who use wheelchairs can use specially equipped vehicles. (Pages 345–346)

3 Aging can affect a driver's reaction time and eyesight. Medications for chronic illnesses may have side effects that interfere with safe driving. (Pages 346–347)

On a separate sheet of paper, write the letter of the answer that best completes each sentence.

1 When drivers are tired, they can
   a. look right at the car's headlights.
   b. experience blurred vision.
   c. increase speed to get to their destination quickly.

2 The body's natural rhythms cause nearly everyone to be less alert in the late
   a. evening.
   b. morning.
   c. afternoon.

3 Drivers who are unable to turn their head or shoulders can use
   a. revolving seats.
   b. extra-large rearview mirrors.
   c. a thickly padded seat cushion.

4 If you cannot avoid driving when you're injured, you should
   a. yell at other drivers.
   b. daydream about pleasant events.
   c. minimize the amount of driving you do.

5 Most of the information you gather about traffic situations comes from
   a. other drivers.
   b. your vision.
   c. your sense of hearing.

6 One of the most deadly forms of impairment is
   a. carbon monoxide poisoning.
   b. measles.
   c. leg injury.

On a separate sheet of paper, write the word or phrase that best completes each sentence.

| recovery | wheelchair lifts |
| medication | compensate |

7 Some _____ for common illnesses can cause conditions such as nausea that are extremely dangerous when you are driving.

8 Repetition, duration, and _____ are important terms to understand to avoid the risks of driving while fatigued.

9 Drivers with a hearing loss may be able to _____ by wearing hearing aids.

10 Modified vehicles for people who are physically disabled may include _____.

Writing

Driver's Log

In this chapter, you have learned about how fatigue and temporary and long-term impairments affect driving. Write two paragraphs based on the following questions.
- What time of day do you experience your greatest fatigue?
- How do you deal with driving or other dangerous activities when you are fatigued?

Projects

1 Fatigue and sleepiness are major factors in motor-vehicle crashes. Research some ways that people can prevent or deal with fatigue or sleepy driving.

2 While you are a passenger, close your eyes. Use your other senses to gather information. Can you identify the sounds you hear? Can you tell whether the car is speeding up, slowing down, or making a turn?

Psychological and Social Readiness

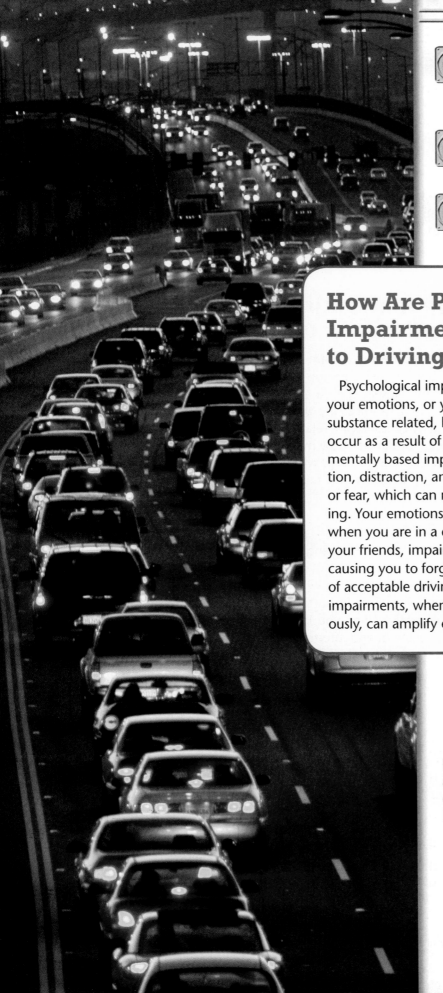

 LESSON 1
Inattention and
Distraction

 LESSON 2
Emotions

 LESSON 3
Norms and Peers

How Are Psychological Impairments Related to Driving?

Psychological impairments affect your mind, your emotions, or your mood. They can be substance related, but most of the time they occur as a result of internal factors. These mentally based impairments include inattention, distraction, and emotions such anger or fear, which can result in aggressive driving. Your emotions can even get out of hand when you are in a car enjoying yourself with your friends, impairing your judgment and causing you to forget the norms and customs of acceptable driving practices. Psychological impairments, when they occur simultaneously, can amplify each other's effect.

Driver Ed
Online

For additional activities, visit drivered.glencoe.com. Here you will find:

◆ **Web Link Exercises**

◆ **eFlashcards**

◆ **Practice Driving Tests**

Inattention and Distraction

LESSON 1

OBJECTIVES
1. **Define** inattention as it relates to driving.
2. **Identify** strategies to focus attention on the driving task.
3. **Name** some distractions that increase driving risk.
4. **Describe** how these distractions can hinder your driving ability.

KEY TERMS
- inattention
- distraction

FYI

Each year in North America, driver inattention plays a part in more than 1 million vehicle crashes. These crashes not only cause serious injuries and fatalities but also cost an estimated $40 billion annually.

Inattention and distraction are two major forms of psychological impairment. While similar and sometimes overlapping, these two impairments lessen your ability to drive and increase driving risk unless you take steps to counter their effects.

How Do Inattention and Distraction Affect Driving?

Inattention and distraction are similar impairments. Sometimes they overlap because both impair a person's ability to drive safely and alertly. If drivers follow others too closely, run off the road, turn left across traffic, and disobey traffic signals, then chances are they have been inattentive while driving, or distracted. Many collisions are related to inattention or distraction, but it is difficult to precisely calculate how many. You can lessen your risk of inattention or distraction if you understand what is happening to you, and you take steps to get your mind back on task.

INATTENTION

Inattention is a lack of paying attention, or the inability to focus on some relevant action such as the task of driving. When you don't pay attention, your mind is somewhere other than where it should be. Having a mental focus on what you are doing is an important part of your ability to get things done efficiently and safely. When you lose this focus, you become inattentive and susceptible to external and internal influences.

Not paying attention puts you at high risk of having a crash. Inattentiveness makes you less likely to remember any rules of conduct and prevents you from acting on your store of knowledge and skill. This is obviously important while driving. Driving without paying attention makes you disconnected from your actions in a way that is similar to drunk driving.

You need to be 100 percent on task when driving. Too many dangers, hazards, and unexpected events lurk in each driving situation you encounter. Driving is more likely to result in disaster if you are not fully focused and attentive.

DISTRACTION

A **distraction** is any thing or situation that draws your mind off the task at hand. Distractions divert your attention in another direction or cause mental confusion.

Distraction is the frequent partner of inattention—especially while driving. Though distractions are frequent while driving, focusing purposefully on what you are doing can help you resist their effects. Even attentive drivers can find themselves pulled from their primary task of driving in the face of strong distractions. These distractions often are important at the time and compelling for the driver. This is when your ability to recognize risk and risky behaviors in yourself becomes important and necessary in order to stop the distraction and return to the primary task of driving. Inattentiveness sets the stage for even small distractions to take your focus off the task of driving.

Inattention and distraction are closely linked factors that impair a person's ability to drive safely and alertly. *What might happen if you are distracted or not paying attention?*

DISTRACTIONS CAN INCREASE DRIVING RISK

To drive, you have to see and know what is going on around you. You need to be sure that other drivers know where you are and be able to communicate what you plan to do. You have to keep adjusting your speed and vehicle position to driving conditions. You have to be alert to any surprises that might turn into emergencies. With all of this going on, you need to minimize your own driving risk.

You can minimize risk by eliminating all distracting items around you. Be sure that there are no distractions inside your vehicle that will take your attention away from your driving and increase your risk.

How Can Distractions Hinder Your Driving Ability?

There are many distractions as you drive—cell phones, audio systems, passengers in the car, and more. It is important to be aware of these distractions so that you can be a safe and responsible driver.

CELL PHONES

Cell phones are a major distraction, and their use increases the risk of a crash. Using a cell phone while driving is not recommended, and it's already illegal in some states. Dialing and talking divert a driver's attention away from controlling the vehicle and watching the road.

Cell phones *can* provide some safety benefits for a motorist. You can, for instance, use a cell phone to get help if your vehicle malfunctions or to report a crash you see on the road. Cell phones have helped keep roads safer by allowing motorists to report bad driving or crashes at the scene and when they happen. But in nonemergency situations, using a cell phone can become a liability.

When driving while using a cell phone, you will often fail to see other highway users approaching your vehicle (especially from the sides or behind), wander from lane to lane, drive too slowly or respond too slowly to changes in traffic, make untimely lane changes, or try to make unsafe turns. Reaction

FYI

At any given time, half a million people are engaged in cell phone conversations while driving motor vehicles.

Talking on a cell phone while driving prevents you from placing your full attention on driving. **Why is this dangerous?**

time while using a cell phone can be worse than the reaction time when driving under the influence of alcohol. The risk is comparable to alcohol impairment while driving at .10 percent blood alcohol concentration level.

The primary issue with cell phones is not the physical distraction that comes with holding, dialing, and viewing the cell phone display. The biggest problem is the mental distraction. The need to think and respond to another person seems to override the necessary attention to the task of driving. And remember that many conversations involve business or planning activities. These activities consume mental energy, energy that is needed for driving.

Research by Stutts et al. in 2002 indicates that crashes involving cell phone use are twice as likely to be rear-end collisions. In crashes involving drivers using cell phones, the most frequent violations were failure to reduce speed, traffic-signal violations, speeding, following too closely, and failure to yield. Drivers engaged in cell phone conversations missed twice as many traffic signals when they were talking on a cell phone, and they took longer to react to traffic signals they didn't miss. Surprisingly, these effects were about the same if cell phone users were actually holding the handset or if the conversation was hands-free.

The best practice is to keep your cell phone in the glove compartment with the ringer off. Let the voicemail system record incoming messages. Get out of traffic and stop at a safe off-road location when you place or receive a phone call, even in an emergency. Never try to do anything difficult while driving. Remember that you need to give driving your full attention.

✓ Tips for New Drivers

USING A CELL PHONE

Driving requires your undivided attention. When you get behind the wheel of a vehicle, your primary responsibility is to ensure the safety of both you and your passengers. Using a cell phone takes your attention away from this responsibility, so it is best not to use a cell phone while driving. If you need to make a call, find a safe place to pull over and park. If you absolutely must make a call while driving, however, follow these guidelines.

▶ Know how to use the cell phone before you start driving.

▶ If possible, ask a passenger to make the call for you.

▶ Use the cell phone only when and where it seems safe to make a call.

▶ Explain to the caller that you are driving.

▶ Finish the conversation as quickly as possible.

▶ Do not mix a phone conversation with other distractions, such as tuning the radio.

VEHICLE AUDIO SYSTEMS

Most vehicles have radios, cassette players, or CD players. These systems supply information and entertainment to the driver and passengers. However, don't become so interested in the music that you forget to pay attention to your driving. Music should be secondary to your driving activities. Remember that loud music can mask useful information you might hear on the road.

Here are two tips for minimizing risk with vehicle sound systems:

- Keep radio volume at a reasonable level. Your concentration must be focused on driving, and lowering the volume of your radio or entertainment system will help keep you on task.
- Do not change tapes or CDs while driving. Looking for and changing tapes or CDs is distracting—and very dangerous. Risk is increased anytime you take your eyes off the road or drive with only one hand on the wheel.

Don't let passengers distract you. *How can you prevent the distraction?*

HEADPHONES

You need your sense of hearing when you drive. In about 20 states, it is against the law to wear stereo headphones while driving. Drivers need to collect and process information continually from all senses, including hearing. You need to hear honking horns, sirens, and other kinds of roadway sounds.

If you are wearing headphones, you may not be able to hear another vehicle honking its horn at you. You may not hear police vehicles, fire trucks, ambulances, or trains approaching. You will miss important information about your own driving, such as road noise, engine noise, and wind noise—all of which help you monitor your vehicle's performance. You may also lose your concentration if you are too absorbed in what you are hearing.

Even if it isn't against the law in your state, put your headphones away. Your job is to pay attention to your driving.

PASSENGERS

Other people can be quite distracting. Sometimes the people in your vehicle want you to pay more attention to them than to your driving. As a driver, you are responsible for the safety of your passengers. It is your responsibility to tell them to sit still or be quiet. As a driver, you have the ability to stop the vehicle if things get out of control with your passengers. Allow things to cool down before driving again, even when you are engaged in a conversation or when children or animals are distracting you.

OTHER DISTRACTIONS

Traffic jams, toll roads, and the need to eat or drink are other common distractions.

Traffic jams. You may become distracted in traffic jams, when the flow of traffic stops or slows to a crawl. When you are stuck for a long time, your mind can wander, and you can lose your concentration. Remember, even when you are stopped, it is important to pay attention to everything that is going on around you. Some people become very agitated in traffic jams and may do

SAFETY TIP

When driving with infants and small children, be sure that they are in safety seats and that the seats are securely fastened in place in the backseat. Do not allow small children to ride in the front seat, especially in vehicles equipped with passenger-side air bags. The powerful force of an inflating air bag can injure or kill small children.

unexpected things, either in or out of their vehicle. Be wary of the things that are happening around you.

Toll roads. Toll roads can be distracting. You have to pay to use a toll road. When you are driving on a toll road, remember that you will need change to pay the toll. Make sure you know how much money you will need, and gather your money *before* you start your trip. If you take a toll road regularly, have a container with plenty of change in it within reach.

Eating and drinking. When you eat or drink while driving, you become distracted when you reach for and consume the item of food or drink. While some foods are designed to be consumed on the go, other foods are either difficult to handle, too hot or cold, or too messy for in-vehicle consumption. Statistically, most food-related crashes happen in the morning on the way to work. While it may be tempting to consume breakfast while driving to work, it's best to do all your eating *outside* the vehicle, thus reducing the chance that you'll be distracted by spills and hot foods. If you spill something on yourself, pull over and clean it off, and avoid a potential crash.

HANDLING DISTRACTIONS

Remember, your job is to concentrate on your driving. Pay attention. Being prepared to handle distractions is part of that job. To be a responsible driver, keep your eyes and ears and body and mind focused on the task of driving. Even under ideal conditions, you will drive safely by giving it your full attention.

?
WHAT WOULD YOU DO?
What steps can you take to avoid distractions when you are driving on a long trip?

Lesson 1 Review

❶ What is the definition of *inattention* as it relates to driving?

❷ What strategies can you use to focus your attention on the driving task?

❸ What distractions can increase your driving risk?

❹ How can these distractions hinder your driving ability?

Emotions

OBJECTIVES
1. **Identify** three effects your emotions can have on your driving.
2. **Describe** three ways to control the effects your emotions may have on your driving.

KEY TERMS
◆ **aggressive driving**
◆ **road rage**
◆ **frustration**

Emotional states, when heightened in any manner, affect a driver's ability to perceive and respond to the threats on the road. Whenever a driver is extremely angry, exuberant, sad, frustrated, upset, or anxious, that driver should not be behind the wheel because his or her decisions may be influenced by strong emotions.

When you are driving, it is not just skill that matters. What's more important is your ability to think clearly and make sound, responsible driving decisions. Thinking clearly involves making rational decisions with your mind, not emotional decisions based on how you feel. Responsible driving involves maturity and self-control.

How Do Emotions Affect Your Driving?

When you experience a strong negative emotion, you may feel the need to do something forceful. If you are behind the wheel of a car and another person does something that makes you angry, you may have an impulse to act out your emotion by driving aggressively. This might take the form of squealing the tires, flooring the gas pedal, taking fast corners, running lights, changing lanes frequently to pass other vehicles, or making a lot of noise. To police officers and other drivers, driving based on your emotions is considered to be aggressive driving. In extreme cases, when the behavior is revengeful or involves violence, it escalates to become road rage. This emotional behavior can sometimes spread to other drivers who may also begin driving aggressively, putting themselves and others at risk. It can be very dangerous to act on your emotions. Emotional behavior is also dangerous and frightening to see in other drivers.

Why Are Young Adults at Greater Risk?

Teens and young adults are particularly at risk when it comes to emotionally related crashes for two important reasons.

First, many powerful new emotions are being experienced during adolescence. These heightened feelings include the sensation of first love, loneliness at home or in school, the frustration or sadness of failed exams, the fear or anxieties about the future, and even the exuberant intensity of speeding down the road in a car or truck. For many young adults, these feelings are so strong that they can do or think about little else.

Second, in the late teen years, the teen brain is being radically rewired and prepared for adulthood. This dramatic rewiring puts teens of driving age in the difficult position of not knowing why they might feel certain ways and of being quite unable to control or manage these feelings.

How Do Emotions Distract You from Driving?

Any strong emotion can get in the way of your ability to drive. This happens because emotional highs and lows can cause you to get lost in thinking about how you feel and to not pay attention to the driving task. Emotional upset also affects your ability to concentrate and to process information.

INATTENTION

Emotions interfere with driving by taking your attention away from the road. You may be so preoccupied with your own feelings that you miss stop signs, speed, or take other risks, without even realizing what you are doing. Strong feelings focus your attention on the object of your emotion. Sometimes these strong emotionally driven thoughts and obsessions are so overpowering that you can't think of anything else. If you are driving a vehicle, these thoughts distract you from driving.

LACK OF CONCENTRATION

You may have moments when you can't seem to concentrate on anything. If you can't concentrate on driving, the best advice is to let someone else drive. If you can't do that, at least wait until you are better able to focus on the driving task.

Dealing with the UNEXPECTED

AGGRESSIVE DRIVING

How can you avoid triggering aggressive driving? Follow these tips:

- ▲ **Don't tailgate.** Riding too close to the vehicle in front of you may make the driver angry. If someone is tailgating you, pull over to allow the vehicle to pass.
- ▲ **Don't drive slowly in the passing lane.** If you are driving in the left lane and someone wants to get by, move over and let the driver pass you.
- ▲ **Don't make gestures.** Making rude gestures will make other drivers angry. If someone makes a rude gesture at you, ignore it.
- ▲ **Be courteous.** Don't cut off other drivers. Use your turn signal to communicate your intentions when changing lanes or turning. Don't use your horn unless you must.
- ▲ **Avoid eye contact.** If a driver becomes angry with you, don't make eye contact. Staring back will only make matters worse.
- ▲ **Don't retaliate.** Stay calm, and don't allow yourself to be drawn into a conflict with an angry driver.

SAFELY PROCESSING INFORMATION

When you experience strong emotion, your ability to receive and process roadway information is diminished. This decreases your ability to manage risk. In some collisions, it is not unusual to hear one of the drivers say that they did not see the other vehicle, despite a clear view, lots of light, and little traffic. In these cases, the drivers were suffering from "attention blindness," brought on by strong emotions or a very distracting train of thought that robbed processing power from the brain. After all, you actually see with your brain; your eyes only receive the image and forward it.

Safe driving is a full-time job for your mind as well as for your body. Drivers have to see and hear the signs and signals of the roadway. As a driver, you also have to use good judgment based on the information you gather and process in your brain.

Strong emotions can affect your driving. *How can they affect your driving?*

Why Is Angry Driving A Major Problem?

Anger is the most troublesome emotion to deal with while driving. Angry feelings can build up quite unexpectedly when driving. Anger is a major emotional impairment because it easily leads to aggressive driving.

Aggressive driving is the most commonly identified driver impairment related to emotional state. There can be serious consequences to **aggressive driving**, which is a combination of dangerous acts committed while driving. Aggressive driving occurs when drivers bully other drivers, tailgate and crowd others, cut people off, use their horns and lights against others, and make rude gestures to others—acts that often involve intimidation. In its most severe form, emotions are so high and volatile that road rage results. **Road rage** is a crime that involves criminal acts directed against another person through physical violence while you are driving, and it often is the culmination of aggressive-driving behaviors.

CONTROLLING ANGER

Knowing how to control your anger and your own aggressive driving first requires that you recognize the warning signs. The better you are at noticing and identifying your own anger, the better you will be at stopping it earlier. Although it is difficult to do, you need to learn how to put your angry feelings aside. Practicing common courtesy, identifying troublesome situations before they become problems, and watching out for aggressive drivers are three ways to control your own anger.

Common courtesy. One of the ways you can avoid aggressive driving is by practicing common courtesy. You can be nice to other people. Here are some examples:
- Keep a safe distance from the vehicles ahead.
- When you make a mistake, apologize with an appropriate gesture.

FYI

In a recent 6-year period, aggressive driving was responsible for more than 200 deaths and more than 12,600 serious injuries in the United States.

Driver Ed
Online

Topic: Aggressive driving

For a link to more information on aggressive driving, go to drivered .glencoe.com.

Activity: Using the information provided in this online brochure, work in small groups to create a public service announcement that provides helpful guidelines for avoiding aggressive driving.

- Always signal when changing lanes.
- Keep your cool. Don't make obscene gestures or flash your headlights because you are angry.

Identify troublesome situations early. Identify situations that may upset or annoy you, and deal with them in a responsible way. When a situation is likely to bother you, take a few deep breaths; say to yourself, "I won't let this get to me." Then focus your attention on driving. You can also try to plan ahead.

Watch out for aggressive drivers. As instances of aggressive driving become more common, there are ways you can anticipate and protect yourself from another driver's frustration and anger. After an extensive study of aggressive driving, AAA (the American Automobile Association) suggests the following:

- Be patient and keep your cool in traffic.
- Never underestimate the other driver's capacity for mayhem.
- Do not assume the other driver's mistakes are directed at you.
- Be polite and courteous, even if another driver is not.
- Avoid all conflict. If another driver challenges you, take a deep breath and get out of the way.
- Reduce your own stress levels by allowing plenty of time for your trip.
- Reduce your own stress levels by listening to soothing music.
- Understand that you can't control the traffic, only your reaction to it.

FRUSTRATION

Frustration is similar to the emotion of anger. **Frustration** is a feeling of disappointment, exasperation, or weariness caused by aims being thwarted or desires unsatisfied. Because driving can be such a changing and complicated task, many people become frustrated as they drive.

As a driver, you can bring frustration into the vehicle with you or develop it while you drive. You need to recognize frustration in yourself and figure out how to deal with it. When you become frustrated to the point of being exasperated, you may do things you might normally not do. When you know you're frustrated, this is the time to take a time-out and regain your composure.

Don't let your emotions get the better of you. Instead, learn ways to control your emotions. *How can you control your emotions?*

SADNESS AND DEPRESSION

You may struggle from time to time with feelings of great sadness, an emotion sometimes referred to as *depression* when it is long lasting or intense. Sadness is a strong emotion that can distract you from matters at hand. It can bring a disconnection from reality, an unwillingness to deal properly with emerging situations, or a lack of motivation or concern about other drivers. All of these factors make a depressed driver a very dangerous individual.

One dangerous aspect of extreme sadness or depression is that you don't care much about yourself and others. People do very foolish and destructive things when they feel depressed. Things that should be important—such as hazardous situations on the road—can seem unimportant and trivial.

If one of your friends is obviously depressed and wants to drive, deal with it in the same way that you would if they had consumed alcohol or other drugs. The friend should not drive! If you are extremely depressed, you shouldn't drive either. You or your friend need to take time in order to sort feelings out. If your friend needs to get somewhere, drive him or her yourself, or have your friend take public transportation.

How Can Positive Emotions Impair Your Driving?

Positive emotions also affect your ability to drive safely in the same way as drugs and alcohol. Your judgments, perceptions, attention span, and reflexes are all affected in a similar way to alcohol or drugs.

EXUBERANCE

Exuberance is an extreme happiness almost to the point of being excessive. It refers to happiness spinning out of control. When your state of joy or happiness energizes you and dominates you to the point where it affects your driving behavior and decisions, it is dangerous. In fact, exuberance can be almost as dangerous as some of the more negative emotions if it causes you to lose focus and make driving mistakes.

PLAYFULNESS

Being playful as a driver means you are not being serious about driving. Playfulness can manifest as goofing off, joking, provoking, and doing the unexpected thing to get a laugh from your friends. Playfulness is generally the pursuit or performance of humor. It's not behavior that is suitable for high-risk, changeable situations such as driving.

You need to recognize when the prevailing mood in the vehicle is getting out of hand and bring it back to the very serious job of driving. A stopped vehicle has an impressive calming effect on soaring emotions, or provides a safe place to play them out. And you certainly can't crash into anything while you are parked.

OVERCONFIDENCE AND COMPLACENCY

Many drivers are overconfident of their own driving ability. Overconfidence is thinking that you have more skill than you actually have. This emotion can lead you into actions and situations beyond your abilities or control, and it may be a significant factor in causing crashes.

New drivers are often even more overconfident than most. This overconfidence helps explain young drivers' disproportionate representation in crash statistics. Young drivers encounter many difficulties on the road because they judge crash risk quite differently than experienced drivers. For example, young drivers do not assess their own personal risk very accurately. In particular, young male drivers generally believe they are less likely to become involved in a crash than other young male drivers. Young male drivers also view their personal risk level as comparable to that of older male drivers, which is statistically proven to be untrue.

HOW CAN YOU CONTROL YOUR EMOTIONS?

Though it may not seem possible, you can learn to control your emotions when you have to. The key is to recognize when emotions are strong and distracting your attention from other important activities. You can take steps to avoid or minimize problems relating to your emotional state. If you feel overwhelmed by emotions at a particular time, before you drive, take a time-out to collect your thoughts and feelings and to bring yourself back to the moment. Sometimes, you just need a little time to sort out your feelings and to let the emotions settle down before you drive. Maintaining a responsible attitude, anticipating mistakes from others, and making a habit of using correct procedures will also help you drive responsibly.

MAINTAIN A RESPONSIBLE ATTITUDE

You exhibit a responsible attitude when you show respect for order and safety and when you take responsibility for your actions. Try to assume a responsible attitude by putting aside strong emotions while you drive. Act courteously, even if you happen to feel angry at that moment. It will help you feel a lot better.

WHAT WOULD YOU DO?
You're already late. How will you deal with your emotions and with getting to your destination in this situation?

EXPECT MISTAKES FROM OTHERS

Don't let yourself get irritated by every instance of bad driving you encounter. It's a better idea to just accept the fact that other drivers make mistakes at one time or another. Other drivers may be distracted, inexperienced, acting on their emotions, or even intoxicated. Never assume that other drivers will drive safely or obey all rules all the time.

TRAIN YOURSELF ALWAYS TO USE CORRECT PROCEDURES

Get into the habit of using safe driving procedures, such as signaling before you make a turn. Make such procedures automatic, no matter what your emotional state may be. These kinds of habits will protect you from the powerful influences of emotion in your driving.

Lesson 2 Review

❶ How can emotions affect your driving?

❷ How can you control your emotions when you drive?

❸ Why is angry driving a major problem?

Norms and Peers

Social impairments can affect your ability to drive safely. Whenever you have a passenger in your car, it's potentially a social occasion because you can talk and joke with your passenger. As a driver, it is good to remember that you are responsible for your safety as well as that of your passengers. Use good judgment to make your decisions and not a desire to "go along" with the crowd when your passengers are doing something risky or dangerous.

Understanding customs and norms can also help you drive safely and avoid other forms of social impairment.

What Is a Social Impairment?

Social impairments often involve peer pressure. **Peer pressure** is the influence that people your age have on you to think and act like them. Your peers are usually your friends or people you know, but on the highway your peers are other drivers. Social impairments can happen when you are driving and having a good time with your peers or when other drivers attempt to involve you in risky behaviors while you are driving.

PEER PRESSURE

As a teen driver, much of your time will be spent in a vehicle with your friends. Sometimes the vehicle gets all of you to school, to work, or to a social event. Sometimes riding in the vehicle *is* the social event. In all cases, the risks and hazards of the road remain the same. While pressure from friends to act or behave in a certain way can be positive or neutral, often peer pressure is negative, especially when it involves risky activities.

For instance, sometimes peer pressure can lead you to believe that risky or reckless driving is cool. Unfortunately, when you are with your friends, you are probably less concerned about the risks and hazards of the road. This reduced level of concern is why novice drivers are at greater risk when passengers are present.

Socially energized situations often create a "time-out" atmosphere, where normal safety behaviors are temporarily suspended and the potential for risky behavior increases.

You can also be affected by peer pressure from other drivers. This might occur after a winning game when honking vehicles full of young people are parading down the street and everyone is shouting back and forth to each other. It might occur in a traffic jam when other drivers begin honking and driving aggressively and you are tempted to follow along. People can get carried away. You need to avoid getting into this kind of situation, because once in, it's very difficult to get out.

OBJECTIVES
1. **Describe** ways to avoid the negative impact of peer pressure.
2. **Define** norms and customs as they relate to driving.
3. **Explain** how laws and norms affect driving risk.

KEY TERMS
- peer pressure
- norm
- custom

SAFETY TIP

Don't let a conversation with passengers distract you while driving. If you have a serious or emotional matter to discuss with a companion, do so after you've parked the car.

● - - - - - - - →

Drivers expect and trust other drivers and passengers to behave in a normal fashion. *What can you do if another driver does not behave in a normal fashion?*

HOW TO AVOID NEGATIVE PEER PRESSURE

If you ever feel trapped or cornered into doing something risky, ask yourself, "Is this something that I would normally do or try by myself?" If not, let the others know how stupid you think it is. Let your friends know that you know what's right for you and that you think too much of yourself to give in to the kind of pressure or influence that leads you to do something you wouldn't normally do.

How Do Norms and Customs Affect Driving Behavior?

Within your community, you know more people at home, school, and work than you do in many other places. One of those places where most of the people you encounter are strangers is the roadway. How is it possible for so many different kinds of people to drive in an orderly way, without the constant presence of walls, fences, police, or lawyers? The answer is found in the normal behaviors, or norms, that prevail in society. There is a common ground upon which all members of a society stand—a set of norms by which everyone lives. These norms help determine how you live with others in a community.

UNDERSTANDING NORMS

Norms are rules or normal standards of behavior that govern how people behave in different situations. These rules and standards are well-known, and they guide behavior. Citizens act toward each other within a permissible zone of conduct that is considered to be "normal." Without norms, people would be continually faced with a great burden of making decisions. Drivers know what normal acceptable behavior is, and most of the time they follow the norms. If you habitually deviate from the driving norms, you become a high-risk driver.

Did You Know **?**

The automatic traffic signal is responsible for the orderly movement of millions of vehicles and pedestrians in today's cities and towns. Garrett A. Morgan, an African American inventor, developed the three-way traffic signal in 1923. Morgan sold the rights to his invention to the General Electric Company for $40,000.

CUSTOMS

Customs are behaviors that satisfy people's needs for comfortably interacting with one another. Each society has different customs, which are part of the pattern of living. But if the law often reinforces the norms, it must be said that the law does not enforce people's customs.

However, people who violate customs are often seen as troublemakers. Violating customs certainly makes other people uncomfortable. As a driver, you may feel very uncomfortable when another driver pushes to the head of a line of vehicles past many others who were in line first.

NORMS AND CUSTOMS IN RELATION TO DRIVING

Driving is a shared experience. You drive a vehicle by taking into account how others drive their vehicles. You and other drivers trust that a predictable set of activities will take place. For example, you don't have to stop and think about driving in the right-hand lane, stopping at red lights, proceeding on green lights, and lowering your high beams when another car approaches. Your choices are based on normative patterns—typical driving behaviors for typical driving situations that try to assure that everything will be okay for everyone. As you learn to drive, you will not memorize the entire book of driving rules, norms, and customs. First, you learn as much as you can of the basic set of rules and laws needed to gain access to the road. As you drive, you observe the normal behavior of other drivers for the rest.

How Do Laws and Norms Affect Risk?

Although laws and norms are sometimes the same, the differences between them need to be understood. Laws seek to fashion and regulate proper driving behavior. Ideally, this helps the majority while harming few others. Implicit in traffic laws is the notion that norms in and of themselves don't always work. Basically, laws are intended to reduce risk and harm. Laws have formal sanctions or official penalties attached, which affect the driver who is caught

The best way to ensure everyone's safety on the road is to obey all traffic laws. *How can you make sure that you are obeying all traffic laws?*

Peter Rothe

University of Alberta
Edmonton, Alberta, Canada

Inattention and distraction are closely linked factors that often impair a person's ability to drive safely. They usually become an issue when your driving experiences become mundane, habitual, and somewhat boring. Therein lies the danger. It's often been said that driving is made up of long periods of boredom punctuated by brief moments of crisis or panic. As a driver, you need to recognize that inattention and distraction are normal parts of driving. To counter the risk, you should be aware of the driving reality as mundane and always be ready to quickly refocus and reengage in the driving task when a crisis disrupts your habitual driving.

How can you resist the urge to let your emotions affect your driving?

? WHAT WOULD YOU DO?
Describe your driving strategy for dealing with this situation.

breaking them. Fines, imprisonment, vehicle impounding, and loss of license are a few of the penalties assigned to violating traffic laws. Laws are enforced by police officers and the highway patrol.

Unlike written laws, norms are unwritten laws enforced by the opinion of other people. A driver who violates a norm is considered immoral, boorish, impolite, or worse.

A better understanding of norms and laws helps you deal with the gray, ambiguous situations that frequently occur in the driving environment. Drivers create and implement patterns that they believe are appropriate, and they don't like to see others step out of the patterns. The repercussions of violating customs, norms, or laws become social impairments if they trigger aggressive, reckless driving or even road rage. The rewards of following the norms and laws include the minimizing of your driving risk and the ability to arrive at your destination safely.

Lesson 3 Review

❶ How can you avoid the negative impact of peer pressure?

❷ What are the definitions of *norms* and *customs* as they relate to driving?

❸ How do laws and norms affect driving risk?

READING CITY MAPS

Driving in a new city is often very confusing. Most maps have insets that show major cities in larger scale. Below is an inset map of Wichita, Kansas. Suppose you are coming into Wichita from the north, on Interstate 135. To get to Wichita State University, you would leave Route 15 at the interchange for 13th Street. Then you would head east to Hillside Avenue. To get from Washington Road to the Historical Museum, you would drive about 1 mile east on Douglas Avenue.

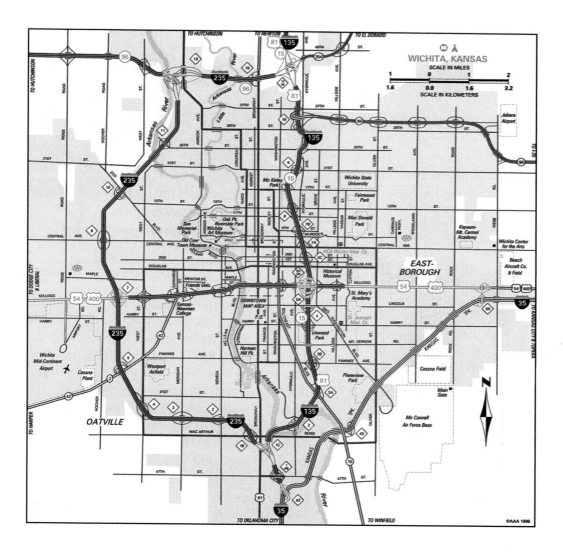

TRY IT YOURSELF

❶ How would you get from Wichita State University to Friends University?

❷ Suppose you are at the airport. How would you drive to Planeview Park?

❸ How would you get from the corner of 25th Street and Amidon Avenue to the Wichita Center for the Arts?

Key Points

Lesson 1

1 Inattention is the inability to focus and/ or attend to some idea, action, or issue. (Page 354)

2 Passengers, cell phones, a vehicle's audio system, food and drink, smoking, and a number of other things are sources of distraction while driving. (Page 355)

3 Distractions hinder your driving ability by drawing your attention away from the road. (Page 355)

4 Strategies to focus your attention include being aware of what distracts you, telling your passengers how you expect them to behave, adjusting the vehicle's audio system before you drive, stopping the vehicle in a safe off-road location to use the cell phone, and not eating, smoking, drinking, or wearing headphones while driving. (Pages 355–358)

? WHAT WOULD YOU DO?
What steps can you take to avoid distractions when you are driving on a long trip?

Lesson 2

1 Emotions, such as joy, sadness, anger, and fear, can cause you to be inattentive, interfere with your ability to concentrate, and hinder your ability to process information while driving. (Page 359)

2 You can make an effort to control your emotions by maintaining a responsible attitude, expecting mistakes from others, and training yourself to always use correct procedures. (Page 364)

Lesson 3

? WHAT WOULD YOU DO?
Describe your driving strategy for dealing with this situation.

1 Ways to avoid negative peer pressure include asking yourself, "Is this something that I would normally do or try by myself"? If not, let others know how you feel. Let your friends know that you know what's right for you and that you think too much of yourself to give in to that kind of pressure or influence. (Page 366)

2 Norms are rules or standards that govern how people behave in different situations. Customs are behaviors that satisfy people's needs for comfortably interacting with one another. (Pages 366–367)

3 Understanding norms and laws affect risk in that they help you deal with gray, ambiguous situations that frequently occur in the driving environment. (Page 368)

On a separate sheet of paper, write the letter of the answer that best completes each sentence.

1 Anything that draws your mind off driving is
  a. an inattention.
  b. a distraction.
  c. an emotion.

2 The best practice for cell phone use while driving is to
  a. use it only when you are sitting in traffic.
  b. use it only if you are wearing a headset.
  c. keep your phone in the glove compartment with the ringer off.

3 The most troublesome emotion when driving is
  a. sadness.
  b. anger.
  c. exuberance.

4 If you cannot concentrate on driving,
  a. let someone else drive.
  b. make a stronger effort to concentrate.
  c. continue driving as if nothing is wrong.

5 Behaviors that satisfy people's needs for comfortably interacting with one another are
  a. laws.
  b. norms.
  c. customs.

6 Standards of behavior that govern how people behave in different situations are
  a. laws.
  b. norms.
  c. customs.

On a separate sheet of paper, write the word or phrase that best completes each sentence.

peer pressure	road rage
inattention	aggressive driving

7 _____ is a combination of dangerous acts committed while driving.

8 A crime that involves criminal acts directed against another person through physical violence while you are driving is _____.

9 The influence that people your own age have on you to think and act like them is known as _____.

10 _____ is the inability to focus on some relevant action.

Writing

Driver's Log

In this chapter, you have learned about how emotional and social factors can affect driving. Write at least two paragraphs giving your ideas on the following questions.
- What "sets you off" emotionally?
- How will you control negative peer influences that adversely affect your driving?

Projects

❶ Emotional factors play an important part in the way people drive. What are some ways that people could be reminded to maintain a responsible attitude and to be courteous and patient while driving?

❷ Inattention and distraction are primary causes of young novice driver crashes. What are some ways you can limit distractions inside and the vehicle and devote more attention to the driving task?

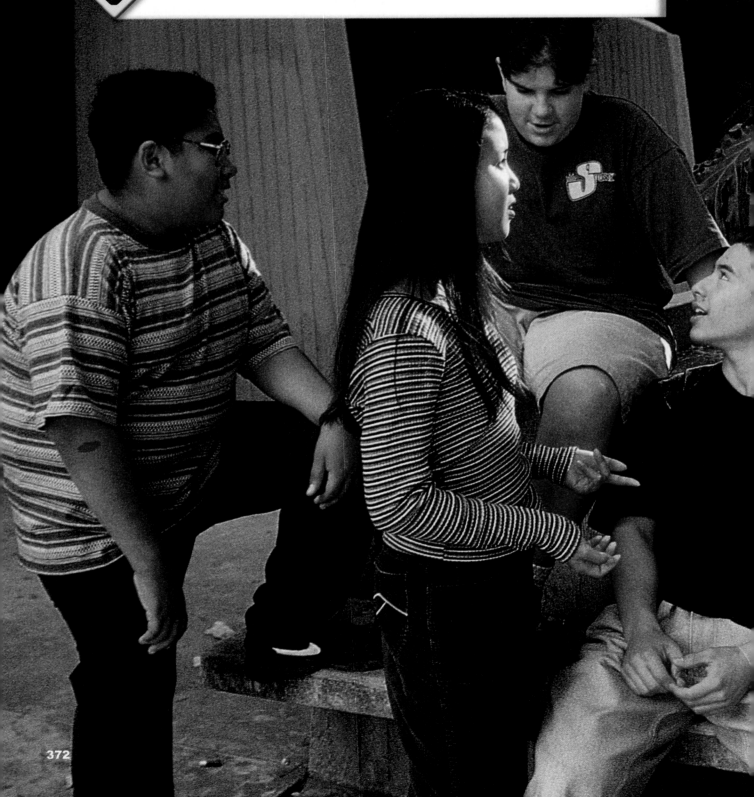

What Are the Effects of Peer Pressure?

Most young people are vulnerable to peer pressure, which is often harmless. However, peer pressure can influence you in ways that can damage you and your future, such as influencing you to experiment with drinking alcohol or even using or misusing other drugs. Understanding how the abuse of alcohol and other drugs can be destructive can help you resist negative peer pressure. This will reduce the risks of impaired driving, which leads to too many accidents.

Driver Ed
Online

For additional
activities, visit
drivered.glencoe.com.
Here you will find:

◆ **Web Link Exercises**

◆ **eFlashcards**

◆ **Practice Driving Tests**

Alcohol and You

OBJECTIVES

1. **Describe** the three major categories of alcoholic drinking.
2. **List** factors that influence the effects of alcohol on the body.

KEY TERM

◆ Blood Alcohol Concentration (BAC)

Alcohol is a potentially dangerous drug, but it is very much a part of society. There is a great deal of drinking of alcoholic beverages by people of all ages, and alcoholic products are constantly advertised on TV and in magazines and newspapers. This pervasiveness is demonstrated by the way the word *drink* is often used to mean "drink alcohol." For example, "I drink too much." Or "I don't drink anymore." Advertising sells alcohol as a desirable, acceptable, and even a romantic drink. Unfortunately, most people have a limited or inaccurate knowledge of the effects of alcohol. Alcohol use can be used recreationally or abused, and its effects are not predictable. There are many misconceptions about alcohol. Often people do not realize how badly they might drive after even a few drinks.

What Are the Types of Alcohol Use?

All drinking increases the amount of alcohol in a person's blood, called **Blood Alcohol Concentration (BAC)**. BAC determines the intensity of the effects a person feels from drinking. But people also drink in different ways. Experimentation, recreational drinking, and alcohol abuse are three major categories of alcoholic drinking to consider.

EXPERIMENTATION

At some time during their lives, most young people in the United States experiment with drinking. People are naturally curious. How much a person may try to drink, and how often, varies from person to person. Since the effects of alcohol are not predictable, particularly in the beginning, this experimentation carries some risk. Many young people do things they would not normally do after they have been drinking. Research has found that the earlier young people begin to drink alcohol, the more likely they are to become an alcohol abuser or alcoholic. For instance, young people who start to drink before age 15 are four times more likely to become alcoholics than those who begin drinking at age 21. The risk of alcoholism decreases by about 14 percent for each year a young person waits to begin drinking.

SAFETY TIP

Resist peer pressure to drink alcohol. Pick friends who share your values and who choose abstinence from alcohol and other drugs.

RECREATIONAL DRINKING

Drinking alcohol for recreation means drinking for what one thinks is fun. A drink or two can help many people think they feel relaxed in social situations, especially if they don't drink to excess. Many people think they feel comfortable after a drink or two, but it is not a substitute for the pleasures of living or for normal social activities. Once the effects of a drug such as alcohol are known, some young people find it easy to seek the artificial mood change instead of naturally changing the way one feels by doing more appropriate activities, such as sports, socializing, or even talking about problems.

ALCOHOL ABUSE

Alcohol is probably the most abused drug in the United States. The definition of *abusive drinking* or *drug abuse* is the definition of the word *abuse*. To abuse a drug means the "wrong, improper or abnormal use" of that drug, whether it's alcohol or any other drug. Therefore, any drinking for persons under the legal drinking age can be termed *abusive* since the activity is clearly illegal, physically harmful, and is more likely to establish a lifelong pattern of problem drinking. Thus, if young people who are underage use alcohol, it is considered abusive drinking, or alcohol abuse. For people of the legal age to drink, alcohol abuse usually means drinking to excess or drinking very frequently.

Other examples of alcohol abuse include:

- Drinking to become intoxicated or get drunk
- Drinking when driving, or driving while intoxicated
- Drinking to relieve stress
- Drinking to change a feeling, mood, or social situation
- Gulping drinks

What Factors Contribute to the Effects of Alcohol?

All people are affected by alcohol. Drinking too much of any beverage containing alcohol will get a person drunk. However, no two humans are exactly the same. This means that two people who drink the same amount may experience effects that are very different. In addition, the effects on a particular person at a particular time differ for a number of reasons. These factors include:

1. **Expectations:** If a person believes one kind of alcoholic beverage will produce a greater effect than another, it probably will, even if the BAC is the same.
2. **Mood:** Anger, depression, and excitement before drinking may all contribute to different effects.
3. **Fatigue:** Since alcohol is a depressant, being tired can affect how you react to alcohol.
4. **Existing medications or medical sensitivities:** Many medications react with alcohol, and some people may be more sensitive than others and have serious drug interactions.

TEN MISCONCEPTIONS ABOUT DRINKING

The public receives a great deal of incorrect information about alcohol. While some of this has been done to make these ideas easy to remember and a couple of these ideas are true in some cases and untrue in others, it is still bad or incomplete information. It is always better to know the whole truth.

Ten of the worst misconceptions about alcohol follow. The first two are the most common. Misconceptions include:

1. **All drinks are equal in alcohol content.**
   Fact: This is true only sometimes. For instance, coolers are popular alcoholic drinks for some young people. A cooler may have 50 percent more alcohol

The body can't eliminate much more than 1/2 ounce of alcohol in an hour. It will take about 2 hours for the body to get rid of a standard-sized drink. This figure will vary, however, depending on the gender, weight, and size of the person.

content than a 1-ounce shot of whiskey. When a 12-ounce can or bottle of regular beer is compared to a 1-ounce shot of 80-proof whiskey (1/2 of the proof = alcohol percentage), the beer actually has 35 percent more alcohol. This knowledge is important for at least two reasons:

a. For a person drinking beer, the more a person drinks, the wider the gap becomes.

b. About 80 percent of persons charged with DWI or DUI were drinking beer prior to their arrest.

The most important concept to remember is that both the size of the drink (ounces) and strength of the drink (percentage of alcohol) have to be known before any meaningful comparison can be made. No matter how big the glass, more alcohol means a stronger drink, with stronger effects.

2. The human body removes one drink per hour.

Fact: This is only true for some people. Alcohol does eventually pass out of your body, but it is a dangerous concept that the human body can always remove one drink per hour. Even if standard drink sizes are used, this removal rate is true only for very obese or very large people. The truth is that the average elimination rate is .015 percent per hour: if one drink raised your BAC to .015 percent, the BAC would be zero after one hour. However, one regular beer for a 120-pound female will raise her BAC up to .03 percent, so only one-half of the alcohol will have been removed in one hour (.03 percent – .015 percent = .015 percent). And for a male weighing 150 pounds, one beer will produce a maximum BAC of .027 percent, so he will still have alcohol in his system after one hour (.027 percent – .015 percent = .012 percent).

If these levels seem very small, consider what happens when a person continues drinking at this pace. The 120-pound female will be at an unsafe driving level in a little over 3 hours and an illegal driving level (.08 percent) in just over 5 hours. For the 150-pound male to reach each of these levels, it takes 4 and 7 hours, respectively. When the drinking rate exceeds the elimination rate, BAC rises, your ability to drive is impaired, and you eventually get drunk.

3. Males and females handle alcohol the same.

Fact: Not true. It is harder for females to handle alcohol because females have much less of an enzyme called *alcohol dehydrogenase* in their stomach than males. Since this enzyme breaks down alcohol, females absorb more alcohol into their bloodstream than males do. Females also tend to have more body fat than males, another factor in blood alcohol concentration.

4. Beer is not as intoxicating as hard liquor.

Fact: Not true. While there is more alcohol in an ounce of liquor than in an ounce of beer, beer contains enough alcohol to intoxicate you.

5. You cannot get drunk on a full stomach.

Fact: A full stomach does mean the alcohol is absorbed into the bloodstream a little more slowly. However, all of that alcohol will still get into the bloodstream and travel to the brain and other parts of the body.

6. Impaired (drinking) driving is not dangerous.

Fact: Not true. Motor-vehicle crashes are the number-one killer of teens. Motor-vehicle crashes kill more 16- to 20-year-olds each year than homicide, suicide, cancer, accidental poisoning, and heart disease combined.

Driver Ed Online

Topic: **Myths about alcohol**

For a link to more information on myths about alcohol, go to drivered.glencoe .com.

Activity: After reviewing the information provided at this link, create your own list of myths about alcohol based on information you have heard from friends or classmates. Then create a list of facts to dispute these myths.

7. You must drink because your friends want you to, even if you are the driver.

Fact: Real friends would not want you to hurt yourself or others. Resist peer pressure in this dangerous situation. Tell your friends the facts about alcohol.

8. Black coffee, a cold shower, lots of exercise, or all three together can quickly sober up a drinker.

Fact: Not true. The body cannot burn much more than ½-ounce of alcohol in an hour. Nothing can really speed up the process.

9. Alcohol makes you feel better when you are depressed.

Fact: Alcohol is a depressant, or "downer." Even if it lifts you up for a minute, it may leave you feeling worse than before.

10. Sometimes, because of peer pressure at a party, there is no other choice but to drink.

Fact: You do have a choice. You do not have to drink alcohol—you can drink something else. Abstinence is the only responsible action for anyone under 21.

?

WHAT WOULD YOU DO?
You and a friend are offered a drink. You say no, but your friend wants to try one. What will you say to your friend?

Lesson 1 Review

❶ What are the different types of alcohol use?

❷ What are the two most common misconceptions about alcohol use?

❸ What factors can contribute to the effects of alcohol?

Alcohol and Its Effects

Alcohol is the deadliest drug in the world when its effects on drivers are considered. Drinking and drunkenness contribute to accidents of all kinds, including those involving motor vehicles, water, recreation, fires, hunting, falls, and more. Alcohol abuse also causes many problems for individuals and society.

Does Alcohol Really Cause Accidents?

The case against drinking and driving is very easily proved. The available statistics tell a terrible story of alcohol-related crashes, deaths, and injuries.

- The 17,419 people who died in alcohol-related crashes during 2002 represent an average of one alcohol-related death every 30 minutes.
- The same year, more than 327,000 people were injured in crashes where police reported that alcohol was present—an average of about one person injured every 2 minutes.
- In 2002, some 25 percent of the 57,803 drivers were involved in fatal alcohol-related crashes.
- In 2002, 24 percent of young drivers 16 to 20 years old who were killed in crashes were intoxicated or drunk.
- About three in every ten Americans will be involved in an alcohol-related crash at some time in their lives.

How Does Alcohol Affect Driving Ability?

Research has shown that drinking alcohol has many adverse effects on driving ability, even at low blood-alcohol concentrations. Other research has shown that all drivers, and particularly young drivers, are at a greatly increased risk of dying as their BAC rises. No matter how good a driver you are, alcohol will decrease your skill and it will damage your judgment behind the wheel.

Being a good driver takes skill and judgment. When you are behind the wheel of a motor vehicle, all of your senses must be on alert. You need to react quickly to potentially threatening conditions and make split-second decisions. As a driver, you must perform many tasks. The ability to divide your attention among these tasks is critical. Even without alcohol, driving can be difficult. This difficulty is increased with even very low levels of alcohol.

One drink of alcohol causes rapid changes in the body because alcohol is absorbed faster than food. As soon as you drink, alcohol is absorbed into the bloodstream through the walls of the stomach and small intestine. Once in the bloodstream, alcohol is quickly carried to all parts of the body. Alcohol has the greatest effect on the brain, the organ that controls all body functions. That is why any drinker's mental and physical abilities become diminished.

Tips for New Drivers

DRINKING AND DRIVING

Keep in mind that people under the age of 21 who drink and drive are breaking not just one but two laws. They are breaking the law against driving while intoxicated and the law against underage drinking. If caught drinking and driving, underage drivers face severe penalties, including suspension of driver's licenses, fines, and possible jail time. Don't take chances—play it safe and smart by choosing not to drink alcohol.

The ability to process information after you receive it is vital. Alcohol interferes with the brain's ability to use information to make good decisions. If you are drinking, you might miss the meaning of a particular sign or lane marking, for example, or not see it at all. Something as simple as maintaining your position in a lane is more difficult since alcohol affects fine-muscle control. Under the influence of alcohol, your steering can become erratic and result in a crash.

Numerous experiments involving drivers who were tested both sober and at various BAC levels have demonstrated information-processing losses even at low BAC levels. Small amounts of drinking affect you. While drivers who have been drinking a little may be able to cope with simple tasks such as weaving between cones, they are unable to successfully handle more complex or emergency situations such as pulling out of skids or sudden lane changes. The risk of being in a fatal crash or dying as a driver in a fatal crash rises rapidly as BAC increases.

It is a misconception that alcohol makes you safer in the event of a crash because your body is limber. The chance of dying as a driver in a crash is much greater for drivers who have been drinking than for sober drivers. Reasons for this include:

- Drinkers often fail to wear safety belts.
- Medical attention becomes more difficult for intoxicated persons.

Blurred or double vision is often the result of a driver having too much to drink. *How can blurred vision affect your ability to drive?*

How Is Your Body Affected by Alcohol?

Alcohol affects your body by acting as a depressant. This means it is a drug that slows down and impairs the central nervous system. The part of the brain that alcohol affects first is the part that allows you to think clearly and make good decisions. Changes in thinking can occur even with small amounts of alcohol. This effect is an impairment that may not be noticed by the drinker. Alcohol can cause a

younger driver to drive too fast, pass when it is unsafe to do so, or make a bad decision in an emergency situation.

YOUR VISION IS AFFECTED

As you know, vision is the most important sense needed in driving. Alcohol impairs several specific areas of vision.

Visual acuity. This is sharpness of vision. Alcohol may make images blurry for the driver. This impairs your ability to identify properly what is in the traffic scene and to make good driving decisions.

Side vision. Alcohol affects your peripheral vision, or what you can see to each side. Normally, most people have 180 degrees of side vision. While looking straight ahead, you can usually notice objects at the side even though you cannot see them clearly. Alcohol reduces your visual field and makes it more difficult to see potential hazards on either side. Side vision is most important when going through intersections or past parked cars where pedestrians may step out.

Color distinction. Alcohol affects your ability to distinguish colors. Drivers get much information from different colors in the traffic scene. Red, for example, means only three things on a traffic sign: stop, yield, or some prohibition of action. If alcohol impedes your ability to determine the color of a sign or traffic light, that is a problem.

Night vision. Alcohol adversely affects your night vision. Seeing at night does not involve so much seeing small details as it does the detection of objects in the field of view. Normally, it takes 1 second for the pupil to constrict and respond to the glare of oncoming headlights. It takes up to 7 seconds after exposure to headlight glare for the pupil to once again adapt to the dark conditions. Any loss of night vision is important because most drinking is done at night.

Distance judgment. Alcohol reduces the ability to judge distance accurately. You must be able to determine how far objects are from your vehicle. The movement of other objects complicates distance judgment or depth perception.

Static and dynamic vision. **Static vision** involves visually interpreting something that is not in motion. This ability may not be significantly affected until a BAC of .10 percent is reached. **Dynamic vision** involves visually interpreting something that is in motion. A blood alcohol concentration as low as .02 percent has been shown to affect dynamic visual acuity.

YOUR REACTION TIME IS AFFECTED

Reaction time is definitely affected by alcohol. Research has also shown that simple reaction time is a stimulus–response reaction such as flinching when you hear a loud sound or taking your hand off a hot object. Simple reaction time is not significantly impaired by alcohol. However, complex reaction time is affected. Complex reaction time includes more complicated responses, such as the ability to react and steer left, steer right, or brake in an emergency. Complex reaction time, critical for driving, is impaired at very low BACs.

How Much Alcohol Affects Your Driving?

Even one drink might be enough to impair your ability to drive safely. From the moment alcohol enters your bloodstream, you begin to lose your ability to think clearly. Even a small amount of alcohol causes changes in your coordination. It should not come as a surprise that approximately 40 percent of all highway deaths are alcohol related.

FACTS ABOUT ALCOHOL AND DRIVING

The facts spelled out in **Figure 18.1** tell you why alcohol-impaired driving is a recipe for disaster.

- As the alcohol concentration goes up, the chance of death goes up.
- Chance of death in a crash goes up even at low BAC.
- Chance of death increases rapidly with BAC above the legal limit.

Information from the National Highway Traffic Safety Administration clearly shows that alcohol-related crashes are a large part of the highway safety problem. It also shows that large numbers of young people are involved in alcohol-related crashes.

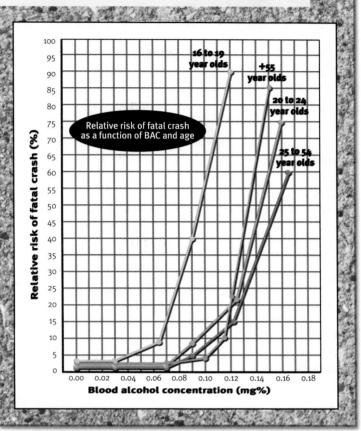

FIGURE 18.1

PROBABILITY OF A FATAL COLLISION

Relative risk of fatal crash as a function of BAC and age

16 to 19 year olds

+55 year olds

20 to 24 year olds

25 to 54 year olds

Relative risk of fatal crash (%)

Blood alcohol concentration (mg%)

WHAT WOULD YOU DO?
The driver has been drinking steadily. How can his companions get home? What is their responsibility to the driver?

Lesson 2 Review

❶ How does alcohol affect your driving?

❷ How does alcohol affect vision?

❸ How is your reaction time affected by alcohol?

Other Drugs' Effect on Driving Ability

LESSON 3

OBJECTIVES

1. **Explain** how drugs can affect your ability to drive.
2. **List** legal and illegal drugs that can impact your driving ability.
3. **Define** *synergism* and its meaning to drivers.

KEY TERMS

- over-the-counter drugs
- prescription drugs
- depressants
- stimulants
- hallucinogens
- narcotics
- synergism

Alcohol is not the only drug that can impair your ability to drive. Both legal and illegal drugs can impair your driving ability. Legal drugs can be bought over the counter or with a prescription. Illegal drugs are against the law, and they greatly impair driving ability too.

How Do Drugs Affect Driving Ability?

Some legal drugs and all illegal drugs impair your ability to drive. How a drug affects you depends on the condition of your own body and on the drug itself. Some drugs decrease your ability to make sound decisions and respond well to situations. Other drugs can actually change the way you think or perceive things. It is important that you know about these drugs and their effects on driving. Once you understand the danger of taking drugs and driving, you can take steps to avoid putting yourself and others at risk.

Figure 18.2 provides some of the major drugs that impair driving ability.

FIGURE 18.2	DRUGS THAT AFFECT DRIVING ABILITY		
Narcotics	*Depressants*	*Stimulants*	*Hallucinogens*
Heroin	Alcohol	Amphetamines (speed)	Marijuana
Codeine	Barbiturates	Cocaine (crack or rock)	LSD
Morphine	Methadone		PCP (angel dust)
	Sleeping pills		Hashish
	Tranquilizers		

Many of the drugs listed above are illegal, but legal drugs can also impair your ability to drive.

What Types of Legal Drugs Impair Driving Ability?

Over-the-counter drugs, prescription drugs, and alcohol and other depressants are all legally available. Even when prescribed by a doctor or purchased legally, many of these drugs can impair driving ability.

OVER-THE-COUNTER DRUGS

Over-the-counter drugs can be purchased legally in drugstores and supermarkets without a doctor's prescription. Many people do not even think of them as drugs. These drugs are heavily advertised for use on colds, flu, headaches, allergies, and other everyday ailments. It is important to read the package label of these drugs. Some over-the-counter drug labels warn that their use may "cause drowsiness or dizziness," or they warn "Do not drive after using." Pay attention to these warnings! They are written because these drugs may impair your ability to drive. It is your responsibility as a driver to know what side effects any medications you are taking might cause.

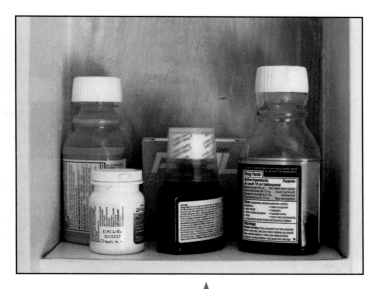

Many of the capsules, tablets, and syrups commonly found in medicine cabinets are over-the-counter drugs. *Why is it important to read the package labels of these drugs before driving?*

PRESCRIPTION DRUGS

You can get **prescription drugs** at a pharmacy or drugstore, but you cannot buy them unless your doctor writes a prescription or prescribes them for you. If your doctor does not tell you about their adverse effects, ask the pharmacist if you can drive safely while you are taking a particular prescription medication. Find out what side effects the drug may have that might affect your driving.

Many prescription drugs have warnings on the package or the bottle. When you pick up the prescription, look carefully at the package insert or container. If the labels advise you not to drive or not to take the medication in combination with alcohol, obey the warnings. It is your responsibility as a driver to know what drugs you are taking and what effects they can have.

DEPRESSANTS

Depressants are prescription drugs that slow down, or depress, the central nervous system. When used properly, their basic effect is to calm you down. Alcohol is a cheap, easily purchased, over-the-counter depressant drug. Doctors also prescribe depressant medications for patients who are experiencing a great deal of tension, who are very anxious, or who are being treated for high blood pressure. These drugs are also sometimes sold illegally.

While depressants can help a patient lessen stress and anxiety, they also slow down the patient's mental and physical activity. These drugs slow down reflexes and have a harmful effect on coordination. Be wary of these effects if you take depressants and need to drive. Do not combine prescription depressants with alcohol.

What Types of Illegal Drugs Impair Driving Ability?

Almost every type of illegal drug can impair your ability to drive and also your ability to think clearly. All these drugs affect your mind and trigger subtle changes in your perception. Most impair how your mind and body work. Three classes of illegal drugs are stimulants, hallucinogens, and narcotics.

Dealing with the UNEXPECTED

UNDER THE INFLUENCE

Be aware of signs that other drivers on the road may be under the influence of alcohol or other drugs. Various signs indicate possible problems.

▲ **Traveling at erratic speeds.** Intoxicated drivers often have trouble driving at a steady speed.
▲ **Running over curbs or turning into the wrong lane.** Intoxicated drivers are often unable to turn smoothly.
▲ **Weaving or swerving.** Intoxicated drivers suffer from loss of coordination and attention, which affects their ability to steer smoothly.
▲ **Ignoring or overshooting traffic signs.** Intoxicated drivers suffer impaired reflexes and vision loss.

STIMULANTS

Stimulants speed up, or stimulate, the central nervous system. Some are legal, but many stimulants are illegal. The caffeine in coffee and most soft drinks, for instance, is a widely available stimulant. Other powerful stimulants, such as amphetamines and cocaine, were once widely prescribed by doctors, but today their hazards are recognized by the medical profession, and they are more often purchased illegally. In addition to cocaine and rock cocaine, some other illegal stimulants include benzedrine, dexedrine, and methamphetamine. Some drivers misuse these drugs and take them to keep awake when driving long distances.

Stimulants can give you a false feeling of well-being and make you think that you are super alert. When abused, these drugs often cause drivers to take foolish and life-threatening risks. When the effects of stimulants wear off, which can happen very suddenly, users can quickly become very tired and quite depressed.

HALLUCINOGENS

Hallucinogens, such as LSD, PCP, marijuana, and hashish, are so powerful and dangerous that selling or using them is always against the law. **Hallucinogens**, or mind-altering drugs, change the way a person thinks, sees, and acts, all of which definitely impair driving ability. They are called hallucinogens because they can cause hallucinations. The abuse of these drugs can result in temporary psychosis or long-term mental damage. These drugs can cause drivers to lose the ability to judge the space and speed at which they are driving or can cause them to hallucinate so that they suddenly react to an obstacle that isn't really there.

No one really knows when the effects of hallucinogens wear off, but it is known that the chemicals in marijuana can stay in the body for 4 to 6 weeks. Drivers may think that the effects have worn off when they are still under the influence, and their driving remains impaired.

NARCOTICS

Narcotics, such as morphine and heroin, have a strong depressant effect and create a euphoria that can quickly become a serious addiction. Illegal forms are injected with a needle, smoked, or inhaled through the nose. The narcotic drugs can cause stupor or a coma. Many narcotic overdoses have resulted in death.

SYNERGISM

It is important to realize that mixing or taking two drugs often has a stronger effect than either drug taken alone. **Synergism** is the interaction of one drug with another to enhance the effect of one or both. For example, if a person drinks alcohol and takes a depressant, the combination could produce a depressive effect on the person greater than the typical effect of either substance. Even a nonprescription drug such as an antihistamine can be dangerous when mixed with alcohol. It is very important, therefore, to avoid combining alcohol and other drugs. In fact, it's a good idea to avoid combining any drugs unless they are prescribed by a physician and you understand their effects.

If you find yourself on the same roadway as a driver who shows any signs of being drug impaired, increase the amount of space between your vehicles. Be alert to the fact that there is an impaired driver sharing the roadway with you. If possible, inform a police officer of what you have noticed.

FYI

Marijuana masks the feeling of nausea that accompanies intoxication. Drinkers who mix marijuana and alcohol may not realize how much alcohol they have consumed. They may continue drinking until they suffer alcohol poisoning, which can result in coma or even death.

WHAT WOULD YOU DO?
You are taking a prescription medicine. Can you drive your sister to the movies? How will you decide if it is safe for you to drive?

Lesson 3 Review

❶ What are some other kinds of drugs besides alcohol?

❷ How do these drugs affect your ability to drive?

❸ What kinds of legal drugs can impair your driving ability?

LESSON 4

Preventing Impaired Driving

OBJECTIVES

1. **Identify** ways to prevent alcoholism and drug abuse.
2. **Describe** the laws that are designed to control impaired driving.

There is no such thing as responsible drinking for an underage person. Illicit drug use is equally irresponsible. There are, however, responsibilities that everyone has regarding impaired drivers. For yourself, you can learn how to avoid driving when drugs impair your driving. You can also learn the warning signs for alcoholism or drug addiction and how to seek help for long-term problems involving alcohol and drugs.

What Are a Person's Responsibilities Regarding Impaired Driving?

Many questions come up regarding a driver or a passenger's responsibilities for their own or another person's impaired driving. It is important to protect yourself and others from these effects. Here are two good things to understand about responsibility:

1. People have a responsibility to protect themselves from the threat that drug use poses to their health and well-being.
2. People also have a responsibility to protect themselves and others from the risk posed by people who drive while impaired.

What this means is to look out for yourself and also for other people. Do not drive while under the influence of any drugs that impair your driving ability. If you are with someone whose driving is obviously impaired by drugs or alcohol, do not let that person drive. In the short-term, you can help another person whose driving is impaired by taking the car keys, driving yourself, calling your parents for a ride, calling a taxi, riding public transportation, or making other arrangements.

If your drug or alcohol use could be a serious problem, consider getting some long-term help. Drinking can turn into alcoholism, and recreational drug use can turn into drug addiction. Be aware of some of the signs that can indicate you have a problem.

How Can Alcoholism or Drug Abuse Be Prevented?

Problem drinking can lead to alcoholism. The attitudes of a young person's friends and relatives and what that person does while drinking all affect what is considered "alcoholism" and "alcoholic." These terms are powerful, distasteful, and very negative, but they also indicate a real problem. Remember that nobody rings a bell and lets someone know when he or she has become an alcoholic or a drug abuser. That person must diagnose his or her problem, or

All 50 states and the District of Columbia have established lower BACs for young drivers. These zero tolerance laws make it illegal for people under 21 to drive with a BAC higher than 0.00 percent to 0.02 percent, depending on the state in which they live.

perhaps friends or family can help tell that person. Pattern of drinking, the amount of alcohol one consumes at any given time, and the reasons for using alcohol are all factors that determine if a person is dependent on alcohol or might be an alcoholic.

SUPPORT GROUPS

There are support groups to help alcoholics, problem users, and their relatives and friends. These self-help groups keep any information you may volunteer confidential. Two such groups for people with problems with alcohol or drugs are Alcoholics Anonymous (AA), and Narcotics Anonymous (NA). Alateen is an important organization for young people who think or know that they have a problem with alcohol and need help. Alanon is a support group for people who have an alcoholic parent, sibling, or friend.

LEGAL MEASURES TO CORRECT PROBLEMS CAUSED BY ALCOHOL

A number of legal measures are in place to deal with drivers who use alcohol or drugs. Several of these have been specifically aimed at young people. The number and scope of laws related to alcohol have increased greatly in recent years.

Administrative License Revocation. Administrative License Revocation (ALR) laws have been passed to provide immediate punishment for persons who fail or refuse a breath or blood test. The punishment is usually the immediate loss of your driver's license. ALR penalties may be in addition to other penalties for motor-vehicle operation while intoxicated.

Zero Tolerance Laws. Prohibiting any drinking until age 21 and "zero tolerance" laws have been enacted to prevent persons under age 21 from either drinking at all or driving a motor vehicle with any measurable alcohol in their system. Research has shown that these measures can be effective. For example, prohibiting drinking by persons under age 21 has resulted in reducing alcohol-related traffic deaths for that age group.

Open Containers. Many states also have laws that prohibit open containers of alcohol in a vehicle. If you are found with an open container such as an open beer can or an open bottle of wine, you will be legally penalized. These laws are designed to get people of legal age to drink at home, not in vehicles.

Blood Alcohol Concentration. Laws are also in place to define intoxication as more than "looking drunk," which can be a very subjective decision. Intoxication is also usually defined as a certain BAC (.08 percent in most cases). Thus a driver can be convicted of DWI/DUI if he or she reaches this level regardless of whether or not that person looks drunk or looks high.

FYI

Since 1982, the number of 15- to 20-year-olds killed in alcohol-related crashes has dropped from 22 to 9 per 100,000 youths—a decrease of more than 50 percent. Zero tolerance laws have been a major factor in this positive trend.

An intoxicated driver will have difficulty focusing on the pen as the officer moves it. *What are some of the physical effects of alcohol?*

Dr. Maury Dennis

Texas A&M University
College Station, TX

While alcohol and other drugs affect all drivers, young drivers are most at risk. Even though their eyesight, reflexes, coordination, and physical condition are usually better than that of older people, they still are in proportionally more alcohol-related fatal crashes than any other age group. This may be because of much night driving and lack of experience with alcohol as well as inexperience as a driver. Learning to drive safely is hard enough; do not make it more risky by driving after drinking or using drugs.

What are some of the consequences of driving after drinking or using drugs?

WHAT WOULD YOU DO?
Your friend offers you an illegal drug. What would you say to your friend?

Legal penalties. A judge can impose several different types of legal penalties for alcohol-related offenses such as driving drunk. These include fines, loss of license, jail time, community service, education courses, and ignition interlocks.

In addition to the legal ramifications, insurance premiums usually shoot up with a DUI conviction. If a crash occurs as a result of the driver's being under the influence, a civil lawsuit may also be filed against the intoxicated driver.

MAKING GOOD DECISIONS

Education is the key to making informed, responsible decisions regarding alcohol and drugs. It is important to remember that alcohol is certainly a drug. Potential losses for young people resulting from drug abuse or alcohol abuse include money, freedom, health, friends/family, driver's license, and life.

Lesson 4 Review

❶ How can alcoholism and drug abuse be prevented?

❷ What laws are designed to control impaired driving?

❸ Why have laws establishing lower BACs for young people been enacted?

BUILDING Skills — Geography

USING THE MILEAGE CHART

Suppose you are planning to drive from Abilene to El Paso. How many miles would you be traveling? One way to find out would be to use a mileage chart such as the one on this page. Using a mileage chart is easy.

First look at the names of cities down the left side of the chart. Find Abilene, and put your left finger over it.

Then look at the cities across the top of the chart. Put your right finger on El Paso.

Now move your left finger across the chart until it reaches the box below El Paso. The number in the box is the distance in miles between Abilene and El Paso. The distance is 450 miles. That's quite a trip.

To estimate how long it will take you if you drive at an average speed of 55 miles per hour, divide 450 by 55. The trip will take between 8 and 9 hours. But don't forget to add in some time for rest stops. Therefore, you can figure on about a 10-hour trip.

MILEAGE CHART	Abilene	Amarillo	Dallas	Eagle Pass	El Paso	Houston	Lubbock	Midland	Odessa	Pecos	San Angelo	San Antonio
Abilene		273	180	302	450	355	171	148	180	245	92	250
Amarillo	273		351	517	421	597	134	237	258	330	310	513
El Paso	450	421	646	479		751	345	312	289	210	415	555
Lubbock	171	134	318	394	345	530		121	142	219	202	406
Odessa	180	258	352	301	289	507	142	20		75	132	345
San Angelo	92	310	262	215	415	374	202	113	132	210		215

TRY IT YOURSELF

❶ How many miles is it between San Angelo and Eagle Pass?

❷ If you are traveling at 55 miles an hour, how long will it take you to drive from El Paso to Pecos?

❸ Which trip would be longer—one from Odessa to Houston or one from Lubbock to San Antonio?

Key Points

Lesson 1

1. The three categories of alcohol use are experimentation (drinking out of curiosity), recreational drinking (drinking for what one thinks is fun), and alcohol abuse (the wrong, improper, or abnormal use of alcohol). (Pages 374–375)

2. Factors that influence alcohol's effects include expectations, mood, fatigue, and existing medications or medical sensitivities. (Page 375)

? WHAT WOULD YOU DO?
You and a friend are offered a drink. You say no, but your friend wants to try one. What will you say to your friend?

Lesson 2

1. Alcohol decreases your skill and damages your judgment behind the wheel. It interferes with the brain's ability to use information to make good decisions and affects fine-muscle control that allows you to stay in your lane or to steer. A person who has had alcohol is also unable to successfully handle more complex or emergency situations. (Pages 378–379)

2. Alcohol can make your vision blurry, reduce your visual field, affect your ability to distinguish colors, adversely affect your night vision, reduce the ability to judge distance accurately, and reduce your static and dynamic vision. (Page 380)

Lesson 3

1. Drugs can decrease your ability to make sound decisions and respond well to situations. They can also change the way you think or perceive things. (Page 382)

2. Over-the-counter drugs, prescription drugs, depressants, stimulants, hallucinogens, and narcotics can affect and impair your driving ability. (Pages 382–385)

? WHAT WOULD YOU DO?
You are taking a prescription medicine. Can you drive your sister to the movies? How will you decide if it is safe for you to drive?

Lesson 4

1. Support groups, legal measures, and good decision making are all ways to combat alcoholism and drug abuse. (Pages 387–388)

2. Legal measures designed to control problems caused by alcohol and drugs include Administrative License Revocation laws, zero tolerance laws, laws prohibiting open containers, laws defining intoxication through BAC, and legal penalties. (Pages 387–388)

On a separate sheet of paper, write the letter of the answer that best completes each sentence.

1 Chance of death in an alcohol-related crash goes up
  a. at low BAC.
  b. when BAC is .10.
  c. only for nonimpaired drivers and passengers.

2 Over-the-counter drugs
  a. may be used when driving short distances.
  b. may impair driving ability.
  c. must be ordered for you by a doctor.

3 You can reduce the effects of alcohol if you
  a. take a very cold shower.
  b. exercise.
  c. allow several hours to pass.

4 To get help with a drinking problem,
  a. drink just once a week.
  b. drink only beer.
  c. join a support group.

5 Alcohol is
  a. a harmless substance.
  b. a potentially dangerous drug.
  c. not addictive.

6 Even a small amount of alcohol can affect your
  a. long-term memory.
  b. ability to pull out of a skid.
  c. hearing.

On a separate sheet of paper, write the word or phrase that best completes each sentence.

synergism   depressants
prescription stimulants

7 Drugs that slow down the central nervous system are called _____.

8 _____ drugs must be ordered by a doctor.

9 _____ often give drivers a false sense of self-confidence and cause them to take foolish and life-threatening risks.

10 The interaction of one drug with another to enhance the effect of one or both is _____.

Writing

Driver's Log

In this chapter, you have learned about how social pressures can cause you to behave in ways that will put you and others at risk. Imagine that a friend has been drinking and wants to drive you home. Your friend says, "Don't worry, I'm just fine." What will you say? How might your friend respond? Write a dialogue showing what might happen.

Projects

1 Many organizations work to educate drivers about the dangers of drinking and driving. Besides SADD, Mothers Against Drunk Driving (MADD) is probably the best known. Find information about MADD.

2 Refer to your state driver's manual or interview a police officer. Discover the circumstances under which a teenage driver can be convicted of DUI or DWI in your state. Find out about the penalties for conviction as well.

Chapter 19

Vehicle Readiness

LESSON 1
Checking Your Vehicle

LESSON 2
Maintaining Vehicle Systems

LESSON 3
Suspension, Steering, Brakes, and Tires

LESSON 4
Child Safety Seats

Why Is Vehicle Maintenance Important?

Driving a well-maintained vehicle will help keep you as safe as possible. Part of being a good driver is making sure that your car is well maintained and safe to drive. Check your vehicle's different operating systems periodically, and make sure that those systems function properly.

Driver Ed
Online

For additional activities, visit drivered.glencoe.com. Here you will find:

◆ **Web Link Exercises**
◆ **eFlashcards**
◆ **Practice Driving Tests**

Checking Your Vehicle

OBJECTIVES

1. **Identify** several items on your vehicle that you can inspect before starting it.
2. **List** several items to check after starting the engine.
3. **Explain** when to have your vehicle serviced.

KEY TERMS

- ◆ **power train**
- ◆ **tune-up**

Before you enter your vehicle, check under the hood for items such as the coolant level. *Why is it important to check your vehicle?*

Spending a little time or money to inspect and care for your vehicle before something goes wrong will save you both money and aggravation later. More importantly, maintaining your vehicle in good working order can help prevent mechanical failures and possibly save your life.

What Can You Inspect Before Entering Your Vehicle?

You do not need to be a mechanic to inspect your vehicle. You can quickly and easily check many items just by lifting the hood and looking around. You should always make these checks at least once a month and before long drives.

To check your particular model properly, refer to the owner's manual. If you do not have the manual, you can obtain a copy from a dealer or order one from the manufacturer. Automotive manuals are also available in many bookstores. Keep the manual in your glove compartment so you will have it handy when you need it. In addition to the guidelines below, refer to Chapter 4 for other important predriving checks and procedures.

Fluid levels, belts, hoses, wiring, and lights should be checked once a month.

FLUID LEVELS

Your vehicle uses a number of fluids to cool and lubricate its moving parts. Engine oil, radiator coolant, transmission fluid, brake fluid, battery fluid, and windshield-wiper fluid can all be used up, evaporate, or leak away. If you need to add a particular fluid very often, this is a sign that you may have a fluid leak or another problem. Have a mechanic check it out.

Each of the fluid levels is checked in a different place, but all are near the engine, under the hood of the car. The engine oil and transmission fluid usually have dipsticks that you can pull out, wipe clean, reinsert, withdraw and examine. Radiator coolant, brake fluid, battery fluid (distilled water), and windshield-wiper fluid can be checked visually in their separate containers or locations. Once a month, or more often if you know you are leaking a particular type of fluid, inspect your vehicle's fluid levels. If they are low, add more of the correct fluid or have a mechanic do it. Check the engine oil (check it when the engine is cool and not running), the level of radiator coolant (check the overflow tank), the brake master cylinder reservoirs (may be visible without removing the cap), the battery fluid (if your battery has removable caps and can be serviced), the transmission fluid (for cars with automatic transmissions), the power-steering fluid (if your vehicle has power-steering), and the windshield-washer fluid (with proper antifreeze capability in winter).

BELTS, HOSES, AND WIRING

When you check the fluid levels, also take a look at the belts, hoses, and wiring under the hood of your car. A running engine is in constant motion, and belts help the engine move power from one part of the engine to another system, such as the fan or air conditioner. Hoses shunt crucial cooling fluids from one part of the engine to another. Wires are important electrical connections. Problems you notice can be double-checked and fixed by a mechanic.

Here are some simple checks you can make:

1. Check the accessory drive belts for fraying, glazing (a shiny appearance), or cracking. Belts may need tightening or adjustment. Replace all the worn or damaged accessory belts as soon as possible.
2. Check all hoses and hose connections for leaks. If one is leaking, have the hose or clamp replaced.
3. Look for loose, broken, or disconnected wiring. Also check for cracked insulation on wires.
4. Make sure the battery cables are tightly connected and the terminals are free of corrosion.

What Can You Check After Starting the Engine?

Once your engine is running, you should make several routine checks to ensure that your vehicle is operating properly and safely. Gauges, brakes, horn, lights, and warning lights can all be checked before you start driving.

GAUGES AND WARNING LIGHTS

Chapter 4 explained the various gauges and warning lights that provide information about your vehicle. Check these gauges and lights regularly as you drive. Warning lights coming on or gauges that read at dangerous levels will warn you of a wide range of problems.

BRAKES

Your vehicle's brake warning light can make you aware of some problems with your brake system, but some problems may occur without the light turning on.

For this reason, always manually test your brakes as soon as you begin driving. Step on the brake pedal. You should feel firm resistance, and your vehicle should come to a smooth, straight stop. The pedal should stay well above the floor. If this doesn't happen, have your brakes checked by a professional.

HORN

You may not use your horn very often, but periodically check it to make sure it works. If you are driving an unfamiliar vehicle, always locate and try the horn before you begin driving.

SAFETY TIP

Always check radiator coolant level by looking at the radiator overflow tank. If additional coolant is needed, add it to the overflow tank, not to the radiator. Rarely should it be necessary to remove the radiator cap. If you do have to remove the radiator cap, **do so only when the radiator is cool.** If you remove the cap when the radiator is hot, boiling water could spurt out and scald you.

Driver Ed Online

Topic: Preparing your car for summer

For a link to more information on preparing your car for summer, go to drivered.glencoe.com.

Activity: Using the information provided at this link, work in small groups to create a brochure with maintenance tips for preparing your car for summer driving.

You don't have to be a mechanic to do your own maintenance on your car. *What are some of the benefits of learning how to do your own maintenance?*

LIGHTS AND TURN SIGNALS

Vehicle-safety checks find that nearly one out of four vehicles has at least one lightbulb or headlight burned out. Check all exterior lights and turn signals before you drive. Periodically have a friend or family member stand outside the vehicle and tell you if your brake lights work when you press the brake pedal.

How Can You Maintain the Engine and Power Train?

The **power train** moves the power of the engine to the wheels. It is crucial to keep your engine and the power train well maintained.

Maintenance is important, and it helps ensure a longer life for your car. Your owner's manual will give you specific recommendations for maintenance on your vehicle. If your vehicle is new, failure to follow the recommended maintenance schedule can void your warranty.

CHECK AND CHANGE THE OIL REGULARLY

Oil is the most important fluid in the car, since it lubricates and helps cool your engine. Check your vehicle's oil every second time you gas up or more often if necessary. If your oil is low, add more of the same weight.

Oil carries away dirt and grime from the moving engine. Change the oil and oil filter regularly, according to the recommendations in your owner's manual. This is usually every 5,000 to 7,500 miles or 6 months.

Most manufacturers now give two schedules for oil changes: one for normal use and one for severe use. Severe use is often described as many short trips, stop-and-go driving, or regular travel in dusty conditions. Most city driving is considered severe use.

 Tips for New Drivers

HAVING YOUR VEHICLE SERVICED OR REPAIRED

▶ To find a reliable mechanic or garage, ask friends and relatives for their recommendations. You can also call your local American Automobile Association.

▶ Ask the mechanic for a cost estimate of the work to be done.

▶ Find out if the mechanic will guarantee the work done and for how long. Save your bill or receipt.

▶ Know what you are paying for. If there is something you do not understand, ask for an explanation.

▶ If the mechanic replaces a part, ask to see the old part.

▶ Warranties may cover many repairs. Know what your warranty does and does not cover.

PERFORM REGULAR MAINTENANCE

Regular maintenance used to involve giving a car a **tune-up**, which involved replacing a number of parts in the ignition system and then making several ignition and fuel adjustments to ensure that the engine ran properly. On modern cars, the electronic ignition system is practically maintenance free except for the spark plugs, and those may not need replacement until 100,000 miles. As for adjustments, whenever a modern engine is running, the electronic engine-control system makes continuous small adjustments to ensure that the engine is always in perfect tune.

Today, the term *tune-up* (while out of date) is sometimes used to describe a maintenance service that may include an oil and filter change, air filter replacement, a quick check of major components, and a safety inspection.

How Do You Know When Your Vehicle Should Be Serviced?

Do you know when your vehicle needs to be serviced? Your owner's manual contains guidelines for servicing and maintaining your vehicle.

Some systems and parts require more frequent attention than others. Recommended intervals for servicing may be based either on time or on miles driven. For example, your manual might recommend changing the oil every 5,000 to 7,500 miles or six months and having the suspension checked every 30,000 miles or once a year. Try to follow your manual's recommendations for maintenance and servicing.

Keeping complete records will help you schedule maintenance. An easy way to keep track of repairs and maintenance is to keep a small notebook in your glove compartment. Each time you or a mechanic services or repairs the vehicle, jot down the date, exactly what was done, and the mileage on your car. Saving your receipts in an envelope in the glove compartment will also help you remember when a part was replaced or when a particular type of servicing was done.

WHAT WOULD YOU DO?
A friend has agreed to let you use her car while she's on vacation. What checks will you make before getting into her car? What checks will you make after starting the engine?

Lesson 1 Review

❶ What kinds of problems might you spot as you check your vehicle before starting it?

❷ What can you check after you start the engine?

❸ What can help you determine when to have your vehicle serviced?

Maintaining Vehicle Systems

OBJECTIVES

1. **Explain** how the fuel, exhaust, electrical, and light systems work and how to maintain them.
2. **Describe** how the lubricating and cooling systems work and how to maintain them.

KEY TERMS

- exhaust manifold
- muffler
- catalytic converter
- battery
- alternator
- engine control module (ECM)
- coolant
- radiator
- antifreeze

Today it is easy to take your car for granted. But it is still one of the most complicated machines ever invented, with hundreds of moving parts. Every time you get behind the wheel, you take control of a network of many different systems that work together to make your vehicle move. Understanding the basic systems utilized by your vehicle and how to keep them in working order will help you drive safely.

What Are the Basic Systems in a Vehicle?

A system is a network of parts and connecting lines that serves a particular function in your vehicle. All the basic systems in a vehicle are important, and they work together. They include the fuel and exhaust system, the electrical and light systems, and the lubricating and cooling systems.

How Do the Fuel and Exhaust Systems Work?

The fuel system takes fuel such as gasoline or diesel fuel to the engine, and the exhaust system takes burned fuel residue away. The fuel and exhaust systems in a vehicle must operate properly to maximize engine efficiency and minimize air pollution.

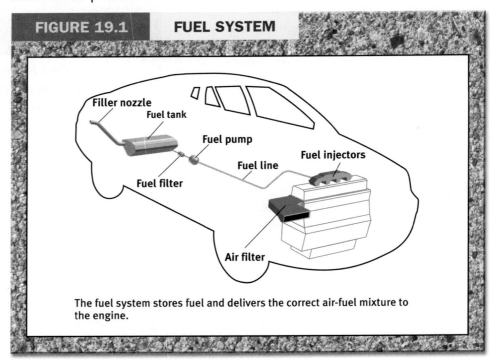

FIGURE 19.1   FUEL SYSTEM

Filler nozzle
Fuel tank
Fuel pump
Fuel injectors
Fuel line
Fuel filter
Air filter

The fuel system stores fuel and delivers the correct air-fuel mixture to the engine.

FIGURE 19.2   EXHAUST SYSTEM

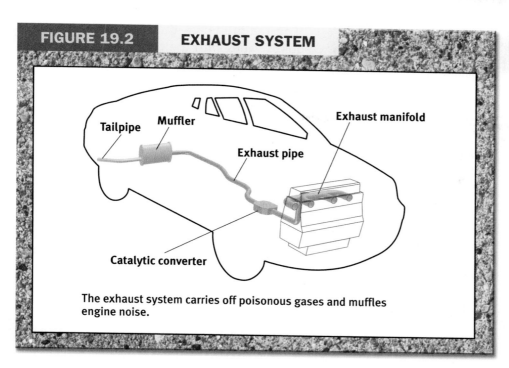

Tailpipe

Muffler

Exhaust manifold

Exhaust pipe

Catalytic converter

The exhaust system carries off poisonous gases and muffles engine noise.

THE FUEL SYSTEM

The fuel system stores fuel and delivers the correct air–fuel mixture to the engine (see **Figure 19.1**). Every vehicle's fuel system includes a fuel tank, fuel lines, a fuel pump, a fuel filter, an electronic fuel-injection (EFI) system or a carburetor, and an air filter. Fuel is stored in the fuel tank. The fuel pump forces fuel through the fuel lines and fuel filter. Near the engine, fuel is mixed with air filtered through an air filter. Fuel is mixed in the EFI system or carburetor. The air-fuel mixture forms a vapor that is injected at a precise time into each cylinder, where it is ignited by a spark plug, a process that repeats hundreds of times per minute.

THE EXHAUST SYSTEM

The exhaust system carries off carbon monoxide and other polluting by-products of gasoline or diesel combustion. The exhaust system also muffles engine noise (see **Figure 19.2**).

The metal pipes of the **exhaust manifold** collect unburned gases as they come from the engine, and these pipes carry the gases and engine noise to the muffler a few feet away. The **muffler** absorbs or muffles noise created from the explosions in the cylinders. Exhaust gases exit through the tailpipe. Pollution-control devices located between the manifold and muffler, such as the **catalytic converter**, reduce the amount of harmful gases coming from the tailpipe that are released into the air.

THE MAINTAINING THE FUEL AND EXHAUST SYSTEMS

To maintain your vehicle's fuel system, replace the air and fuel filters as recommended. This helps keep your vehicle running cleanly and efficiently. Use the type of fuel recommended by the manufacturer for your vehicle. Remember that most vehicles today require lead-free gasoline; leaded gas will destroy the catalytic converter.

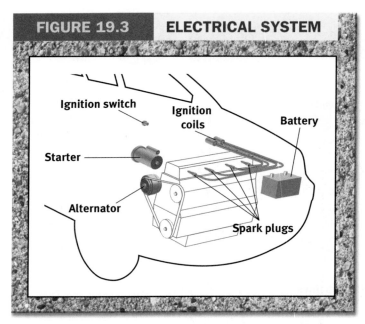

FIGURE 19.3   ELECTRICAL SYSTEM

Ignition switch
Ignition coils
Battery
Starter
Alternator
Spark plugs

The maintenance that the exhaust system requires varies with the conditions under which you drive. Short trips, for example, are harder on a vehicle than long highway drives. Be on the lookout for loose, rusting, or damaged parts, and replace as necessary. Always have your exhaust system thoroughly inspected as part of a tune-up.

How Do the Electrical and Light Systems Work?

Electricity from the battery starts the car, and electricity generated as you drive keeps the lights, the radio, and other accessories working. The electrical system, including the light system, helps keep your vehicle running smoothly and safely (see **Figure 19.3**).

THE ELECTRICAL SYSTEM

The heart of your vehicle's electrical system is the battery. The **battery** stores electricity to start the car. After you turn the ignition key, the battery provides the power to start the engine. It also enables you to operate, for a short time, such equipment as your radio and lights when the engine is not running.

After the battery supplies the electricity to start the spark plugs firing, it helps produce power to operate the stereo, air-conditioning, and other systems.

Dealing with the UNEXPECTED

WORKING A SELF-SERVICE GAS PUMP

To operate a self-service gas pump, pull up to the pump that dispenses the kind of fuel your vehicle uses. If a sign says "Pay Cashier Before Pumping," the pumps will not operate until you pay. Otherwise, pump the amount you need, and pay when you are done.

▲ Open the fuel-filler door, and remove the gas cap.
▲ Take the pump nozzle off its cradle, and place the nozzle in the fuel-tank opening.
▲ Turn on the pump switch. It is usually located near the pump nozzle cradle.
▲ Squeeze the lever on the pump nozzle to begin pumping the fuel.
▲ If you have prepaid or when the tank is full, the pump will shut off automatically. Otherwise, release the lever, and put the nozzle back on its cradle. Turn off the pump switch. Then put the gas cap back on, and shut the fuel-filler door.

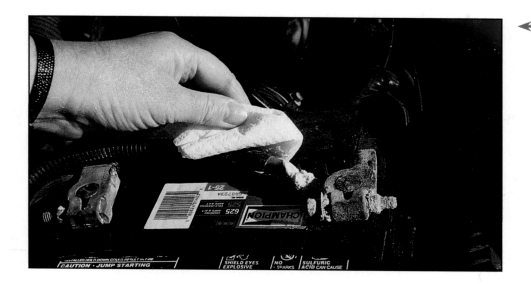

← – – – – – – ●

Keep battery terminals free of corrosion. *Why is this important?*

The **alternator** and generator, working together, provide a constant charge back to the battery when your engine is running. The **engine control module (ECM)** controls the electrical and other engine systems in many cars.

Electricity is powerful. To prevent electrical overloads and damage to delicate electronic components, the electrical system is equipped with safety devices called fuses, usually located in a clearly labeled pod or fuse box beneath the instrument panel or under the hood. When an electrical overload occurs, a fuse blows as a safety measure. If a fuse blows, it must be replaced before that part of the electrical system will work again.

THE LIGHT SYSTEM

Your vehicle's light system is the part of the electrical system that enables you to see and be seen as you are driving.

Exterior lights include headlights, taillights, side-marker lights, brake lights, signal lights, parking lights, and emergency flashers. Interior lights include the dome light on the inside roof of the vehicle and the various dashboard and warning lights that provide you with information about the vehicle or warn you of malfunctions.

MAINTAINING THE ELECTRICAL AND LIGHT SYSTEMS

The first step in maintaining the electrical and light systems is to keep your battery in top working condition. Keep the battery terminals free of corrosion and the battery cables firmly connected. Most current batteries are maintenance-free, but if you have an older one, check the fluid level at least once a month, and add distilled water when needed.

The engine control module or computer constantly monitors the electrical system. If it detects a problem, the "check engine" light on the instrument panel may come on.

Keep headlights clean and properly aligned. Even a thin layer of dirt can cut light output by as much as 90 percent. Misaligned lights can reduce your ability to see the roadway and can momentarily blind oncoming drivers.

Check exterior lights at least once a week, and promptly replace any burned-out bulbs.

> **FYI**
>
> If the "check engine" light comes on, make sure that the gas cap or lid is fully tightened to the point of at least one click or notch. The emission control equipment is so sensitive that it can detect if the cap is not correctly tightened and will cause the warning light to come on. You may or may not need the computer to reset it.

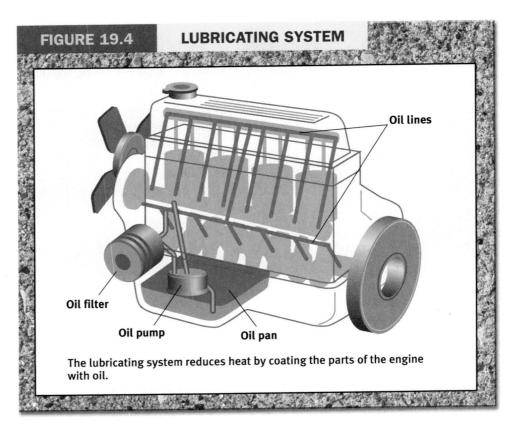

FIGURE 19.4 **LUBRICATING SYSTEM**

Oil lines

Oil filter

Oil pump

Oil pan

The lubricating system reduces heat by coating the parts of the engine with oil.

How Do the Lubricating and Cooling Systems Work?

When you lift the hood of your vehicle after it has been running for a while, you will feel a lot of heat from the engine. That is because the engine and other moving parts get hot as they work. The metal parts of your vehicle's engine move very rapidly, and they rub against each other, which produces friction and heat. The constant fuel–air explosions in all cylinders also create more heat. This explains why the engine temperature may exceed 4,000°F.

Too much heat can destroy your vehicle's engine. The lubricating and cooling systems are designed to keep that from happening by providing a system of circulating liquids that absorb, diffuse, and carry away engine heat.

THE LUBRICATING SYSTEM

Most engines are constantly lubricated by oil. Oil is the key lubricating element in your vehicle's lubricating system. The moving parts of your engine are continually bathed in oil, which absorbs some heat. Continually coating engine parts with oil reduces friction and wear. Oil also helps clean internal engine surfaces and prevents rust and corrosion (see **Figure 19.4**).

The lubricating system centers on an oil pump that moves oil from the oil pan under the engine, where it drains down to be stored, to all moving engine parts, and back again. An oil filter cleans the oil as it circulates over and over again.

In addition to oil, a thick grease is used to lubricate other moving parts of the vehicle, such as the steering system. Like oil, grease reduces friction and helps parts move smoothly. Grease is injected into appropriate places under your car during a tune-up or other service.

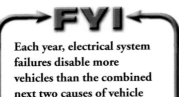

Each year, electrical system failures disable more vehicles than the combined next two causes of vehicle breakdowns.

THE COOLING SYSTEM

The cooling system keeps the engine from overheating by bathing the outside of the engine in a heat-absorbing liquid that is cooled in the radiator. The cooling system uses **coolant**, usually a mixture of water and antifreeze. Coolant is circulated around and through the engine by means of a network of pipes, channels, and connecting hoses (see **Figure 19.5**).

Much of your vehicle's coolant is stored in the radiator and in the radiator overflow tank. When you start the car, a water pump pumps the coolant through the radiator and all around the engine. Air from the moving vehicle and a fan force air through the **radiator** to cool the circulating coolant. A thermostat imbedded in the system controls the flow of the coolant in order to maintain the best operating temperature.

Cooling systems in old cars used water. **Antifreeze** is now used in cooling systems because it has a lower freezing point and higher boiling point than pure water. Without antifreeze, the water in the cooling system would freeze in very cold weather and could boil over in hot weather, especially in traffic jams and on long trips. Since frozen or boiling coolant does not circulate, this can cause the engine to overheat and stop working.

MAINTAINING THE LUBRICATING AND COOLING SYSTEMS

The fluids that lubricate and cool your car should be kept clean and filled up to the proper level.

Checking and changing the oil and oil filter regularly is the key to maintaining your vehicle's lubricating system. To check the actual level of oil, use the oil dipstick. The engine-oil level can only be checked after the engine has been turned off for some period of time, preferably an hour or more. This is necessary to give the oil time to drain back into the oil pan from throughout the engine. Checking it before that has happened will give you a false low

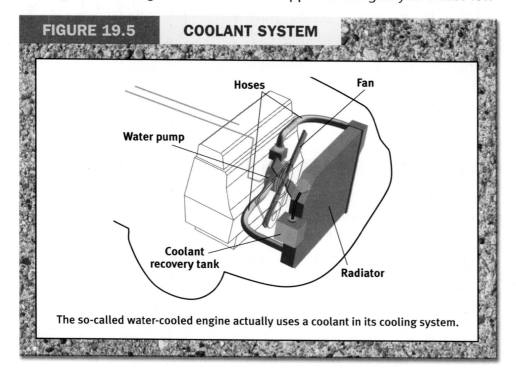

FIGURE 19.5   **COOLANT SYSTEM**

Hoses

Fan

Water pump

Coolant recovery tank

Radiator

The so-called water-cooled engine actually uses a coolant in its cooling system.

reading. Never drive your vehicle with insufficient oil: you could destroy the engine.

Low oil pressure allows the engine to become too hot, which may cause excessive wear of moving parts. Keep in mind that the oil-pressure gauge or warning light does not indicate how much oil is in the engine, but it will signal a drop in oil pressure.

Driving with an overheated engine due to cooling system problems can also damage your vehicle. If the temperature gauge or warning light indicates overheating, stop driving as soon as possible. Open the hood and let the engine cool before you look for the cause of the problem. If you are low on coolant, add some as soon as possible, but never attempt to remove the radiator cap on a hot engine: superheated coolant and steam can erupt from the radiator and cause severe burns. If your engine overheats from time to time, consider keeping some coolant in the vehicle.

To maintain the cooling system, use the proper coolant, and check the fluid level whenever the vehicle is serviced. Also check the fan belt and connecting hoses. Have the cooling system completely drained, flushed, and refilled every 2 years.

You can learn to use a dipstick to check whether or not your vehicle needs more oil. **When is a good time to check your oil level?**

? WHAT WOULD YOU DO?
You've been stuck in bumper-to-bumper traffic for nearly an hour on a hot summer day. The temperature warning light has just come on. How will you handle this situation? What safety precautions will you take?

Lesson 2 Review

❶ Why is it important to keep the fuel and exhaust systems of your vehicle in good condition?

❷ Explain how your vehicle uses electricity, and name the source of electrical power in your vehicle and how to maintain this system.

❸ What do the lubricating and cooling systems do, and how should they be maintained?

LESSON 3

Suspension, Steering, Brakes, and Tires

Your safety and comfort in a vehicle depend not only on how well you drive but also on how your vehicle handles. To protect yourself and others, make sure your vehicle's suspension, steering, and brake systems as well as all four tires are in good operating condition.

What Vehicle Systems Are Important for Comfort and Safety?

The suspension system, steering system, brake system, and tires all contribute to giving you control over your vehicle and to provide a comfortable ride.

THE SUSPENSION SYSTEM

The suspension system supports the weight of the vehicle, cushions the ride, and helps keep the vehicle stable when you drive over bumps or uneven roadway surfaces. Heavy metal springs and shock absorbers help keep the vehicle level during changes in the surface of the road (see **Figure 19.6**).

The springs soften the impact of bumps in the roadway. If your vehicle had only springs, however, it would continue bouncing after hitting a bump. This bouncing would reduce the contact between the tires and the road and make it harder for you to control the vehicle.

The **shock absorbers**—or shocks, as they are commonly called—work to control bouncing. By absorbing the shocks of driving, the up and down movements of tires meeting variations in the road, shock absorbers make the ride smoother and help you maintain steering and braking control.

Most vehicles today use suspensions—especially in the front of the vehicle—where the spring and shock absorber are contained in one unit called a **strut**.

THE STEERING SYSTEM

The steering system enables you to turn the front wheels. The steering wheel is at one end of a steering shaft. At the other end of the shaft, movable rods swing back and forth to change the direction of both front wheels at the same time.

For the comfort and safety of the driver and passengers in the vehicle, front wheels are designed to remain in an upright position and move up and down over bumps, even when they are turned.

OBJECTIVES

1. **Identify** four vehicle systems that are important for comfort and safety.
2. **Describe** warning signs of possible problems with the suspension, steering, or tires.

KEY TERMS

- **shock absorber**
- **strut**
- **hydraulic pressure**
- **disc brake**
- **drum brake**
- **tread**

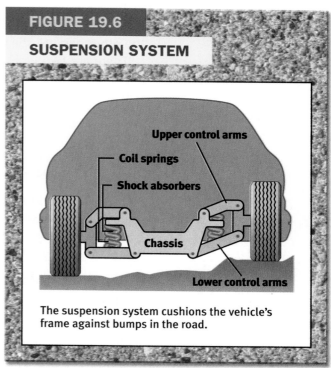

FIGURE 19.6

SUSPENSION SYSTEM

Upper control arms
Coil springs
Shock absorbers
Chassis
Lower control arms

The suspension system cushions the vehicle's frame against bumps in the road.

AVOIDING SUSPENSION AND STEERING PROBLEMS

Most problems affecting the suspension and steering system develop gradually as a result of wear. Watch for the following warning signs:

- There is too much play (free movement) in the steering wheel. With rack-and-pinion power steering, there should be virtually no play in the wheel. In a manual system, there should be no more than 2 inches of play.
- The steering wheel vibrates or is difficult to turn.
- The front end of the vehicle wobbles or shimmies.
- The vehicle bumps as you turn the wheel while driving on a smooth road.
- The vehicle pulls to one side as you drive.
- The vehicle bounces too much after hitting a bump.
- Tread wear on the front tires is uneven.

Have a mechanic check the vehicle if any warning signs of suspension or brake problems appear. **Why is this important?**

Have a mechanic check your vehicle if any of those warning signs appear. The front end of your vehicle may need to be aligned or some other problem may need to be corrected.

THE BRAKING SYSTEM

Brakes slow or stop a vehicle by **hydraulic pressure**—force created by pressurizing a liquid. The liquid is brake fluid, which is stored in the master brake cylinder. When you press the brake pedal, the pressure that builds up creates a stopping pressure on all four wheels. Stepping on the brake pedal forces brake fluid from the master brake cylinder through the brake-fluid lines to the wheel cylinders. The wheel cylinders activate the brakes, which stop the car by pulling against the moving wheels using friction (see **Figure 19.7**).

To minimize the risk of brake failure, brake systems are designed so that front and rear brakes are controlled independently. If one pair of brakes fails, the other pair will still work to stop the vehicle.

There are two types of brakes: disc brakes and drum brakes. Power brakes and antilock brakes are options that are common on new cars. All vehicles are equipped with parking brakes, which is a separate braking system.

Disc brakes. All new vehicles now have **disc brakes** on the front wheels. Many have them on the rear wheels as well. In a disc brake, pressure squeezes the brake pads against a flat metal wheel disc, producing the friction needed to stop the wheel from turning.

Drum brakes. In a **drum brake**, the fluid pressure causes the brake shoes to push out against the brake lining. The lining then presses against the round hollow metal drum spinning as part of the wheel. Friction slows and stops the wheel's turning motion.

Power brakes. Most new vehicles now also have power brakes, which require less pressure on the brake pedal than older nonpower systems. Power brakes take less foot pressure to use. They do not, however, shorten a vehicle's stopping distance. They have the disadvantage of fading when your engine suddenly stops running, which does not happen with nonpower brakes.

Antilock brakes. Many newer vehicles also have an antilock brake system (ABS), which is designed to keep the wheels from locking when the driver presses too hard on the brake pedal in an emergency. Since the wheels do not lock, the driver can continue to steer the vehicle without skidding. Antilock brakes do not shorten the stopping distance of a vehicle.

Parking brake. A parking brake is a mechanically operated brake that is separate from the hydraulic brake system. The driver can operate this with either a lever or a foot pedal. Attached by cable to the rear wheels, it is mostly used to prevent a parked vehicle from rolling.

AVOIDING BRAKE PROBLEMS

Neglecting a problem with the brake system can have fatal consequences. If your vehicle isn't stopping properly, or if you feel something is beginning to go wrong, check with a mechanic. See Chapter 15 for a description of brake failure.

THE TIRES

A driver's traction on the road depends largely on the condition of the tires. Good tires help you steer and stop safely. Surprisingly, more than 40 percent of nearly 250,000 vehicles inspected over a 10-year period had defective tires. All four tires should be in good condition, properly inflated, with an adequate amount of tread.

Tire inflation. Tires are filled with pressurized air. Tires must be inflated at the right density to provide maximum traction and control. Tire pressure is measured in pounds per square inch, or PSI. Most air-pressure machines at service stations and car washes have gauges that allow you to check the air pressure level as you inflate the tires.

To find the recommended maximum air pressure levels for your vehicle's tires, check your owner's manual or look for a sticker that may be affixed to a doorpost or inside the fuel filler door. Usually two tire pressures are listed—one for normal and a higher number for long trips or when carrying heavy loads. The lower number may result in a softer ride but will likely mean lower tread life. The higher number will improve both handling and wear at the cost of some ride quality. Tires also have a recommended air pressure listed on them, but this may be different than your owner's manual recommends. If there is a conflict, go with what the vehicle manufacturer recommends. Some manufacturers recommend different pressures for the front and rear tires.

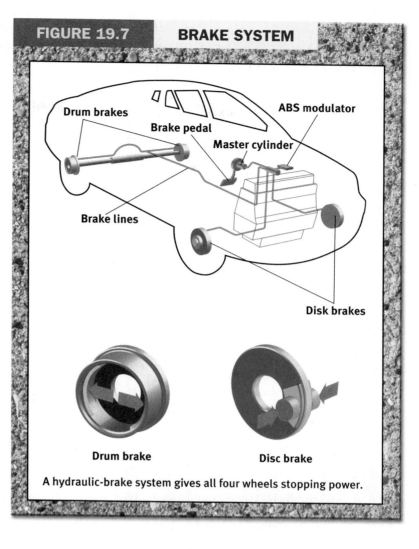

FIGURE 19.7   BRAKE SYSTEM

Drum brakes
Brake pedal
ABS modulator
Master cylinder
Brake lines
Disk brakes

Drum brake   Disc brake

A hydraulic-brake system gives all four wheels stopping power.

SAFETY TIP

You can check for sufficient tread depth by inserting a quarter in the tread. It should at least come to the top of Washington's head. If there is less tread than this, the tire will not function safely in even a light rain.

Charles A. Butler

President, National Driving Solutions
Orlando, FL

How well you manage risk is determined by what you do before you start driving. Make sure all vehicle-system devices are working properly. At least once a month, check fluid levels, belts and hoses, and connections. Service your vehicle according to the kind and amount of driving you do and manufacturer recommendations. Good risk managers always make predriving vehicle-systems checks.

Why are predriving vehicle-system checks important?

Tire tread. The grooved outer surface of a tire is called the **tread**. The tread is the part of the tire that interfaces with the road, and it wears down over time. When there is no visible tread remaining on the tire, the tire is called "bald." It's very dangerous to drive on bald or nearly bald tires.

Tires should be rotated because front tires generally wear faster than rear tires. To equalize tire wear, have your vehicle's tires rotated about every 5,000 to 7,500 miles. Rotating tires means switching their position from front to rear and sometimes from one side to the other. Check your owner's manual for the recommended tire-rotation pattern.

When new tires are put on the car, they need to be balanced. Balancing helps ensure that weight is evenly distributed as the wheel turns. Balanced tires provide better steering control, a smoother ride, and longer tire life.

AVOIDING TIRE PROBLEMS

Check the inflation of your tires periodically, and keep them up to recommended levels. Get in the habit of inspecting your tires regularly before you drive. Watch for the following warning signs of tire troubles: tread wear bars appear, indicating less than $1/16$ inch tread; areas of little or no tread ("bald" spots); uneven wear; bulges anywhere on the tire; embedded nails, glass, or metal; and frequent pressure loss in one particular tire, suggesting a slow leak.

? WHAT WOULD YOU DO?
You just test drove this car. As you stepped on the brake, the car pulled to the right. What could cause this problem? Would you buy this car?

Lesson 3 Review

❶ How are the steering, suspension, brakes, and tires important to your safety?

❷ What are some warning signs that indicate tire problems?

❸ What are the different types of braking systems?

Child Safety Seats

While safety belts are appropriate for adults, they are not adequate for young children. Depending upon the size of the child, seating restraints are necessary.

How Can You Restrain Children Until Age Four?

All 50 states have laws that require children, at least up to age four, to be properly secured in safety-tested and safety-approved child safety seats. Rear-facing infant seats are designed for infants, usually from birth to 20 to 22 pounds (see **Figure 19.8A**). After a baby has outgrown the infant seat, less than one year old but weighing more than 20 pounds, a convertible child safety seat should be used to secure the baby (see **Figure 19.8B**).

Babies should be kept facing the rear until they are at least 20 pounds *and* one year old. The best practice is to leave them facing the rear until they reach the upper weight limits of the rear-facing child safety seat. A rear-facing child safety seat should never be placed in front of an airbag, which could cause serious injury or even death if deployed.

Children over one year old and weighing more than 20 pounds should be properly secured in a forward-facing approved toddler seat (see **Figure 19.8C** on page 410). Most child safety seat harnesses have a weight limit up to 40 pounds and are unsafe for use with children who weigh more.

OBJECTIVES
1. **Identify** the child safety seats.
2. **Describe** the age and/or weight limitations for each type of child safety seat.

FIGURES 19.8A–B

A. Children who are under one year old and who weigh less than 20 pounds must ride in a rear-facing seat.

B. Children who are under one year old and who weigh more than 20 pounds ride in a convertible child safety seat.

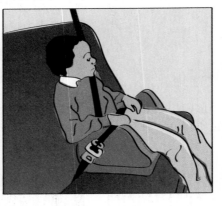

C. Children who are over one year old and who weigh more than 20 pounds ride in forward-facing safety seats.

D. Children who are over one year old and who weigh more than 40 pounds ride in booster seats.

How Can You Protect Children Who Have Outgrown the Safety Seat?

Seat belts are not designed for children. Young children are too small for seat belts and too large for toddler seats. A booster seat raises your child up so that the seat belt fits correctly and can better protect your child (see **Figure 19.8D**). The shoulder belt should cross the child's collarbone and rest snugly on the shoulder and chest, and the lap belt should rest low across the pelvis or hip area—never across the stomach area. A child's ears shouldn't be higher than the vehicle's seat back cushion or the back of a high-back booster seat. Children are also safest in the vehicle's back seat. They should sit in the back seat until the age of 13 whenever possible.

How Should a Safety Belt Fit an Older Child?

The child must be tall enough to sit without slouching, with knees bent at the edge of the seat, with feet on the floor. The lap belt must fit low and tight across the upper thighs. The shoulder belt should rest over the shoulder and across the chest. Never put the shoulder belt under the arm or behind the child's back. The adult lap and shoulder belt system alone will not fit most children until they are at least 4'9" tall and weigh about 80 pounds.

Lesson 4 Review

❶ What are the age and/or weight limitations for the various types of child passenger seats?

❷ How can you protect children who have outgrown their safety seat?

❸ How should a safety belt fit an older child?

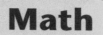
GRAPHING BRAKING DISTANCES

After you apply the brakes, the distance it takes to come to a stop depends in part on the speed at which your vehicle is moving.

The formula for computing braking distance is:

$D = S \times \frac{1}{10}S \div 2.4$

where S = speed, and D = distance in feet.

Here is how you would figure braking distance at 35 mph.

$D = 35 \times (\frac{1}{10} \times 35) \div 2.4$

$D = 35 \times 3.5 \div 2.4$

$D = 51.04$

Thus, braking distance at 35 mph is 51.04 feet, or a little more than 17 yards. Make a graph to show how braking distance changes in relation to speed.

TRY IT YOURSELF

❶ First, use the formula to figure the stopping distance for these speeds: 20 mph, 30 mph, 40 mph, 50 mph, 60 mph.

❷ On a sheet of graph paper, write the speeds along the bottom of the graph at regular intervals, as shown below.

❸ On the left side of the graph, write distances in regular intervals, as shown below.

❹ For each distance you figure, put a dot at the appropriate place on your graph.

❺ Finally, draw a line from the first dot to the second, from the second to the third, and so on, beginning with the dot at the shortest braking distance.

What conclusion can you draw from your graph?

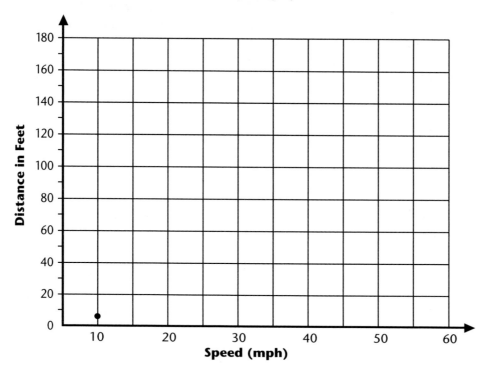

Key Points

Lesson 1

1 At least once a month, before entering your vehicle, check fluid levels, belts and hoses, and connections. (Page 394)

2 After starting the engine, check gauges and warning lights, and test your brakes and horn. (Page 395–396)

3 Service your vehicle according to the kind and amount of driving and manufacturer recommendations. Regularly check and change the oil, check the transmission fluid, and change filters. (Page 396–397)

WHAT WOULD YOU DO?
A friend has agreed to let you use her car while she's on vacation. What checks will you make before getting into her car? What checks will you make after starting the engine?

Lesson 2

1 The fuel pump forces fuel from the tank to the fuel-injection system to mix with air. The vapor is ignited in the cylinders. Unburned engine gases exit through the tailpipe. Replace filters as needed. Have your exhaust system inspected at least twice a year. (Page 398–400)

2 The battery is the source of electrical power. Keep headlights clean and aligned, and replace any burned-out bulbs. (Page 400–401)

3 Lubricating and cooling systems keep heat from destroying the engine by sending oil to moving engine parts. A mixture of fluid and antifreeze cools the engine. Change oil and oil filters regularly. Use coolant, and check the fluid level when the vehicle is serviced. (Page 402–404)

Lesson 3

1 The suspension supports a vehicle's weight, cushions the ride, and stabilizes the vehicle; the steering system enables the front wheels to turn; brakes stop the vehicle; tires help it grip the road. (Page 405–406)

2 Warnings of possible suspension problems include too much play in the wheel, front-end wobble, and pulling to one side. (Page 406)

WHAT WOULD YOU DO?
You just test drove this car. As you stepped on the brake, the car pulled to the right. What could cause this problem? Would you buy this car?

Lesson 4

1 Rear-facing infant seats are for infants from birth to 20 to 22 pounds. Convertible child safety seats are for babies under one year old but larger than 20 pounds. Forward-facing toddler seats are for one-year-olds weighing more than 20 pounds and less than 40 pounds. Booster seats are for children too big for toddler seats and too small for seat belts. (Page 409–410)

On a separate sheet of paper, write the letter of the answer that best completes each sentence.

1 A catalytic converter is part of a vehicle's
   a. transmission.
   b. exhaust system.
   c. fuel system.

2 You should check your engine oil
   a. while your engine is running.
   b. before starting your engine.
   c. every 12,000 miles.

3 Springs and shock absorbers are parts of a vehicle's
   a. transmission.
   b. front-end alignment.
   c. suspension system.

4 When you step on your brake pedal, you should feel
   a. firm resistance.
   b. no resistance.
   c. the floor.

5 A toddler seat should be used for children who weigh
   a. less than 20 pounds.
   b. between 20 and 40 pounds.
   c. more than 40 pounds.

6 You should rotate your vehicle's tires to
   a. equalize tire wear.
   b. increase fuel efficiency.
   c. improve suspension.

On a separate sheet of paper, write the word or phrase that best completes each sentence.

muffler   electrical system

hydraulic pressure   power train

7 The parts of a vehicle that transmit the engine's power to the wheels make up the _____.

8 The heart of a vehicle's _____ is called the battery.

9 Brakes slow or stop a vehicle by applying _____ against the four wheels.

10 The pipes that make up the exhaust manifold collect unburned gases from the engine and carry them to the _____.

Writing

Driver's Log

In this chapter, you have learned how the systems that operate a vehicle function and what the maintenance requirements of these systems are. Based on your observations, do most drivers pay attention to these maintenance requirements? Write a paragraph about what you would tell those who do not.

Projects

❶ In an owner's manual, find the sections that deal with the vehicle systems discussed in this chapter. What information does the manual provide that applies specifically to the particular make and model vehicle? In what other ways does the manual help the owner maintain the vehicle?

❷ Research and report on the various types of tires, including summer, all-season, and winter or snow tires. What are the advantages and limitations of each? Where should you put two new tires or snow tires on a vehicle with front-wheel drive?

This review tests your knowledge of the material in Chapters 16–19, and will help you review for your state driving test. On a separate sheet of paper, select the answer that best completes each statement.

1. Impaired driving can be the result of
   a. wearing prescription sunglasses.
   b. using and abusing drugs or alcohol.
   c. making a quick change in direction.

2. Being fatigued when you drive may cause you to
   a. miss critical information.
   b. be more mindful of driving rules.
   c. drive late at night.

3. To avoid being impaired by carbon monoxide poisoning,
   a. turn on the air-conditioning system.
   b. maintain your car's exhaust system.
   c. refrain from taking prescription medications

4. If you have a chronic disease, you should
   a. secure your doctor's permission to drive if you take certain medications.
   b. drive only during the daylight hours.
   c. drive no more than 25 miles at a time.

5. Aggressive driving behaviors
   a. only affect people who have had too many driving citations.
   b. can become criminal acts when directed toward other drivers.
   c. do not usually affect people who drive on heavily traveled roadways.

6. You can avoid being an aggressive driver by
   a. practicing common courtesies such as keeping a safe distance from the vehicles ahead.
   b. playing the music loudly so you will not be distracted by other drivers.
   c. using your horn and lights when another driver gets too close to you.

7. The best way to control your emotions when you drive is to
   a. expect other drivers to always drive as safely as you drive.
   b. always drive with confidence.
   c. get into the habit of always using safe-driving procedures.

8. Young drivers are at a greater risk when
   a. they have other young passengers in the vehicle with them.
   b. their level of concern for risks and road hazards is greater.
   c. they park their vehicles beside the vehicles of other teen drivers.

9. If you have been drinking alcohol, your driving ability is affected in that
   a. your chances of dying in a crash are decreased because your body is limber.
   b. your BAC is raised only when you consume alcohol on an empty stomach.
   c. your ability to process information and make critical decisions is impaired.

10. If you take a medication, be aware that
    a. only over-the-counter drugs have no adverse affects that will impair your driving ability.
    b. some prescription drugs may make you drowsy and therefore impair your driving ability.
    c. depressant drugs are used to lessen stress and anxiety and therefore will not impair your driving ability.

11. To be sure your vehicle is in good running order,
    a. check the fluid levels, belts, hoses, and wires periodically.
    b. check the engine oil while the engine is running.
    c. have a mechanic check your vehicle only when a warning light flashes.

12. You can keep your vehicle's engine running smoothly by
    a. changing the oil every time you add fuel to the fuel tank.
    b. changing the oil and oil filter regularly, according to the maintenance manual.
    c. washing the dirt and grime from the engine periodically.

13 When your vehicle's fuel and exhaust system work properly, your vehicle is able to
a. clear the air as the engine runs.
b. pump the fuel into the air filter properly.
c. minimize air pollution.

14 When your vehicle's electrical system is in good working order,
a. the fuses keep the battery charged.
b. the battery produces the power to start the engine and to operate the other systems of your car.
c. the "check engine" light shows that the engine is running properly.

15 You must make sure that your vehicle's lubricating and cooling systems work properly so that
a. the metal parts of your vehicle's engine will not rub against each other and overheat.
b. your vehicle's system of circulating liquids can help absorb, diffuse, and carry away the excess engine heat.
c. your vehicle's heating and air-conditioning system will keep you comfortable.

16 To control your vehicle more easily on a rough road surface, make sure that
a. the tread wear on the back tires is uneven but even on the front tires.
b. you have at least 2 inches of play in the steering wheel.
c. your vehicle's suspension system is in good condition.

17 The best way to overcome fatigue when driving is to
a. listen to soothing music.
b. continue driving so you can get to your destination more quickly.
c. get out of the car and walk or jog for a few minutes.

18 If you have a temporary injury,
a. secure a driving permit.
b. drive normally without focusing on your injury.
c. allow extra time to get to your destination.

19 Drivers can compensate for declining physical conditions by
a. wearing sunglasses and hearing aids.
b. using rearview and sideview mirrors to search the roadways for traffic.
c. driving vehicles equipped with special lighting features.

20 A psychological impairment that may affect your driving ability may be caused by
a. a distraction such as talking on a cell phone or to another passenger.
b. the inability to hear approaching road traffic.
c. a malfunctioning traffic signal.

Challenge Question

After two hours, a person who consumes alcoholic beverages at the rate of one drink per hour is most likely to have a lower blood alcohol concentration if he or she
a. waits at least three hours after drinking before driving.
b. chooses to drink beer rather than whiskey.
c. drinks black coffee and exercises after drinking.

GLOSSARY

A

acceleration An increase in speed.

accelerator pedal The gas pedal; controls speed by adjusting the flow of gasoline to the engine.

active safety device A safety feature that requires driver and passenger to take action to protect themselves.

adhesion Sticking together; in automotive terms, traction or friction.

administrative laws Laws that regulate driver licensing, vehicle registration, financial responsibility of drivers and vehicle owners, or minimum equipment and vehicle standards.

advisory speed limit A speed limit that interrupts normal driving speed for a limited time and provides guidelines for adjusting speed.

aggressive driving A combination of dangerous acts committed while driving.

air bag A safety bag that automatically inflates upon impact in a collision.

alternator A generator that produces the electricity needed to run a vehicle and its electrical devices.

angle parking Parking so that a vehicle is positioned at a 30- to 90-degree angle with a curb or other boundary.

antifreeze A substance with a low freezing point, usually added to the liquid in a vehicle's radiator to prevent freezing.

antilock brake system (ABS) A braking system that is designed to keep a vehicle's wheels from locking when the driver brakes abruptly.

antitheft device Any device used to protect a vehicle from being stolen or entered.

assumption Events you assume might happen.

B

balance Balance is controlled by the inner ear. It helps make you aware of your movement as well as the vehicle's movements.

banked curve A curve that slopes up from the inside edge.

battery A unit that stores an electrical charge and furnishes current.

blind spot An area outside a vehicle that is not visible to the driver in the rearview or sideview mirrors.

Blood Alcohol Concentration (BAC) The percentage of alcohol in a person's blood.

blowout A sudden loss of air pressure in a tire.

blowout skid A skid occurring when a tire suddenly loses air pressure.

brake pedal A pedal that enables a driver to slow or stop a vehicle.

braking skid A skid caused when the brakes are applied so hard that one or more wheels lock.

C

carbon monoxide A colorless, odorless, highly poisonous gas; a by-product of burning fuel.

catalytic converter An antipollution device, part of the exhaust system, that reduces harmful emissions.

center of gravity The point around which all the weight of an object is evenly distributed.

central vision The 3-percent cone at the center of your focus. Focusing on objects is done with the help of central vision.

centrifugal force The force that tends to push a moving object out of a curve and into a straight path.

choice A choice is the selection between two or more possible options.

cloverleaf interchange The classic cloverleaf interchange looks like a four-leaf clover from above.

clutch In a vehicle with a manual transmission, a device that engages and disengages the engine and is connected to the drive shaft; the pedal by which the device is operated.

clutch pedal A car with a manual transmission has a clutch pedal, a third foot pedal located to the left of the brake pedal.

collision A crash; the result of one object hitting another with sudden force.

color vision A crucial aspect in traffic safety is color vision. Color vision is the ability to see colors.

commentary driving Commentary driving is "saying" aloud what you sense in real-world traffic situations.

comparison When determining your options, you make comparisons of the information you have.

compensate To make allowances, as in compensating while driving impaired with a cold or the flu.

controlled-access expressway See limited-access expressway.

coolant A liquid added to a motor vehicle's radiator to reduce heat.

cornering skid A skid on a turn or curve.

cost Costs are measured in dollars and lives.

cost-benefit ratio The way you weigh the benefits you receive from driving versus what driving a vehicle actually costs.

crash When a motor vehicle hits another motor vehicle, a pedestrian, an animal, a bicyclist, or a fixed object, this is called a crash.

crowned road A road that is higher in the center than at either edge.

cruise control A vehicle feature that allows a driver to maintain a desired speed without manually pressing the accelerator; intended for highway driving.

customs are behaviors that satisfy people's needs for comfortably interacting with one another.

—————————— D ——————————

deceleration A decrease in speed.

defroster A heating unit that clears moisture from the inside of the front and/or rear windows and ice from the outside surfaces.

depth perception Vision that gives objects their three-dimensional appearance and that enables a person to judge the relative distance between two objects.

depressants Depressants are drugs that slow down, or depress, the central nervous system.

diamond interchange The basic diamond interchange is often chosen for lower-traffic interchanges without special constraints.

directional control The ability of a motor vehicle to hold to a straight line.

directional signal A device that allows drivers to communicate their intentions to move right or left by means of a blinking light; an arm or a hand signal.

disc brake A brake in which pressure squeezes the brake pads against a flat metal wheel disc, producing the friction needed to stop the wheel from turning.

disease A condition of not being at ease.

distance vision The ability to see in the distance.

distraction Any thing or situation that draws your mind off the task at hand.

downshift To shift to a lower gear from a higher one.

driver evaluation facility A special center where individuals with physical disabilities undergo a comprehensive medical assessment to determine their potential to drive.

drum brake A brake in which fluid pressure causes the brake shoes to push against the brake lining, which then presses against the round hollow metal drum inside the wheel. This creates friction, which slows and stops the wheel's turning motion.

duration The length of time you engage in a specific task.

dynamic vision Visually interpreting something that is in motion.

—————————— E ——————————

emergency flashers A signaling device that makes all four turn signals flash at once; used to warn other drivers that a vehicle has stopped or is moving slowly.

engine control module (ECM) Controls electrical and other engine systems in many cars.

entrance ramp Where you enter the freeway.

exhaust manifold Metal pipes that collect unburned gases as they come from the engine and carry those gases to the muffler.

—————————— F ——————————

fatigue Weariness resulting from too much physical or mental exertion.

fixed speed limit A posted speed limit that cannot legally be exceeded.

flashing traffic signal A signal providing information on whether you should stop, slow down or go, depending on the color of the light.

following interval The safe amount of time you should allow when following another vehicle or when being followed.

friction Resistance to motion between two objects when they touch.

friction point The point at which the clutch pedal and other parts of the power train begin to work together as the driver releases the clutch pedal.

frustration A feeling of disappointment, exasperation, or weariness caused by aims being thwarted or desires unsatisfied.

—————————— G ——————————

gear selector lever The lever in a vehicle with an automatic transmission that allows the driver to choose a gear.

giving meaning Giving meaning is a mental process that has to do with understanding what you perceive. It relies heavily on sensing.

glare recovery The ability of your eyes to quickly adjust from headlights back to the dark.

glare vision The ability to see when there is a rapid increase in light.

gravity The invisible force that pulls all objects on Earth toward its center.

grip A tire's ability to change the speed or direction of the vehicle.

ground viewing Searching beneath parked vehicles and other objects for signs of movement.

guide sign A sign, including a route marker or destination, mileage, recreational area, or roadside service sign, used to guide and direct drivers.

H

hand-over-hand steering A steering method in which the driver's hands cross when turning.

hallucinogens Mind altering drugs that change the way a person thinks, sees, and acts, all of which impair driving ability.

head restraint A safety device attached to the back of the seat that is designed to prevent injury to the head and neck.

hearing The ability to hear or listen to sounds.

high-occupancy-vehicle (HOV) sign A lane reserved for use by vehicles having two or more occupants.

highway transportation system (HTS) A system made up of roadways, motor vehicles, and people.

human-perception time The total time needed for a human being to think about an option and choose one.

hydraulic pressure The pressure created by a liquid being forced through an opening or tube.

hydroplaning Skimming on top of a film of water.

I

idle To operate the engine without engaging the gears or applying pressure on the accelerator.

ignition switch A switch, usually found on the steering column but sometimes located on the dashboard to the right of the steering wheel, that starts the car's engine.

illegal per se law A rule making it unlawful for a person to operate a motor vehicle with a blood alcohol concentration (BAC) above a certain level.

implied consent A law stating that any licensed driver charged with driving under the influence or while intoxicated cannot legally refuse to be tested for blood-alcohol concentration.

inattention The lack of paying attention, or the inability to focus on some relevant action.

inertia The tendency of an object in motion to stay in motion and for an object at rest to stay at rest.

interchange A point at which a driver can enter or exit an expressway or connect with a highway going in another direction.

international sign A road sign that conveys meaning through symbols, not words.

intersection The place where two or more roadways cross.

J

jaywalking The pedestrian practice of crossing a roadway without regard for traffic rules or signals.

judgment call A situation in which the driver should size up the situation and then use good judgment.

jump-start To attach a vehicle's dead battery by cables to a charged battery to start the vehicle.

K

kinetic energy The energy of motion.

L

lane-use light An electronic signal mounted above a reversible lane that indicates whether the lane can or cannot be used at a particular time.

limited-access expressway An expressway that has fixed points of entry and exit.

M

margin of safety Areas of roadway large enough to allow you the space, time, and visibility needed for safe movement at anytime.

merging traffic Traffic that is entering an expressway.

mobility The ability to move or be moved.

momentum The energy of motion; the product of weight and speed.

muffler A device in the exhaust system that reduces engine noise.

N

narcotics Narcotics have a strong depressant effect and create a euphoria that can quickly become a serious addiction.

night vision The ability to see in low and variable light conditions.

norm Rules or normal standards of behavior that govern how people behave in different situations.

O

odometer A device that measures distance traveled by a vehicle; its gauge.

option A potential choice.

over-the-counter drugs Drugs that can be purchased legally in drugstores and supermarkets with a doctor's prescription.

overdriving one's headlights Driving so fast at night that the driver is unable to stop within the range of the headlights.

P

parallel parking Parking parallel and close to the edge of the road.

parking brake The brake that holds the rear wheels. It is used to keep a parked vehicle from moving.

passive safety device A device, such as an air bag or head restraint, that functions without the user having to operate it.

pedestrian signal A signal at busy intersections using words or signals to tell pedestrians, or people on foot, how to proceed.

peer pressure The influence of friends who are in your age group.

peripheral vision The area of vision to the left and right of the area of central vision.

perpendicular parking Parking so that a vehicle forms a 90-degree angle with a curb or line.

pitch The forward/backward movement of the car.

point system A system used to keep track of traffic violations by individual drivers.

potential immediate crash zone The area directly in front and to the rear of your vehicle that will likely cause you to crash when a potential hazard becomes a real hazard.

power brakes Brakes that make it easier to slow or stop without intense foot pressure on the brake pedal.

power skid A skid caused when the accelerator is pressed too hard and suddenly.

power train The parts of a motor vehicle that transmit power from the engine to the wheels; the engine, transmission, and clutch.

prescription drugs Drugs you can purchase at a pharmacy or drugstore after receiving a doctor's prescription.

push-pull-feed steering A steering method in which the driver's hands do not cross even when changing lanes or turning.

R

radiator A cooling device that air-cools liquid pumped from the engine.

rate of acceleration The time it takes to speed up from a stop or from one speed to a higher one.

rate of deceleration The time it takes to slow down from one speed to a lower one or to a stop.

recovery time A break from activity that created fatigue.

regulatory sign A sign that controls the flow of traffic.

repetition The number of times an activity is repeated.

response zone The zone where you begin to respond to what you perceive.

reversible lane A lane on which the direction of traffic changes at certain times of day.

revoke To cancel a person's license to drive a vehicle, usually for the period of a year or more, after which time the driver can apply for another license.

right-of-way The right of one roadway user to go first or to cross in front of another; right-of-way must be yielded to others in many situations.

risk The chance of injury to oneself or others and of damage to vehicles and property.

road rage A criminal act directed against another person through physical violence while driving.

roll The feeling that occurs after a vehicle goes through a left-right combination turn on a corner.

roundabout A traffic circle used to control traffic through certain intersections; traffic is routed in one direction around a circle and drivers exit where they like.

S

scanning Picking up bits of information quickly, with glances and quick looks.

searching focusing and looking at everything in the driving environment.

shared left-turn lane A lane that drivers moving in either direction use to make a left turn.

shock absorber A device that cushions a vehicle's frame against the impact of bumps in the road.

skid A driver's loss of control over the direction in which the vehicle is moving.

sound Noise you hear such as sirens from emergency vehicles alerting you to pull over.

space The distance between your vehicle and other vehicles or highway users.

space cushion A safe space margin.

space margin The amount of space that should be allowed in front of, behind, and to both sides of a vehicle.

speedometer A device that measures the speed of a vehicle in miles per hour or kilometers per hour; its gauge.

sport utility vehicle (SUV) A vehicle designed for a variety of uses, usually incorporating four- or all-wheel drive, and featuring increased ground clearance and a cargo area included within the interior.

stall A sudden stop of a vehicle's engine.

static vision Interpreting something that is not in motion.

steering system The system that enables a driver to turn a vehicle's front wheels.

steering wheel The steering wheel controls the direction of the car.

stick shift When operating a manual transmission, the stick shift enables you to manually move the gearshift from place to place.

stimulants Drugs that speed up, or stimulate, the central nervous system.

strut A suspension unit that contains both a spring and a shock absorber.

suspend To take away a person's driver's license for a specified period of time, usually 30 to 90 days.

synergism The interaction of one drug with another to enhance the effect of one or both.

T

T-intersection An intersection where one road ends and forms a "T" with a crossroad.

tailgate To drive too closely behind another vehicle.

three-point turn A turnabout made by turning left, backing to the right, then moving forward.

threshold braking A braking technique in which the driver firmly presses the brake pedal to a point just before the wheels lock.

time The ability to judge your speed and the speed of other vehicles and highway users. Time can also refer to how long it will take your vehicle or another vehicle to stop or intersect paths.

total stopping distance The distance covered by a vehicle from the perception distance to the moment that the vehicle comes to a stop.

tracking Steering; keeping a vehicle steadily and smoothly on a desired course.

traction The friction between a vehicle's tires and the road surface.

traffic control signal An electronic signal, such as a colored light, used to keep traffic moving in an orderly manner.

transmission The gears and related parts that carry power from the engine to the driving axle.

tread The outer surface of a tire, with its pattern of grooves and ridges.

trumpet interchange The point where one road loops off either to the right or left to join another roadway.

tune-up Replacing a number of parts in the ignition system and making several ignition and fuel adjustments to ensure that the engine runs properly.

turnabout Any turning maneuver by which a driver moves a vehicle to face in the opposite direction.

two-point turn A turnabout made by first backing or heading into a driveway or alley and then heading or backing into the street.

U

U-turn A turnabout carried out by making a U-shaped left turn.

V

vehicle-reaction time The time it takes a vehicle to respond.

vehicular homicide Reckless driving causing the death of another person.

vibration Shaking that the driver can sense.

visibility The distance and area a driver can see and the ability of a vehicle or pedestrian to be seen.

visual acuity The ability to see clearly.

visual control zone The zone where you identify objects/conditions that may require a response or continuous attention.

visual lead The distance you can see ahead of your vehicle.

W

warning sign A sign that alerts drivers to potential dangers or conditions ahead.

Y

yaw The spinning action resulting from the back tire sliding sideways toward the front tire.

Photo Credits

2–3: David Young-Wolff/PhotoEdit; 4–5: Tim Fuller Photography; 6, 9: The Terry Wild Studio; 12: Tim Fuller Photography; 13: Tony Freeman/PhotoEdit; 14: Superstock; 15: Tim Fuller Photography; 16: Tony Freeman/PhotoEdit; 18: Tim Fuller Photography; 20 (l): The Terry Wild Studio; 20 (r), 22–23, 25 : Tim Fuller Photography; 29: Tony Freeman/PhotoEdit; 30: Jonathan Nourak/PhotoEdit; 31: Tony Freeman/PhotoEdit; 32 The Terry Wild Studio; 35, 36: Tim Fuller Photography; 38 (l): Tony Freeman/PhotoEdit; 38 (r): Tim Fuller Photography; 40-41: Photovault; 44: Tim Fuller Photography; 45 (t): Michael Newman/PhotoEdit; 45 (b): Spencer Grant/PhotoEdit; 47: Sara Matthews/Visual Education; 49: David Young-Wolff/PhotoEdit; 51: Tim Fuller Photography; 52: Sara Matthews/Visual Education; 53, 55, 58: Tim Fuller Photography; 60 (l): Sara Matthews/Visual Education; 60 (r), 64–65, 66–67, 73, 75: Tim Fuller Photography; 79: The Terry Wild Studio; 83: Tim Fuller Photography; 84: Tony Freeman/PhotoEdit; 85, 86, 88, 90–91, 94, 97: Tim Fuller Photography; 98, 99: Tony Freeman/PhotoEdit; 101: Sara Matthews/Visual Education; 104: Tony Freeman /PhotoEdit; 108, 110, 112–113: Tim Fuller Photography; 114: Tony Freeman/PhotoEdit; 115: Tim Fuller Photography; 116: The Terry Wild Studio; 117, 118, 122, 128: Tim Fuller Photography; 134: Mark Richards/PhotoEdit; 142–143, 144–145: Tim Fuller Photography; 146, 149: The Terry Wild Studio; 151, 152, 153: Tim Fuller Photography; 154: Sara Matthews/Visual Education; 155: Tim Fuller Photography; 156: Sara Matthews/Visual Education; 157: The Terry Wild Studio; 159, 160, 162, 164–165, 167, 168: Tim Fuller Photography; 171: Getty Images; 172, 174, 175, 178, 180, 182: Tim Fuller Photography; 186–187: Tim Fuller Photography; 188–189: The Terry Wild Studio; 190, 191, 192, 193, 195, 196, 198, 199: Tim Fuller Photography; 200: John Henley; 201: Tony Freeman/PhotoEdit; 203: Stephen Simpson; 204: Mason Morfit; 205: Tim Fuller Photography; 206 (l): Tim Fuller Photography; 206 (r): Mason Morfit; 208–209, 211, 212, 213, 214: Tim Fuller Photography; 216: Bill Baranowski/RoundaboutsUSA; 219: Tim Fuller Photography; 222: Mary Kate Denny/PhotoEdit; 224, 226–227, 228, 229: Tim Fuller Photography; 231: Tony Freeman/PhotoEdit; 234: Sara Matthews/Visual Education; 235, 236: Tim Fuller Photography; 238: Tony Freeman/PhotoEdit; 241: Tim Fuller Photography; 242: The Terry Wild Studio; 243, 244 (l): Sara Matthews/Visual Education; 244 (r): The Terry Wild Studio; 248–249: Michael Goodman Photography; 250–251: Kent Knudson/Index Stock; 253, 256: Tim Fuller Photography; 259 (b): Steve Smith/Getty Images; 261, 262, 266, 268: Tim Fuller Photography; 270–271: Carmen Northen/Index Stock; 273: Dick Luria; 274: Tony Freeman/PhotoEdit; 275 (t): The Terry Wild Studio; 275 (b): Sara Matthews/Visual Education; 278: Addison Geary/Stock Boston; 279: Superstock; 280: Rachel Epstein/PhotoEdit; 281: Steve Bloom/Getty Images; 282: Wolfgang Spunbarg/PhotoEdit; 284 (l): Sara Matthews/Visual Education; 284 (r): Wolfgang Spunbarg/PhotoEdit; 286–287: The Terry Wild Studio; 288 (l): Sara Matthews/Visual Education; 288 (r): Frank Siteman/PhotoEdit; 290: Christine Osborne/Visual Education; 291: Mark Richards/PhotoEdit; 293: Corbis; 295: Tim Fuller Photography; 299: The Terry Wild Studio; 300: Tim Fuller Photography; 304: Tom Prettyman/PhotoEdit; 306 (l): Mark Richards/PhotoEdit; 306 (r): The Terry Wild Studio; 308–309: Robert Brenner/PhotoEdit; 310, 311: Tim Fuller Photography; 312: Reza Estakhrian/Getty Images; 315 (t): Robert Ginn/PhotoEdit; 315 (b): Tim Fuller Photography; 317: David Young-Wolff/PhotoEdit; 318: Robert Brenner/PhotoEdit; 322: Tony Freeman/PhotoEdit; 323: Michelle Bridwell/PhotoEdit; 324, 326: Tony Freeman/PhotoEdit; 328: Jeff Greenberg/PhotoEdit; 330 (l): Tim Fuller Photography; 330 (r): Tony Freeman/PhotoEdit; 334–335: The Terry Wild Studio; 336–337, 340: Tim Fuller Photography; 341: The Terry Wild Studio; 342, 343, 344: Tim Fuller Photography; 346: The Terry Wild Studio; 347: Tim Fuller Photography; 348: Getty Images; 349: Corbis; 350 (l): The Terry Wild Studio; 350 (r): Getty Images; 352–353, 355, 356: Tim Fuller Photography; 357: Mary Kate Denny/PhotoEdit; 358: Tim Fuller Photography; 361: Michael Newman/PhotoEdit; 362: David Young-Wolff/PhotoEdit; 364, 366, 367, 368, 370: Tim Fuller Photography; 372–373: Michael Newman/PhotoEdit; 377: The Terry Wild Studio; 379: Rudi Von Briel/PhotoEdit; 381: The Terry Wild Studio; 383: Tim Fuller Photography; 385, 387: The Terry Wild Studio; 388: Tim Fuller Photography; 390 (l, r): The Terry Wild Studio; 392-393: Sara Matthews/Visual Education; 394: David Young-Wolff/PhotoEdit; 396: Tony Freeman/PhotoEdit; 397: Tim Fuller Photography; 401: Sara Matthews/Visual Education; 404 (tl): Tony Freeman/PhotoEdit; 404 (b), 406, 408, 412: Tim Fuller Photography.

All remaining photographs courtesy of AAA.

Illustration Credits
Anthony Cericola/Animated Graphics

Maps courtesy of AAA.